尾田栄一郎

It's the 20th anniversary of *One Piece!*
Maybe it's time…I actually take this
seriously*!!!* Here comes volume 86*!!*

—Eiichiro Oda, 2017

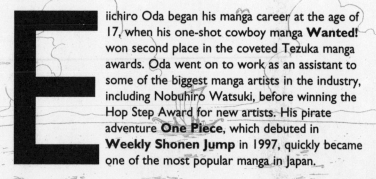

iichiro Oda began his manga career at the age of 17, when his one-shot cowboy manga **Wanted!** won second place in the coveted Tezuka manga awards. Oda went on to work as an assistant to some of the biggest manga artists in the industry, including Nobuhiro Watsuki, before winning the Hop Step Award for new artists. His pirate adventure **One Piece**, which debuted in **Weekly Shonen Jump** in 1997, quickly became one of the most popular manga in Japan.

ONE PIECE VOL. 86
NEW WORLD PART 26

SHONEN JUMP Manga Edition

STORY AND ART BY EIICHIRO ODA

Translation/Stephen Paul
Touch-up Art & Lettering/Vanessa Satone
Design/Yukiko Whitley
Editor/Alexis Kirsch

Printed in the U.S.A.

Published by VIZ Media, LLC
P.O. Box 77010
San Francisco, CA 94107

10 9 8 7 6 5 4 3 2 1
First printing, May 2018

www.viz.com

THE WORLD'S
MOST POPULAR MANGA
www.shonenjump.com

SHONEN JUMP MANGA

ONE PIECE

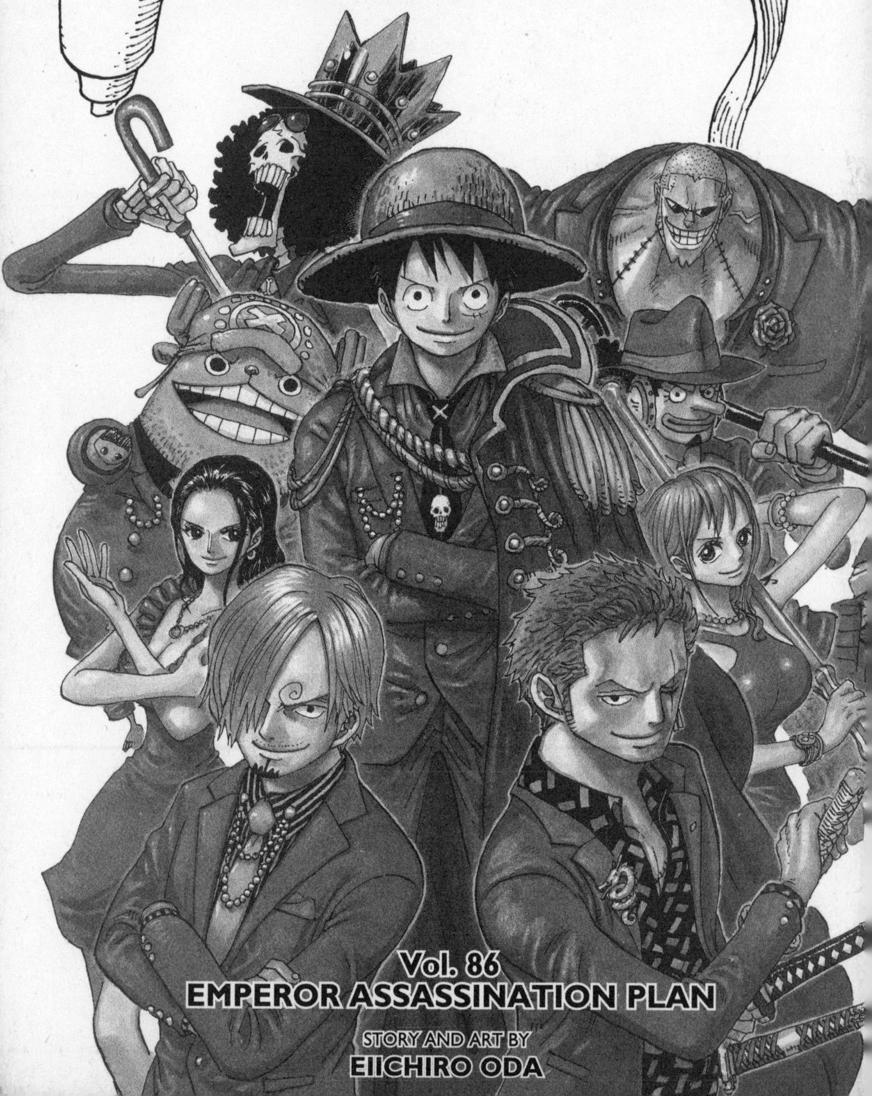

Vol. 86

EMPEROR ASSASSINATION PLAN

STORY AND ART BY

EIICHIRO ODA

The Straw Hat Crew

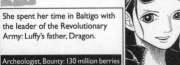

Tony Tony Chopper

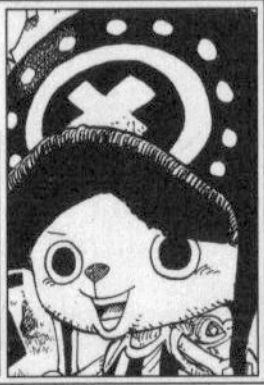

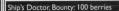

After researching powerful medicine in Birdie Kingdom, he reunited with the rest of the crew.

Ship's Doctor, Bounty: 100 berries

Monkey D. Luffy

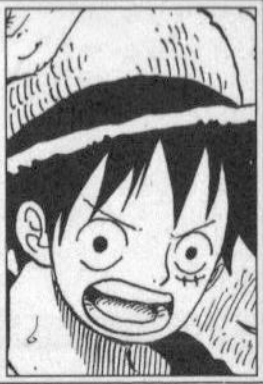

A young man who dreams of becoming the Pirate King. After training with Rayleigh, he and his crew head for the New World!

Captain, Bounty: 500 million berries

Nico Robin

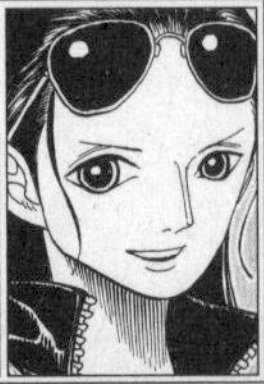

She spent her time in Baltigo with the leader of the Revolutionary Army: Luffy's father, Dragon.

Archeologist, Bounty: 130 million berries

Roronoa Zolo

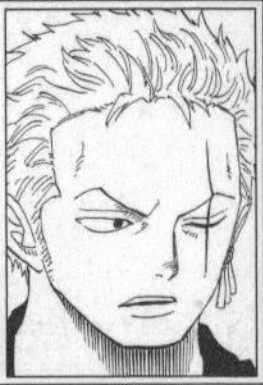

He swallowed his pride and asked to be trained by Mihawk on Gloom Island before reuniting with the rest of the crew.

Fighter, Bounty: 320 million berries

Franky

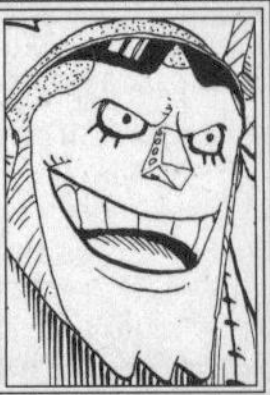

He modified himself in Future Land Baldimore and turned himself into Armored Franky before reuniting with the rest of the crew.

Shipwright, Bounty: 94 million berries

Nami

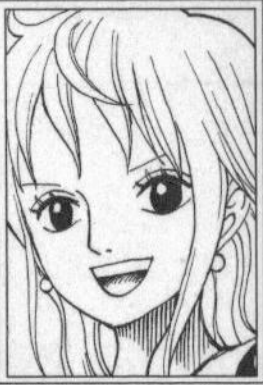

She studied the weather of the New World on the small Sky Island Weatheria, a place where weather is studied as a science.

Navigator, Bounty: 66 million berries

Brook

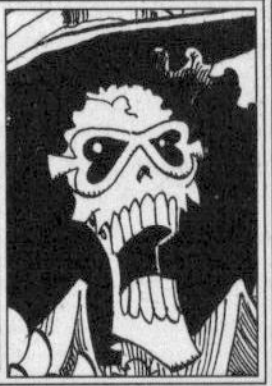

After being captured and used as a freak show by the Longarm Tribe, he became a famous rock star called "Soul King" Brook.

Musician, Bounty: 83 million berries

Usopp

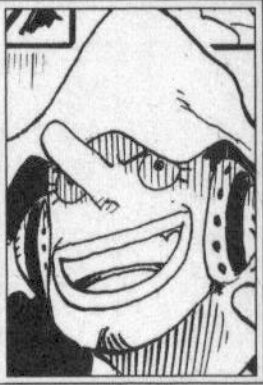

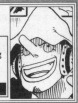

He trained under Heracles at the Bowin Islands to become the King of Snipers.

Sniper, Bounty: 200 million berries

Shanks

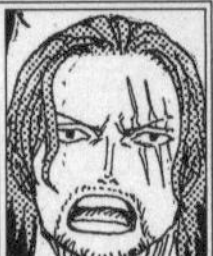

One of the Four Emperors. Waits for Luffy in the "New World," the second half of the Grand Line.

Captain of the Red-Haired Pirates

Sanji

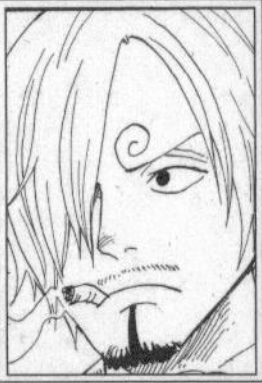

After fighting the New Kama Karate masters in the Kamabakka Kingdom, he returned to the crew.

Cook, Bounty: 177 million berries

As a mere cog of secret plots from both Mama and his own family, Sanji is trapped in a bad situation with no apparent way out. When Luffy comes to get him back, Sanji clashes with his former captain, unable to speak his true feelings. Eventually, he breaks down and admits that he wants to return to the *Sunny*. But in order to do that, he needs to prevent Big Mom's true goal—the slaughter of his family! Jimbei's suggestion to tackle this tremendous challenge is to join forces with Bege, who has goals of his own...

The story of ONE PIECE 1»86

Big Mom Pirates

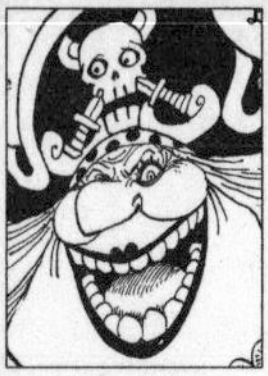

Charlotte Linlin

Captain, Big Mom Pirates

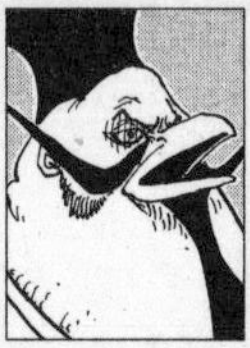

Count Niwatori

Fighter, Big Mom Pirates

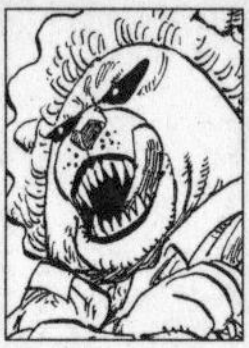

Pekoms

Fighter, Big Mom Pirates

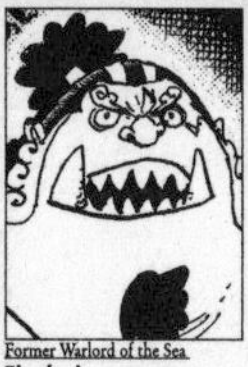

Former Warlord of the Sea
Jimbei

Captain of the Sun Pirates

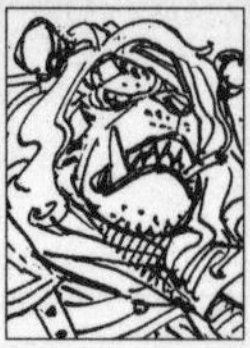

Treetop Pedro (Jaguar Mink)

Leader of the Guardians

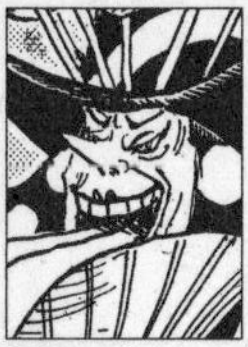

C. Perospero

1st Son of Charlotte

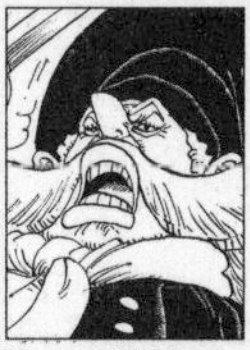

"Gourmet Knight" Streusen

Head Chef, Big Mom Pirates

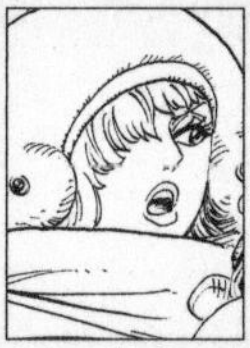

C. Smoothie (Sweet 3)

14th Daughter of Charlotte

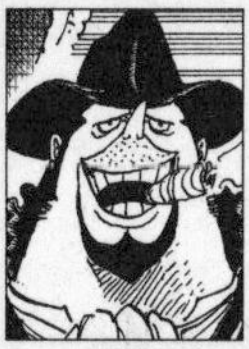

Capone "Gang" Bege

Captain of the Firetank Pirates

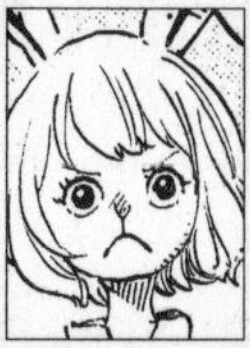

Carrot (Bunny Mink)

Battlebeast Tribe

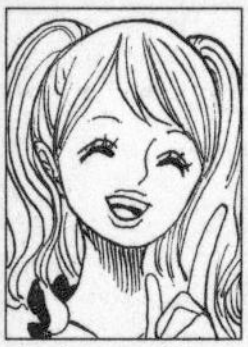

Charlotte Pudding

35th Daughter of Charlotte

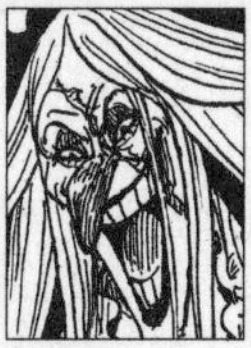

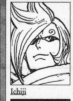

C. Brulee

8th Daughter of Charlotte

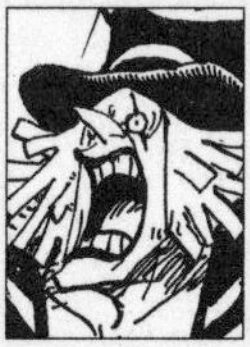

C. Montd'or

19th Son of Charlotte

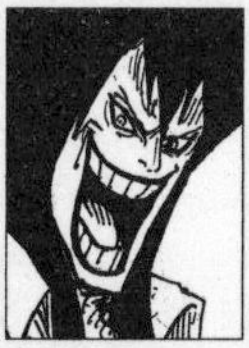

"Gangster" Gastino

Evil Scientist

Germa 66

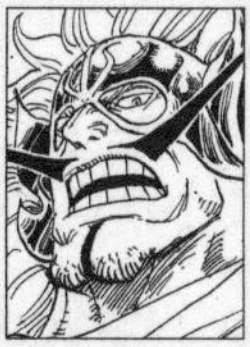

Vinsmoke Judge

King of Germa Kingdom

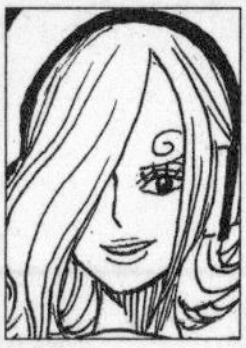

Reiju

Eldest Daughter of Vinsmoke

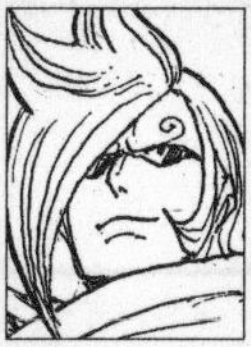

Ichiji

Eldest Son of Vinsmoke

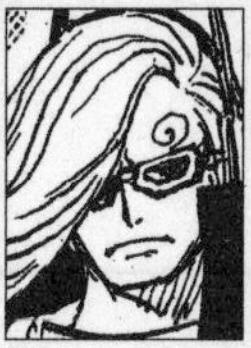

Niji

Second Son of Vinsmoke

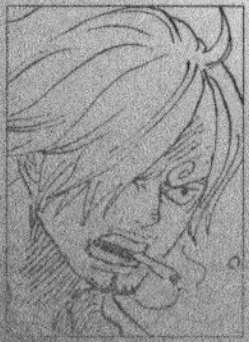

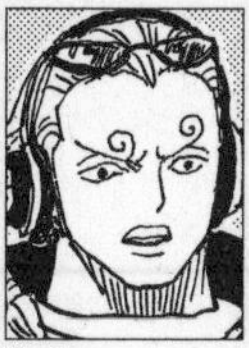

Yonji

Fourth Son of Vinsmoke

Story

After two years of hard training, the Straw Hat pirates are back together, first at the Sabaody Archipelago and then through Fish-Man Island to their next stage: the New World!!

After defeating Doflamingo, Luffy and crew's next goal is to topple Kaido, an Emperor of the Sea. But a wrench is thrown into the works when Sanji leaves the crew because he's part of a political marriage to Big Mom's daughter.

Vol. 86
EMPEROR ASSASSINATION PLAN

CONTENTS

Chapter 859:
EMPEROR ASSASSINATION PLAN

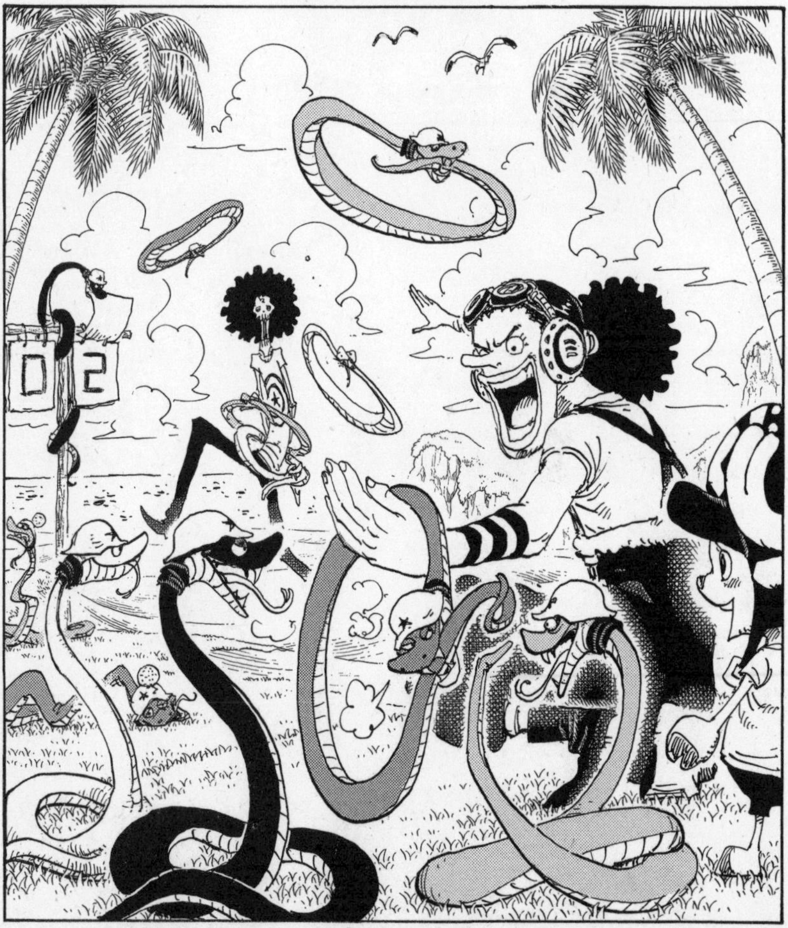

REQUEST: "USOPP PLAYING SNAKE RING-TOSS WITH BROOK" BY ORANGE PENGUIN FROM TOKYO

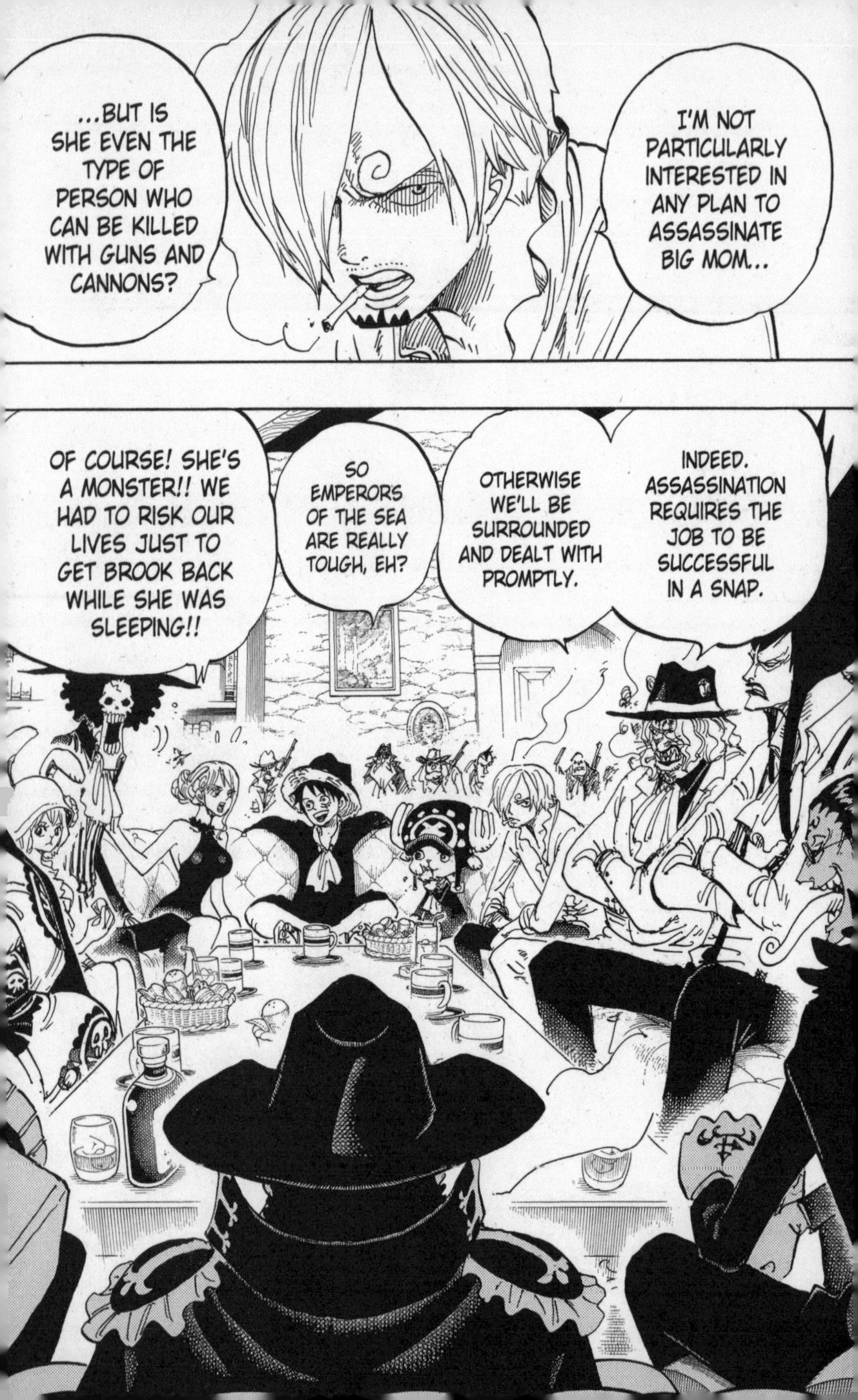
I'M NOT PARTICULARLY INTERESTED IN ANY PLAN TO ASSASSINATE BIG MOM...
...BUT IS SHE EVEN THE TYPE OF PERSON WHO CAN BE KILLED WITH GUNS AND CANNONS?
INDEED. ASSASSINATION REQUIRES THE JOB TO BE SUCCESSFUL IN A SNAP.
OTHERWISE WE'LL BE SURROUNDED AND DEALT WITH PROMPTLY.
SO EMPERORS OF THE SEA ARE REALLY TOUGH, EH?
OF COURSE! SHE'S A MONSTER!! WE HAD TO RISK OUR LIVES JUST TO GET BROOK BACK WHILE SHE WAS SLEEPING!!

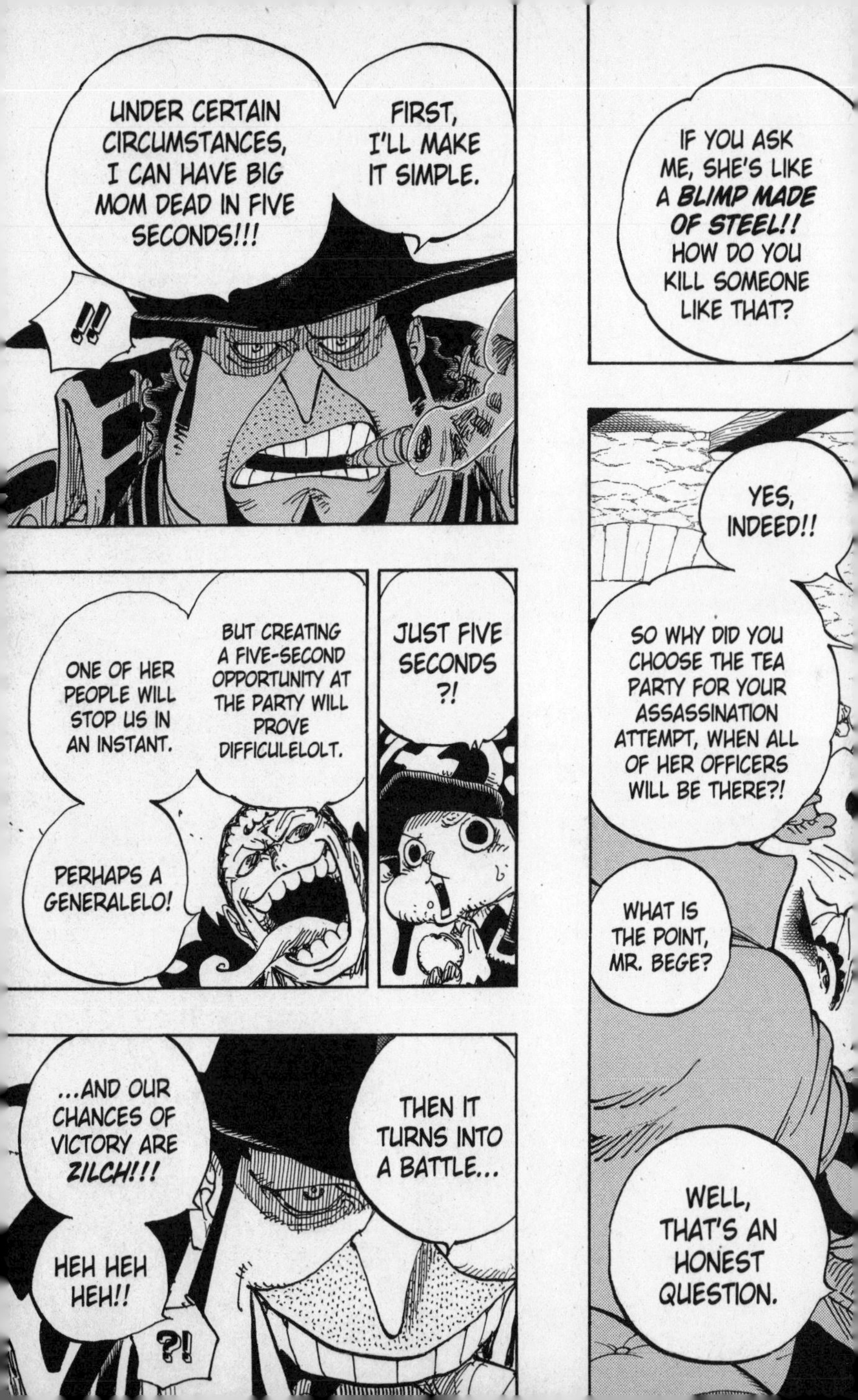
IF YOU ASK ME, SHE'S LIKE A ***BLIMP MADE OF STEEL!!*** HOW DO YOU KILL SOMEONE LIKE THAT?
YES, INDEED!!
SO WHY DID YOU CHOOSE THE TEA PARTY FOR YOUR ASSASSINATION ATTEMPT, WHEN ALL OF HER OFFICERS WILL BE THERE?!
WHAT IS THE POINT, MR. BEGE?
WELL, THAT'S AN HONEST QUESTION.
FIRST, I'LL MAKE IT SIMPLE.
UNDER CERTAIN CIRCUMSTANCES, I CAN HAVE BIG MOM DEAD IN FIVE SECONDS!!!
!!
JUST FIVE SECONDS ?!
BUT CREATING A FIVE-SECOND OPPORTUNITY AT THE PARTY WILL PROVE DIFFICULELOLT.
ONE OF HER PEOPLE WILL STOP US IN AN INSTANT.
PERHAPS A GENERALELO!
THEN IT TURNS INTO A BATTLE...
...AND OUR CHANCES OF VICTORY ARE ***ZILCH!!!***
HEH HEH HEH!!
?!

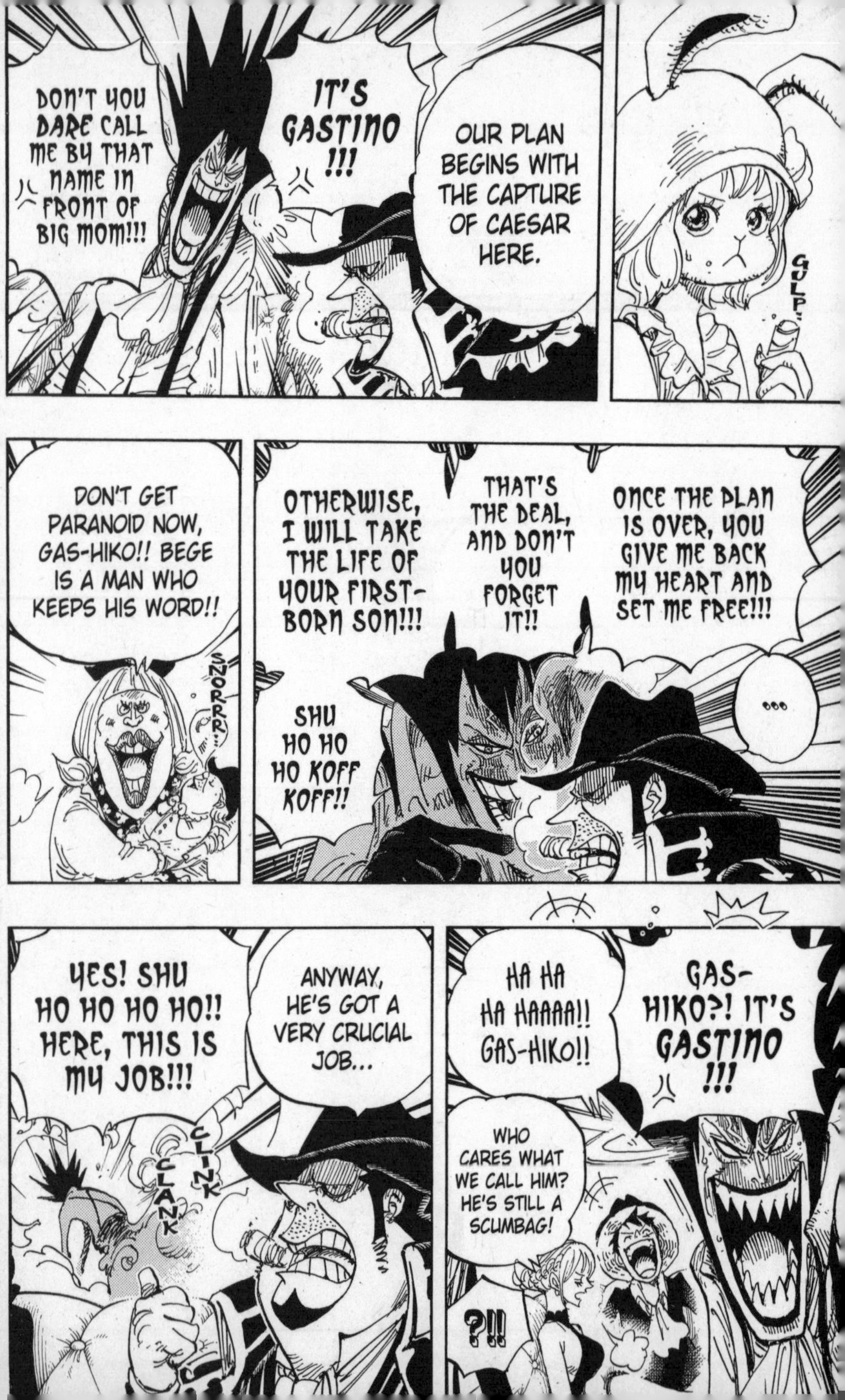
GULP!!
OUR PLAN BEGINS WITH THE CAPTURE OF CAESAR HERE.
IT'S GASTINO!!!
DON'T YOU DARE CALL ME BY THAT NAME IN FRONT OF BIG MOM!!!
ONCE THE PLAN IS OVER, YOU GIVE ME BACK MY HEART AND SET ME FREE!!!
THAT'S THE DEAL, AND DON'T YOU FORGET IT!!
OTHERWISE, I WILL TAKE THE LIFE OF YOUR FIRST-BORN SON!!!
...
SHU HO HO HO KOFF KOFF!!
DON'T GET PARANOID NOW, GAS-HIKO!! BEGE IS A MAN WHO KEEPS HIS WORD!!
SNORRRR...
GAS-HIKO?! IT'S GASTINO!!!
HA HA HA HAAAA!! GAS-HIKO!!
WHO CARES WHAT WE CALL HIM? HE'S STILL A SCUMBAG!
?!!
ANYWAY, HE'S GOT A VERY CRUCIAL JOB...
YES! SHU HO HO HO HO!! HERE, THIS IS MY JOB!!!
CLINK
CLANK

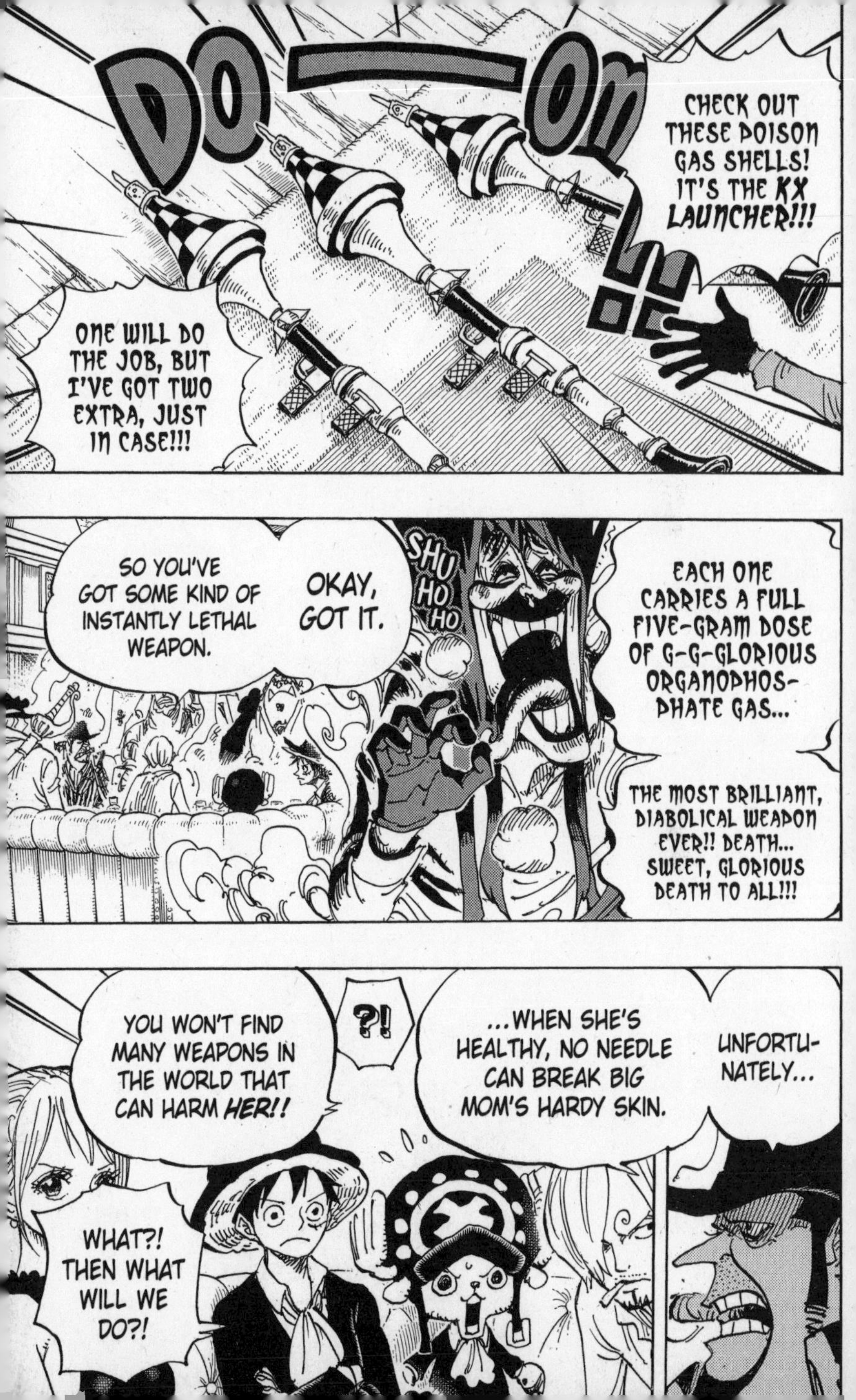
DO—OM
CHECK OUT THESE POISON GAS SHELLS! IT'S THE KX LAUNCHER!!!
ONE WILL DO THE JOB, BUT I'VE GOT TWO EXTRA, JUST IN CASE!!!
EACH ONE CARRIES A FULL FIVE-GRAM DOSE OF G-G-GLORIOUS ORGANOPHOS-PHATE GAS...
THE MOST BRILLIANT, DIABOLICAL WEAPON EVER!! DEATH... SWEET, GLORIOUS DEATH TO ALL!!!
SHU HO HO
OKAY, GOT IT.
SO YOU'VE GOT SOME KIND OF INSTANTLY LETHAL WEAPON.
UNFORTU-NATELY...
...WHEN SHE'S HEALTHY, NO NEEDLE CAN BREAK BIG MOM'S HARDY SKIN.
?!
YOU WON'T FIND MANY WEAPONS IN THE WORLD THAT CAN HARM HER!!
WHAT?! THEN WHAT WILL WE DO?!

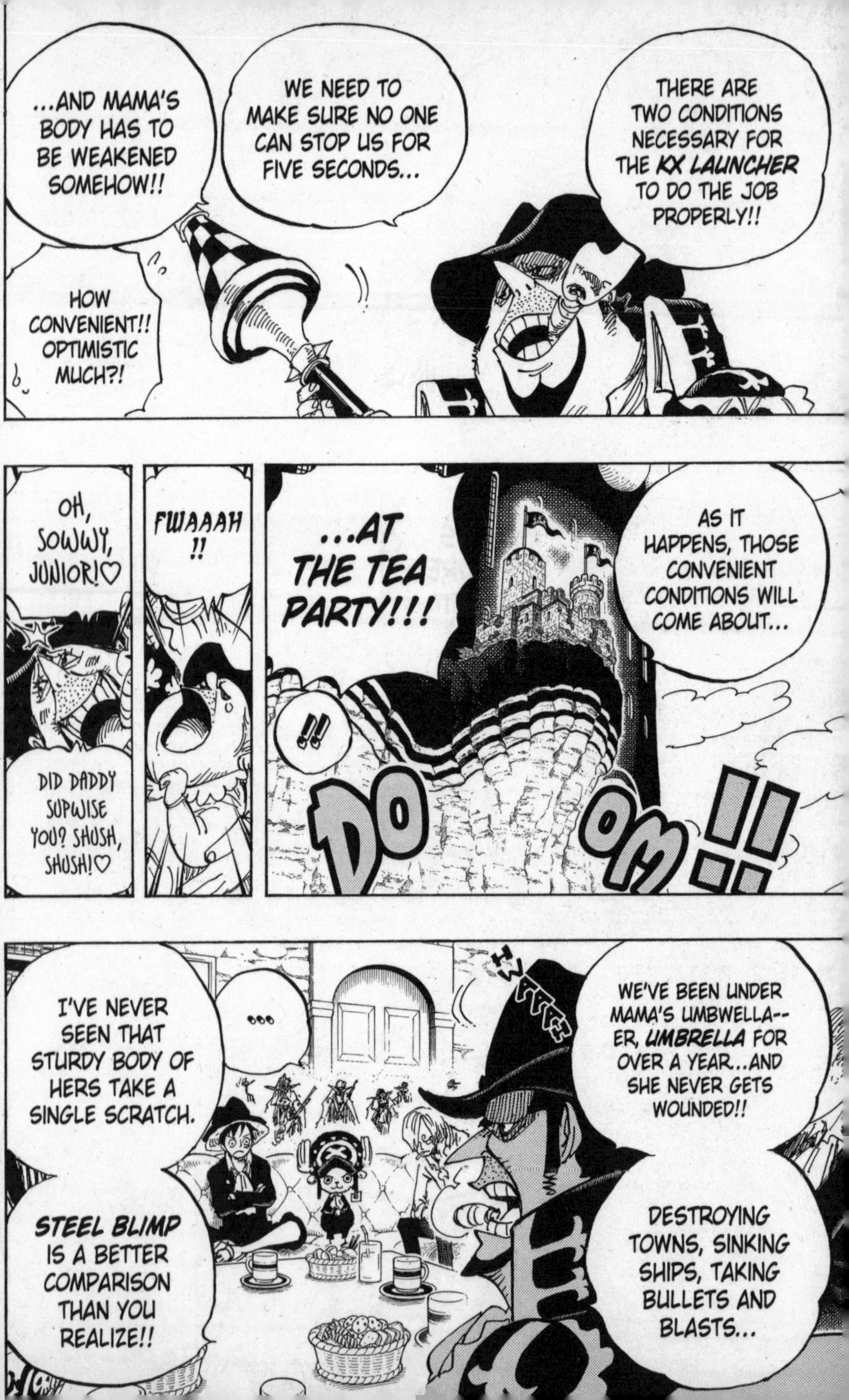
THERE ARE TWO CONDITIONS NECESSARY FOR THE *KX LAUNCHER* TO DO THE JOB PROPERLY!!
WE NEED TO MAKE SURE NO ONE CAN STOP US FOR FIVE SECONDS...
...AND MAMA'S BODY HAS TO BE WEAKENED SOMEHOW!!
HOW CONVENIENT!! OPTIMISTIC MUCH?!
AS IT HAPPENS, THOSE CONVENIENT CONDITIONS WILL COME ABOUT...
...AT THE TEA PARTY!!!
!!
DOOM!!
FWAAAH !!
OH, SOWWY, JUNIOR!♡
DID DADDY SUPWISE YOU? SHUSH, SHUSH!♡
WE'VE BEEN UNDER MAMA'S UMBWELLA-- ER, *UMBRELLA* FOR OVER A YEAR...AND SHE NEVER GETS WOUNDED!!
...
I'VE NEVER SEEN THAT STURDY BODY OF HERS TAKE A SINGLE SCRATCH.
DESTROYING TOWNS, SINKING SHIPS, TAKING BULLETS AND BLASTS...
STEEL BLIMP IS A BETTER COMPARISON THAN YOU REALIZE!!

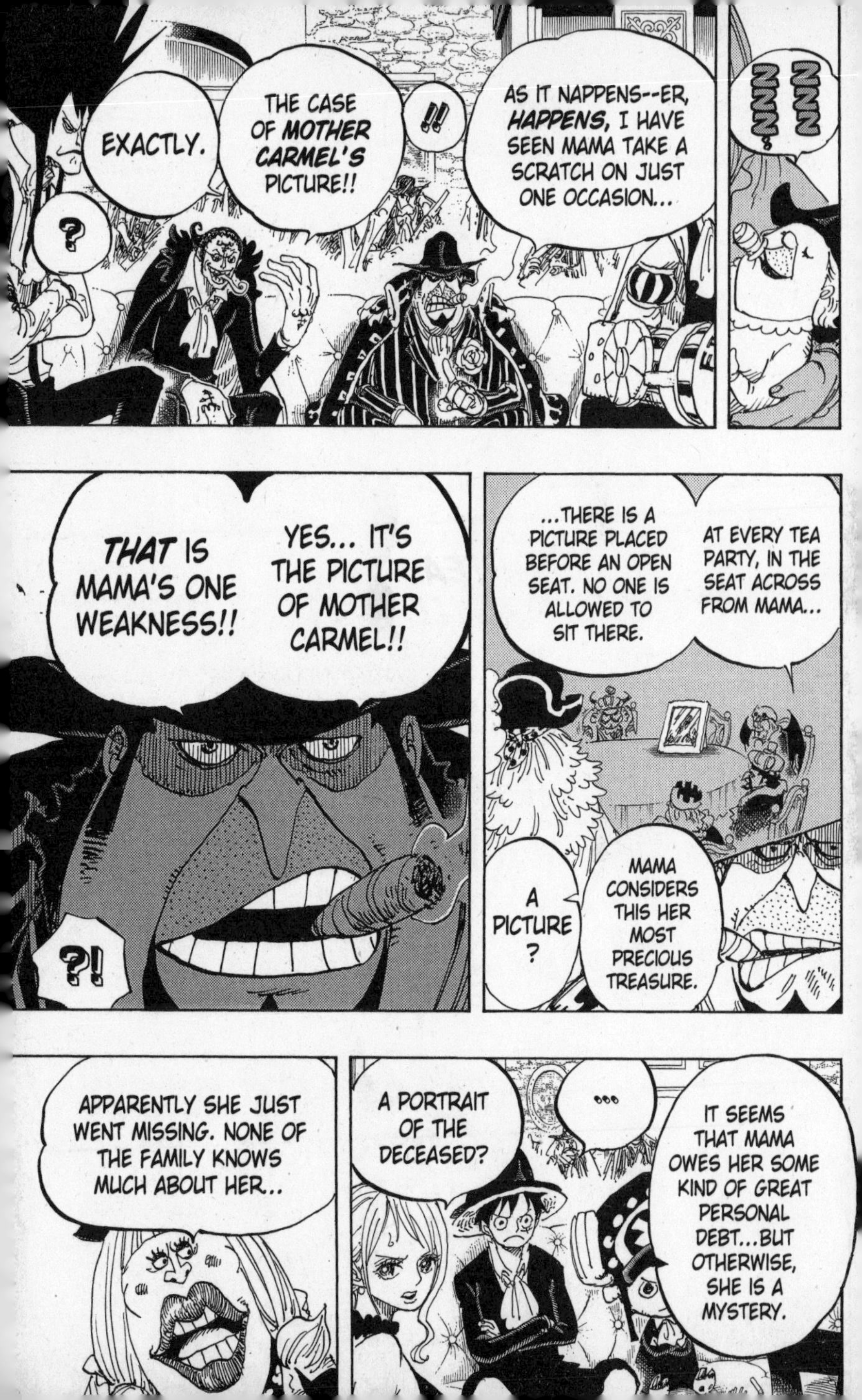
NNN NNN
AS IT NAPPENS--ER, HAPPENS, I HAVE SEEN MAMA TAKE A SCRATCH ON JUST ONE OCCASION...
!!
THE CASE OF MOTHER CARMEL'S PICTURE!!
EXACTLY.
?
AT EVERY TEA PARTY, IN THE SEAT ACROSS FROM MAMA...
...THERE IS A PICTURE PLACED BEFORE AN OPEN SEAT. NO ONE IS ALLOWED TO SIT THERE.
MAMA CONSIDERS THIS HER MOST PRECIOUS TREASURE.
A PICTURE?
YES... IT'S THE PICTURE OF MOTHER CARMEL!!
THAT IS MAMA'S ONE WEAKNESS!!
?!
IT SEEMS THAT MAMA OWES HER SOME KIND OF GREAT PERSONAL DEBT...BUT OTHERWISE, SHE IS A MYSTERY.
...
A PORTRAIT OF THE DECEASED?
APPARENTLY SHE JUST WENT MISSING. NONE OF THE FAMILY KNOWS MUCH ABOUT HER..

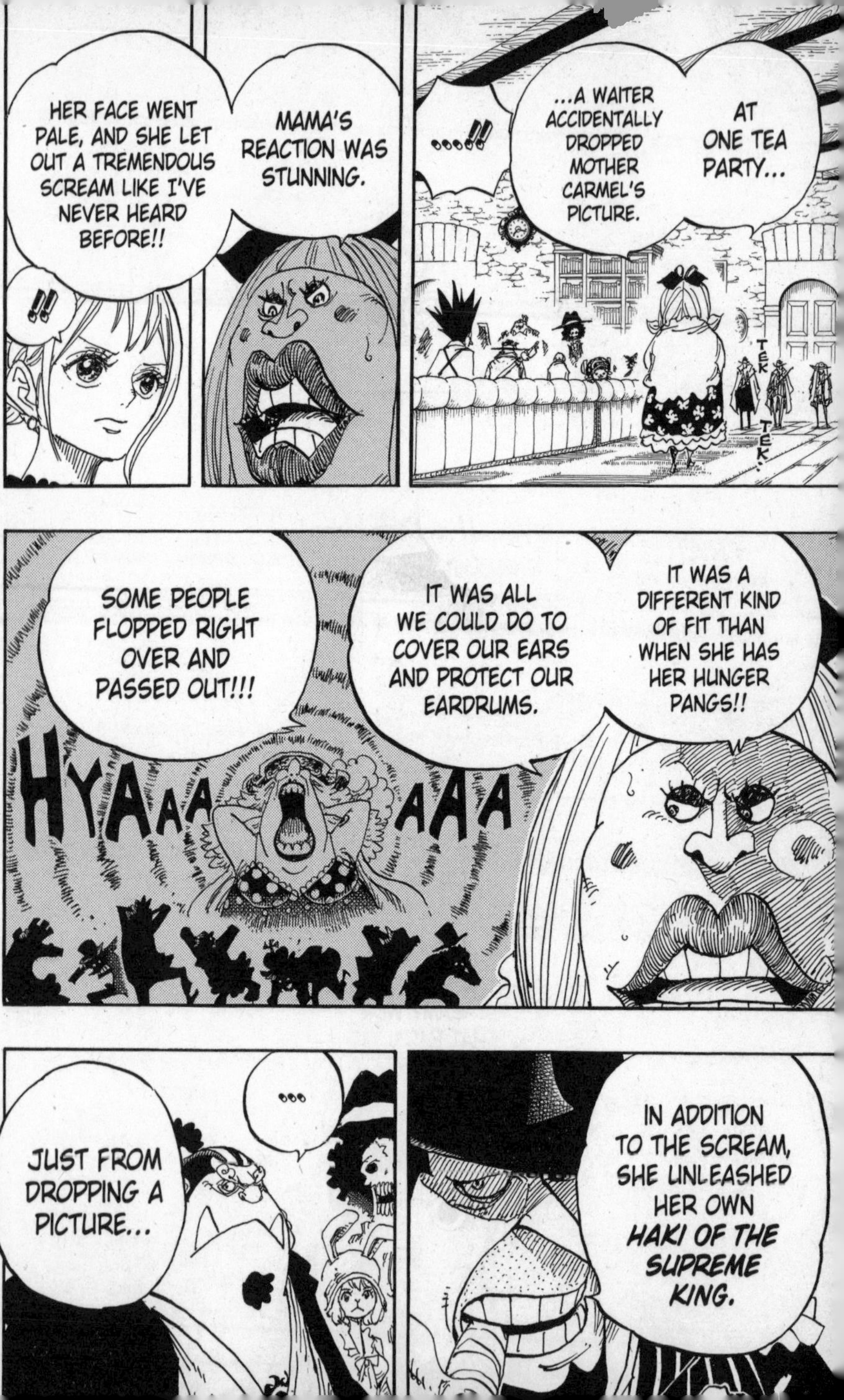
AT ONE TEA PARTY...
...A WAITER ACCIDENTALLY DROPPED MOTHER CARMEL'S PICTURE.
....!!
TEK
TEK
MAMA'S REACTION WAS STUNNING.
HER FACE WENT PALE, AND SHE LET OUT A TREMENDOUS SCREAM LIKE I'VE NEVER HEARD BEFORE!!
!!
IT WAS A DIFFERENT KIND OF FIT THAN WHEN SHE HAS HER HUNGER PANGS!!
IT WAS ALL WE COULD DO TO COVER OUR EARS AND PROTECT OUR EARDRUMS.
SOME PEOPLE FLOPPED RIGHT OVER AND PASSED OUT!!!
HYAAAAAAA
IN ADDITION TO THE SCREAM, SHE UNLEASHED HER OWN *HAKI OF THE SUPREME KING.*
...
JUST FROM DROPPING A PICTURE...

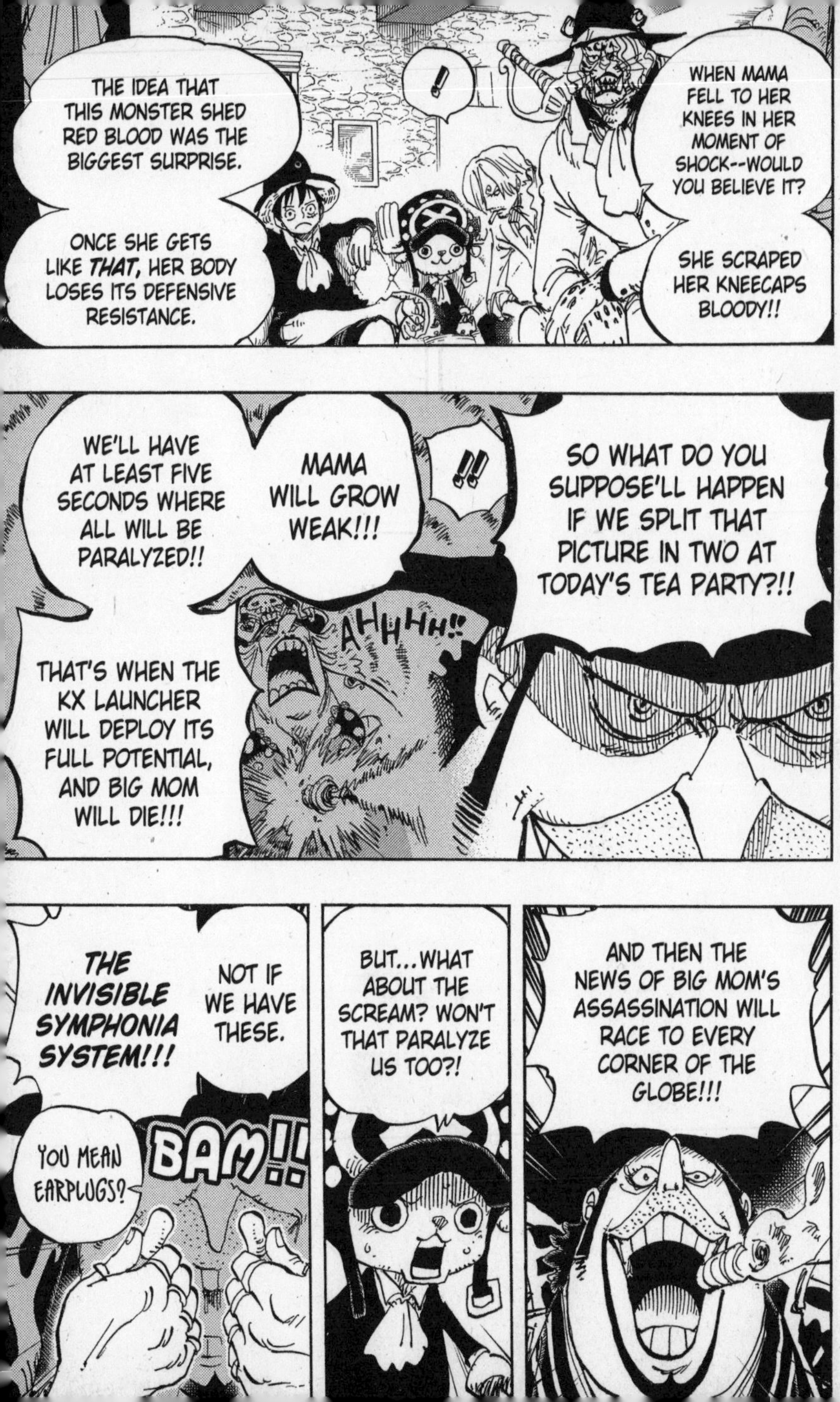
WHEN MAMA FELL TO HER KNEES IN HER MOMENT OF SHOCK--WOULD YOU BELIEVE IT?
SHE SCRAPED HER KNEECAPS BLOODY!!
!
THE IDEA THAT THIS MONSTER SHED RED BLOOD WAS THE BIGGEST SURPRISE.
ONCE SHE GETS LIKE *THAT*, HER BODY LOSES ITS DEFENSIVE RESISTANCE.
SO WHAT DO YOU SUPPOSE'LL HAPPEN IF WE SPLIT THAT PICTURE IN TWO AT TODAY'S TEA PARTY?!!
!!
MAMA WILL GROW WEAK!!!
WE'LL HAVE AT LEAST FIVE SECONDS WHERE ALL WILL BE PARALYZED!!
AHHHHH!!
THAT'S WHEN THE KX LAUNCHER WILL DEPLOY ITS FULL POTENTIAL, AND BIG MOM WILL DIE!!!
AND THEN THE NEWS OF BIG MOM'S ASSASSINATION WILL RACE TO EVERY CORNER OF THE GLOBE!!!
BUT...WHAT ABOUT THE SCREAM? WON'T THAT PARALYZE US TOO?!
NOT IF WE HAVE THESE.
THE INVISIBLE SYMPHONIA SYSTEM!!!
BAM!!
YOU MEAN EARPLUGS?

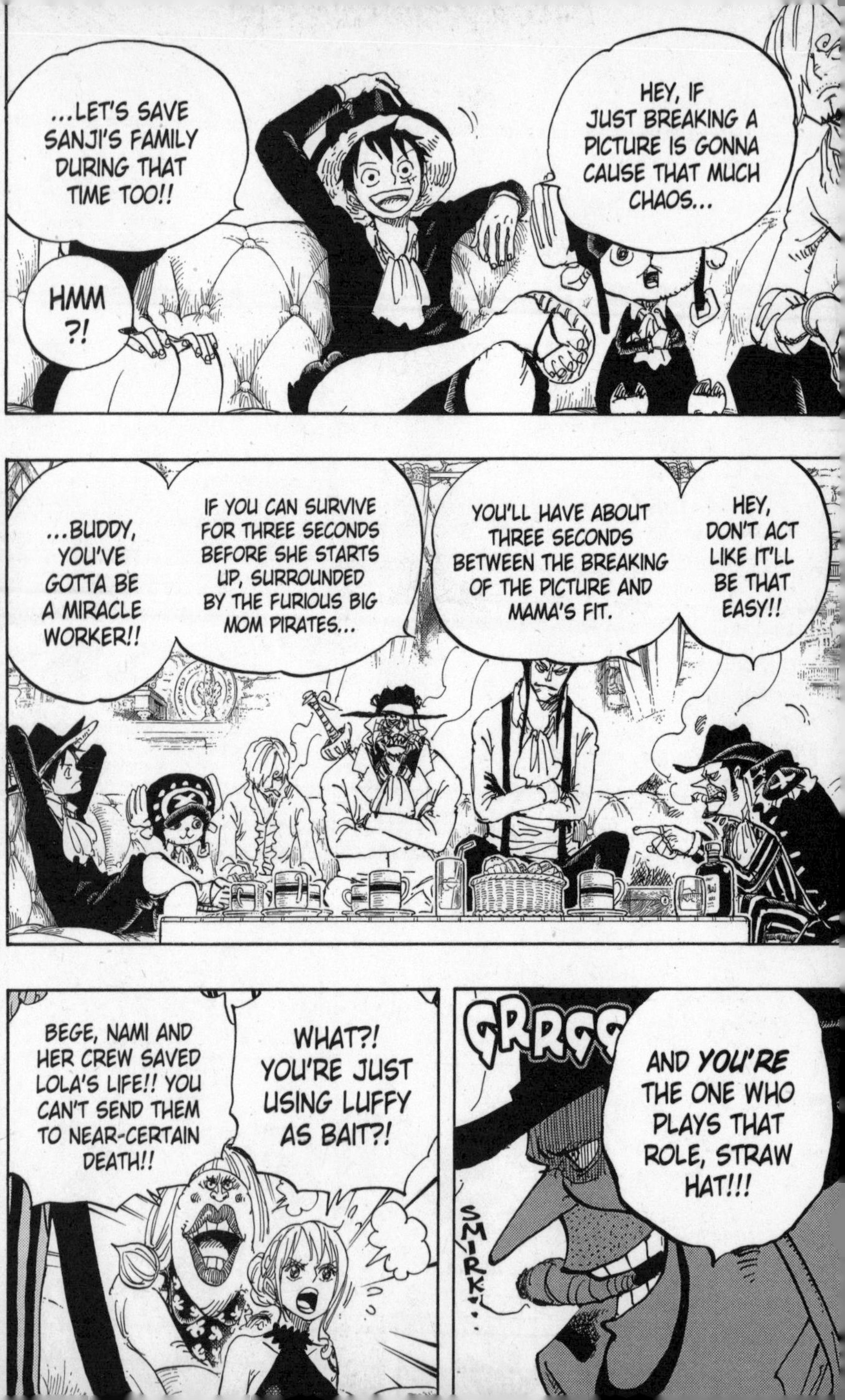
HEY, IF JUST BREAKING A PICTURE IS GONNA CAUSE THAT MUCH CHAOS...
...LET'S SAVE SANJI'S FAMILY DURING THAT TIME TOO!!
HMM ?!
HEY, DON'T ACT LIKE IT'LL BE THAT EASY!!
YOU'LL HAVE ABOUT THREE SECONDS BETWEEN THE BREAKING OF THE PICTURE AND MAMA'S FIT.
IF YOU CAN SURVIVE FOR THREE SECONDS BEFORE SHE STARTS UP, SURROUNDED BY THE FURIOUS BIG MOM PIRATES...
...BUDDY, YOU'VE GOTTA BE A MIRACLE WORKER!!
GRRGG
AND *YOU'RE* THE ONE WHO PLAYS THAT ROLE, STRAW HAT!!!
SMIRK
WHAT?! YOU'RE JUST USING LUFFY AS BAIT?!
BEGE, NAMI AND HER CREW SAVED LOLA'S LIFE!! YOU CAN'T SEND THEM TO NEAR-CERTAIN DEATH!!

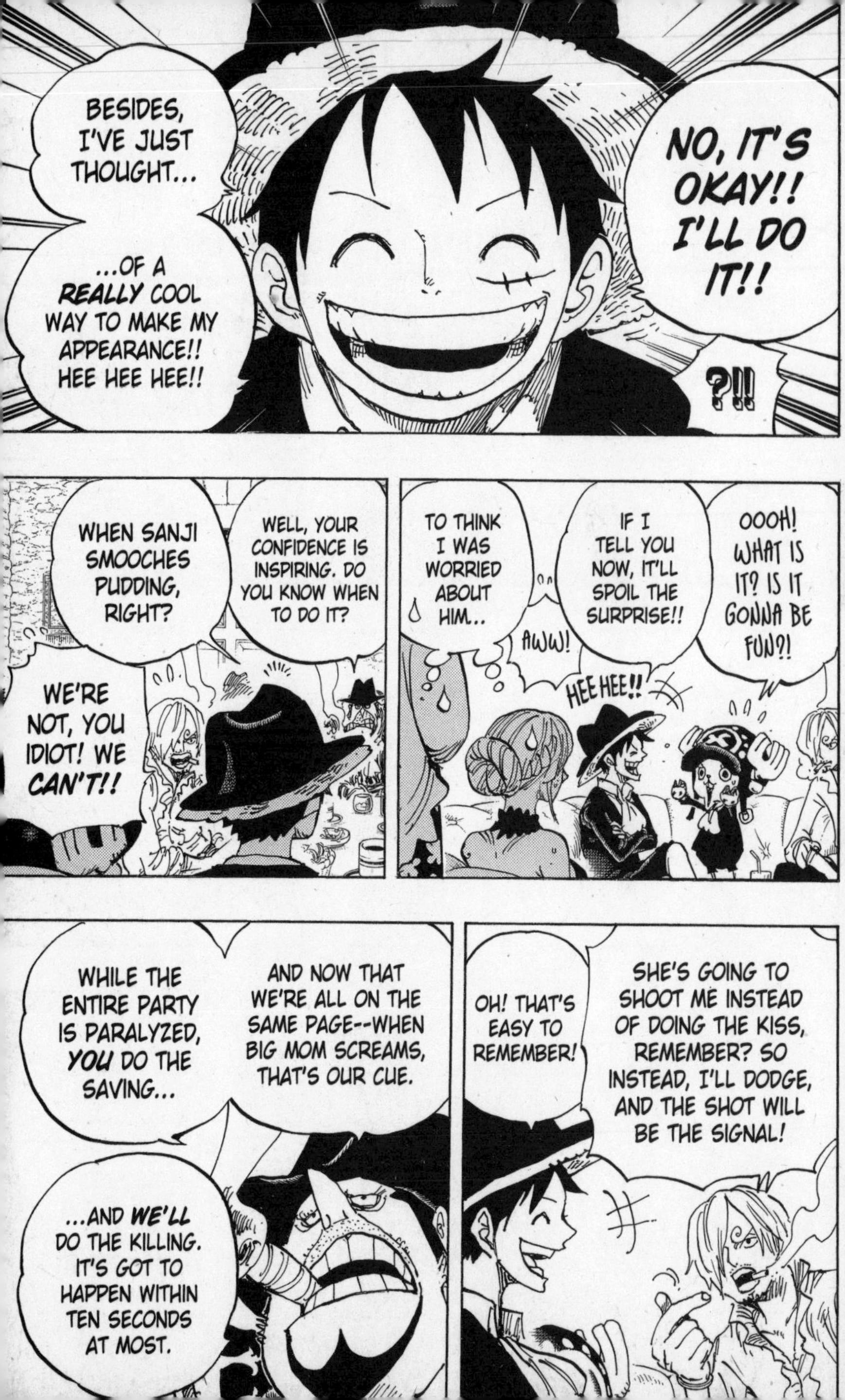
NO, IT'S OKAY!! I'LL DO IT!!
BESIDES, I'VE JUST THOUGHT...
...OF A REALLY COOL WAY TO MAKE MY APPEARANCE!! HEE HEE HEE!!
?!!
OOOH! WHAT IS IT? IS IT GONNA BE FUN?!
IF I TELL YOU NOW, IT'LL SPOIL THE SURPRISE!!
HEE HEE!!
AWW!
TO THINK I WAS WORRIED ABOUT HIM...
WELL, YOUR CONFIDENCE IS INSPIRING. DO YOU KNOW WHEN TO DO IT?
WHEN SANJI SMOOCHES PUDDING, RIGHT?
WE'RE NOT, YOU IDIOT! WE CAN'T!!
SHE'S GOING TO SHOOT ME INSTEAD OF DOING THE KISS, REMEMBER? SO INSTEAD, I'LL DODGE, AND THE SHOT WILL BE THE SIGNAL!
OH! THAT'S EASY TO REMEMBER!
AND NOW THAT WE'RE ALL ON THE SAME PAGE--WHEN BIG MOM SCREAMS, THAT'S OUR CUE.
WHILE THE ENTIRE PARTY IS PARALYZED, YOU DO THE SAVING...
...AND WE'LL DO THE KILLING. IT'S GOT TO HAPPEN WITHIN TEN SECONDS AT MOST.

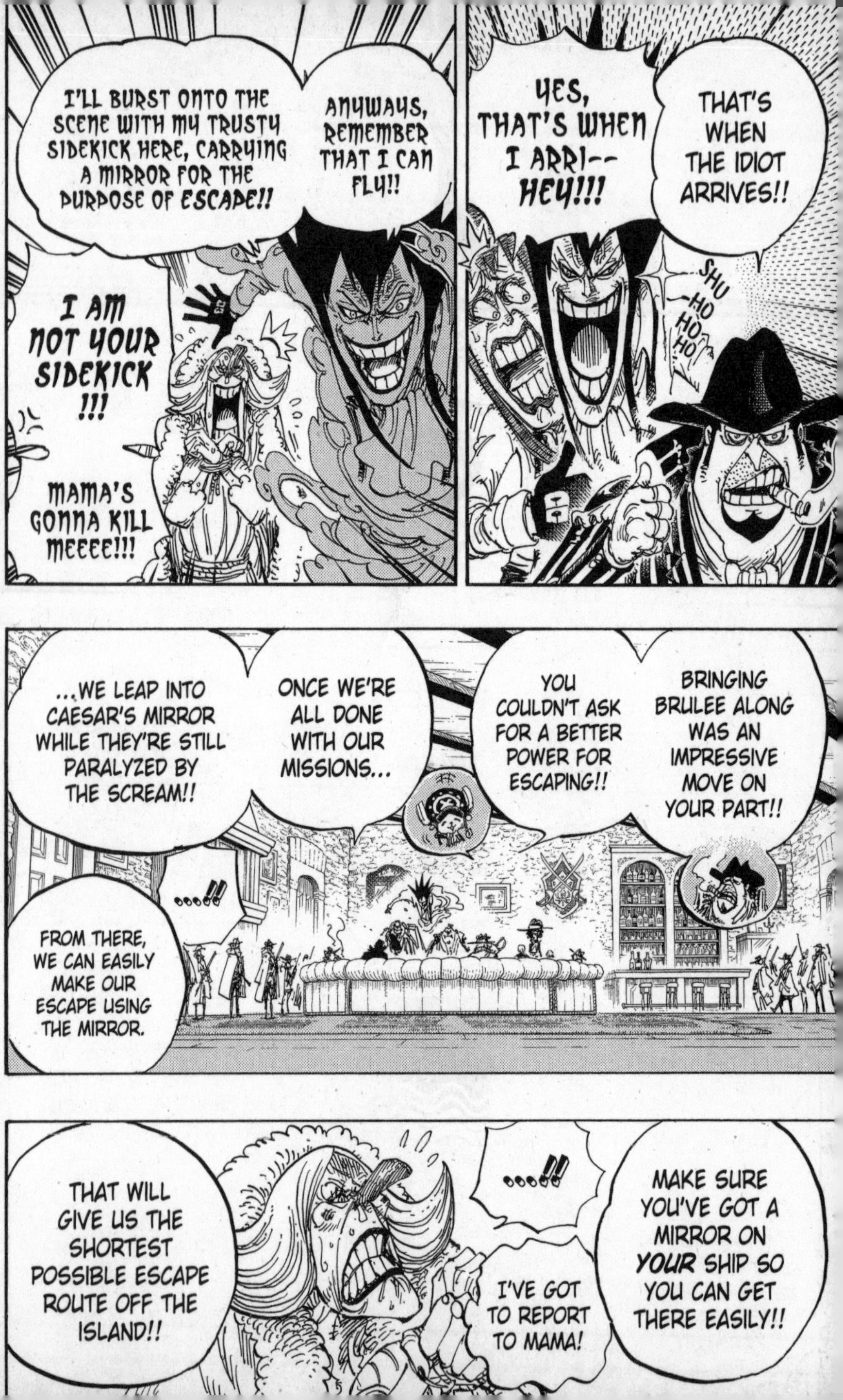
THAT'S WHEN THE IDIOT ARRIVES!!
YES, THAT'S WHEN I ARRI-- HEY!!!
SHU HO HO HO HO
ANYWAYS, REMEMBER THAT I CAN FLY!!
I'LL BURST ONTO THE SCENE WITH MY TRUSTY SIDEKICK HERE, CARRYING A MIRROR FOR THE PURPOSE OF ESCAPE!!
I AM NOT YOUR SIDEKICK!!!
MAMA'S GONNA KILL MEEEE!!!
BRINGING BRULEE ALONG WAS AN IMPRESSIVE MOVE ON YOUR PART!!
YOU COULDN'T ASK FOR A BETTER POWER FOR ESCAPING!!
ONCE WE'RE ALL DONE WITH OUR MISSIONS...
...WE LEAP INTO CAESAR'S MIRROR WHILE THEY'RE STILL PARALYZED BY THE SCREAM!!
.....!!
FROM THERE, WE CAN EASILY MAKE OUR ESCAPE USING THE MIRROR.
MAKE SURE YOU'VE GOT A MIRROR ON YOUR SHIP SO YOU CAN GET THERE EASILY!!
.....!!
I'VE GOT TO REPORT TO MAMA!
THAT WILL GIVE US THE SHORTEST POSSIBLE ESCAPE ROUTE OFF THE ISLAND!!

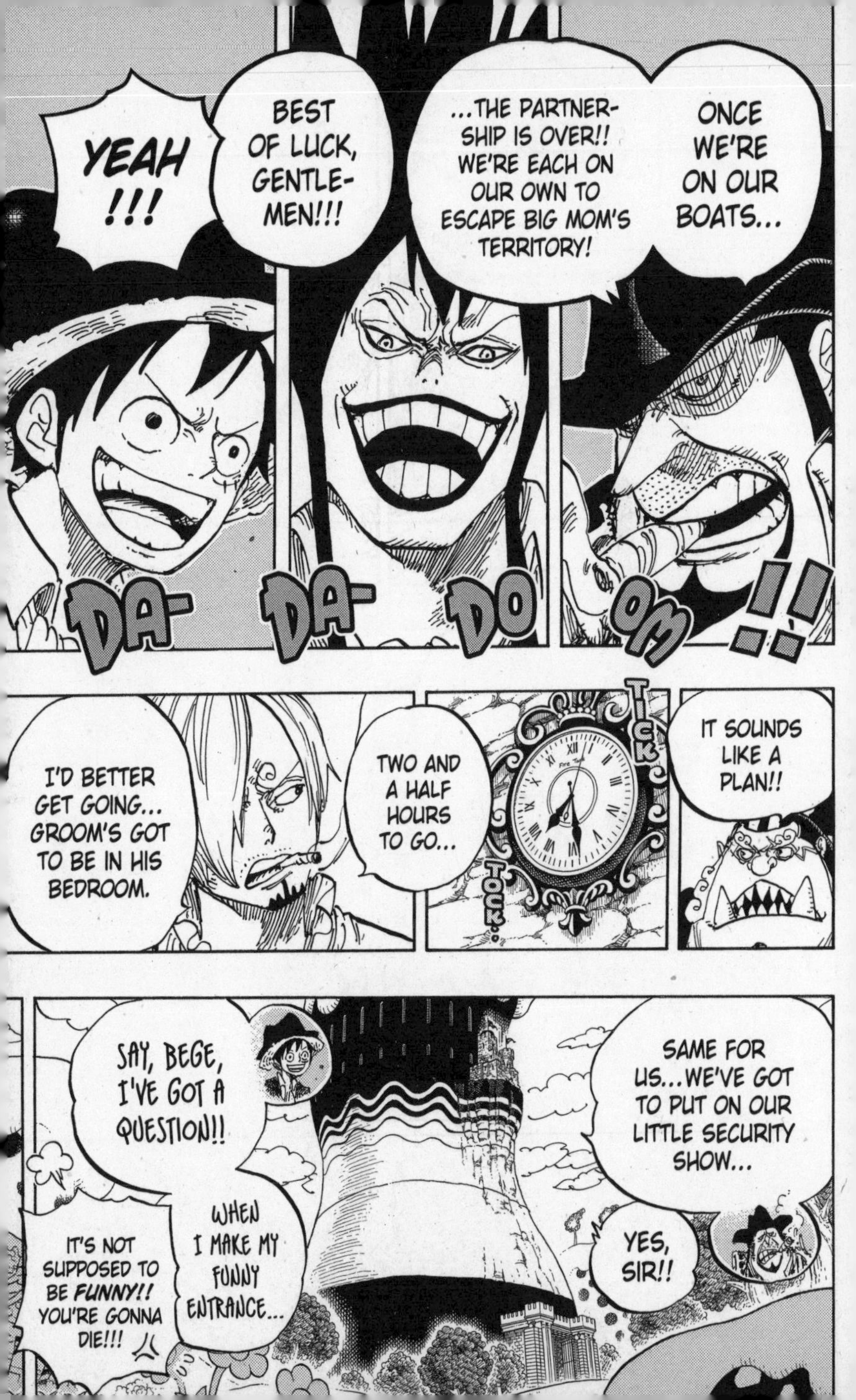
ONCE WE'RE ON OUR BOATS...
...THE PARTNERSHIP IS OVER!! WE'RE EACH ON OUR OWN TO ESCAPE BIG MOM'S TERRITORY!
BEST OF LUCK, GENTLEMEN!!!
YEAH!!!
DA-DA-DOOM!!
IT SOUNDS LIKE A PLAN!!
TICK
TOCK..
TWO AND A HALF HOURS TO GO...
I'D BETTER GET GOING... GROOM'S GOT TO BE IN HIS BEDROOM.
SAME FOR US...WE'VE GOT TO PUT ON OUR LITTLE SECURITY SHOW...
YES, SIR!!
SAY, BEGE, I'VE GOT A QUESTION!!
WHEN I MAKE MY FUNNY ENTRANCE...
IT'S NOT SUPPOSED TO BE FUNNY!! YOU'RE GONNA DIE!!!

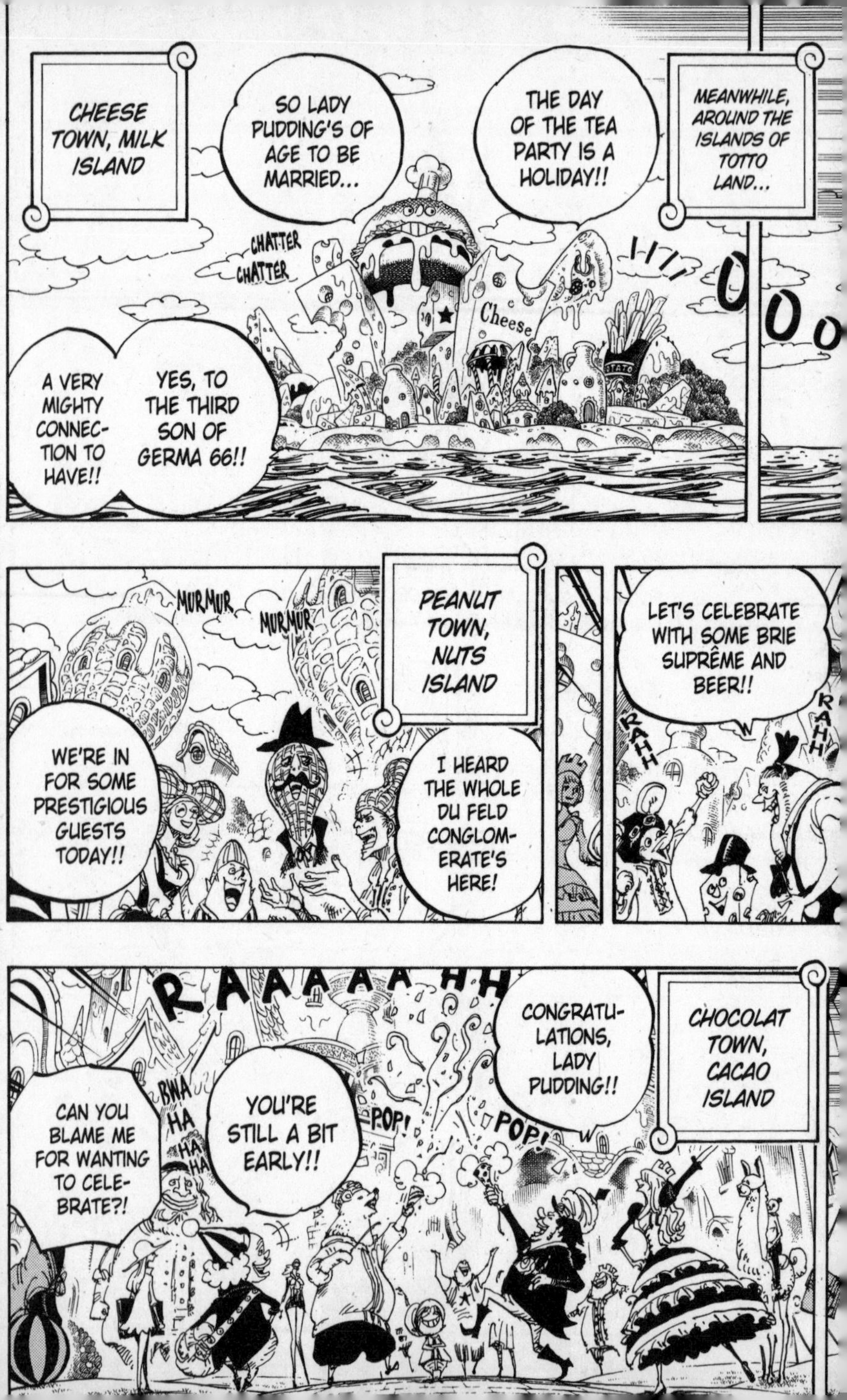
MEANWHILE, AROUND THE ISLANDS OF TOTTO LAND...
OOO
THE DAY OF THE TEA PARTY IS A HOLIDAY!!
SO LADY PUDDING'S OF AGE TO BE MARRIED...
CHEESE TOWN, MILK ISLAND
CHATTER CHATTER
Cheese
YES, TO THE THIRD SON OF GERMA 66!!
A VERY MIGHTY CONNEC-TION TO HAVE!!
LET'S CELEBRATE WITH SOME BRIE SUPRÊME AND BEER!!
RAHH
RAHH
PEANUT TOWN, NUTS ISLAND
I HEARD THE WHOLE DU FELD CONGLOM-ERATE'S HERE!
MURMUR
MURMUR
WE'RE IN FOR SOME PRESTIGIOUS GUESTS TODAY!!
CHOCOLAT TOWN, CACAO ISLAND
CONGRATU-LATIONS, LADY PUDDING!!
RAAAAAHH
POP!
POP!
YOU'RE STILL A BIT EARLY!!
BWA HA HA HA
CAN YOU BLAME ME FOR WANTING TO CELE-BRATE?!

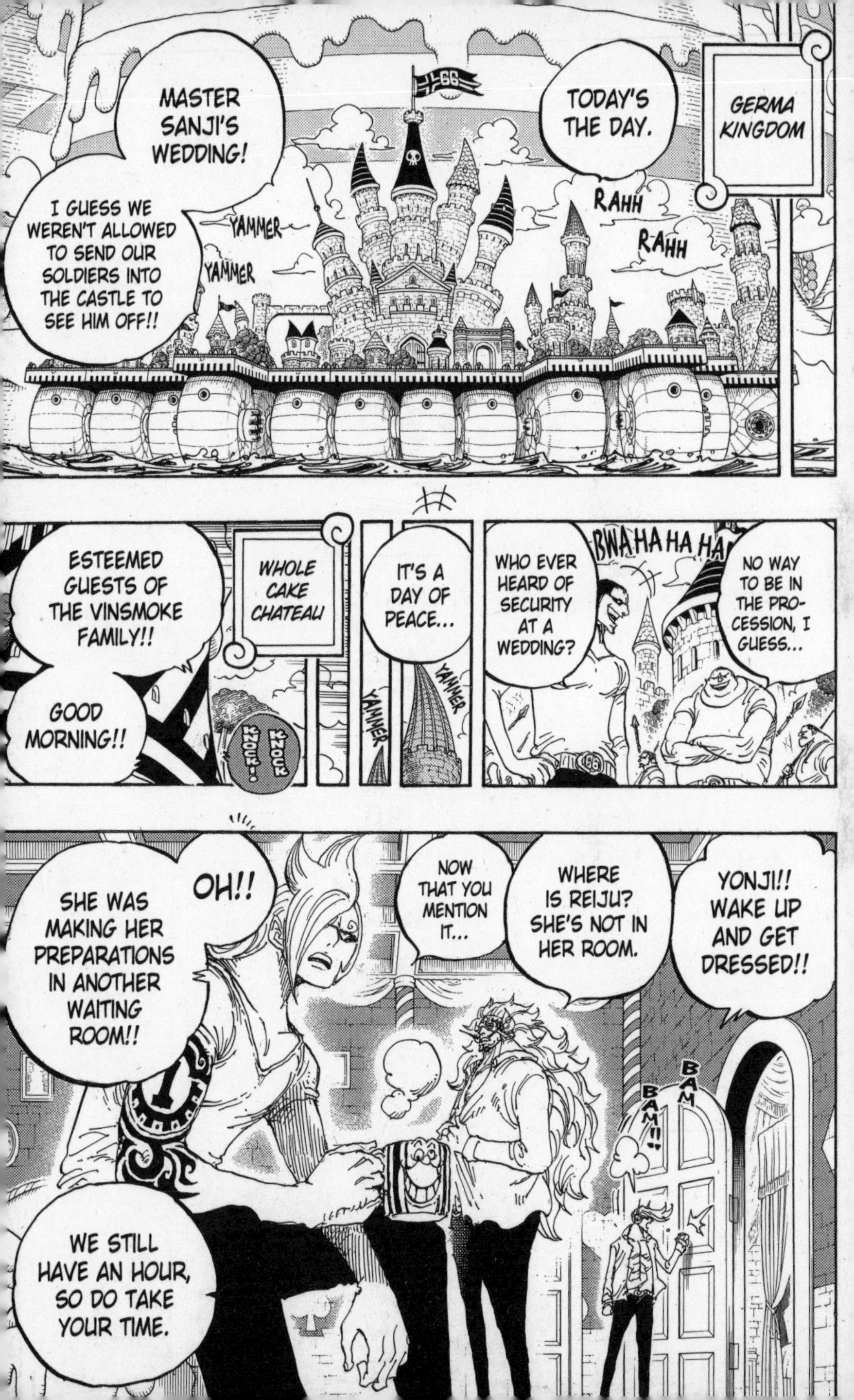
GERMA KINGDOM
TODAY'S THE DAY.
RAHH
RAHH
MASTER SANJI'S WEDDING!
YAMMER
YAMMER
I GUESS WE WEREN'T ALLOWED TO SEND OUR SOLDIERS INTO THE CASTLE TO SEE HIM OFF!!
BWAHAHAHA HA
NO WAY TO BE IN THE PRO-CESSION, I GUESS...
WHO EVER HEARD OF SECURITY AT A WEDDING?
IT'S A DAY OF PEACE...
YAMMER
YAMMER
WHOLE CAKE CHATEAU
KNOCK KNOCK
ESTEEMED GUESTS OF THE VINSMOKE FAMILY!!
GOOD MORNING!!
YONJI!! WAKE UP AND GET DRESSED!!
BAM BAM!!
WHERE IS REIJU? SHE'S NOT IN HER ROOM.
NOW THAT YOU MENTION IT...
OH!!
SHE WAS MAKING HER PREPARATIONS IN ANOTHER WAITING ROOM!!
WE STILL HAVE AN HOUR, SO DO TAKE YOUR TIME.

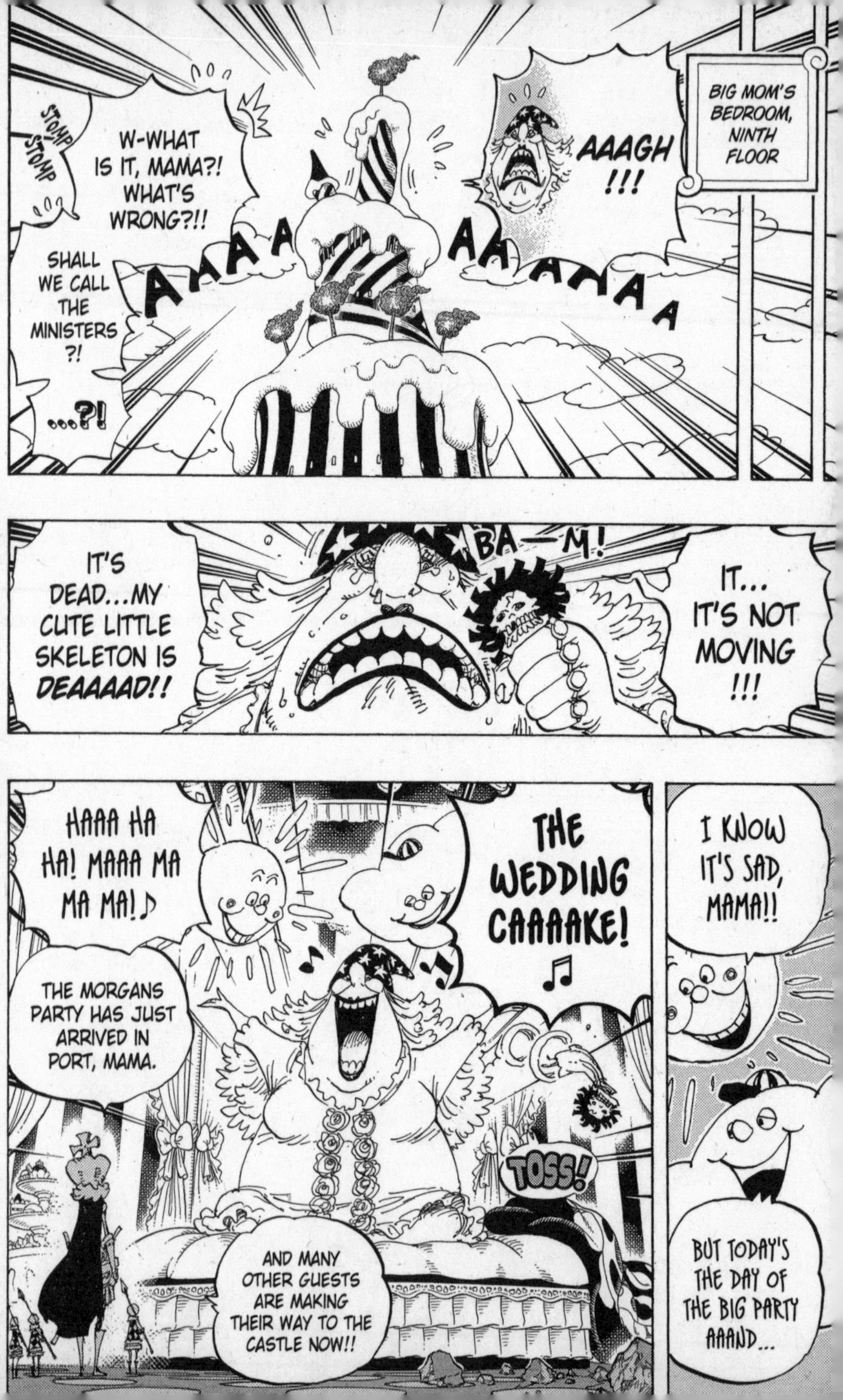
BIG MOM'S BEDROOM, NINTH FLOOR
AAAGH !!!
AAAAAAAAAAAA
W-WHAT IS IT, MAMA?! WHAT'S WRONG?!!
STOMP STOMP
SHALL WE CALL THE MINISTERS ?!
...?!
BA—M!
IT... IT'S NOT MOVING !!!
IT'S DEAD...MY CUTE LITTLE SKELETON IS DEAAAAD!!
I KNOW IT'S SAD, MAMA!!
BUT TODAY'S THE DAY OF THE BIG PARTY AAAND...
THE WEDDING CAAAAKE! ♫
HAAA HA HA! MAAA MA MA MA!♪
TOSS!
THE MORGANS PARTY HAS JUST ARRIVED IN PORT, MAMA.
AND MANY OTHER GUESTS ARE MAKING THEIR WAY TO THE CASTLE NOW!!

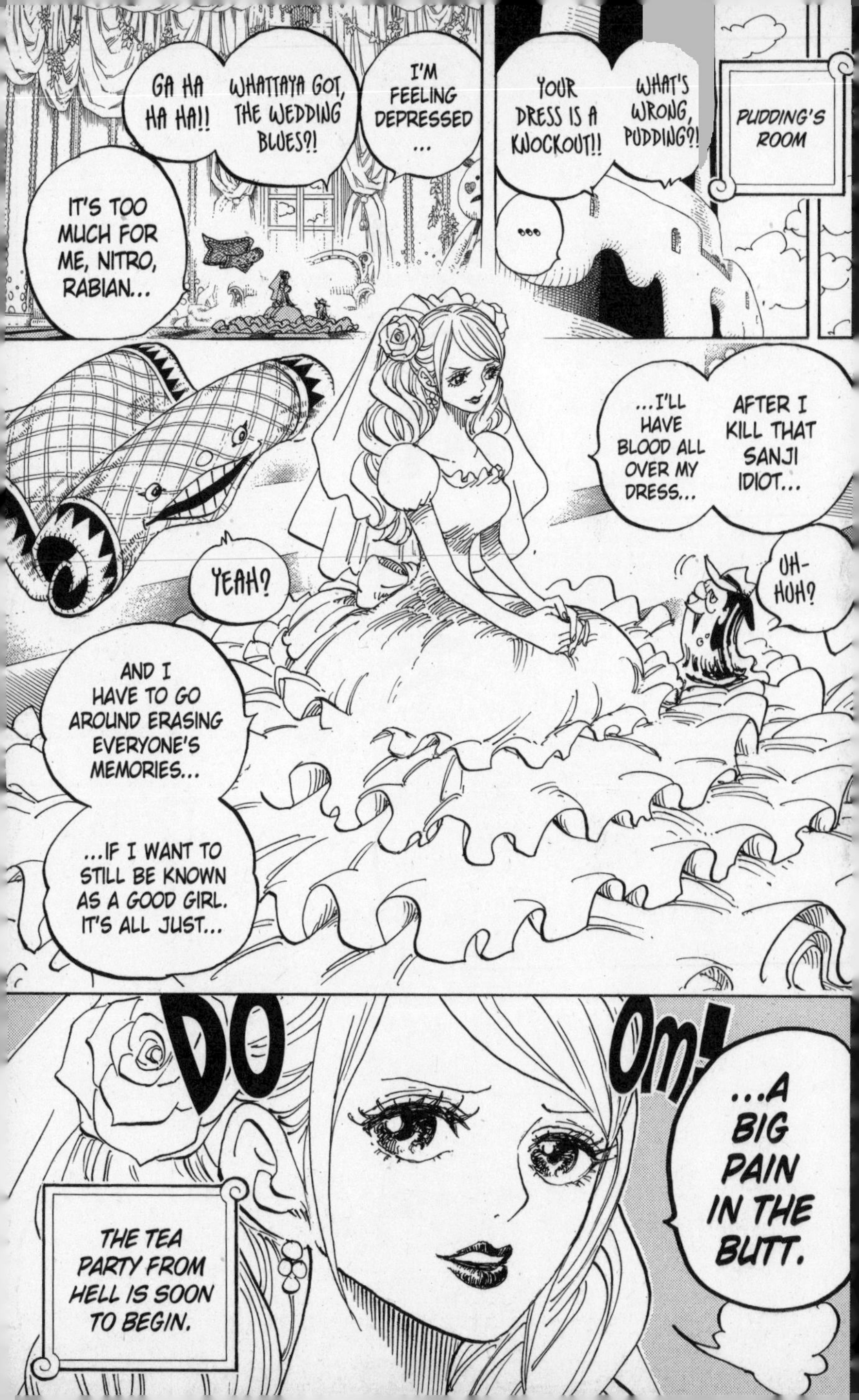
PUDDING'S ROOM
WHAT'S WRONG, PUDDING?!
YOUR DRESS IS A KNOCKOUT!!
...
I'M FEELING DEPRESSED ...
WHATTAYA GOT, THE WEDDING BLUES?!
GA HA HA HA!!
IT'S TOO MUCH FOR ME, NITRO, RABIAN...
AFTER I KILL THAT SANJI IDIOT...
...I'LL HAVE BLOOD ALL OVER MY DRESS...
UH-HUH?
YEAH?
AND I HAVE TO GO AROUND ERASING EVERYONE'S MEMORIES...
...IF I WANT TO STILL BE KNOWN AS A GOOD GIRL. IT'S ALL JUST...
DOOM!
...A BIG PAIN IN THE BUTT.
THE TEA PARTY FROM HELL IS SOON TO BEGIN.

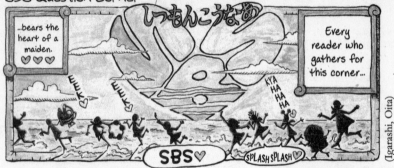

SBS Question Corner

Every reader who gathers for this corner...
...bears the heart of a maiden. ♡♡♡
KYA HA HA HA HA ♡
EEK ♡
EEK ♡
SPLASH SPLASH ♡
SBS ♡

(Igarashi, Oita)

Q: Hello, I'm Eiichiro Oda. I'm here to answer all of your dirty questions. Now, let us begin the SBS. ♡

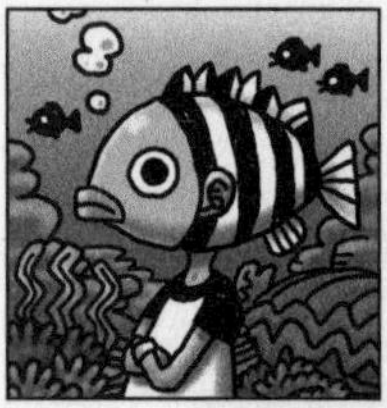

A: Im-pos-ter!!! Knock it off!! Stop trying to impersonate me!! I am innocent! The SBS is not a segment for perverted frivolity! It's entirely wholesome! This is the worst intro ever!!

6

Q: Oda Sensei, I'm sure that you've gotten plenty of letters ever since you revealed Reiju's panties. But don't let it bother you. All of humanity was naked once. If panties are all it takes to get their panties in a bunch, then they need to learn some self-control.

--Heart-Racing Nosebleed

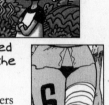

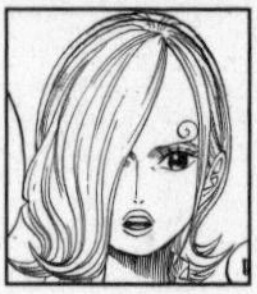

A: Your pen name is the least wholesome thing about this!!!

SCRUB
SCRUB
BUT REALLY, I DON'T KNOW WHAT I'D HAVE

Q: Hello, Oda Sensei. In chapter 858, there's a bathing scene for Nami. If the whole family sees this on the anime, it's going to be incredibly awkward… (laughs) What do you suppose I should do?

--Sanadacchi

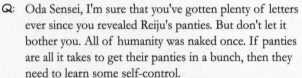

A: Man, what's with all the naughty questions this time?! It's so strange. Okay, listen up, Sanadacchi. All of humanity was naked once! If a bathing scene is going to get you all a-twitter, maybe you just need to learn some self-control!
P.S. I got a heart-racing nosebleed while drawing this scene.

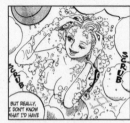

Chapter 860: 10:00 START

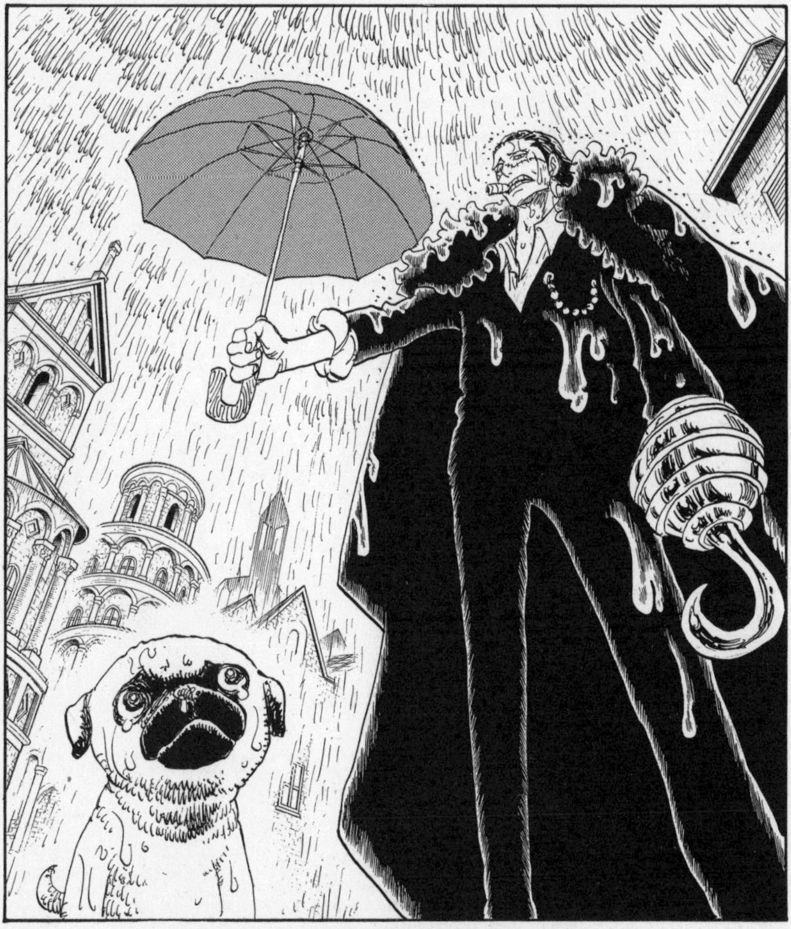

REQUEST: "CROCODILE HOLDING AN UMBRELLA OVER A PUPPY SHIVERING IN THE RAIN" BY HIYU MORI FROM HYOGO

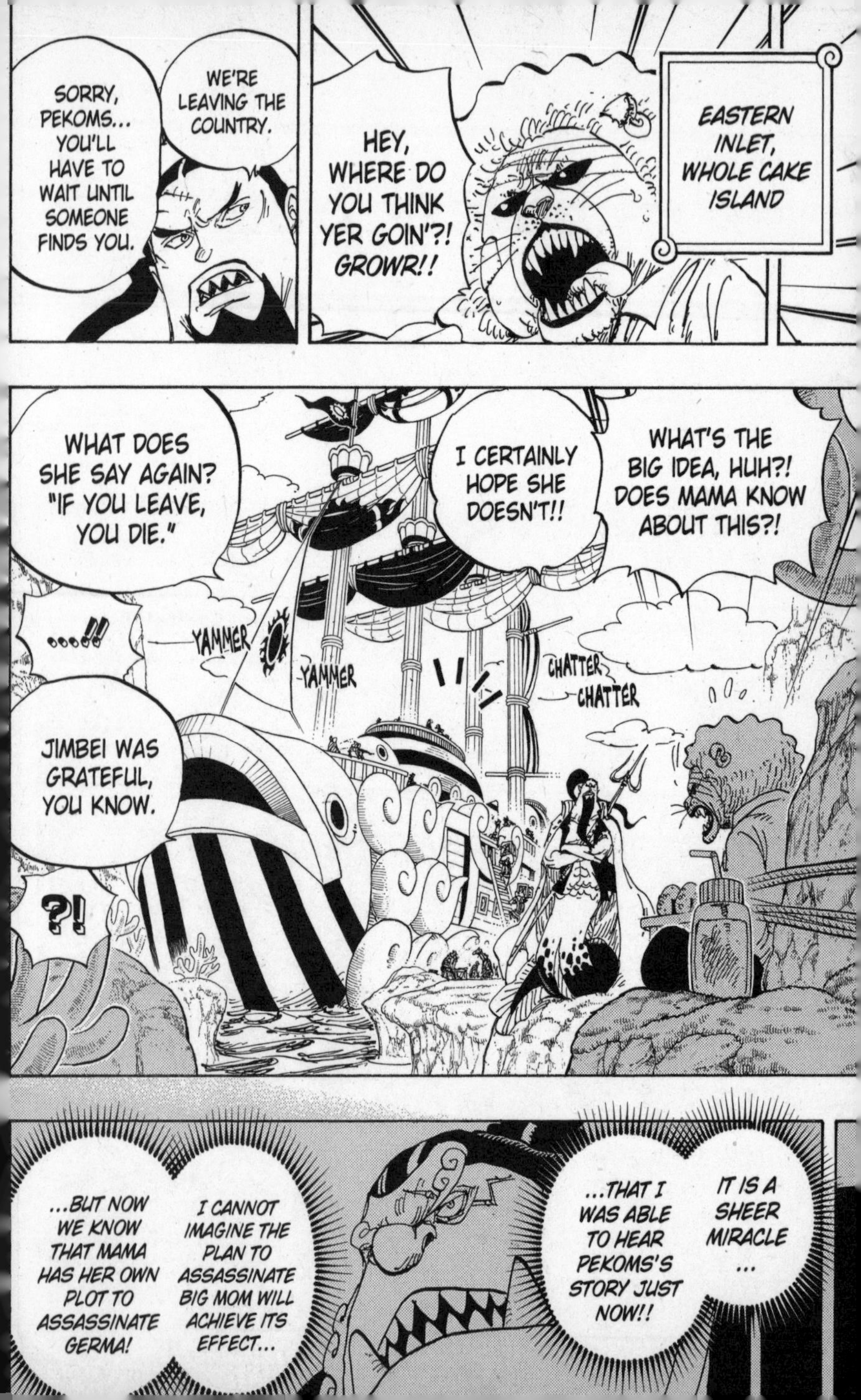

EASTERN INLET, WHOLE CAKE ISLAND
HEY, WHERE DO YOU THINK YER GOIN'?! GROWR!!
WE'RE LEAVING THE COUNTRY.
SORRY, PEKOMS... YOU'LL HAVE TO WAIT UNTIL SOMEONE FINDS YOU.
WHAT'S THE BIG IDEA, HUH?! DOES MAMA KNOW ABOUT THIS?!
I CERTAINLY HOPE SHE DOESN'T!!
WHAT DOES SHE SAY AGAIN? "IF YOU LEAVE, YOU DIE."
CHATTER CHATTER
YAMMER YAMMER
....!!
JIMBEI WAS GRATEFUL, YOU KNOW.
?!
IT IS A SHEER MIRACLE ...
...THAT I WAS ABLE TO HEAR PEKOMS'S STORY JUST NOW!!
I CANNOT IMAGINE THE PLAN TO ASSASSINATE BIG MOM WILL ACHIEVE ITS EFFECT...
...BUT NOW WE KNOW THAT MAMA HAS HER OWN PLOT TO ASSASSINATE GERMA!

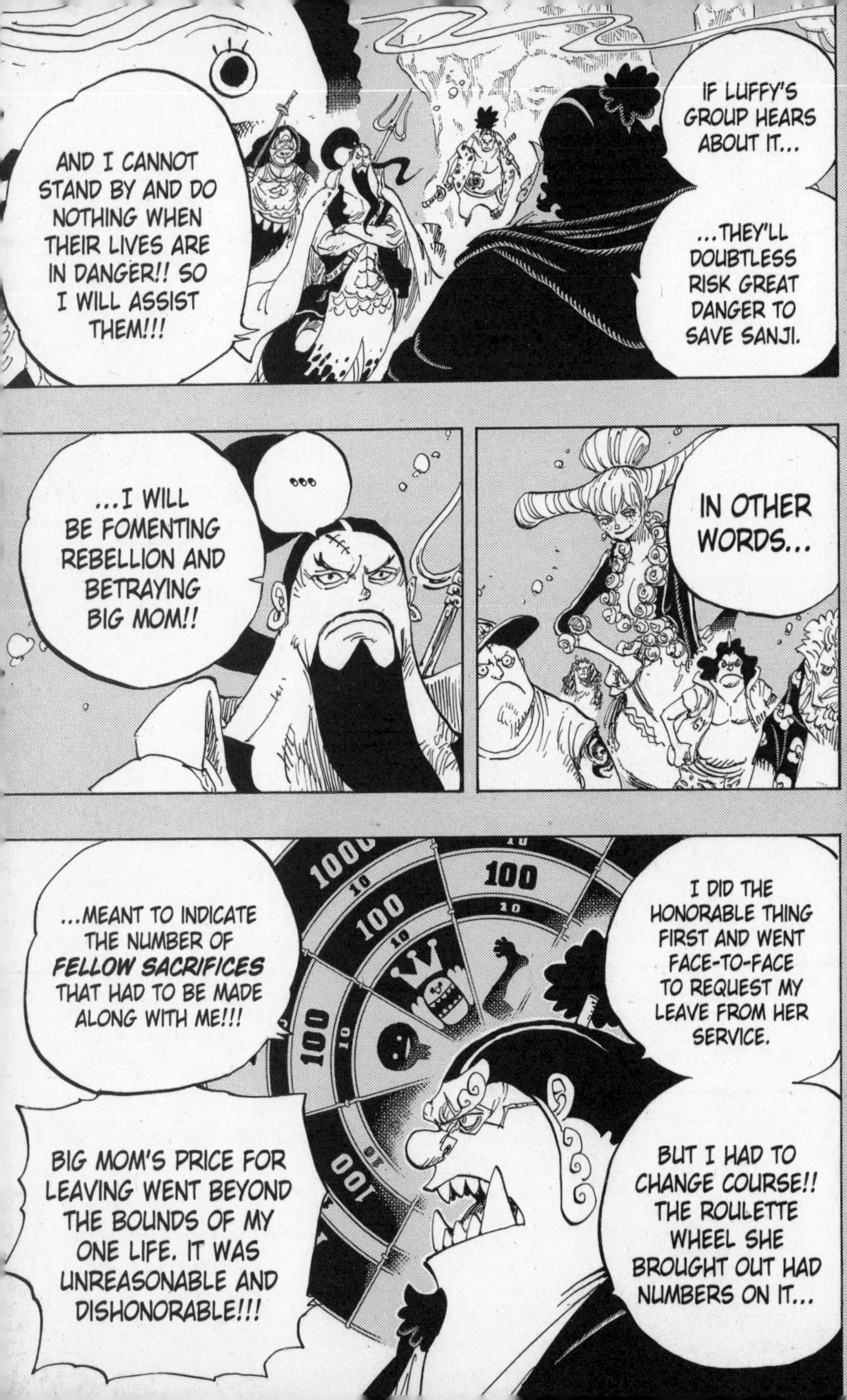
IF LUFFY'S GROUP HEARS ABOUT IT...
...THEY'LL DOUBTLESS RISK GREAT DANGER TO SAVE SANJI.
AND I CANNOT STAND BY AND DO NOTHING WHEN THEIR LIVES ARE IN DANGER!! SO I WILL ASSIST THEM!!!
IN OTHER WORDS...
...
...I WILL BE FOMENTING REBELLION AND BETRAYING BIG MOM!!
I DID THE HONORABLE THING FIRST AND WENT FACE-TO-FACE TO REQUEST MY LEAVE FROM HER SERVICE.
BUT I HAD TO CHANGE COURSE!! THE ROULETTE WHEEL SHE BROUGHT OUT HAD NUMBERS ON IT...
...MEANT TO INDICATE THE NUMBER OF *FELLOW SACRIFICES* THAT HAD TO BE MADE ALONG WITH ME!!!
BIG MOM'S PRICE FOR LEAVING WENT BEYOND THE BOUNDS OF MY ONE LIFE. IT WAS UNREASONABLE AND DISHONORABLE!!!

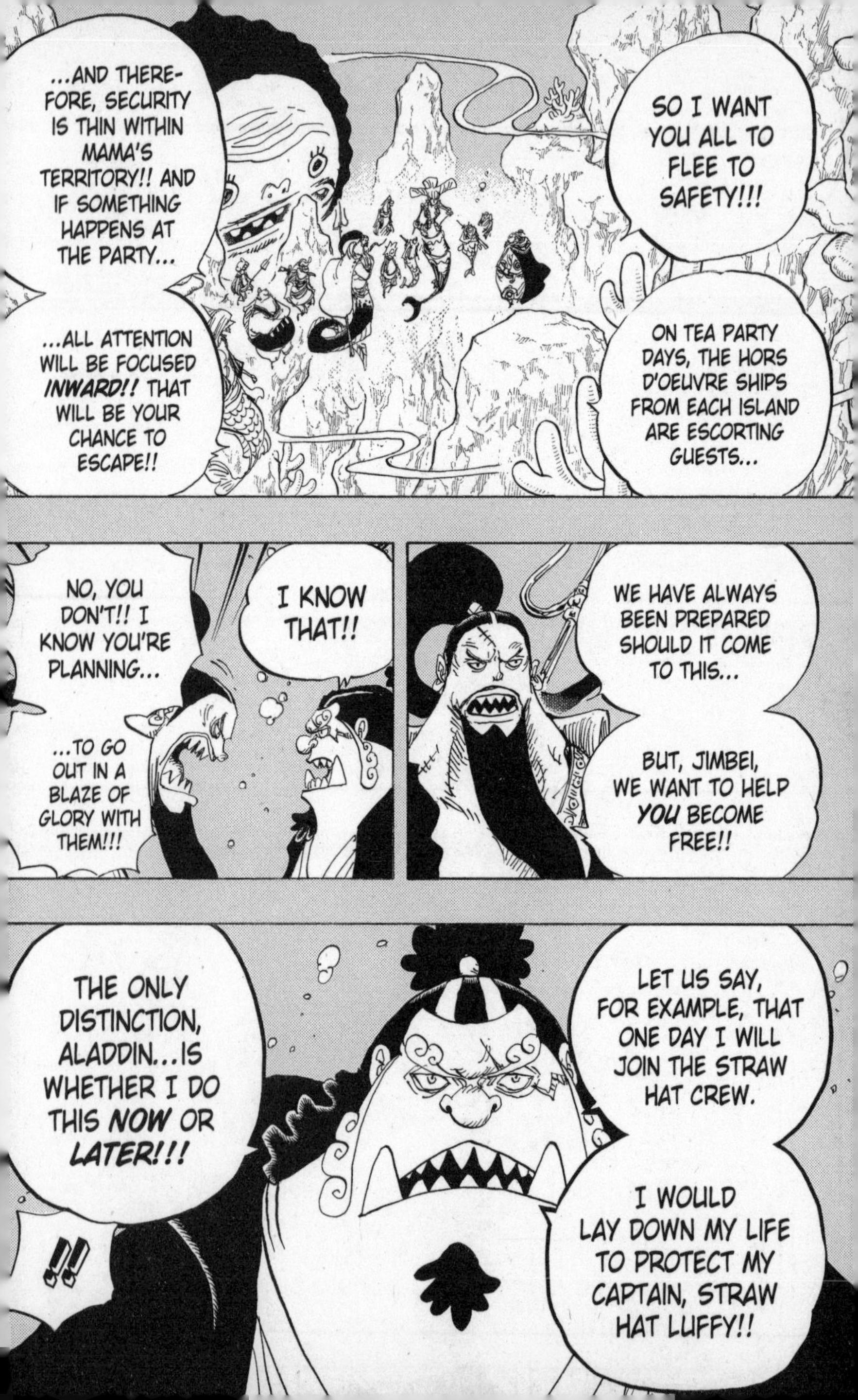
SO I WANT YOU ALL TO FLEE TO SAFETY!!!
ON TEA PARTY DAYS, THE HORS D'OEUVRE SHIPS FROM EACH ISLAND ARE ESCORTING GUESTS...
...AND THEREFORE, SECURITY IS THIN WITHIN MAMA'S TERRITORY!! AND IF SOMETHING HAPPENS AT THE PARTY...
...ALL ATTENTION WILL BE FOCUSED *INWARD!!* THAT WILL BE YOUR CHANCE TO ESCAPE!!
WE HAVE ALWAYS BEEN PREPARED SHOULD IT COME TO THIS...
BUT, JIMBEI, WE WANT TO HELP *YOU* BECOME FREE!!
I KNOW THAT!!
NO, YOU DON'T!! I KNOW YOU'RE PLANNING...
...TO GO OUT IN A BLAZE OF GLORY WITH THEM!!!
LET US SAY, FOR EXAMPLE, THAT ONE DAY I WILL JOIN THE STRAW HAT CREW.
I WOULD LAY DOWN MY LIFE TO PROTECT MY CAPTAIN, STRAW HAT LUFFY!!
THE ONLY DISTINCTION, ALADDIN...IS WHETHER I DO THIS *NOW* OR *LATER!!!*
!!

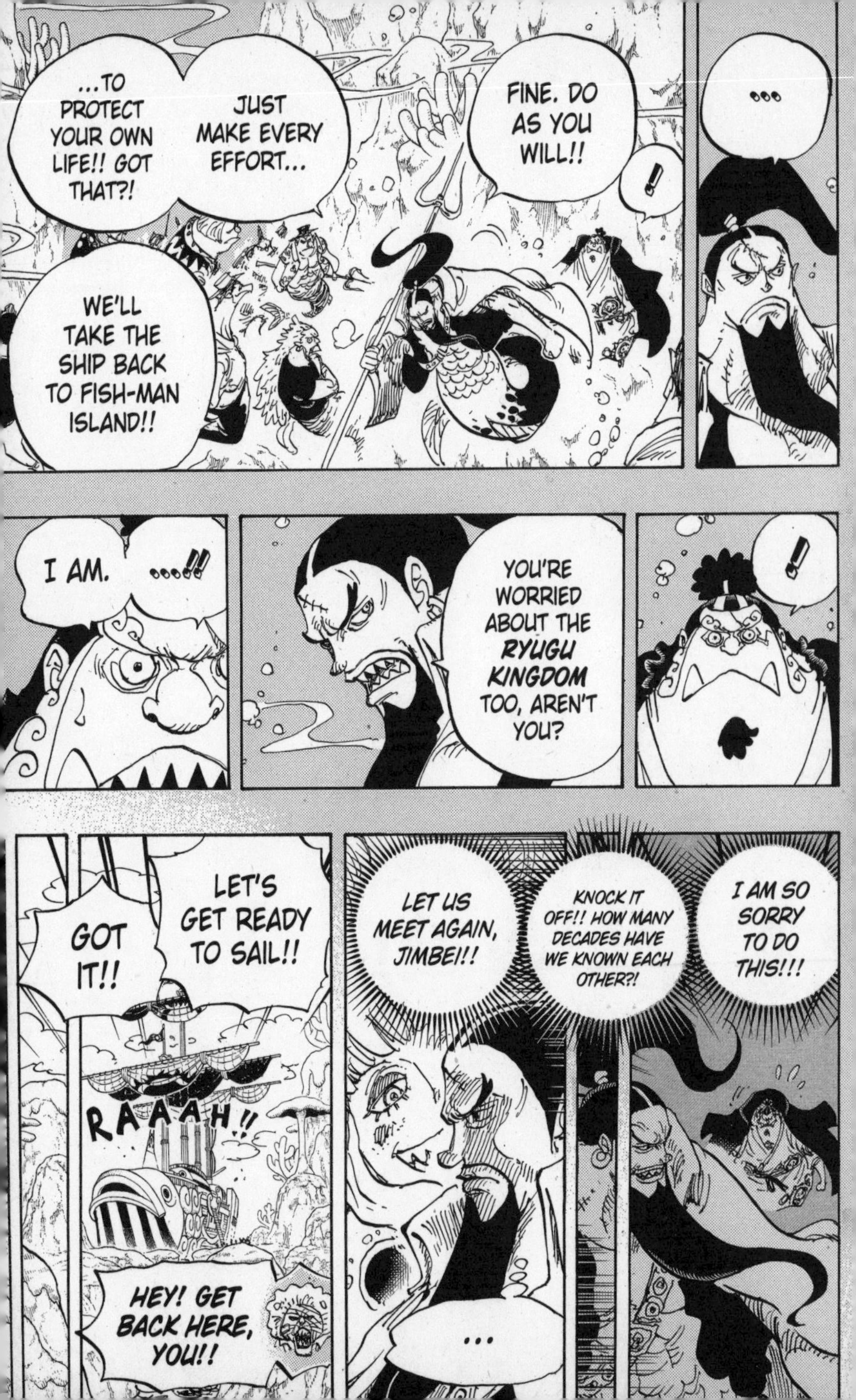
...
FINE. DO AS YOU WILL!!
!
JUST MAKE EVERY EFFORT...
...TO PROTECT YOUR OWN LIFE!! GOT THAT?!
WE'LL TAKE THE SHIP BACK TO FISH-MAN ISLAND!!
!
YOU'RE WORRIED ABOUT THE *RYUGU KINGDOM* TOO, AREN'T YOU?
...!!
I AM.
I AM SO SORRY TO DO THIS!!!
KNOCK IT OFF!! HOW MANY DECADES HAVE WE KNOWN EACH OTHER?!
LET US MEET AGAIN, JIMBEI!!
...
LET'S GET READY TO SAIL!!
GOT IT!!
RAAAH!!
HEY! GET BACK HERE, YOU!!

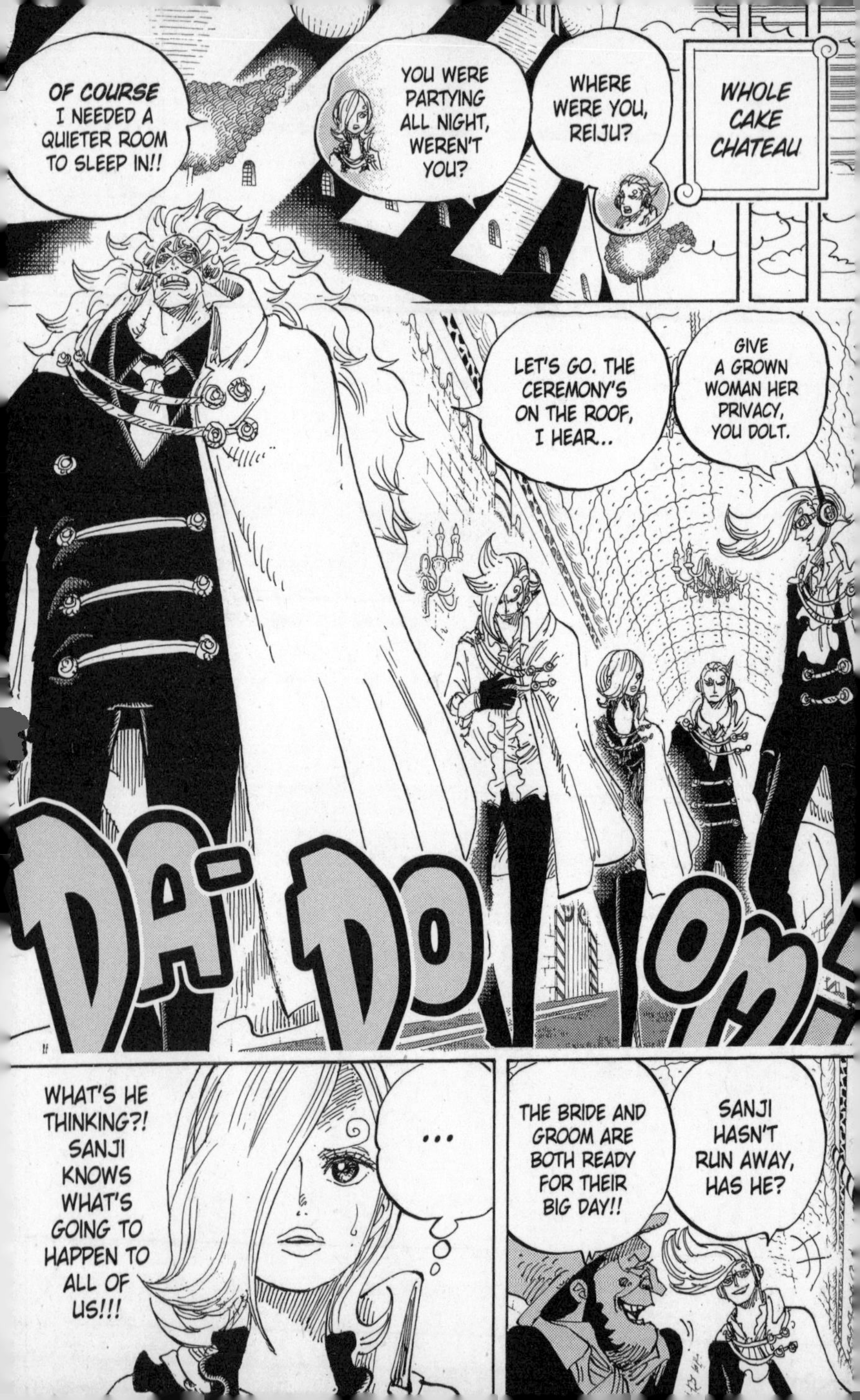
WHOLE CAKE CHATEAU
WHERE WERE YOU, REIJU?
YOU WERE PARTYING ALL NIGHT, WEREN'T YOU?
OF COURSE I NEEDED A QUIETER ROOM TO SLEEP IN!!
GIVE A GROWN WOMAN HER PRIVACY, YOU DOLT.
LET'S GO. THE CEREMONY'S ON THE ROOF, I HEAR..
DA-DOOM
SANJI HASN'T RUN AWAY, HAS HE?
THE BRIDE AND GROOM ARE BOTH READY FOR THEIR BIG DAY!!
...
WHAT'S HE THINKING?! SANJI KNOWS WHAT'S GOING TO HAPPEN TO ALL OF US!!!

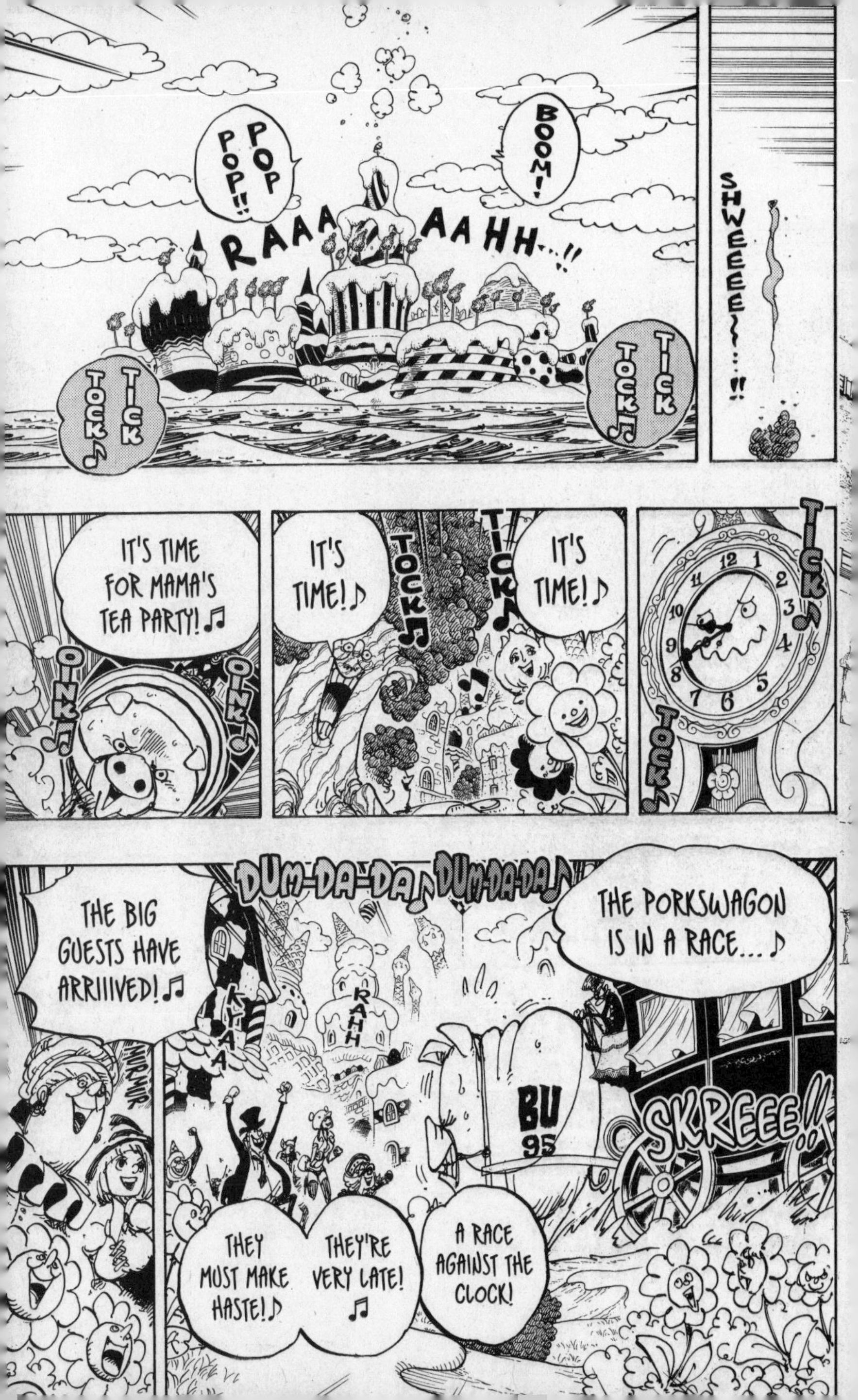
SHWEEEE~...!!
BOOM!
TICK TOCK♫
RAAAAAHH...!!
POP POP!!
TICK TOCK♪
TICK♪
TOCK♪
IT'S TIME!♪
TICK♪
TOCK♫
IT'S TIME!♪
IT'S TIME FOR MAMA'S TEA PARTY!♫
OINK♪
OINK♪
THE PORKSWAGON IS IN A RACE...♪
DUM-DA-DA♪
DUM-DA-DA♪
SKREEE!!
BU 95
A RACE AGAINST THE CLOCK!
THEY'RE VERY LATE!♫
RAHH
KYAA
THE BIG GUESTS HAVE ARRIIIVED!♫
MURMUR
THEY MUST MAKE HASTE!♪

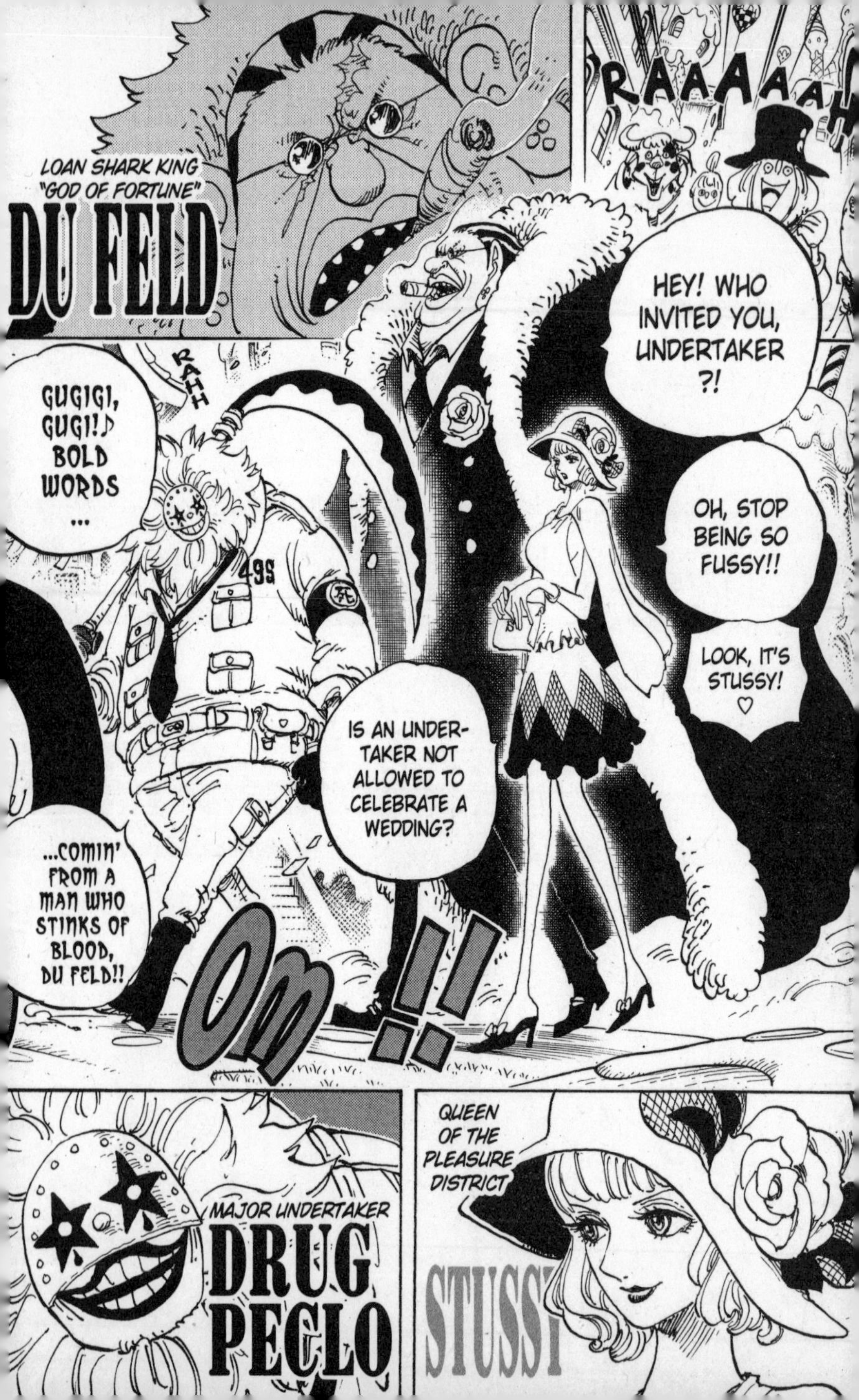

RAAAAAH
LOAN SHARK KING "GOD OF FORTUNE"
DU FELD
HEY! WHO INVITED YOU, UNDERTAKER ?!
OH, STOP BEING SO FUSSY!!
LOOK, IT'S STUSSY! ♡
GUGIGI, GUGI!♪ BOLD WORDS ...
RAHH
IS AN UNDER-TAKER NOT ALLOWED TO CELEBRATE A WEDDING?
...COMIN' FROM A MAN WHO STINKS OF BLOOD, DU FELD!!
OM!!
QUEEN OF THE PLEASURE DISTRICT
STUSSY
MAJOR UNDERTAKER
DRUG PECLO

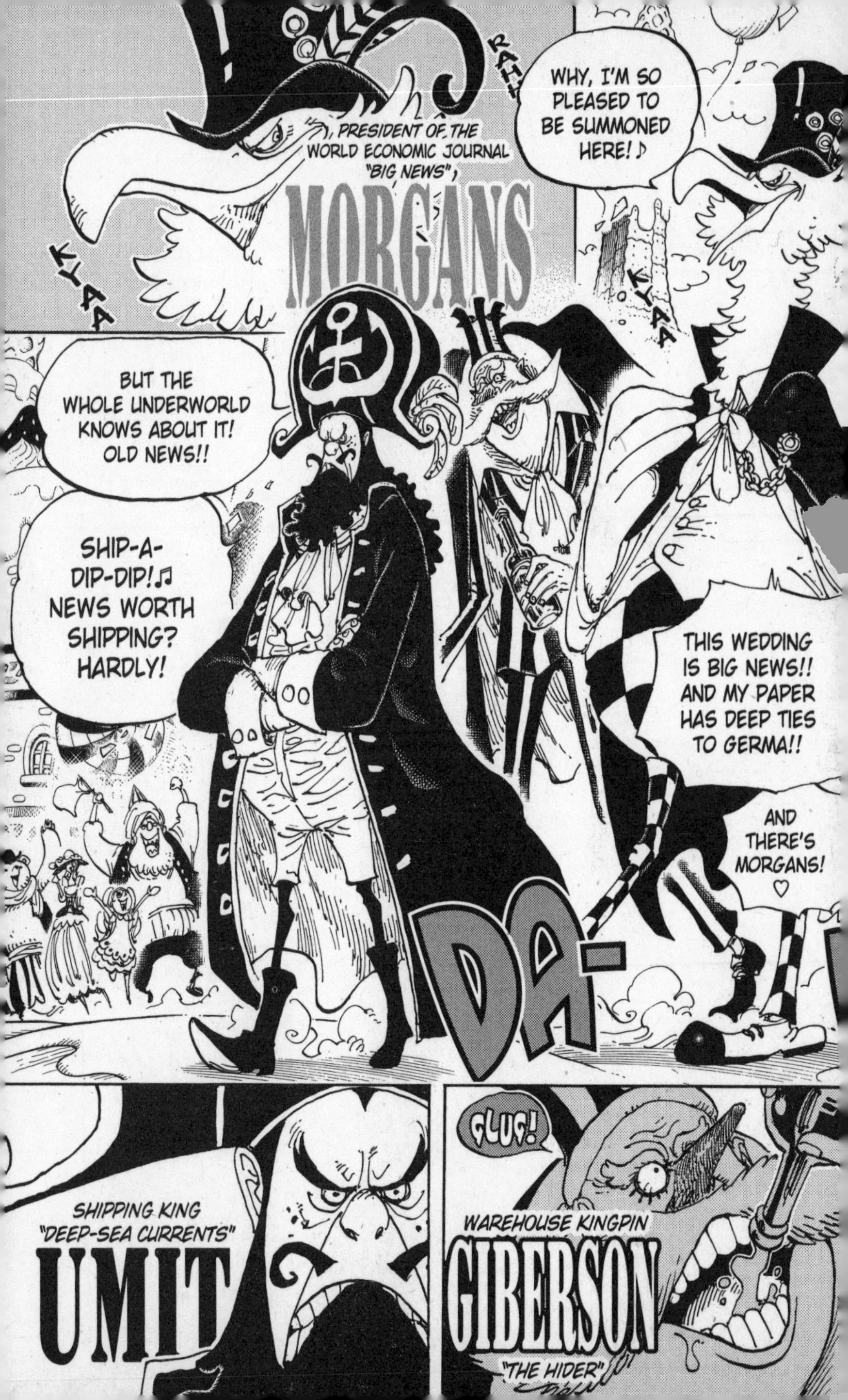

WHY, I'M SO PLEASED TO BE SUMMONED HERE! ♪
KYAA
RAHH
PRESIDENT OF THE WORLD ECONOMIC JOURNAL "BIG NEWS",
MORGANS
KYAA
THIS WEDDING IS BIG NEWS!! AND MY PAPER HAS DEEP TIES TO GERMA!!
AND THERE'S MORGANS! ♡
DA-
BUT THE WHOLE UNDERWORLD KNOWS ABOUT IT! OLD NEWS!!
SHIP-A-DIP-DIP!♫ NEWS WORTH SHIPPING? HARDLY!
GLUG!
WAREHOUSE KINGPIN
GIBERSON
"THE HIDER"
SHIPPING KING
"DEEP-SEA CURRENTS"
UMIT

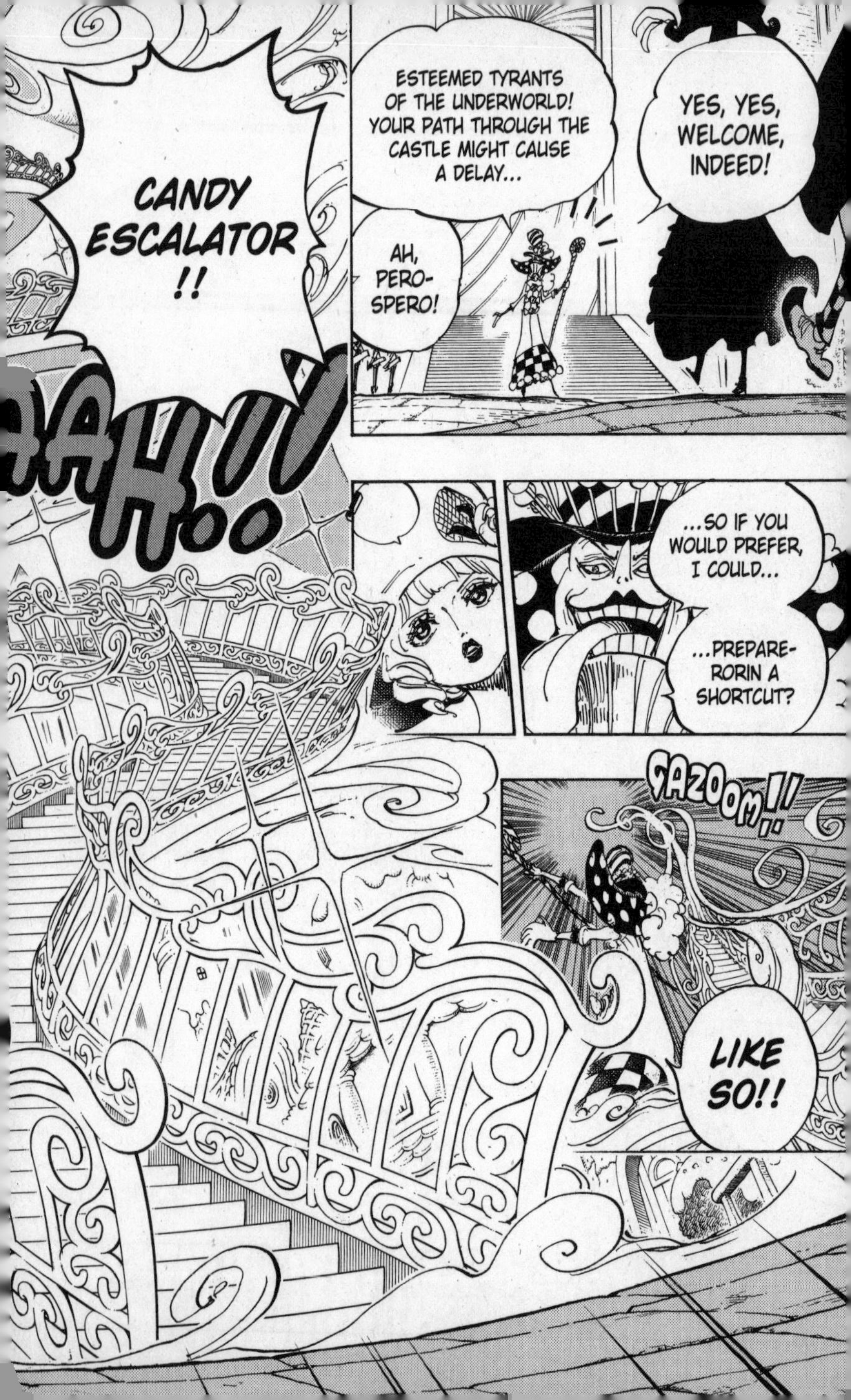
YES, YES, WELCOME, INDEED!
ESTEEMED TYRANTS OF THE UNDERWORLD! YOUR PATH THROUGH THE CASTLE MIGHT CAUSE A DELAY...
AH, PERO-SPERO!
...SO IF YOU WOULD PREFER, I COULD...
...PREPARE-RORIN A SHORTCUT?
GAZOOM!!
LIKE SO!!
CANDY ESCALATOR!!
AAH!!

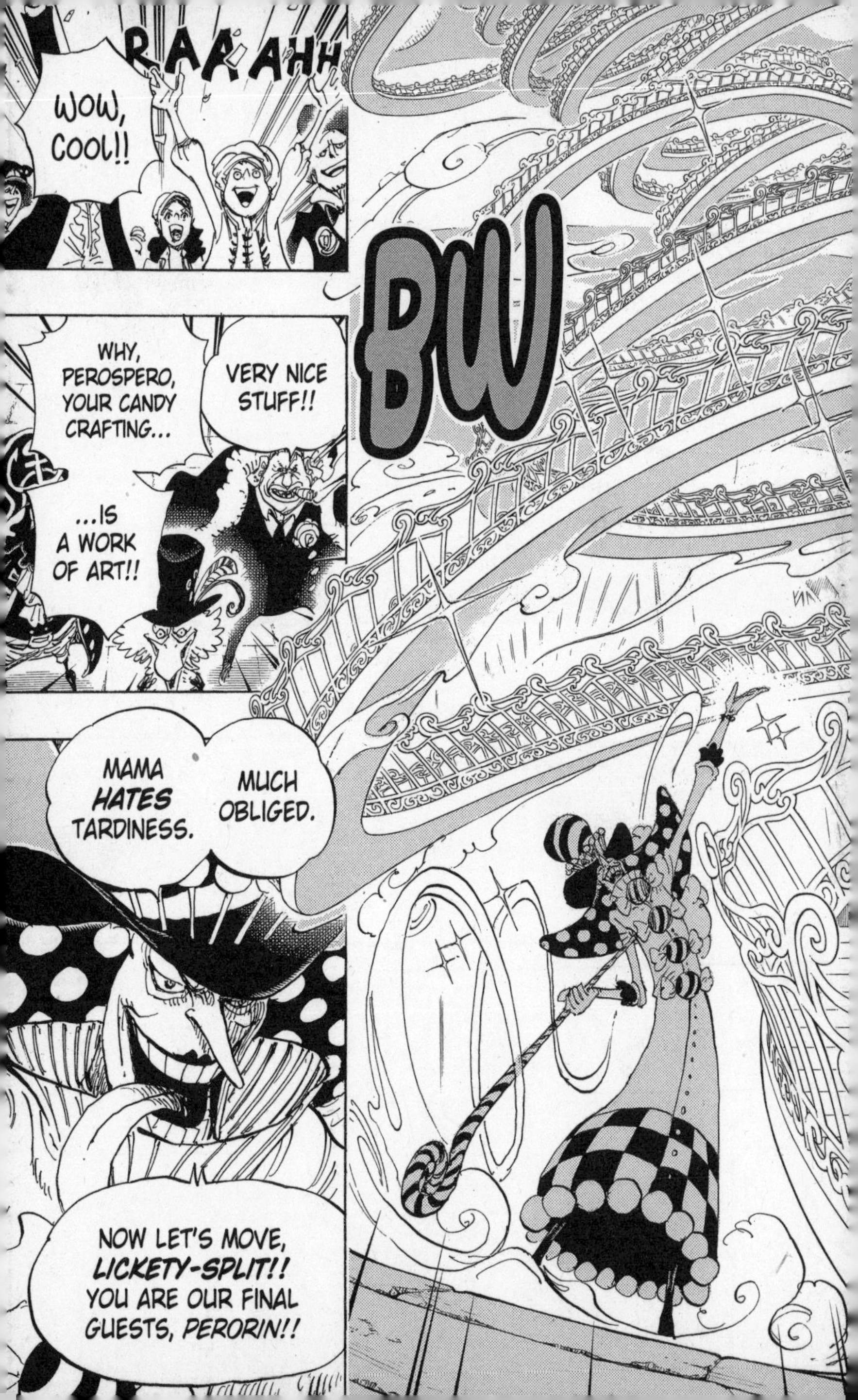
BW
RAR AHH
WOW, COOL!!
VERY NICE STUFF!!
WHY, PEROSPERO, YOUR CANDY CRAFTING...
...IS A WORK OF ART!!
MUCH OBLIGED.
MAMA *HATES* TARDINESS.
NOW LET'S MOVE, *LICKETY-SPLIT!!* YOU ARE OUR FINAL GUESTS, *PERORIN!!*

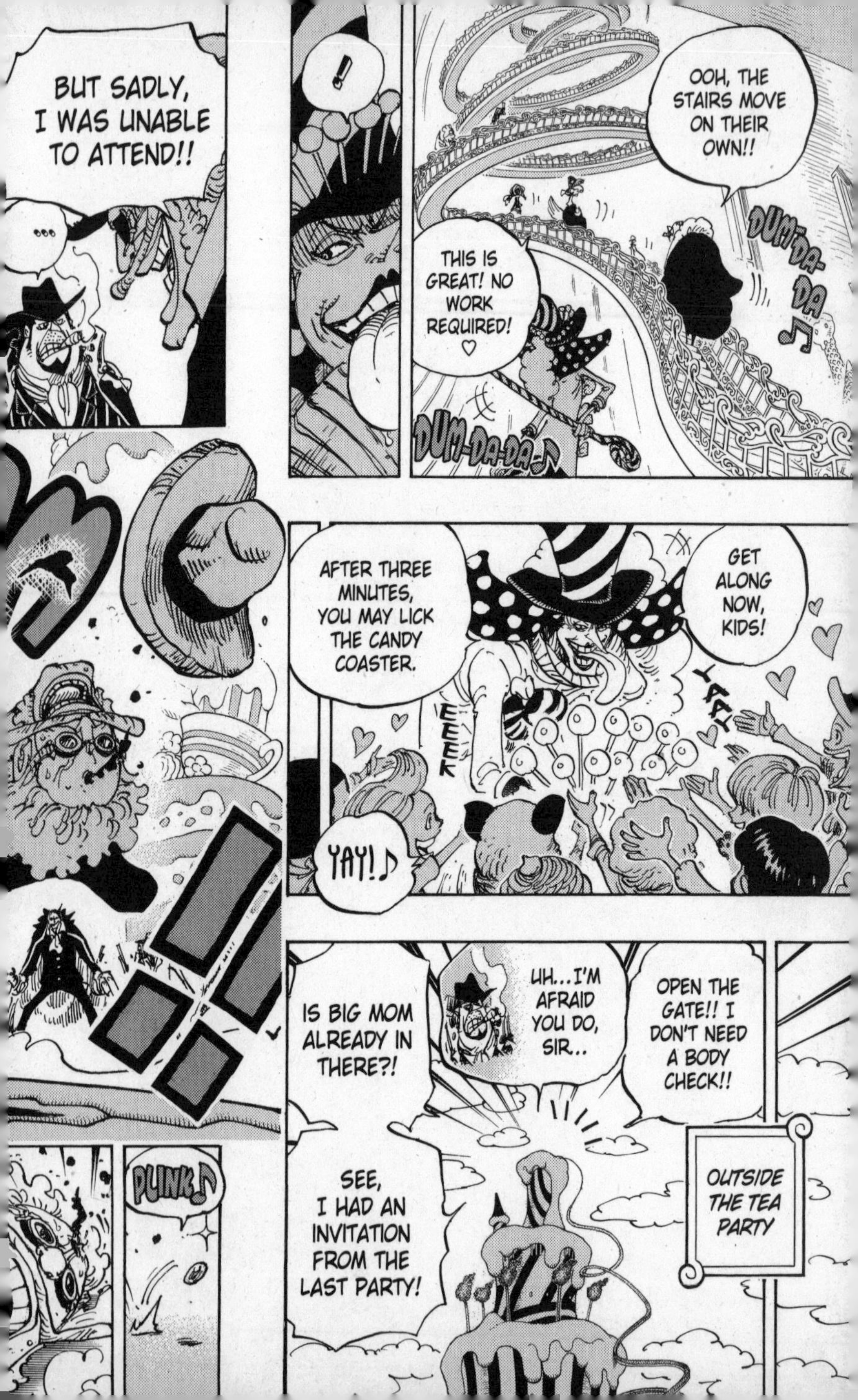
OOH, THE STAIRS MOVE ON THEIR OWN!!
DUM-DA-DA♪
THIS IS GREAT! NO WORK REQUIRED! ♡
DUM-DA-DA♪
!
BUT SADLY, I WAS UNABLE TO ATTEND!!
...
GET ALONG NOW, KIDS!
YAY
AFTER THREE MINUTES, YOU MAY LICK THE CANDY COASTER.
EEEK
YAY!♪
OPEN THE GATE!! I DON'T NEED A BODY CHECK!!
UH...I'M AFRAID YOU DO, SIR...
IS BIG MOM ALREADY IN THERE?!
OUTSIDE THE TEA PARTY
SEE, I HAD AN INVITATION FROM THE LAST PARTY!
PLUNK♪

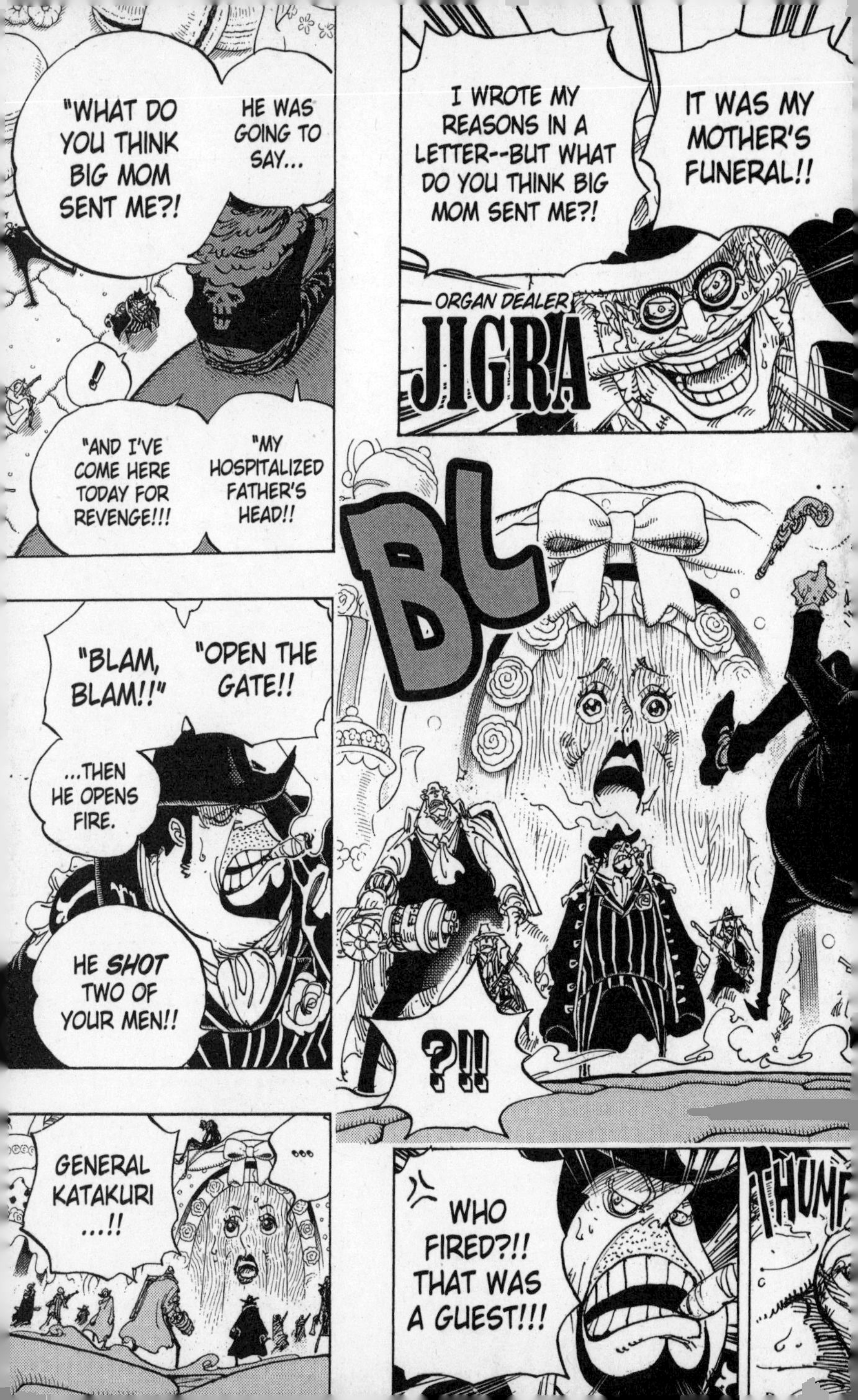
IT WAS MY MOTHER'S FUNERAL!!
I WROTE MY REASONS IN A LETTER--BUT WHAT DO YOU THINK BIG MOM SENT ME?!
ORGAN DEALER
JIGRA
HE WAS GOING TO SAY...
"WHAT DO YOU THINK BIG MOM SENT ME?!
!
"MY HOSPITALIZED FATHER'S HEAD!!
"AND I'VE COME HERE TODAY FOR REVENGE!!!
BL
?!!
WHO FIRED?!! THAT WAS A GUEST!!!
THUMP
"OPEN THE GATE!!
"BLAM, BLAM!!"
...THEN HE OPENS FIRE.
HE SHOT TWO OF YOUR MEN!!
...
GENERAL KATAKURI ...!!

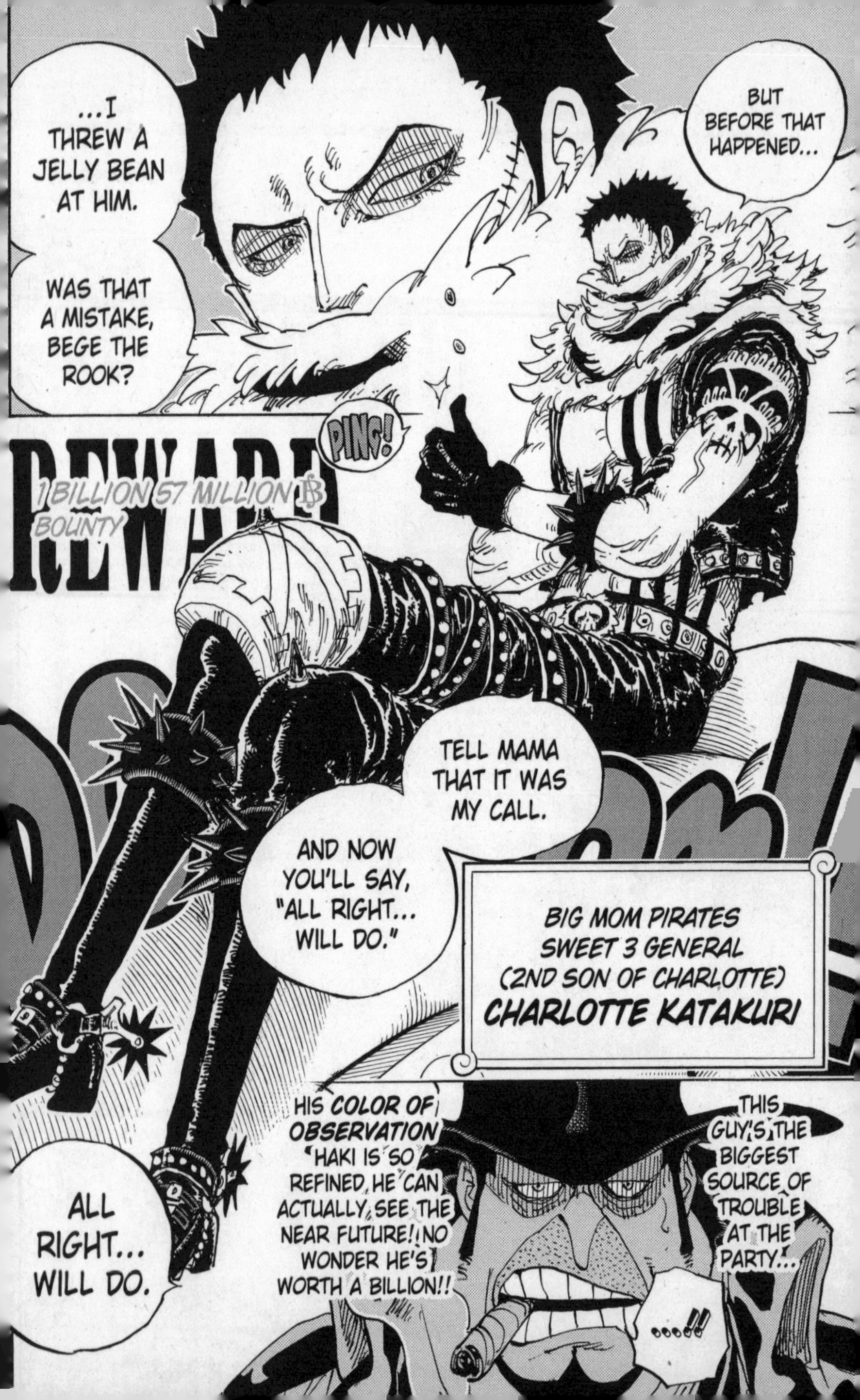
BUT BEFORE THAT HAPPENED...
...I THREW A JELLY BEAN AT HIM.
WAS THAT A MISTAKE, BEGE THE ROOK?
PING!
1 BILLION 57 MILLION ฿ BOUNTY
TELL MAMA THAT IT WAS MY CALL.
AND NOW YOU'LL SAY, "ALL RIGHT... WILL DO."
BIG MOM PIRATES SWEET 3 GENERAL (2ND SON OF CHARLOTTE) CHARLOTTE KATAKURI
THIS GUY'S THE BIGGEST SOURCE OF TROUBLE AT THE PARTY...
HIS COLOR OF OBSERVATION HAKI IS SO REFINED HE CAN ACTUALLY SEE THE NEAR FUTURE!! NO WONDER HE'S WORTH A BILLION!!
....!!
ALL RIGHT... WILL DO.

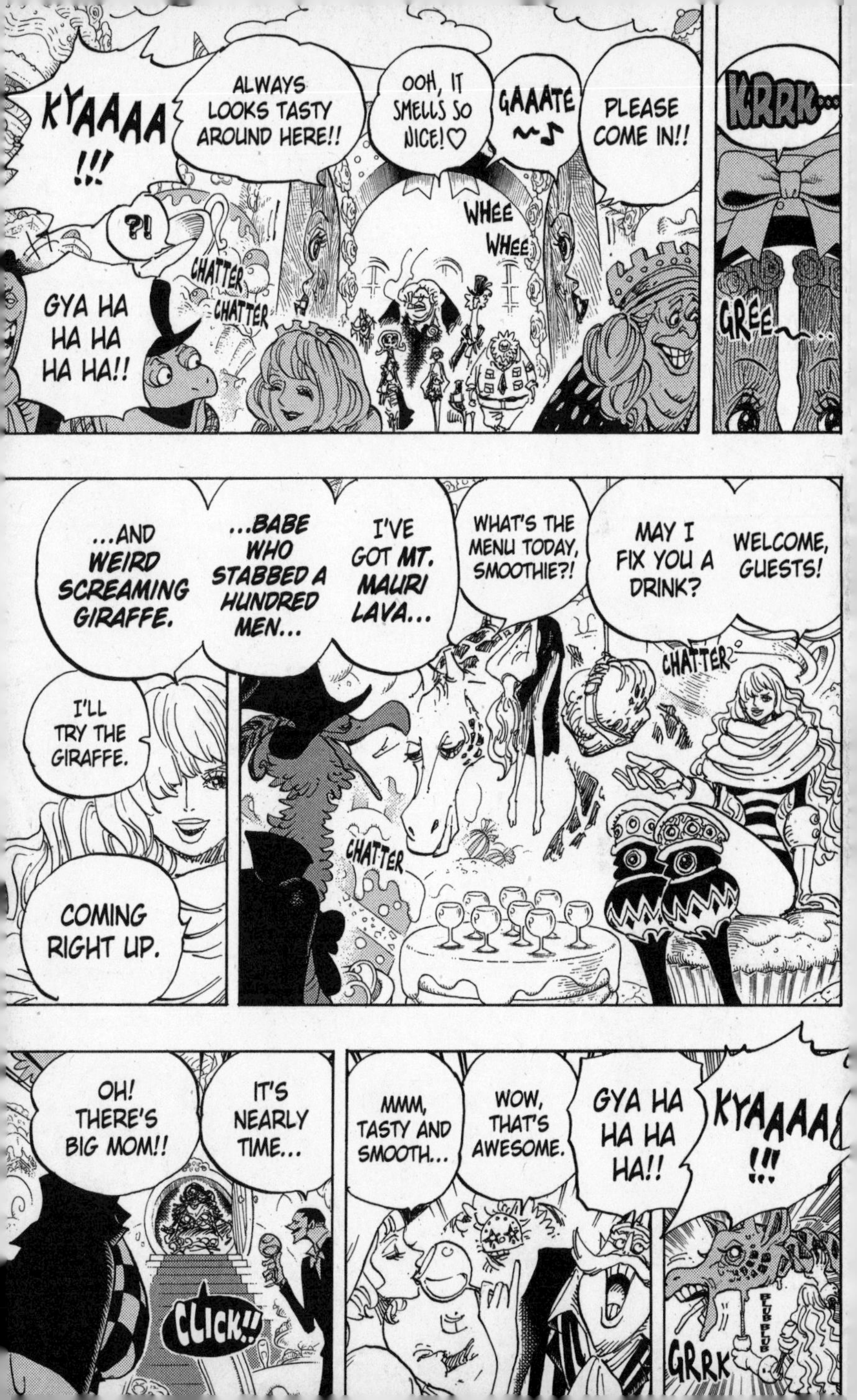

KRRK...
GREE~...
PLEASE COME IN!!
GAAATE ~♪
OOH, IT SMELLS SO NICE!♡
ALWAYS LOOKS TASTY AROUND HERE!!
KYAAAA !!!
WHEE WHEE
?!
CHATTER CHATTER
GYA HA HA HA HA HA!!
WELCOME, GUESTS!
MAY I FIX YOU A DRINK?
WHAT'S THE MENU TODAY, SMOOTHIE?!
I'VE GOT MT. MAURI LAVA...
...BABE WHO STABBED A HUNDRED MEN...
...AND WEIRD SCREAMING GIRAFFE.
CHATTER
CHATTER
I'LL TRY THE GIRAFFE.
COMING RIGHT UP.
KYAAAA !!!
GYA HA HA HA HA!!
WOW, THAT'S AWESOME.
MMM, TASTY AND SMOOTH...
BLUB BLUB
GRRK
IT'S NEARLY TIME...
OH! THERE'S BIG MOM!!
CLICK!!

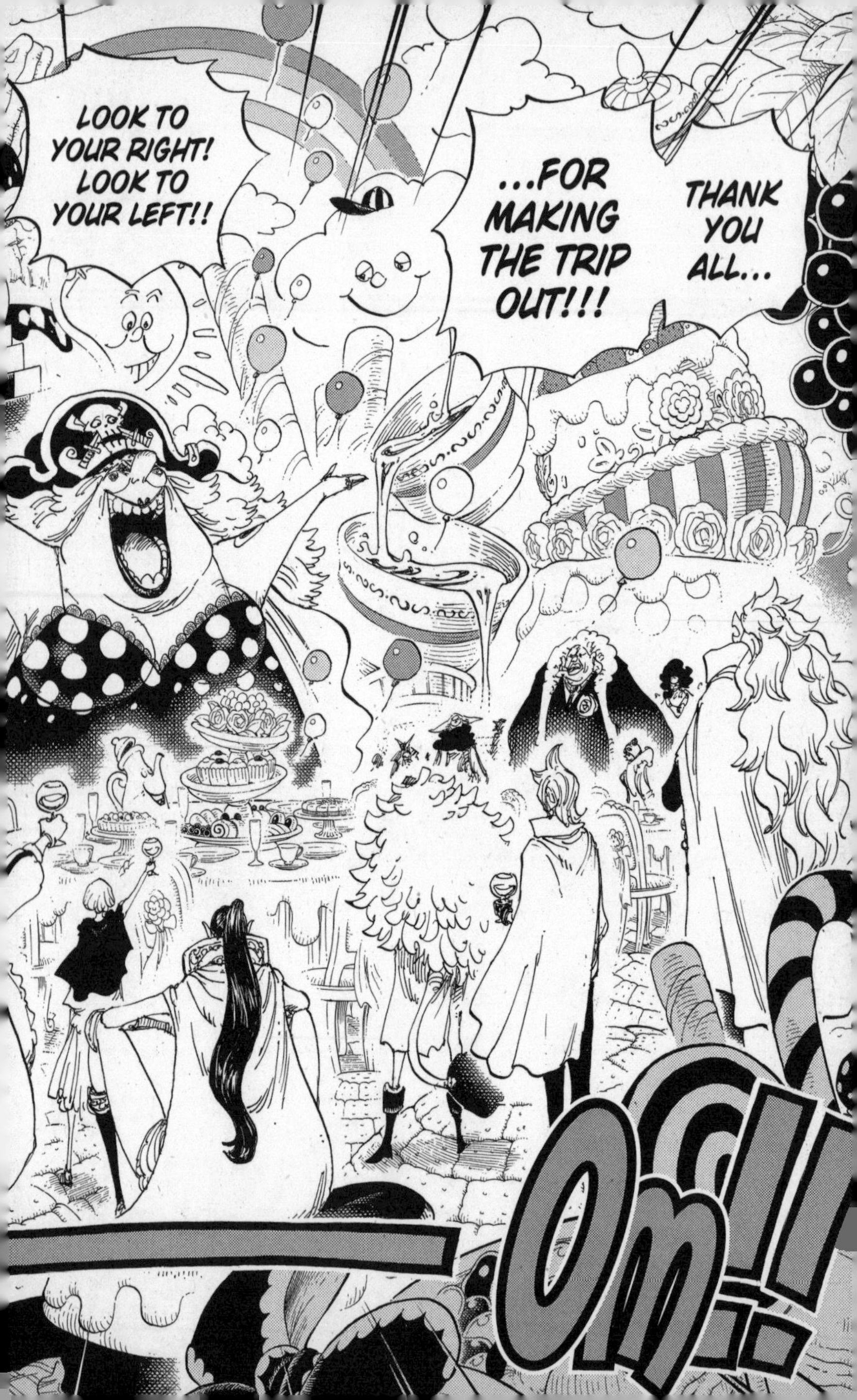
THANK YOU ALL...
...FOR MAKING THE TRIP OUT!!!
LOOK TO YOUR RIGHT! LOOK TO YOUR LEFT!!
OM!!

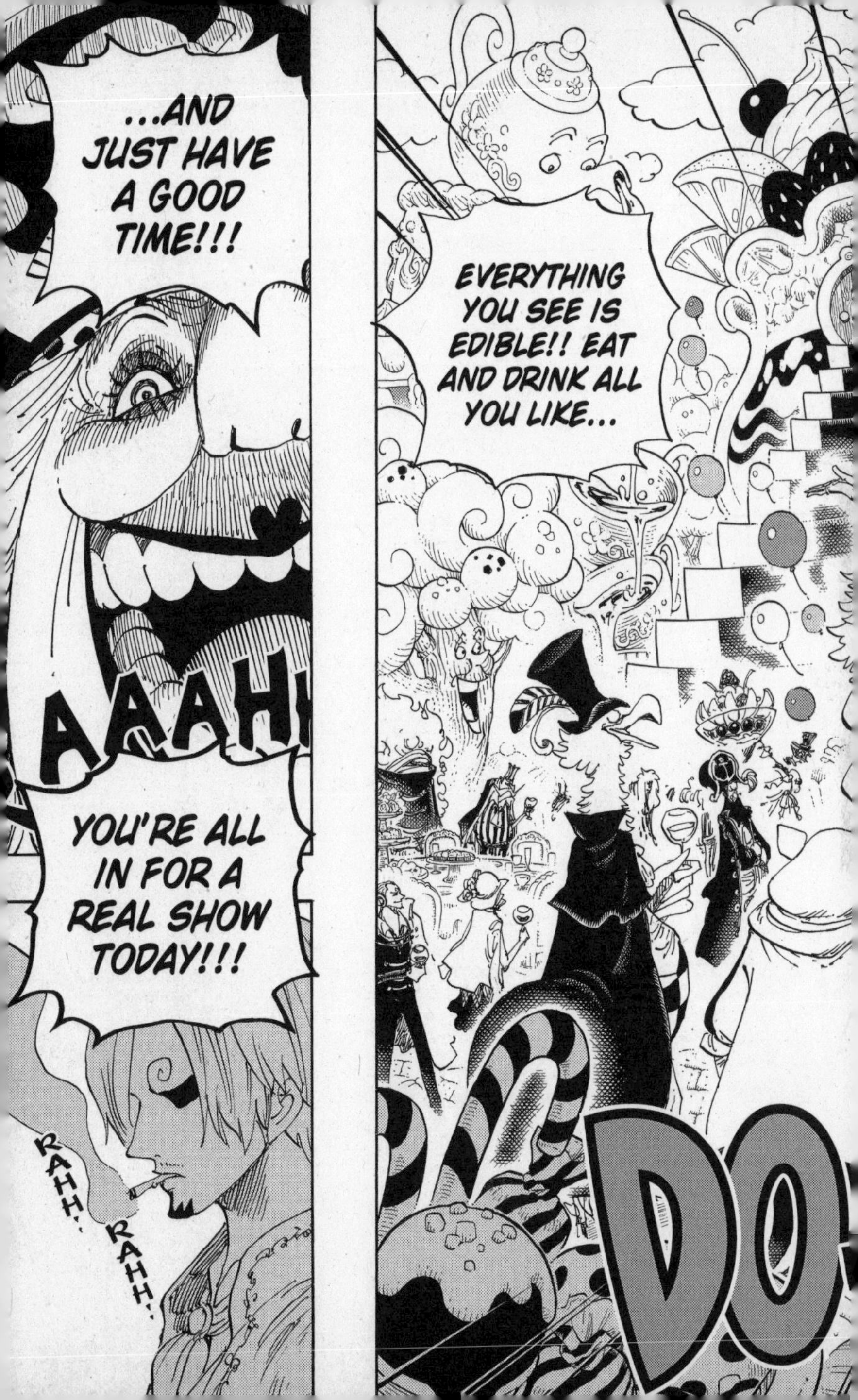
EVERYTHING YOU SEE IS EDIBLE!! EAT AND DRINK ALL YOU LIKE...
DO-
...AND JUST HAVE A GOOD TIME!!!
AAAH
YOU'RE ALL IN FOR A REAL SHOW TODAY!!!
RAHH! RAHH!

質問コーナー

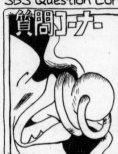

He thrust the young women aside, and commanded them, "Find some younger man to cavort with!!"
"Eek!"
"But, Señor!" they lamented.
He was Señor Pink, senior officer of the Doflamingo Family's Diamante forces.
"I ain't--*smuk!*--into kids," he said, his baritone voice warm with the glow of love.
And the girls...screamed. "Eeek! ♡ Señor! ♡"
THE END

SBS Hard Boiled 4

(Igarashi, Oita)

Q: Please make Urouge cute.

--Ajishio

A: It didn't work.

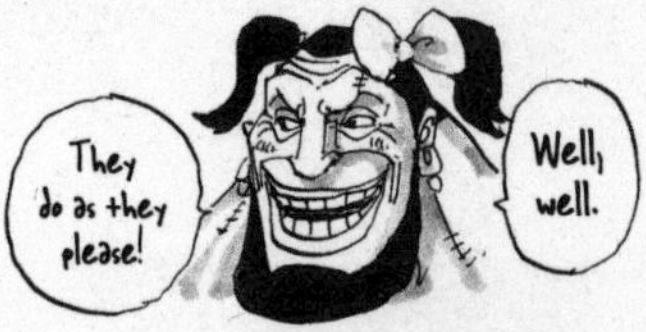

They do as they please!
Well, well.

Q: Odacchi!! I've decided to display my Nami figure on my TV stand.

--Captain Nobuo

A: I see. Next question.

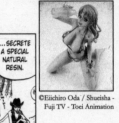

©Eiichiro Oda / Shueisha - Fuji TV - Toei Animation

...SECRETE A SPECIAL NATURAL RESIN.
YUCK. IT'S STICKY.
DON'T WIPE IT ON ME!

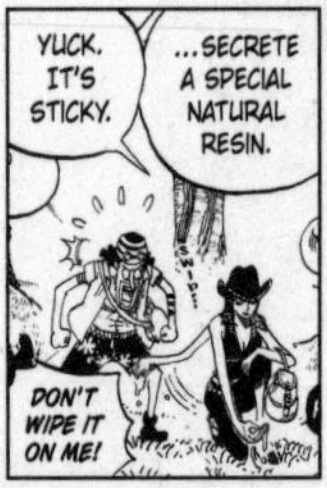

Q: Odacchi Sensei!! Sum up your current feeling with a famous *One Piece* quote! Three, two, one, **go!!**

A: Yuck. It's sticky. (Unforgettable quote)

Q: Tell me the name of the big black cat in Hawkins' pirate crew. I can't get over how cute it is. Is that black cat a mink?

--Law's Design Is Cool

A: Umm...Black? Black cat? That looks...Black to you? Can we just agree that it's a cat? You're right, this cat is a mink. He's a crew member on Hawkins' crew. His name is Faust, and he seems to be a sorcerer...but what kind of sorcery does he command? What kind of saucery does he catmand? (That's a little joke for you folks.)

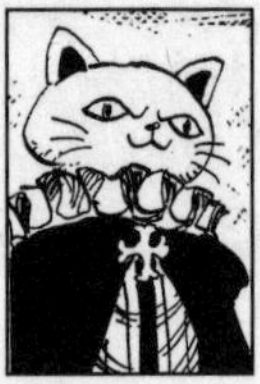

Q: Hello, Oda Sensei. Whitebeard always wore a bandana around his head. Was he hiding his baldness? Please draw what he looked like underneath.

--Sanadacchi

A: It's like this. According to rumor.

But I...
...still love you.

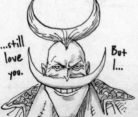

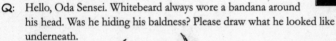

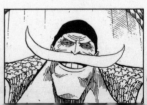

Chapter 861:
THE ACTOR

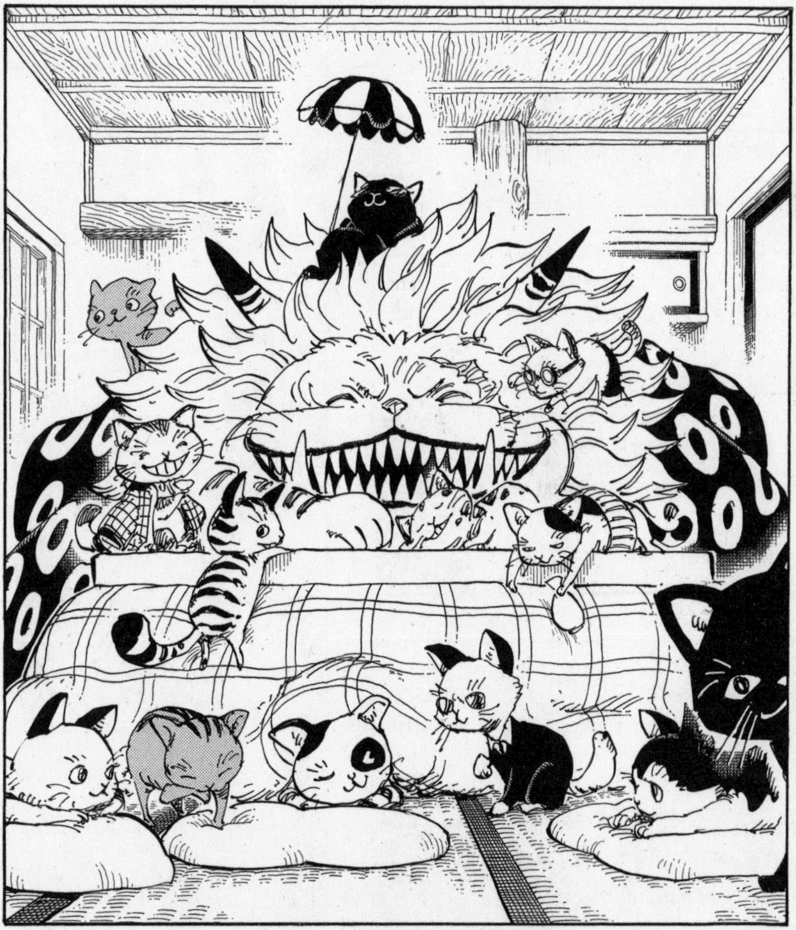

REQUEST: "CAT VIPER LOUNGING IN A KOTATSU WITH A BUNCH OF CATS" BY NODA SKYWALKER FROM OSAKA

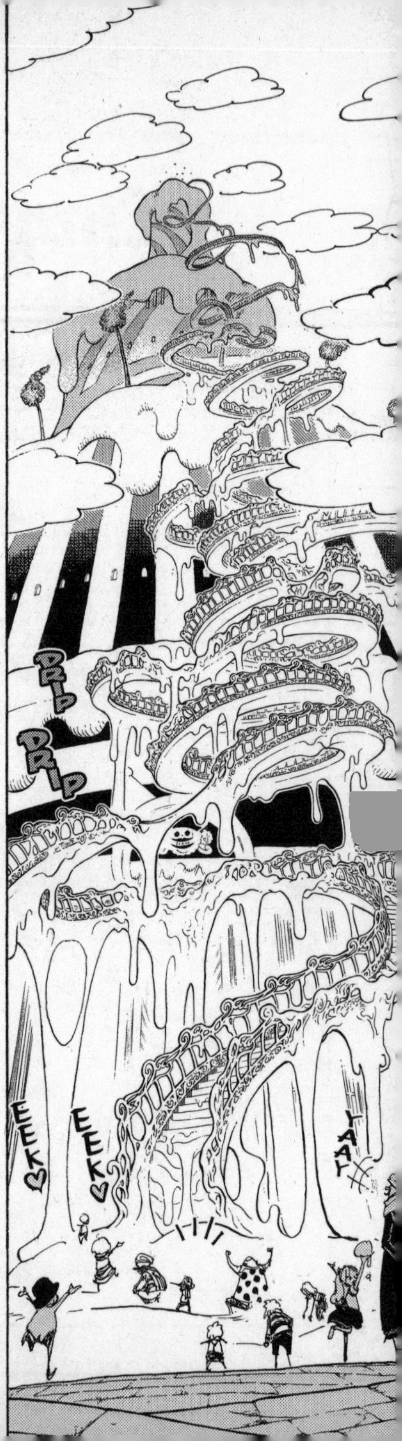
DRIP
DRIP
YAAY
EEK♡
EEK♡

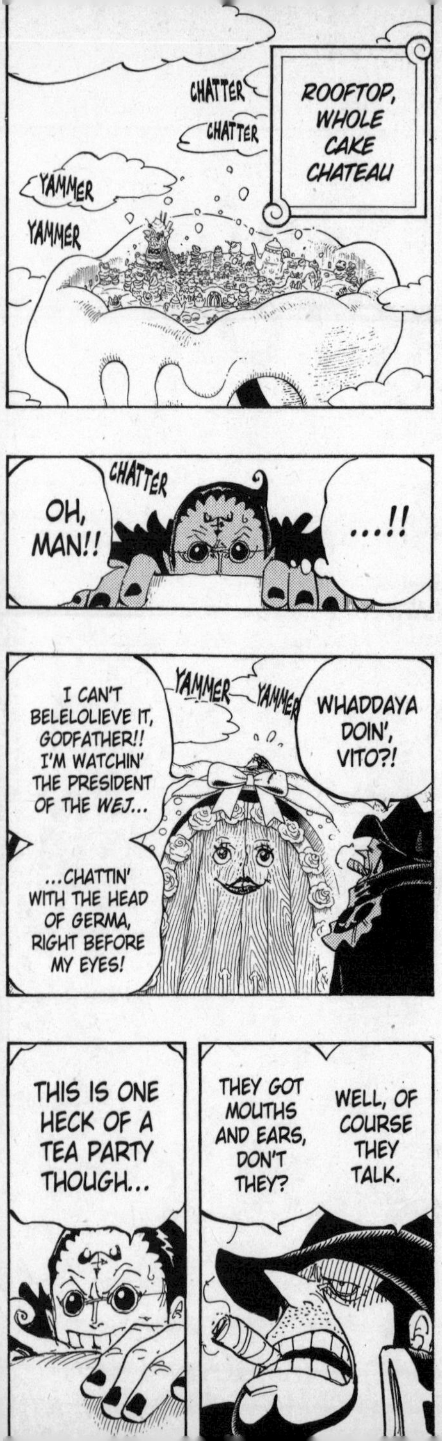
ROOFTOP, WHOLE CAKE CHATEAU
CHATTER
CHATTER
YAMMER
YAMMER
...!!
CHATTER
OH, MAN!!
WHADDAYA DOIN', VITO?!
YAMMER
YAMMER
I CAN'T BELELOLIEVE IT, GODFATHER!! I'M WATCHIN' THE PRESIDENT OF THE WEJ...
...CHATTIN' WITH THE HEAD OF GERMA, RIGHT BEFORE MY EYES!
WELL, OF COURSE THEY TALK.
THEY GOT MOUTHS AND EARS, DON'T THEY?
THIS IS ONE HECK OF A TEA PARTY THOUGH...

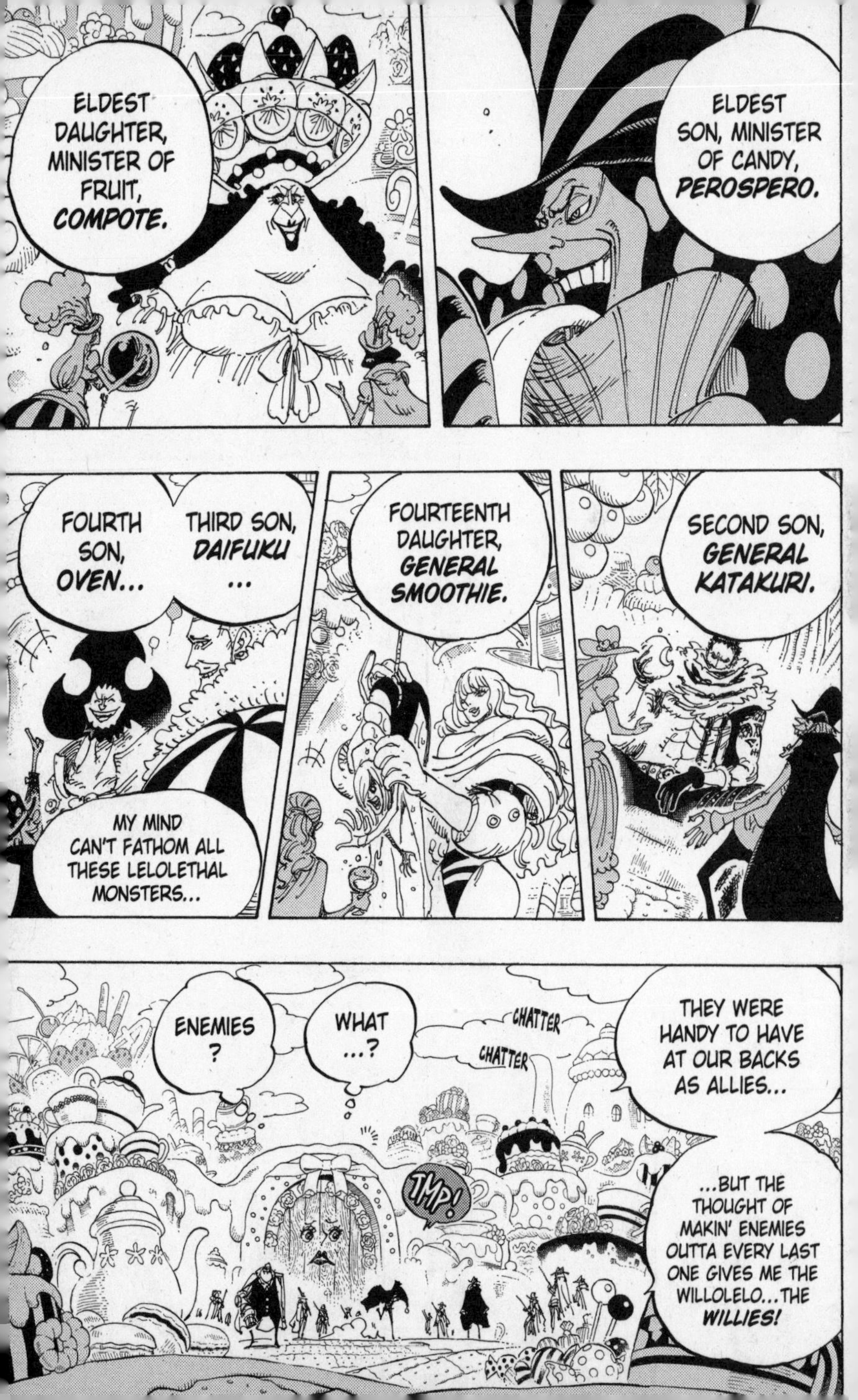
ELDEST SON, MINISTER OF CANDY, PEROSPERO.
ELDEST DAUGHTER, MINISTER OF FRUIT, COMPOTE.
SECOND SON, GENERAL KATAKURI.
FOURTEENTH DAUGHTER, GENERAL SMOOTHIE.
THIRD SON, DAIFUKU ...
FOURTH SON, OVEN...
MY MIND CAN'T FATHOM ALL THESE LELOLETHAL MONSTERS...
THEY WERE HANDY TO HAVE AT OUR BACKS AS ALLIES...
CHATTER
CHATTER
WHAT ...?
ENEMIES ?
...BUT THE THOUGHT OF MAKIN' ENEMIES OUTTA EVERY LAST ONE GIVES ME THE WILLOLELO...THE WILLIES!
TMP!

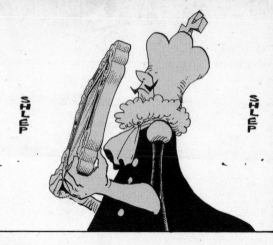

SHLEP

SHLEP

AHA...

KTUNK..

MAMA...

MURMUR

MURMUR

...OF MOTHER CARMEL.

THE ENTRANCE...

DO

O
MI

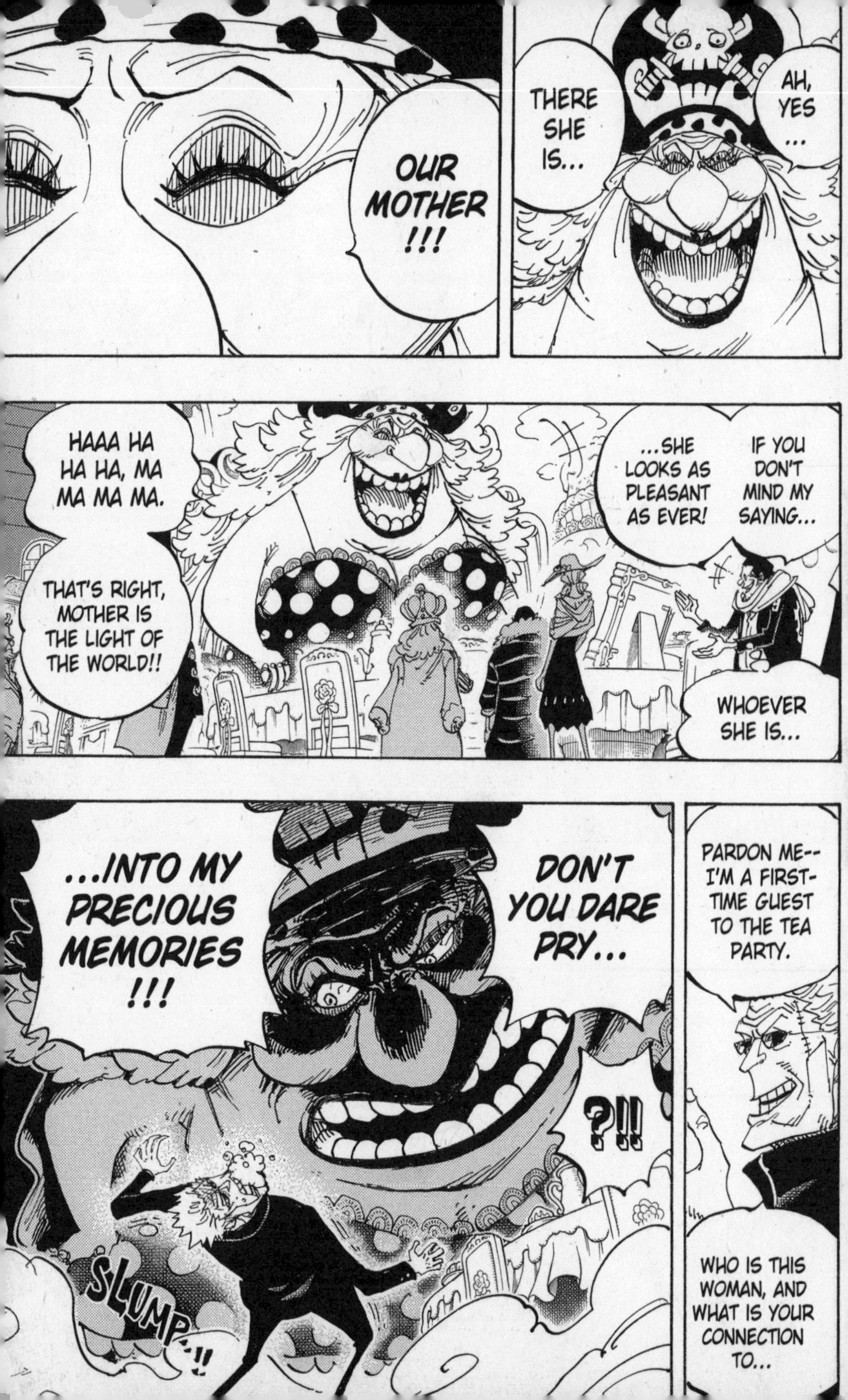
AH, YES ...
THERE SHE IS...
OUR MOTHER !!!
IF YOU DON'T MIND MY SAYING...
...SHE LOOKS AS PLEASANT AS EVER!
WHOEVER SHE IS...
HAAA HA HA HA, MA MA MA MA.
THAT'S RIGHT, MOTHER IS THE LIGHT OF THE WORLD!!
PARDON ME-- I'M A FIRST-TIME GUEST TO THE TEA PARTY.
WHO IS THIS WOMAN, AND WHAT IS YOUR CONNECTION TO...
DON'T YOU DARE PRY...
...INTO MY PRECIOUS MEMORIES !!!
?!!
SLUMP..!!

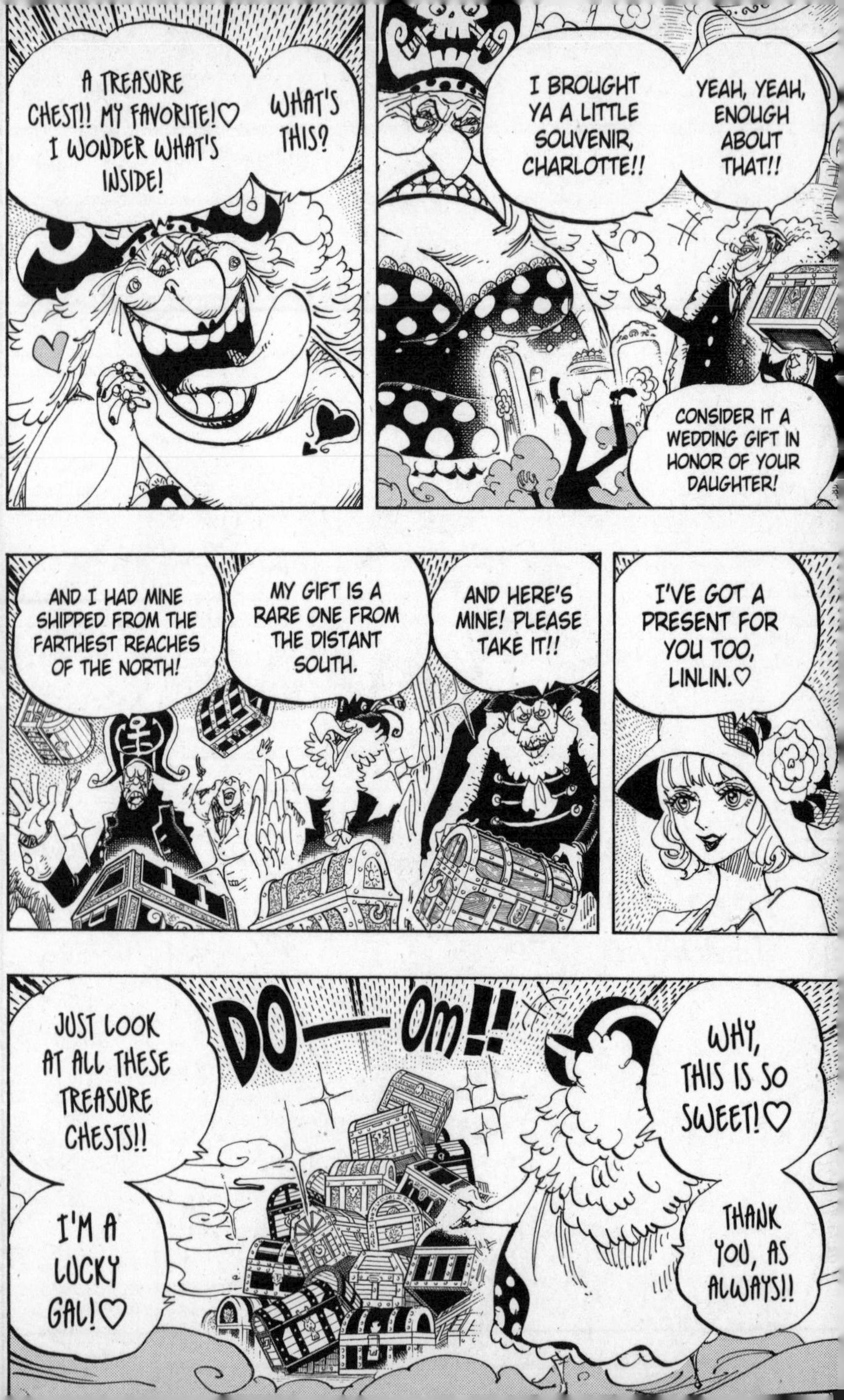
YEAH, YEAH, ENOUGH ABOUT THAT!!
I BROUGHT YA A LITTLE SOUVENIR, CHARLOTTE!!
CONSIDER IT A WEDDING GIFT IN HONOR OF YOUR DAUGHTER!
WHAT'S THIS?
A TREASURE CHEST!! MY FAVORITE!♡ I WONDER WHAT'S INSIDE!
I'VE GOT A PRESENT FOR YOU TOO, LINLIN.♡
AND HERE'S MINE! PLEASE TAKE IT!!
MY GIFT IS A RARE ONE FROM THE DISTANT SOUTH.
AND I HAD MINE SHIPPED FROM THE FARTHEST REACHES OF THE NORTH!
WHY, THIS IS SO SWEET!♡
DO—OM!!
JUST LOOK AT ALL THESE TREASURE CHESTS!!
THANK YOU, AS ALWAYS!!
I'M A LUCKY GAL!♡

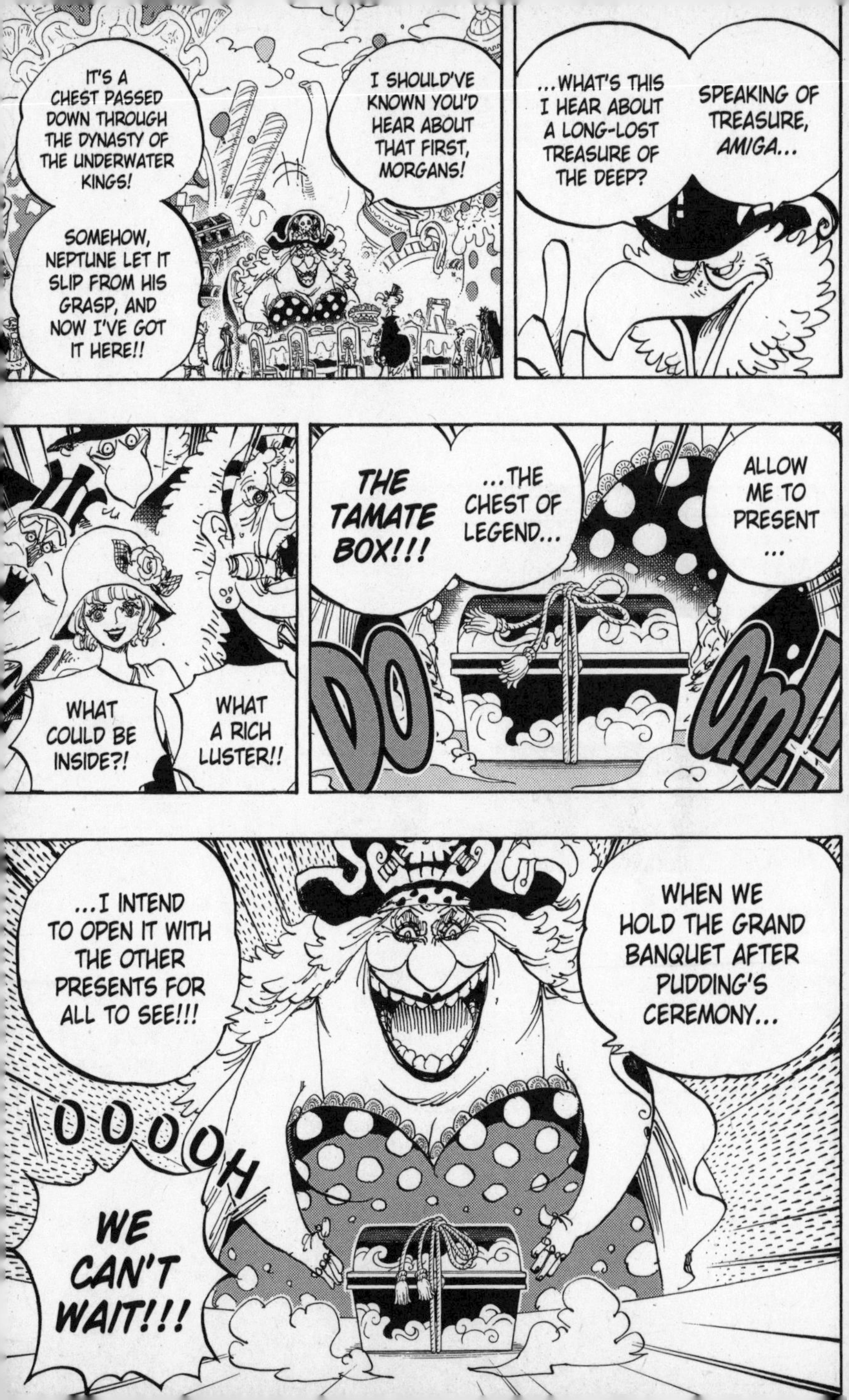
SPEAKING OF TREASURE, AMIGA...
...WHAT'S THIS I HEAR ABOUT A LONG-LOST TREASURE OF THE DEEP?
I SHOULD'VE KNOWN YOU'D HEAR ABOUT THAT FIRST, MORGANS!
IT'S A CHEST PASSED DOWN THROUGH THE DYNASTY OF THE UNDERWATER KINGS!
SOMEHOW, NEPTUNE LET IT SLIP FROM HIS GRASP, AND NOW I'VE GOT IT HERE!!
ALLOW ME TO PRESENT ...
...THE CHEST OF LEGEND...
THE TAMATE BOX!!!
DO
OM!!
WHAT A RICH LUSTER!!
WHAT COULD BE INSIDE?!
WHEN WE HOLD THE GRAND BANQUET AFTER PUDDING'S CEREMONY...
...I INTEND TO OPEN IT WITH THE OTHER PRESENTS FOR ALL TO SEE!!!
OOOOOH
WE CAN'T WAIT!!!

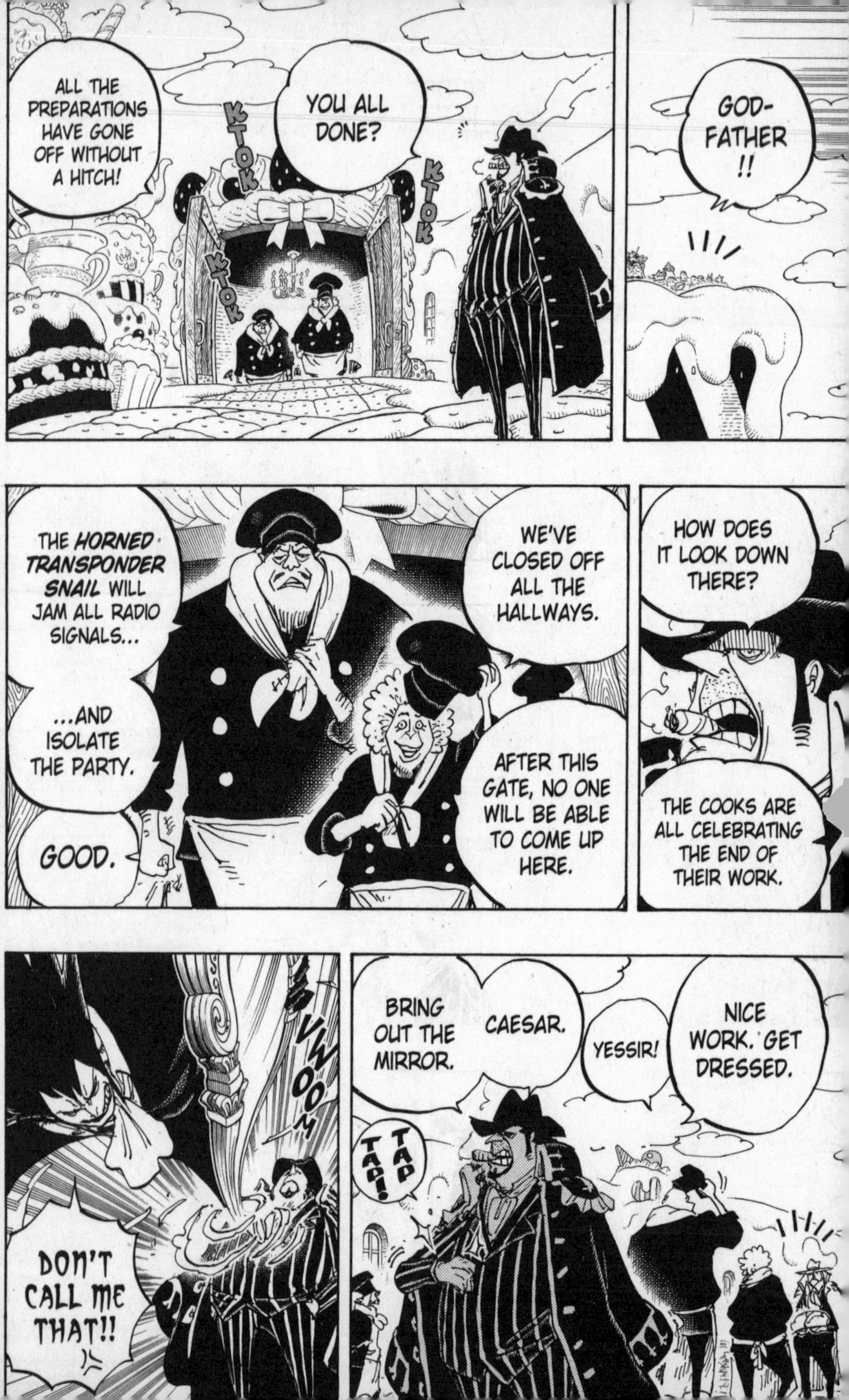
GOD-FATHER!!
YOU ALL DONE?
KTOK KTOK KTOK
ALL THE PREPARATIONS HAVE GONE OFF WITHOUT A HITCH!
HOW DOES IT LOOK DOWN THERE?
THE COOKS ARE ALL CELEBRATING THE END OF THEIR WORK.
WE'VE CLOSED OFF ALL THE HALLWAYS.
THE HORNED TRANSPONDER SNAIL WILL JAM ALL RADIO SIGNALS...
AFTER THIS GATE, NO ONE WILL BE ABLE TO COME UP HERE.
...AND ISOLATE THE PARTY.
GOOD.
NICE WORK. GET DRESSED.
YESSIR!
CAESAR.
BRING OUT THE MIRROR.
TAP TAP
VWOOOM
DON'T CALL ME THAT!!

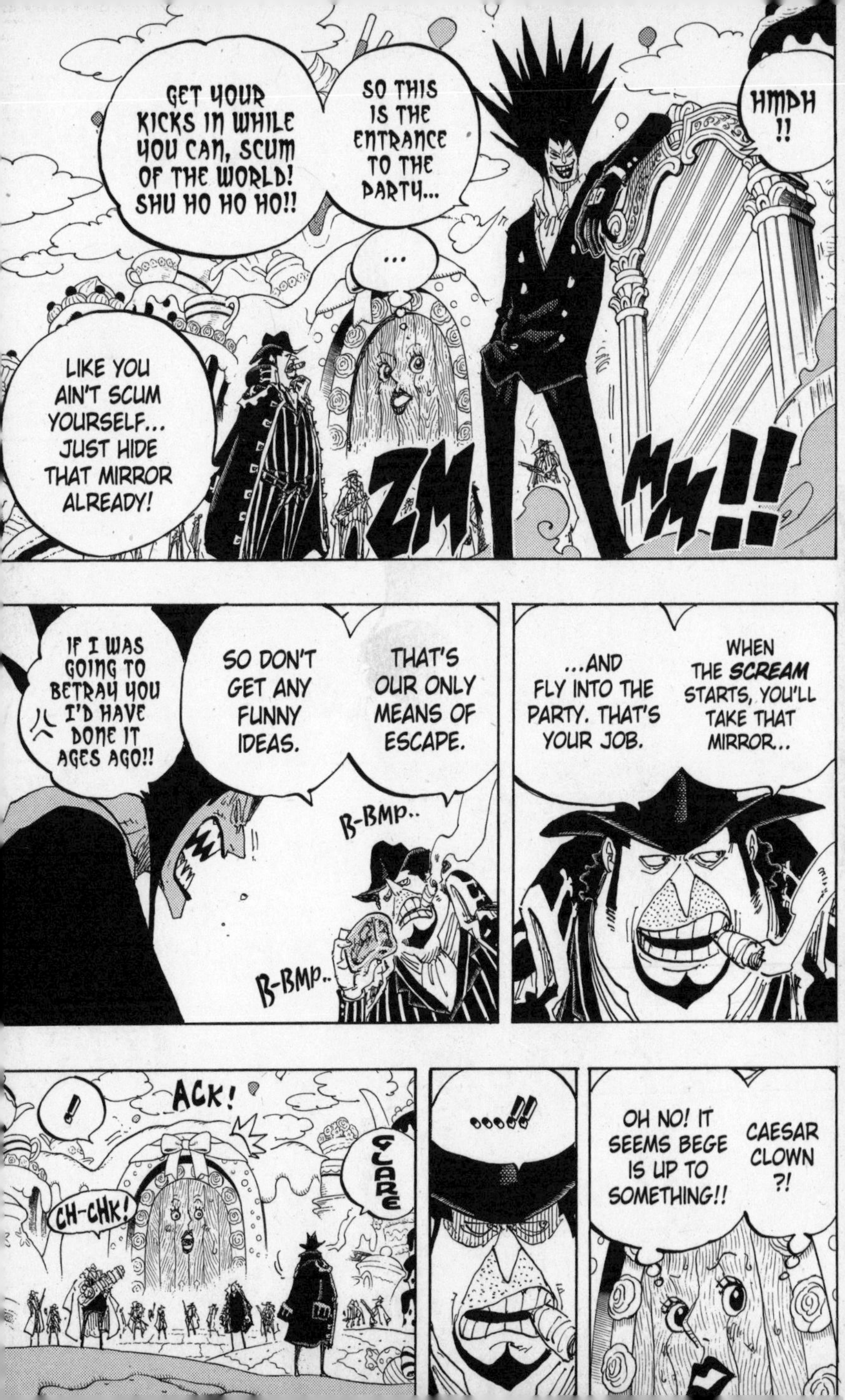
HMPH!!
SO THIS IS THE ENTRANCE TO THE PARTY...
GET YOUR KICKS IN WHILE YOU CAN, SCUM OF THE WORLD! SHU HO HO HO!!
...
LIKE YOU AIN'T SCUM YOURSELF... JUST HIDE THAT MIRROR ALREADY!
ZM MM!!
WHEN THE SCREAM STARTS, YOU'LL TAKE THAT MIRROR..
...AND FLY INTO THE PARTY. THAT'S YOUR JOB.
THAT'S OUR ONLY MEANS OF ESCAPE.
SO DON'T GET ANY FUNNY IDEAS.
B-BMP..
IF I WAS GOING TO BETRAY YOU I'D HAVE DONE IT AGES AGO!!
B-BMP..
CAESAR CLOWN?!
OH NO! IT SEEMS BEGE IS UP TO SOMETHING!!
....!!
GLARE
ACK!
!
CH-CHK!

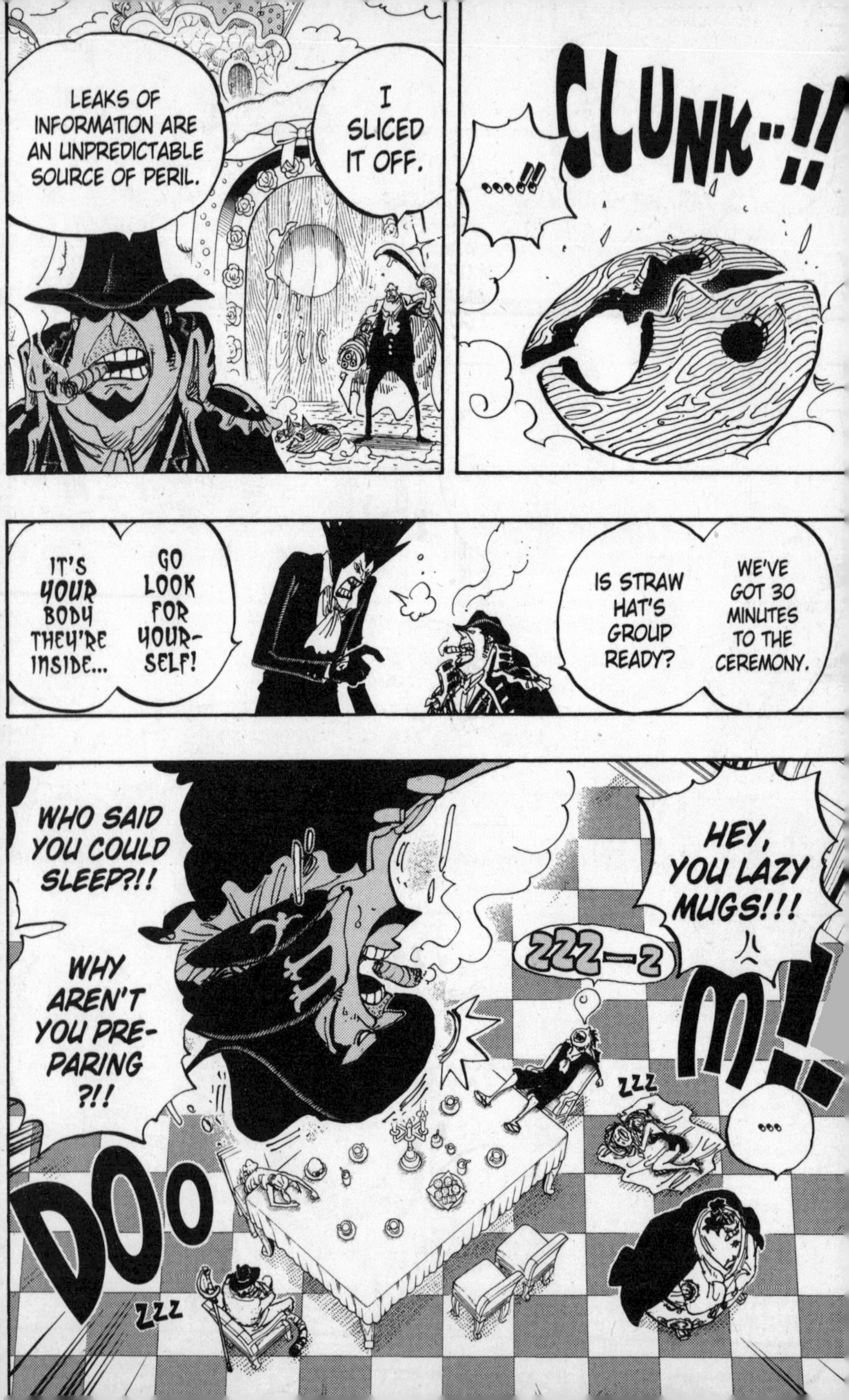
CLUNK..!!
....!!
I SLICED IT OFF.
LEAKS OF INFORMATION ARE AN UNPREDICTABLE SOURCE OF PERIL.
WE'VE GOT 30 MINUTES TO THE CEREMONY.
IS STRAW HAT'S GROUP READY?
GO LOOK FOR YOURSELF!
IT'S YOUR BODY THEY'RE INSIDE...
HEY, YOU LAZY MUGS!!!
M!!
ZZZ—Z
WHO SAID YOU COULD SLEEP?!!
WHY AREN'T YOU PREPARING?!!
...
ZZZ
DOO
ZZZ

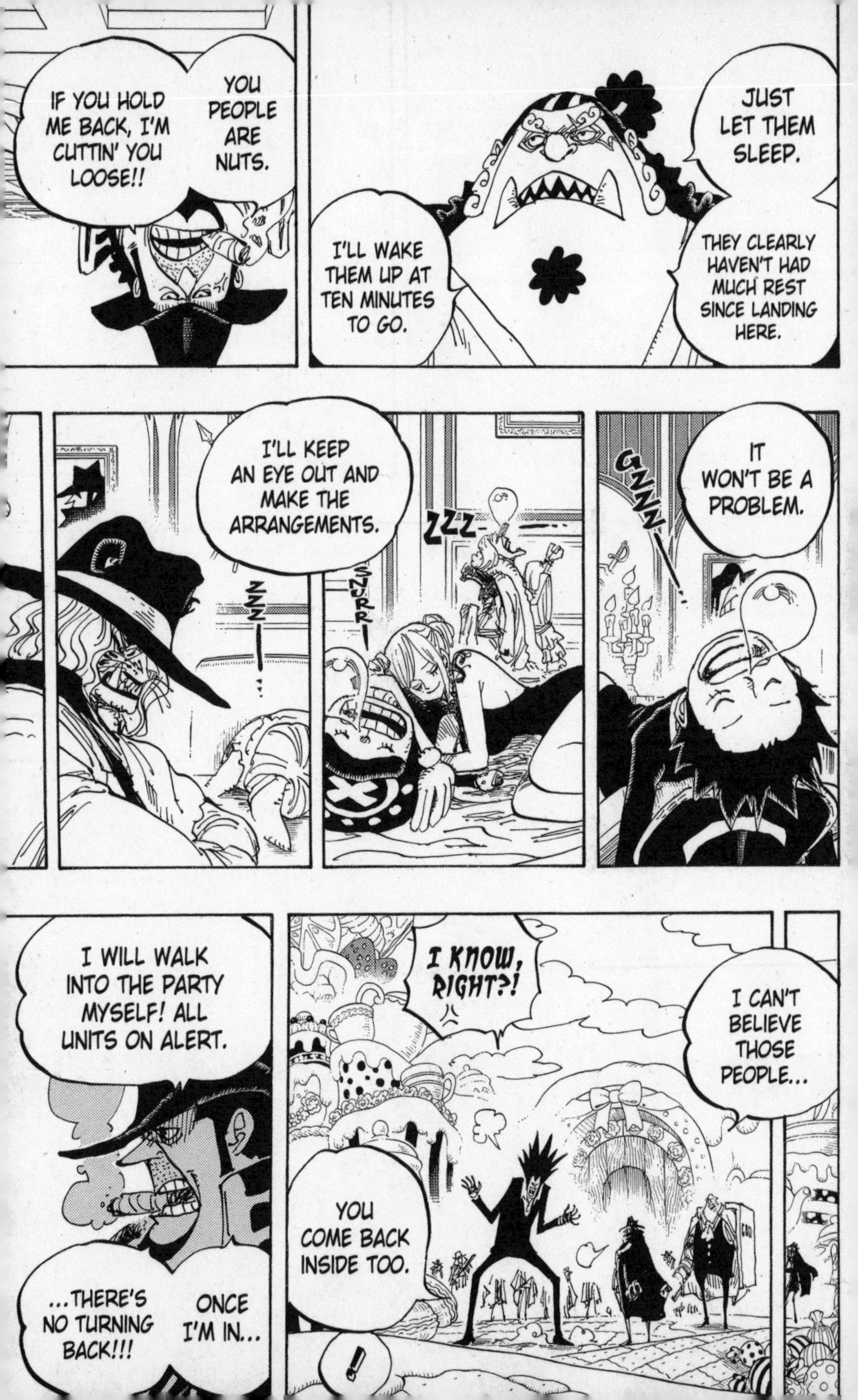
JUST LET THEM SLEEP.
THEY CLEARLY HAVEN'T HAD MUCH REST SINCE LANDING HERE.
I'LL WAKE THEM UP AT TEN MINUTES TO GO.
YOU PEOPLE ARE NUTS.
IF YOU HOLD ME BACK, I'M CUTTIN' YOU LOOSE!!
GZZZ
IT WON'T BE A PROBLEM.
ZZZ
SNURR
I'LL KEEP AN EYE OUT AND MAKE THE ARRANGEMENTS.
ZZZ
I CAN'T BELIEVE THOSE PEOPLE...
I KNOW, RIGHT?!
YOU COME BACK INSIDE TOO.
!
I WILL WALK INTO THE PARTY MYSELF! ALL UNITS ON ALERT.
ONCE I'M IN...
...THERE'S NO TURNING BACK!!!

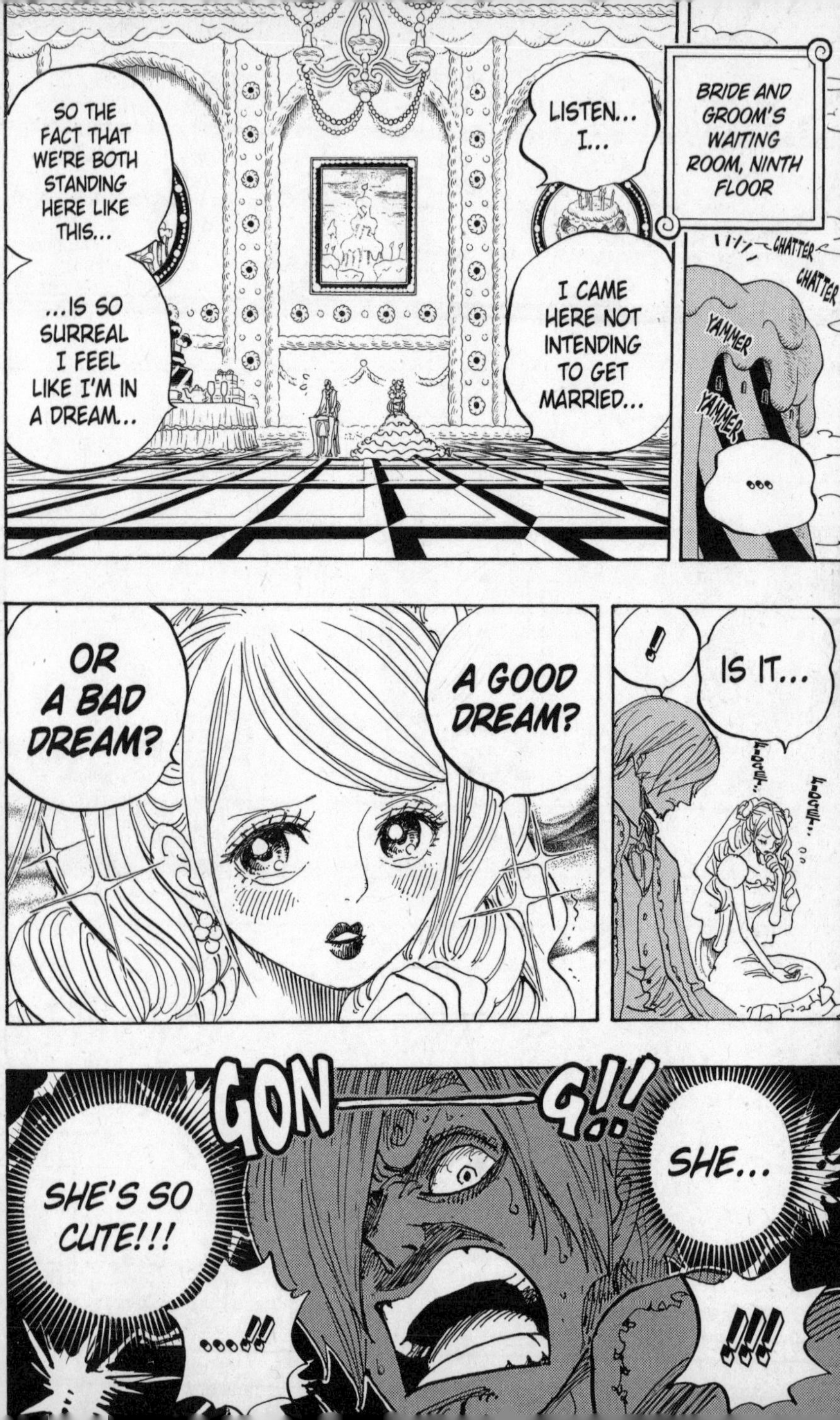
BRIDE AND GROOM'S WAITING ROOM, NINTH FLOOR
CHATTER
CHATTER
YAMMER
YAMMER
...
LISTEN... I...
I CAME HERE NOT INTENDING TO GET MARRIED...
SO THE FACT THAT WE'RE BOTH STANDING HERE LIKE THIS...
...IS SO SURREAL I FEEL LIKE I'M IN A DREAM...
!
IS IT...
FIDGET...
FIDGET...
A GOOD DREAM?
OR A BAD DREAM?
GON—G!!
SHE...
SHE'S SO CUTE!!!
!!!
...!!

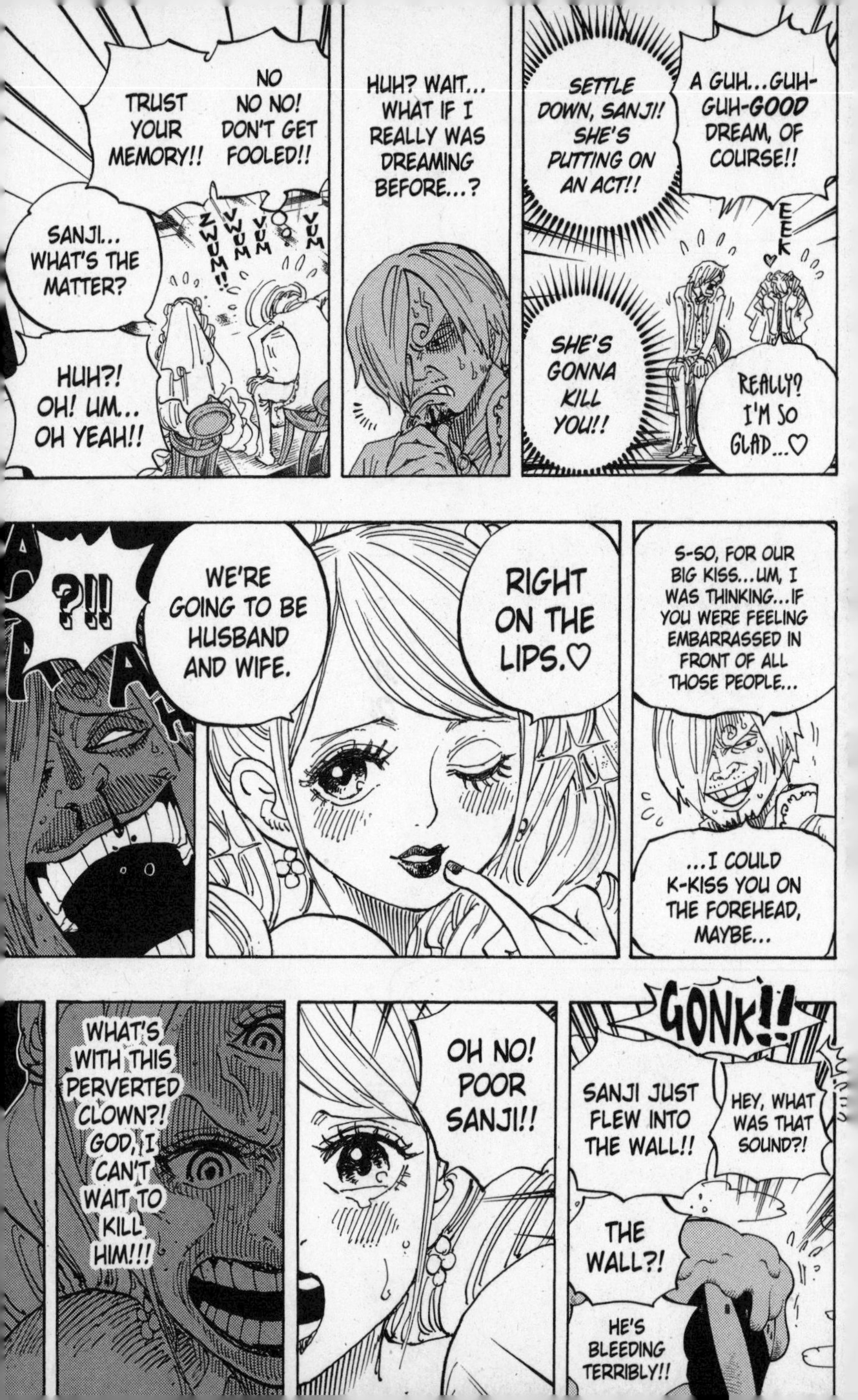
A GUH...GUH-GUH-GOOD DREAM, OF COURSE!!
SETTLE DOWN, SANJI!! SHE'S PUTTING ON AN ACT!!
EEK
SHE'S GONNA KILL YOU!!
REALLY? I'M SO GLAD...♡
HUH? WAIT... WHAT IF I REALLY WAS DREAMING BEFORE...?
NO NO NO! DON'T GET FOOLED!!
TRUST YOUR MEMORY!!
VUM
VUM
VWUM
ZWUUM!!
SANJI... WHAT'S THE MATTER?
HUH?! OH! UM... OH YEAH!!
S-SO, FOR OUR BIG KISS...UM, I WAS THINKING...IF YOU WERE FEELING EMBARRASSED IN FRONT OF ALL THOSE PEOPLE...
...I COULD K-KISS YOU ON THE FOREHEAD, MAYBE...
RIGHT ON THE LIPS.♡
WE'RE GOING TO BE HUSBAND AND WIFE.
?!!
GONK!!
HEY, WHAT WAS THAT SOUND?!
SANJI JUST FLEW INTO THE WALL!!
THE WALL?!
HE'S BLEEDING TERRIBLY!!
OH NO! POOR SANJI!!
WHAT'S WITH THIS PERVERTED CLOWN?! GOD, I CAN'T WAIT TO KILL HIM!!!

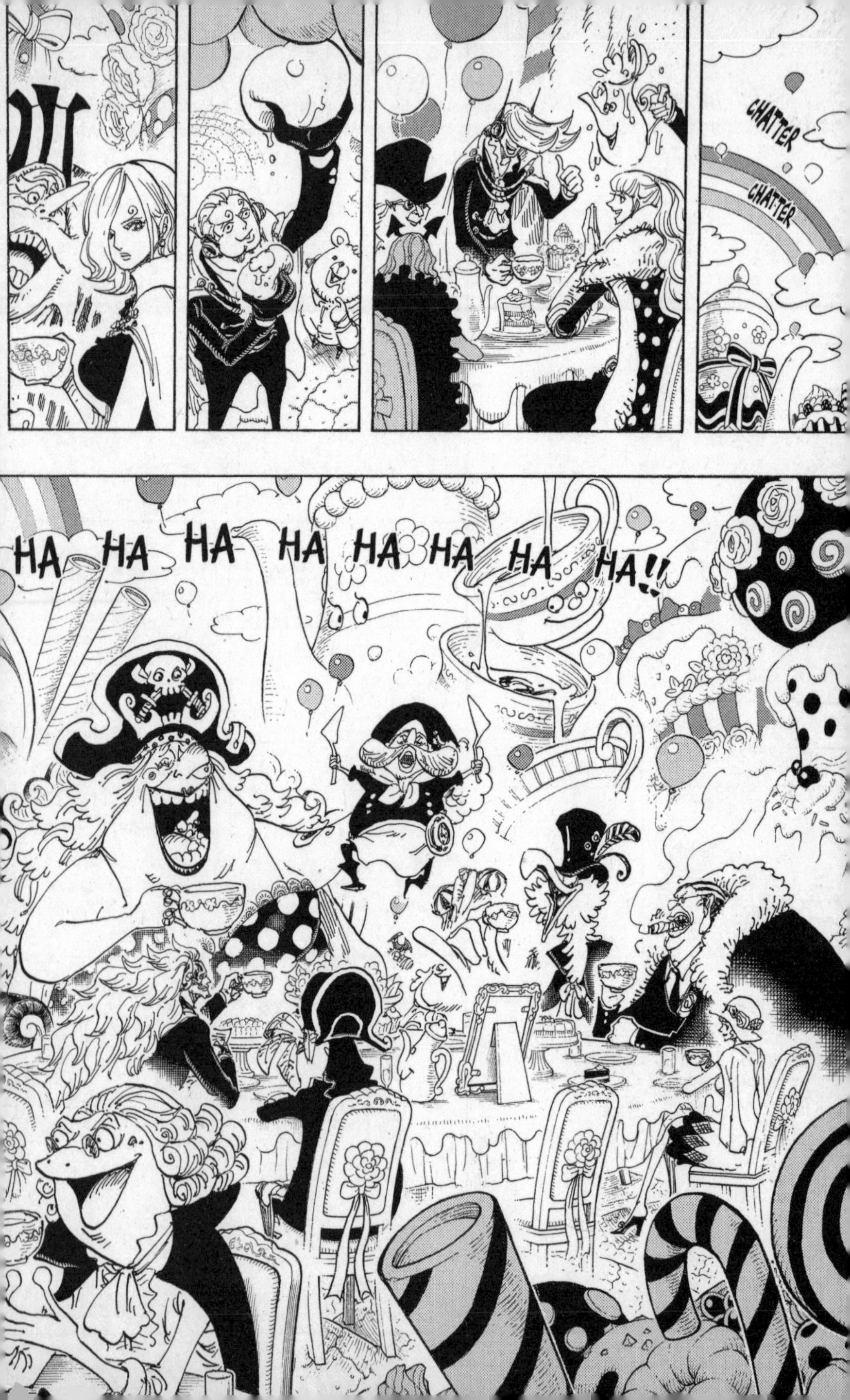
CHATTER
CHATTER
HA HA HA HA HA HA HA HA!!

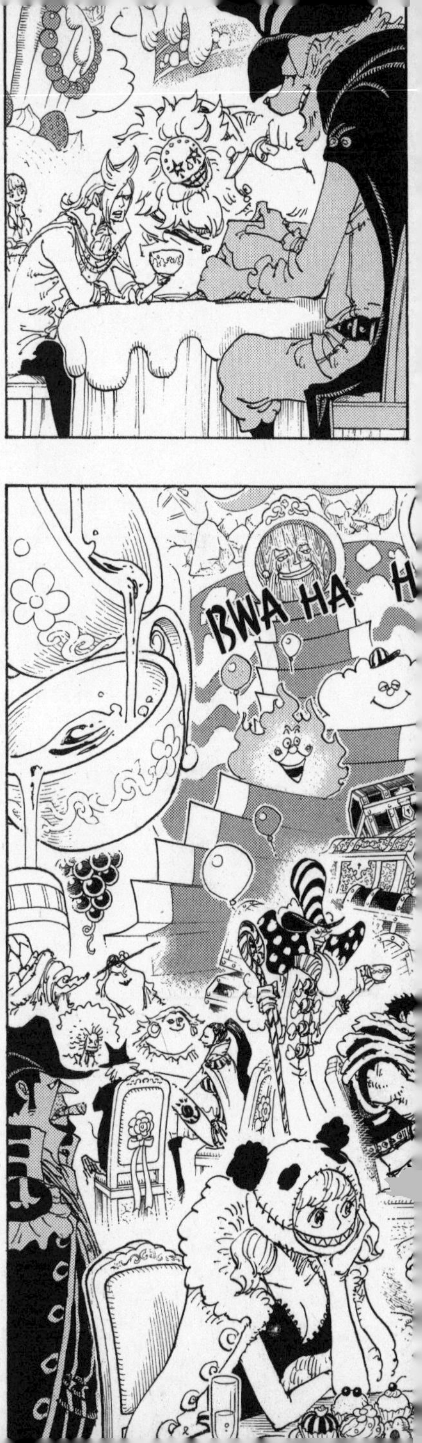
BWA HA H

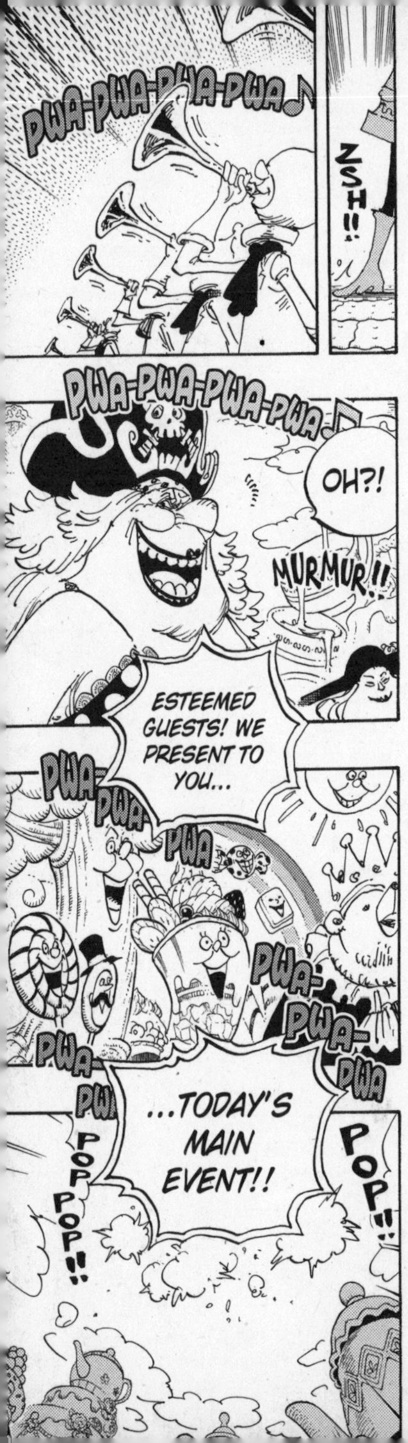
ZSH!!
PWA-PWA-PWA-PWA♪
PWA-PWA-PWA-PWA♪
OH?!
MURMUR!!
ESTEEMED GUESTS! WE PRESENT TO YOU...
PWA-PWA-PWA
PWA-PWA-PWA
PWA-PWA
...TODAY'S MAIN EVENT!!
POP POP!!
POP POP!!

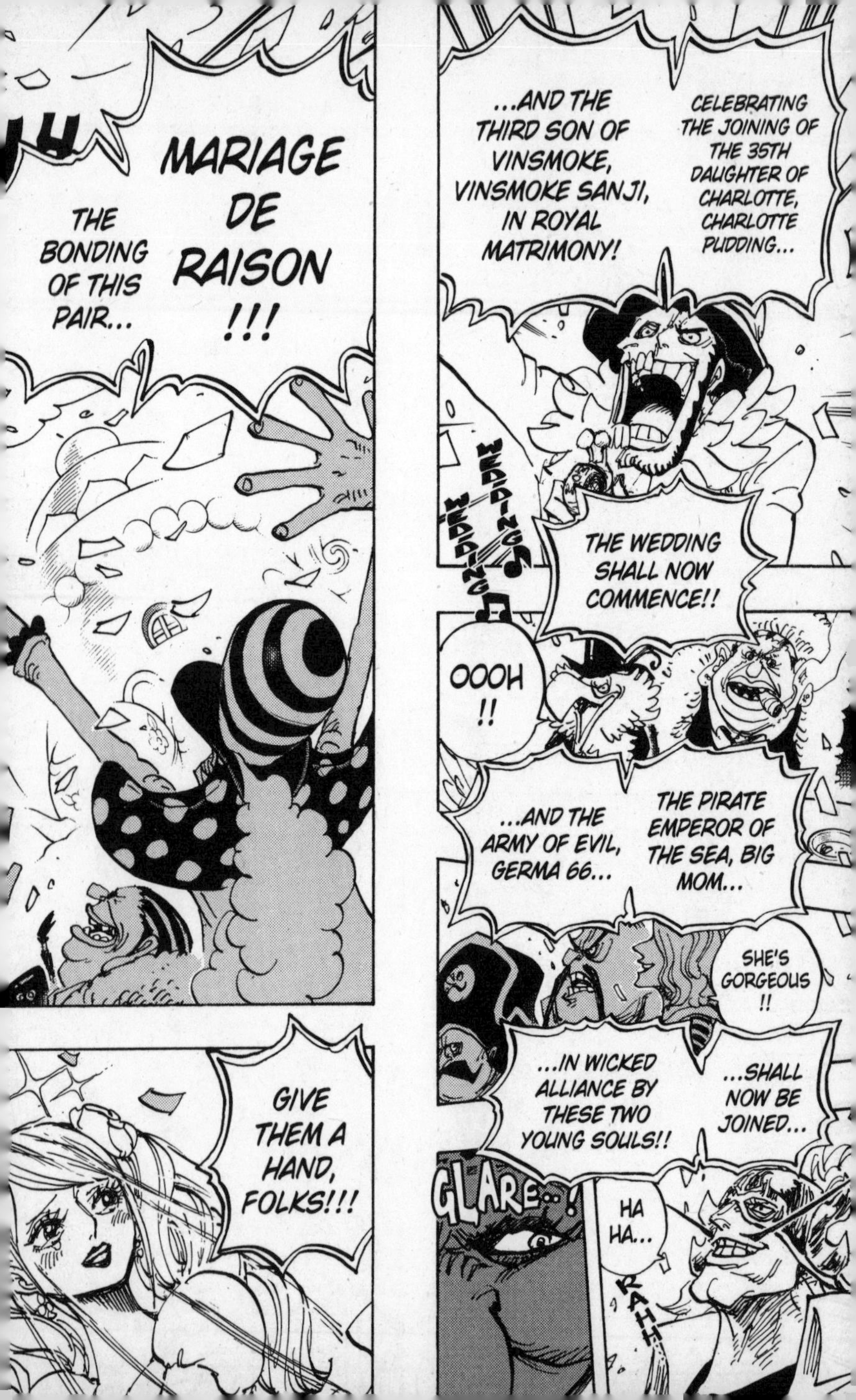
CELEBRATING THE JOINING OF THE 35TH DAUGHTER OF CHARLOTTE, CHARLOTTE PUDDING...
...AND THE THIRD SON OF VINSMOKE, VINSMOKE SANJI, IN ROYAL MATRIMONY!
WEDDING WEDDING
THE WEDDING SHALL NOW COMMENCE!!
OOOH !!
THE PIRATE EMPEROR OF THE SEA, BIG MOM...
...AND THE ARMY OF EVIL, GERMA 66...
SHE'S GORGEOUS !!
...SHALL NOW BE JOINED...
...IN WICKED ALLIANCE BY THESE TWO YOUNG SOULS!!
GLARE..!
HA HA...
RAHH
MARIAGE DE RAISON !!!
THE BONDING OF THIS PAIR...
GIVE THEM A HAND, FOLKS!!!

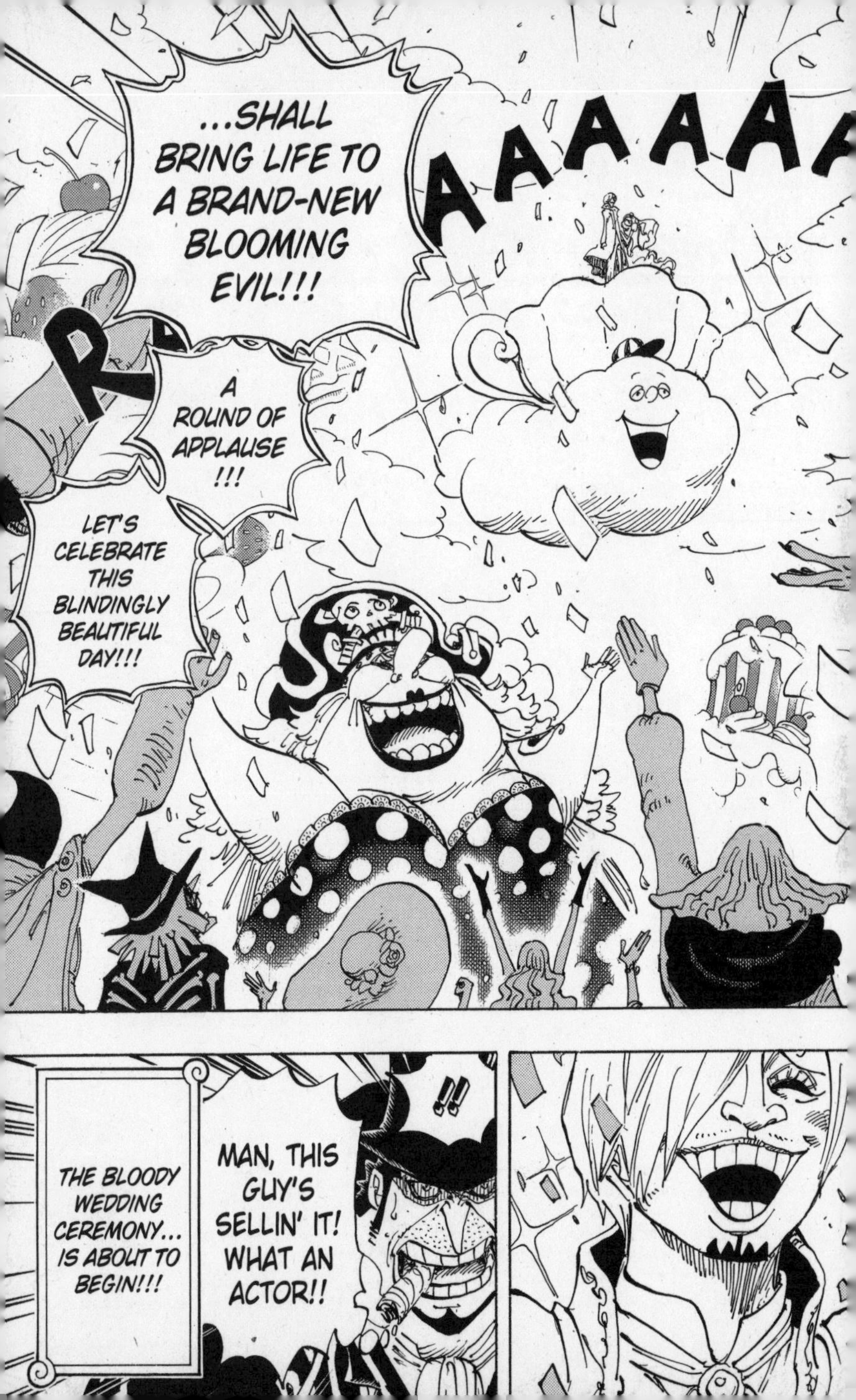
AAAAA
...SHALL BRING LIFE TO A BRAND-NEW BLOOMING EVIL!!!
A ROUND OF APPLAUSE!!!
R
LET'S CELEBRATE THIS BLINDINGLY BEAUTIFUL DAY!!!
!!
MAN, THIS GUY'S SELLIN' IT! WHAT AN ACTOR!!
THE BLOODY WEDDING CEREMONY... IS ABOUT TO BEGIN!!!

SBS Question Corner

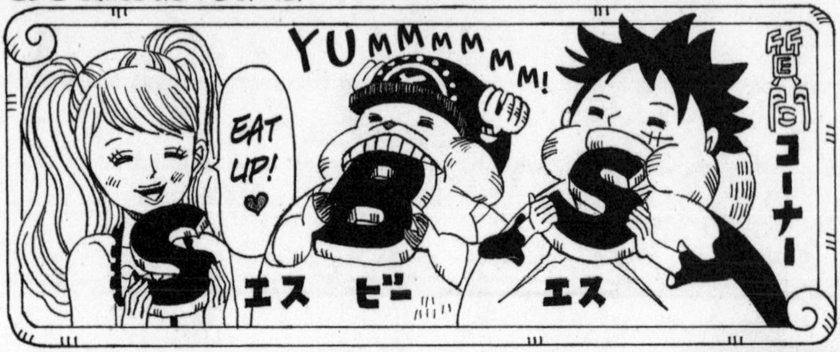
質問コーナー
YUMMMMMMMM!
EAT UP!
エス
ビー
エス

(Hana Usagi, Ibaraki)

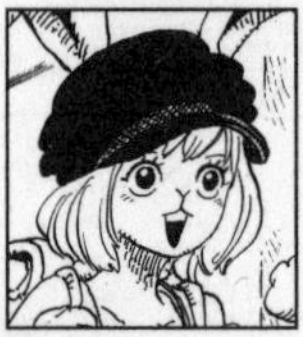

Q: Hi, Oda Sensei! I have a request for our talented artist, Carrot. Can she draw a picture of Lola and Chiffon? Thank you! ♡♡

--Kimochi-chan

A: Ah, I see. I'll ask her.

C: Yeah! Sure!

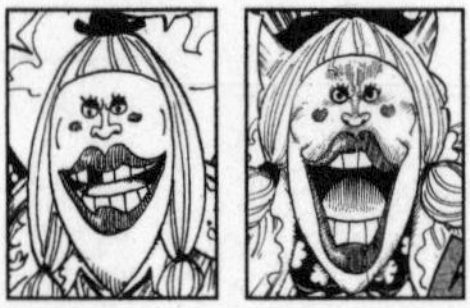

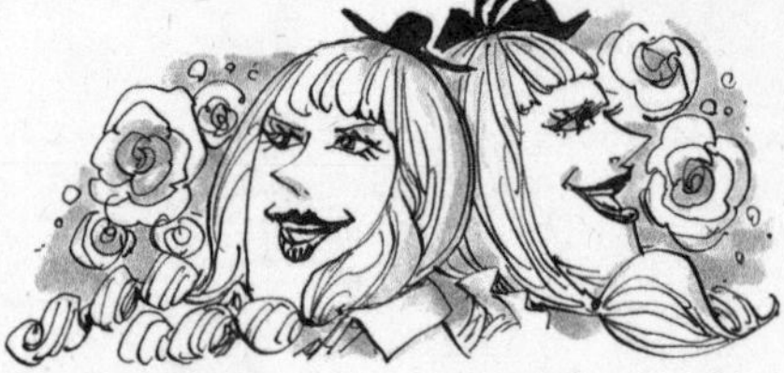

A: Oh...Oh.

Q: I'm 16 years old, and a huge fan of Charlotte Katakuri. So I have a question--there are some people in Totto Land with very long necks. Are these the Snakeneck people? If I'm right, please use the Germa 66 press tool to stretch out my neck too.

--Minogorilla

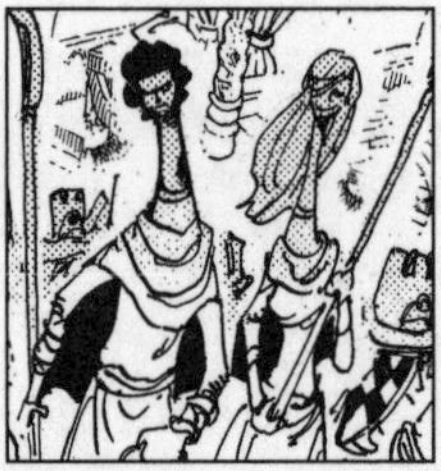

A: Ah yes. The Snakeneck people appeared on the slave auction list in the Sabaody Archipelago, but we didn't didn't see them until now. Some of Big Mom's children are snakenecks, even. They're 34th son Mascarpone and 29th daughter Joscarpone. These twins are inseparable.

Q: Is it the style among the Longleg people to get leg tattoos?

--Macchi and Takeshi

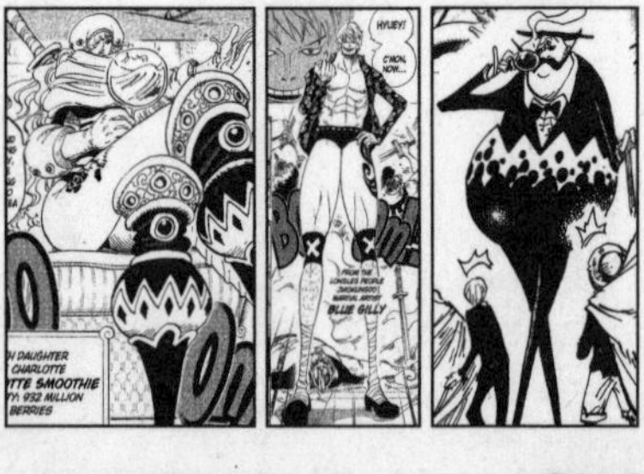
HYUEY!
C'MON, NOW...
BLUE GILLY

A: It is. The Longlegs are very proud of their long and beautiful limbs. As we saw with Blue Gilly back in Dressrosa, it's a fashion choice to have openly visible tattoos on their legs. Baron Tamago does not seem to fall under this type, however.

Chapter 862:
THE THINKER

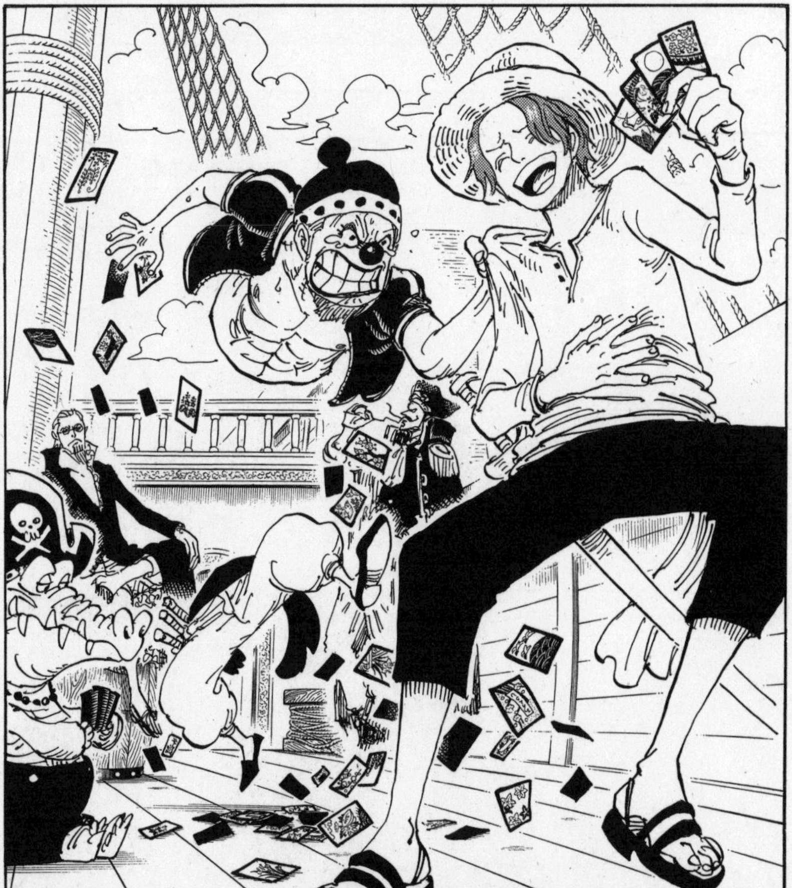

REQUEST: "YOUNG BUGGY AND SHANKS PLAYING CARDS" BY INTERDIMENSIONAL PORK RIBS FROM MIE

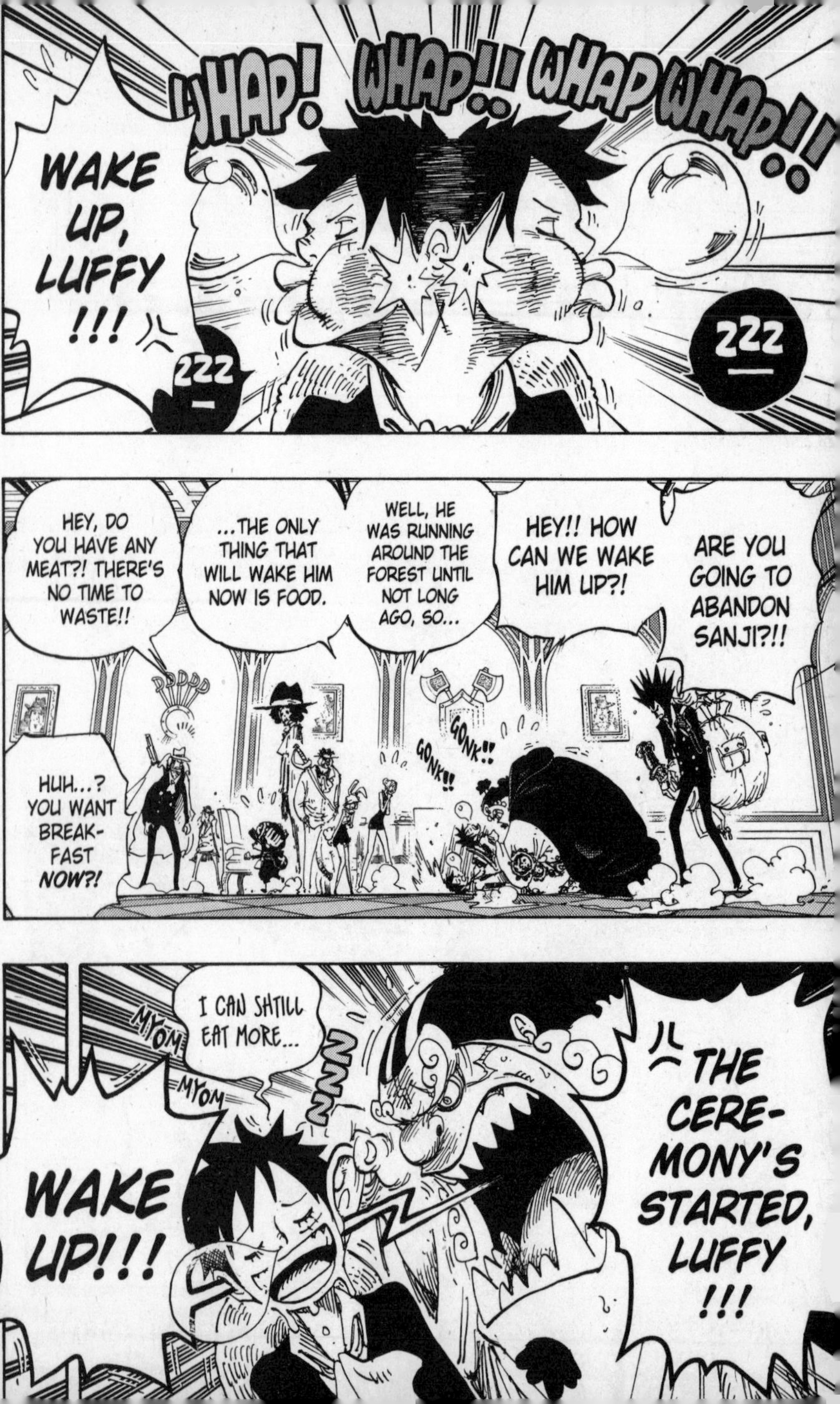
zzz
WHAP! WHAP!! WHAP WHAP!!
WAKE UP, LUFFY!!!
zzz
ARE YOU GOING TO ABANDON SANJI?!!
HEY!! HOW CAN WE WAKE HIM UP?!
WELL, HE WAS RUNNING AROUND THE FOREST UNTIL NOT LONG AGO, SO...
...THE ONLY THING THAT WILL WAKE HIM NOW IS FOOD.
HEY, DO YOU HAVE ANY MEAT?! THERE'S NO TIME TO WASTE!!
GONK!!
GONK!!
HUH...? YOU WANT BREAK-FAST NOW?!
THE CERE-MONY'S STARTED, LUFFY!!!
I CAN SHTILL EAT MORE...
MYOM
MYOM
WAKE UP!!!

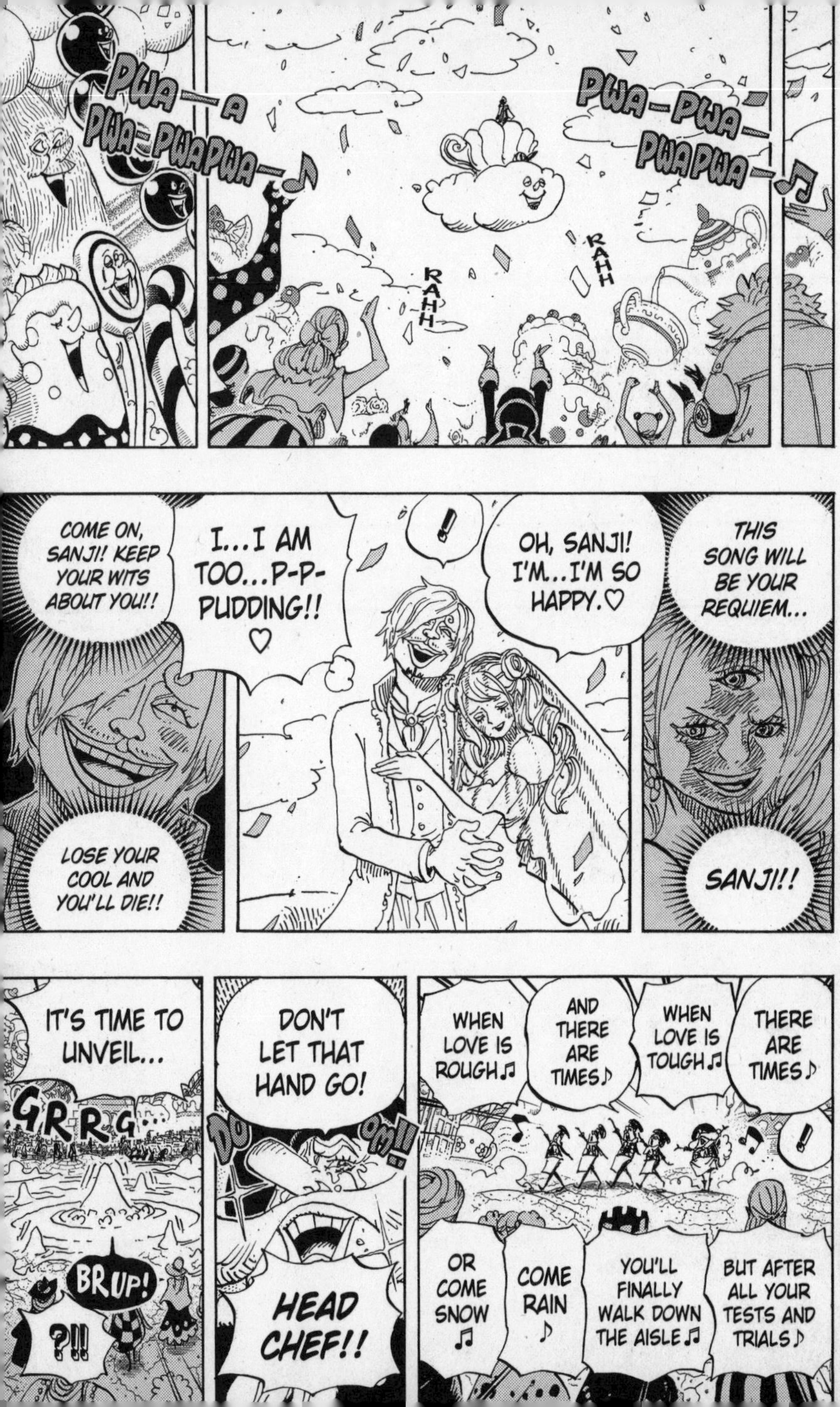
PWA-PWA-PWAPWA-♫
RAHH
RAHH
PWA-A PWA-PWAPWA-♪
THIS SONG WILL BE YOUR REQUIEM...
SANJI!!
OH, SANJI! I'M...I'M SO HAPPY.♡
!
I...I AM TOO...P-P-PUDDING!! ♡
COME ON, SANJI! KEEP YOUR WITS ABOUT YOU!!
LOSE YOUR COOL AND YOU'LL DIE!!
THERE ARE TIMES♪
WHEN LOVE IS TOUGH♫
AND THERE ARE TIMES♪
WHEN LOVE IS ROUGH♫
!
BUT AFTER ALL YOUR TESTS AND TRIALS♪
YOU'LL FINALLY WALK DOWN THE AISLE♫
COME RAIN ♪
OR COME SNOW ♫
DON'T LET THAT HAND GO!
DOOM!!
HEAD CHEF!!
IT'S TIME TO UNVEIL...
GRRG...
BRUP!
?!!

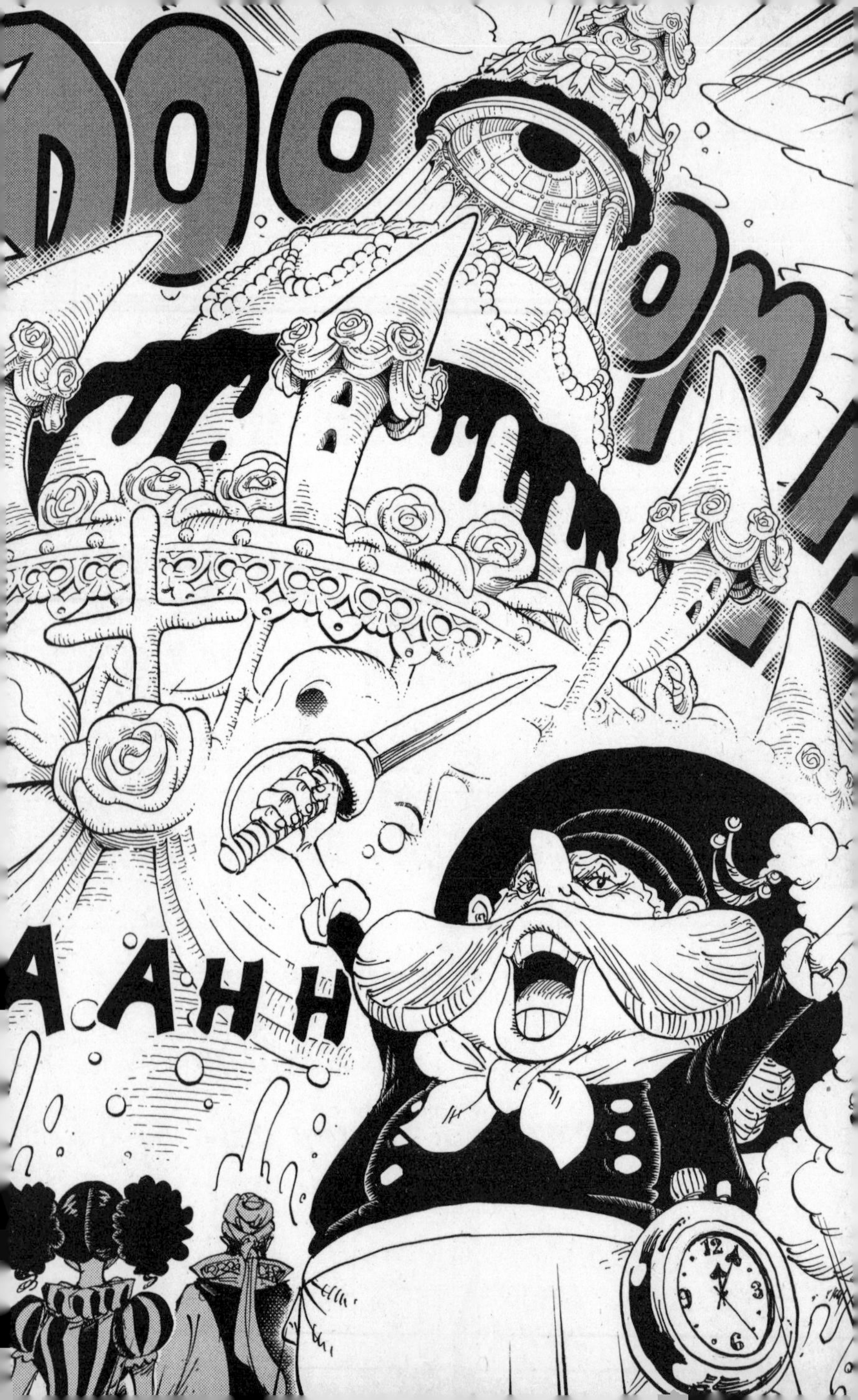
DOOOM!!
AAHH

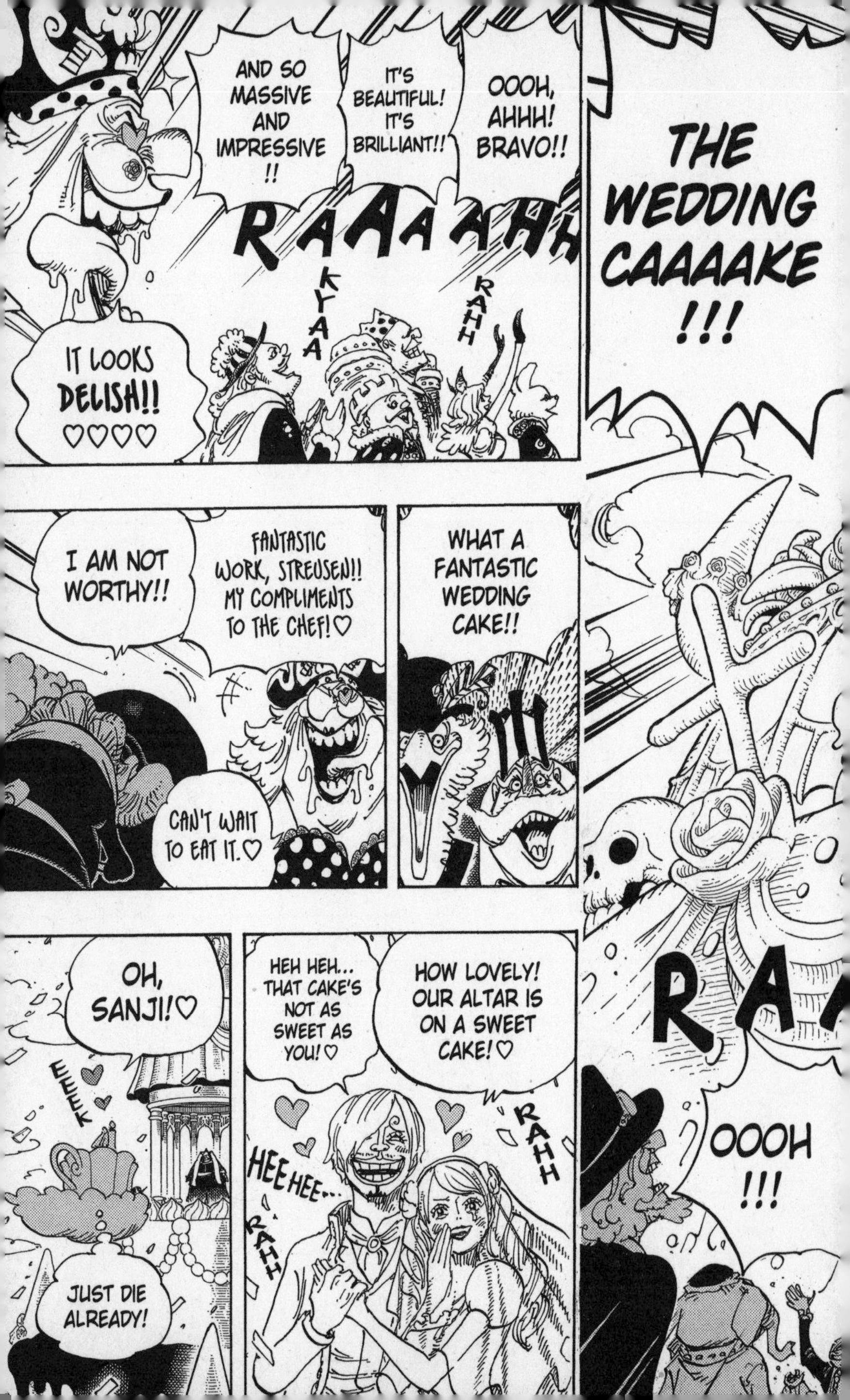
THE WEDDING CAAAAKE !!!
RA
OOOH !!!
OOOH, AHHH! BRAVO!!
IT'S BEAUTIFUL! IT'S BRILLIANT!!
AND SO MASSIVE AND IMPRESSIVE !!
RAAAAHH
RAHH
KYAAA
IT LOOKS DELISH!! ♡♡♡♡
WHAT A FANTASTIC WEDDING CAKE!!
FANTASTIC WORK, STREUSEN!! MY COMPLIMENTS TO THE CHEF!♡
I AM NOT WORTHY!!
CAN'T WAIT TO EAT IT.♡
HOW LOVELY! OUR ALTAR IS ON A SWEET CAKE!♡
HEH HEH... THAT CAKE'S NOT AS SWEET AS YOU!♡
RAHH
HEE HEE...
RAHH
OH, SANJI!♡
EEEK
JUST DIE ALREADY!

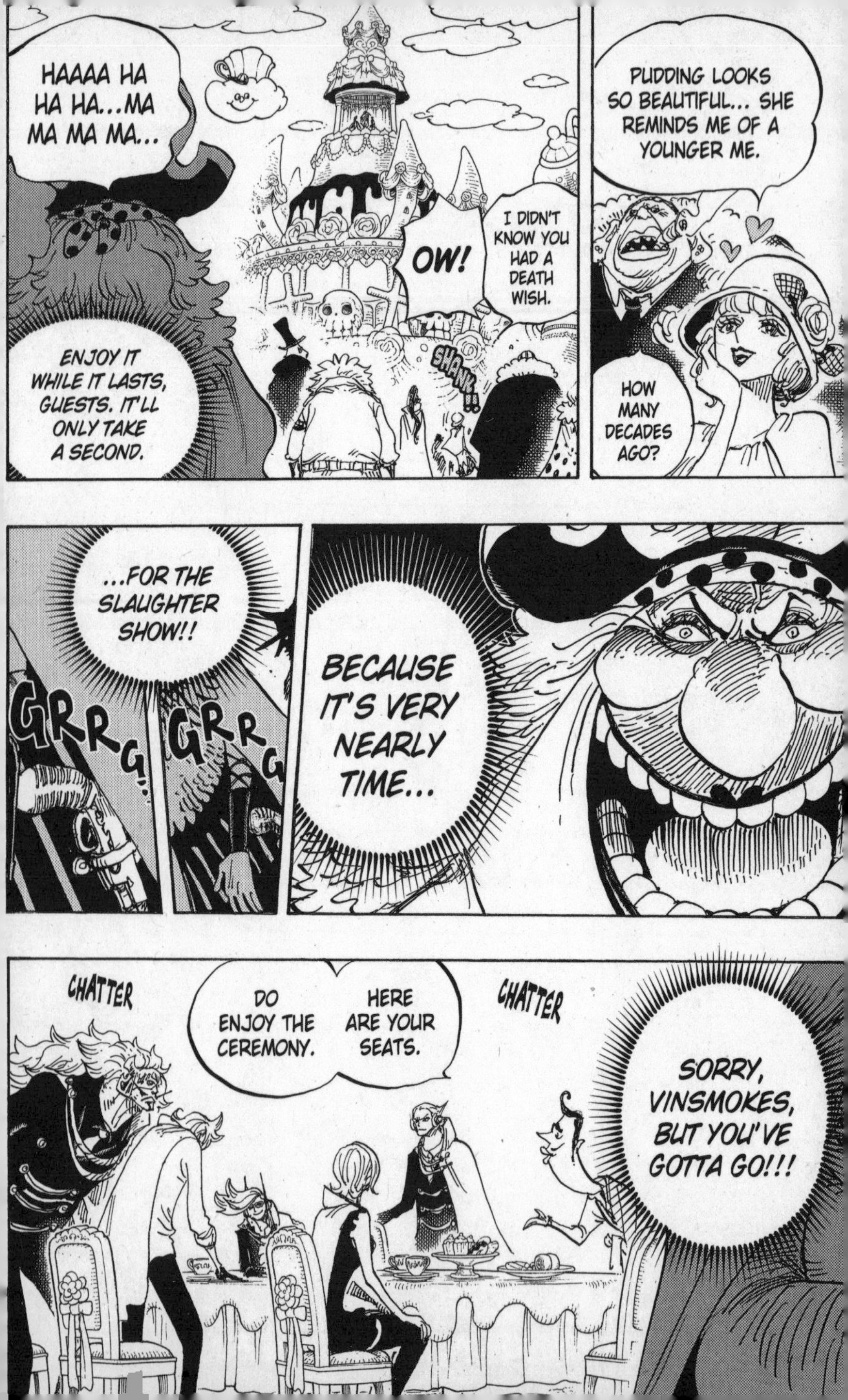
PUDDING LOOKS SO BEAUTIFUL... SHE REMINDS ME OF A YOUNGER ME.
HOW MANY DECADES AGO?
I DIDN'T KNOW YOU HAD A DEATH WISH.
OW!
SHANK!!
HAAAA HA HA HA...MA MA MA MA...
ENJOY IT WHILE IT LASTS, GUESTS. IT'LL ONLY TAKE A SECOND.
BECAUSE IT'S VERY NEARLY TIME...
...FOR THE SLAUGHTER SHOW!!
GRRG
GRRG
CHATTER
SORRY, VINSMOKES, BUT YOU'VE GOTTA GO!!!
HERE ARE YOUR SEATS.
DO ENJOY THE CEREMONY.
CHATTER

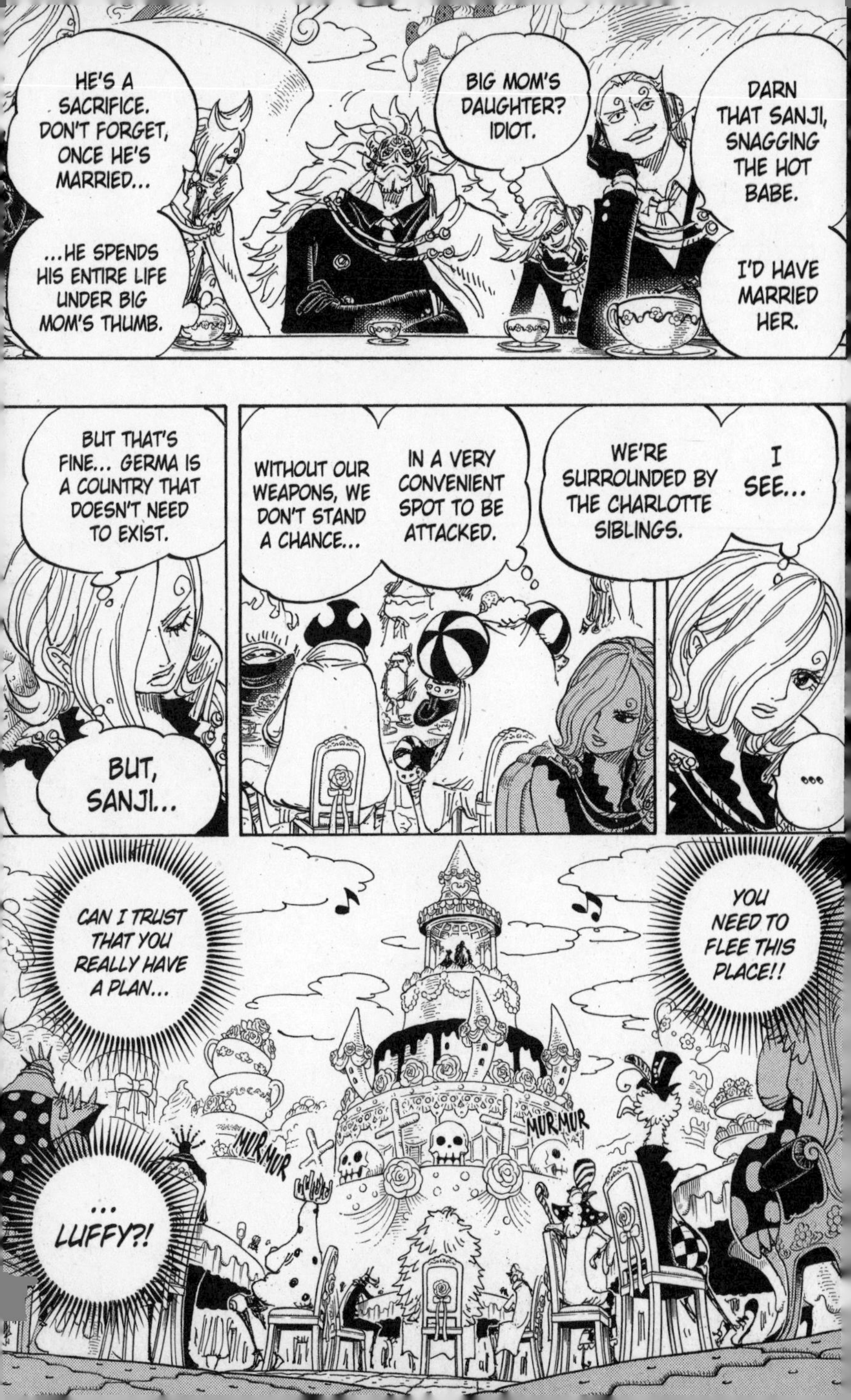
DARN THAT SANJI, SNAGGING THE HOT BABE.
I'D HAVE MARRIED HER.
BIG MOM'S DAUGHTER? IDIOT.
HE'S A SACRIFICE. DON'T FORGET, ONCE HE'S MARRIED...
...HE SPENDS HIS ENTIRE LIFE UNDER BIG MOM'S THUMB.
I SEE...
WE'RE SURROUNDED BY THE CHARLOTTE SIBLINGS.
...
IN A VERY CONVENIENT SPOT TO BE ATTACKED.
WITHOUT OUR WEAPONS, WE DON'T STAND A CHANCE...
BUT THAT'S FINE... GERMA IS A COUNTRY THAT DOESN'T NEED TO EXIST.
BUT, SANJI...
YOU NEED TO FLEE THIS PLACE!!
MURMUR
MURMUR
CAN I TRUST THAT YOU REALLY HAVE A PLAN...
... LUFFY?!

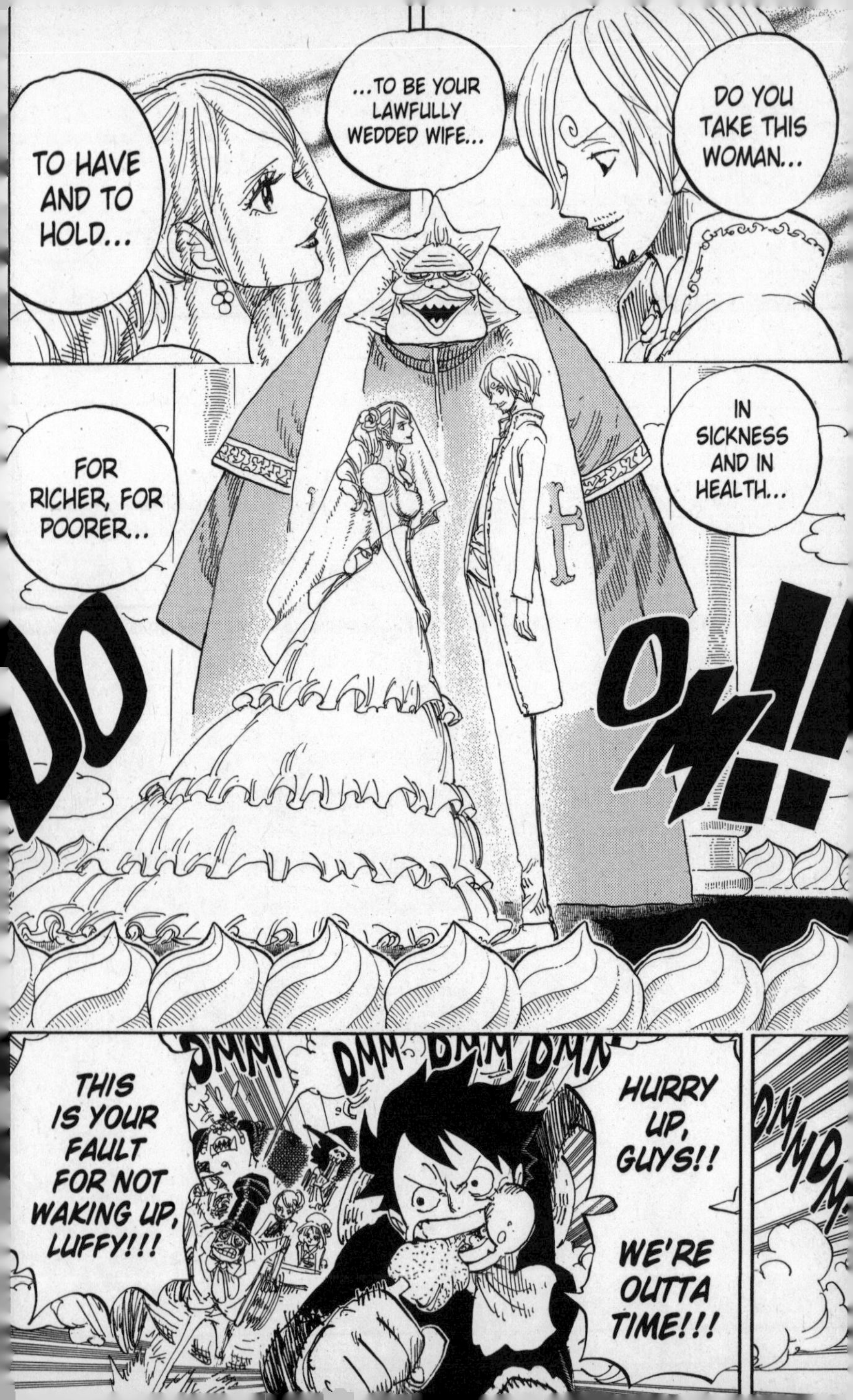
DO YOU TAKE THIS WOMAN...
...TO BE YOUR LAWFULLY WEDDED WIFE...
TO HAVE AND TO HOLD...
IN SICKNESS AND IN HEALTH...
FOR RICHER, FOR POORER...
DOON!!
HURRY UP, GUYS!!
WE'RE OUTTA TIME!!!
DMM DMM DMM DMM
THIS IS YOUR FAULT FOR NOT WAKING UP, LUFFY!!!

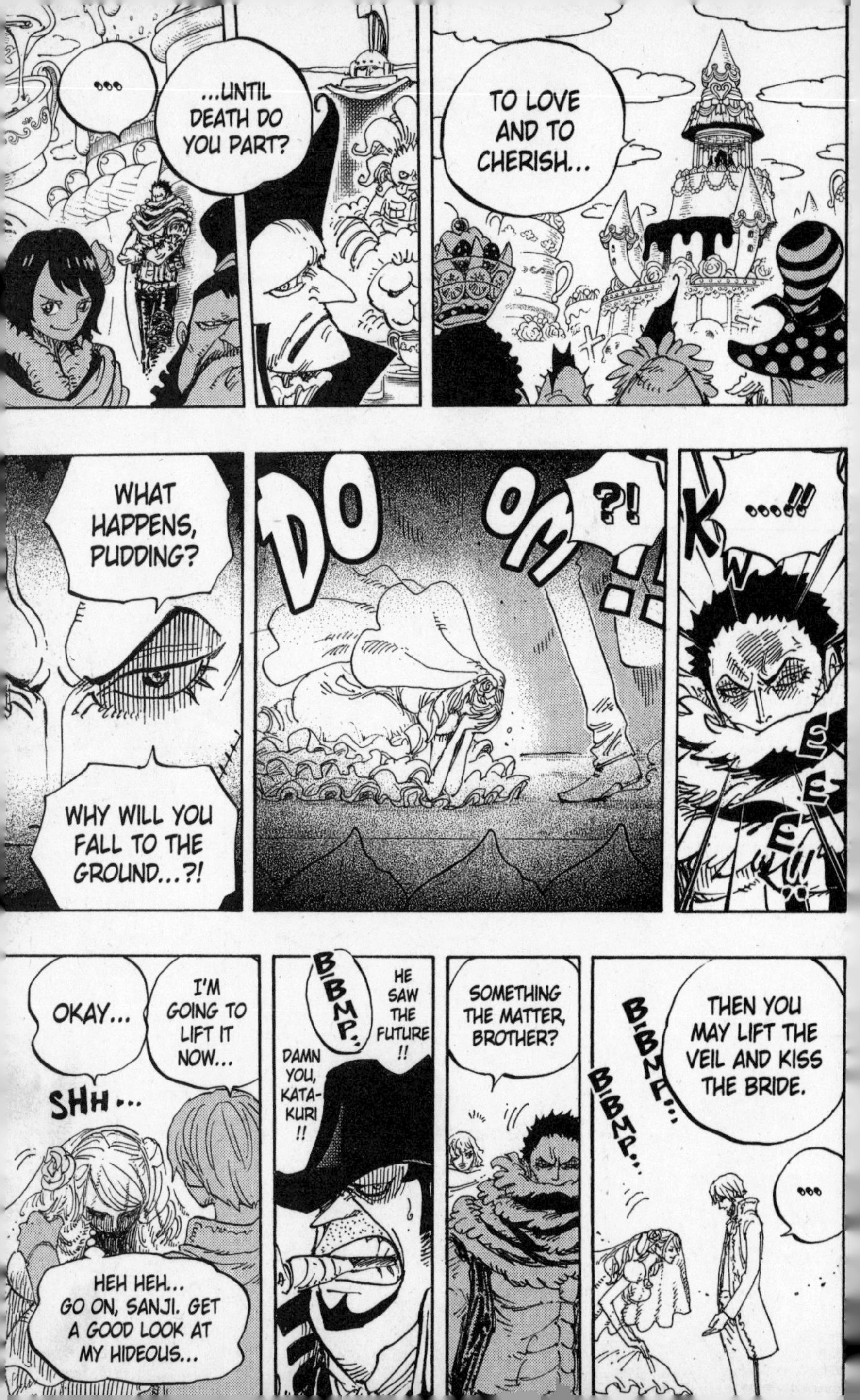

TO LOVE AND TO CHERISH...
...UNTIL DEATH DO YOU PART?
...
...!!
KWEEEE!!
?!
DOOM!!
WHAT HAPPENS, PUDDING?
WHY WILL YOU FALL TO THE GROUND...?!
THEN YOU MAY LIFT THE VEIL AND KISS THE BRIDE.
B-BMP...
B-BMP...
...
SOMETHING THE MATTER, BROTHER?
HE SAW THE FUTURE!!
B-BMP..
DAMN YOU, KATA-KURI!!
I'M GOING TO LIFT IT NOW...
OKAY...
SHH...
HEH HEH... GO ON, SANJI. GET A GOOD LOOK AT MY HIDEOUS...

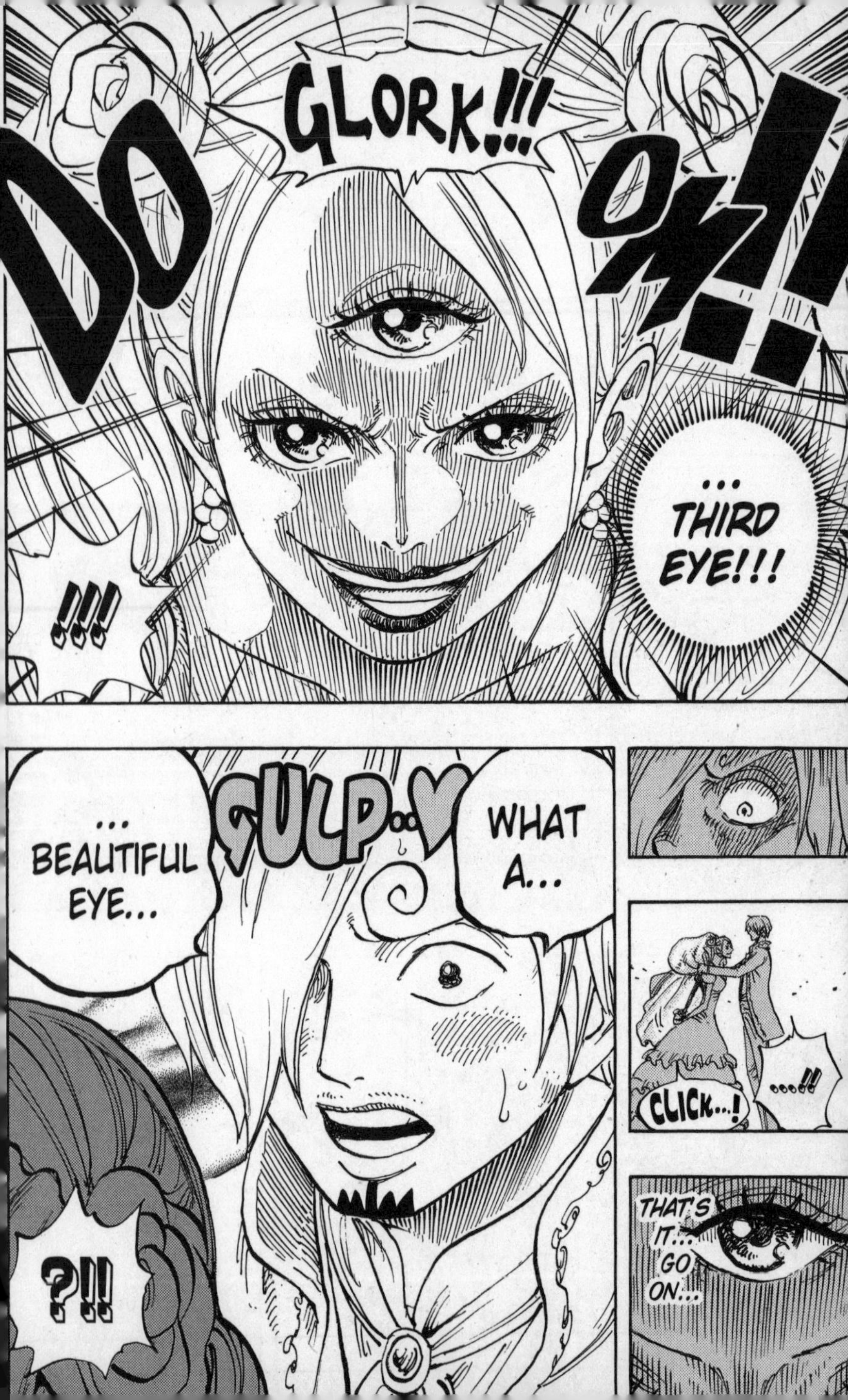
GLORK!!!
DOOM!!
... THIRD EYE!!!
!!!
...!!
CLICK...!
THAT'S IT... GO ON...
WHAT A...
GULP..♥
... BEAUTIFUL EYE...
?!!

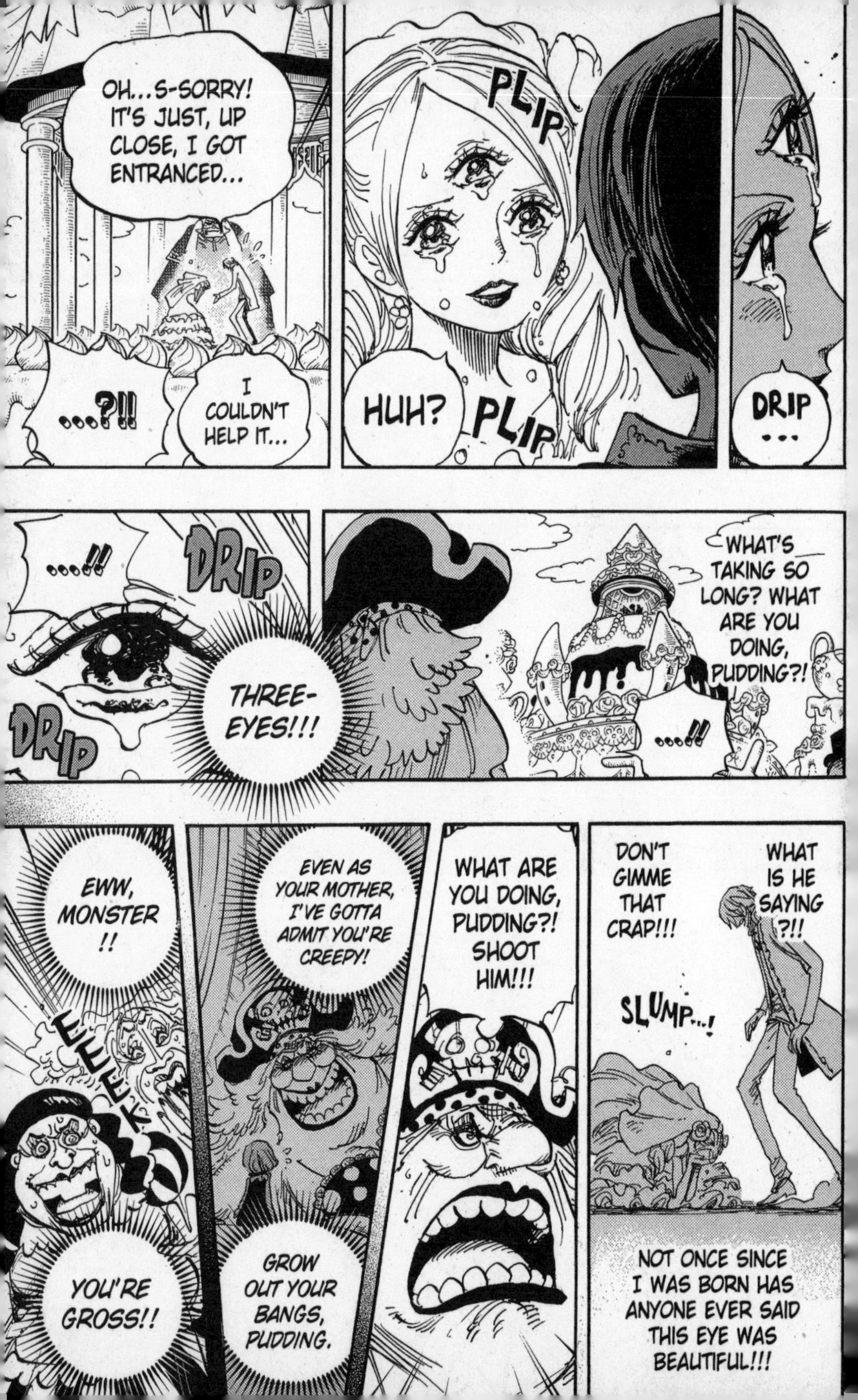
DRIP
...
PLIP
HUH?
PLIP
OH...S-SORRY! IT'S JUST, UP CLOSE, I GOT ENTRANCED...
I COULDN'T HELP IT...
...?!!
WHAT'S TAKING SO LONG? WHAT ARE YOU DOING, PUDDING?!
...!!
DRIP
...!!
THREE-EYES!!!
DRIP
WHAT IS HE SAYING?!!
DON'T GIMME THAT CRAP!!!
SLUMP...!
NOT ONCE SINCE I WAS BORN HAS ANYONE EVER SAID THIS EYE WAS BEAUTIFUL!!!
WHAT ARE YOU DOING, PUDDING?! SHOOT HIM!!!
EVEN AS YOUR MOTHER, I'VE GOTTA ADMIT YOU'RE CREEPY!
GROW OUT YOUR BANGS, PUDDING.
EWW, MONSTER!!
EEEEK
YOU'RE GROSS!!

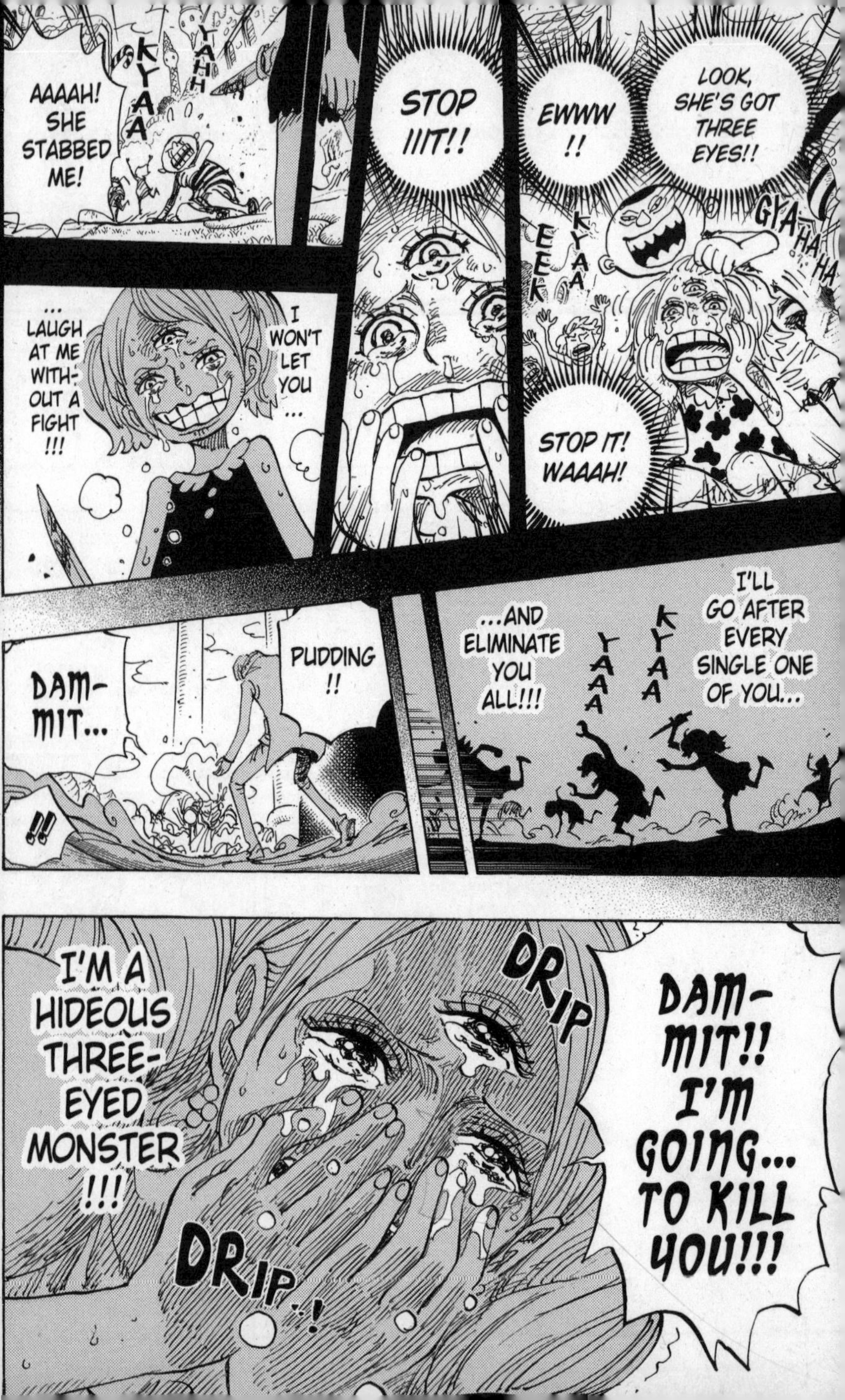

LOOK, SHE'S GOT THREE EYES!!
EWWW !!
GYAHAHA
KYAA
EEK
STOP IT! WAAAH!
STOP IIIT!!
AAAAH! SHE STABBED ME!
YAHH
KYAA
I WON'T LET YOU ...
... LAUGH AT ME WITHOUT A FIGHT !!!
I'LL GO AFTER EVERY SINGLE ONE OF YOU...
KYAA
YAAA
...AND ELIMINATE YOU ALL!!!
PUDDING !!
DAM-MIT...
!!
DAM-MIT!! I'M GOING... TO KILL YOU!!!
DRIP
I'M A HIDEOUS THREE-EYED MONSTER !!!
DRIP

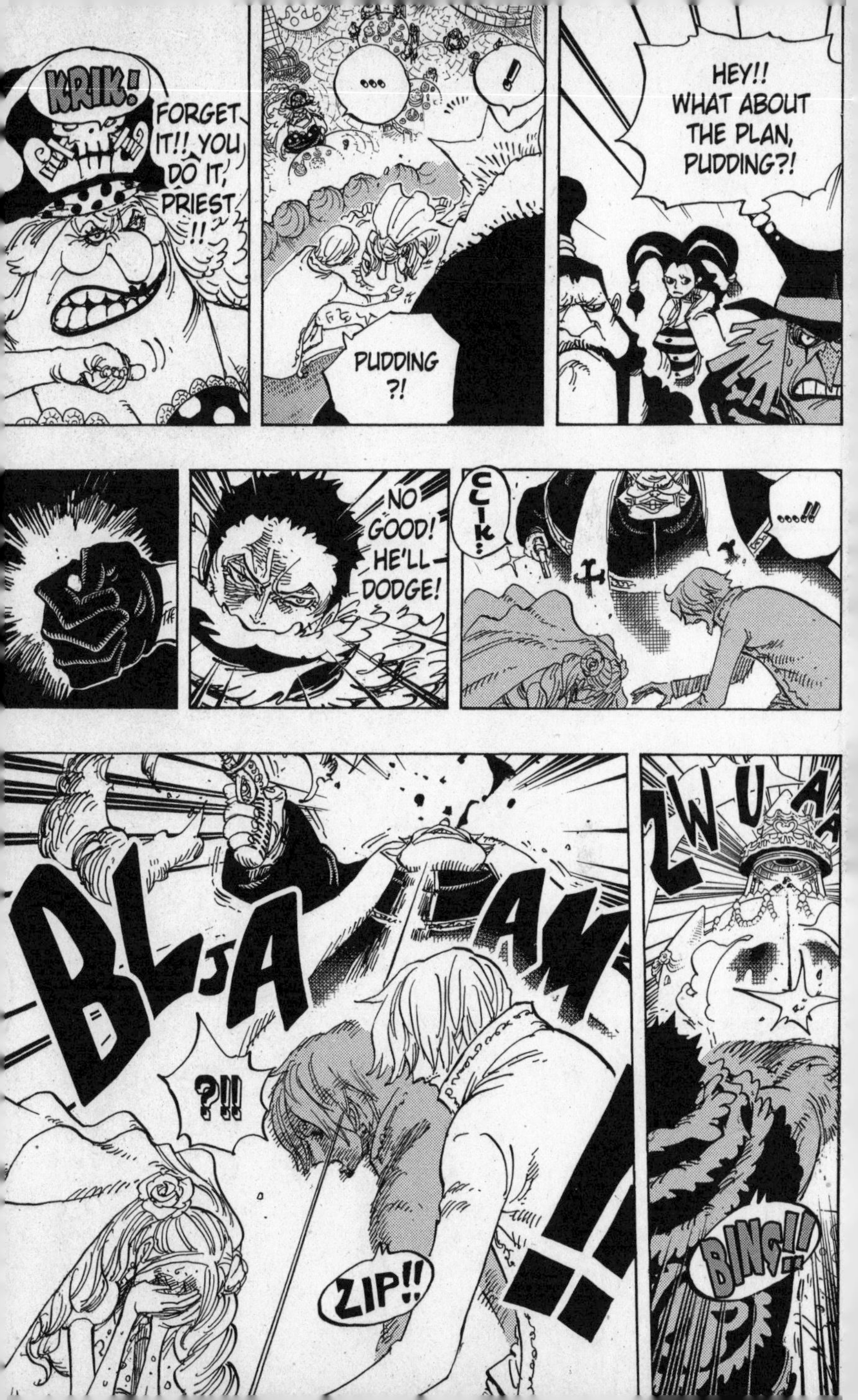
HEY!! WHAT ABOUT THE PLAN, PUDDING?!
!
...
PUDDING ?!
KRIK!
FORGET IT!! YOU DO IT, PRIEST!!
...!!
CLIK
NO GOOD! HE'LL DODGE!
ZWUAA
BING!!
BLAM!!
?!!
ZIP!!

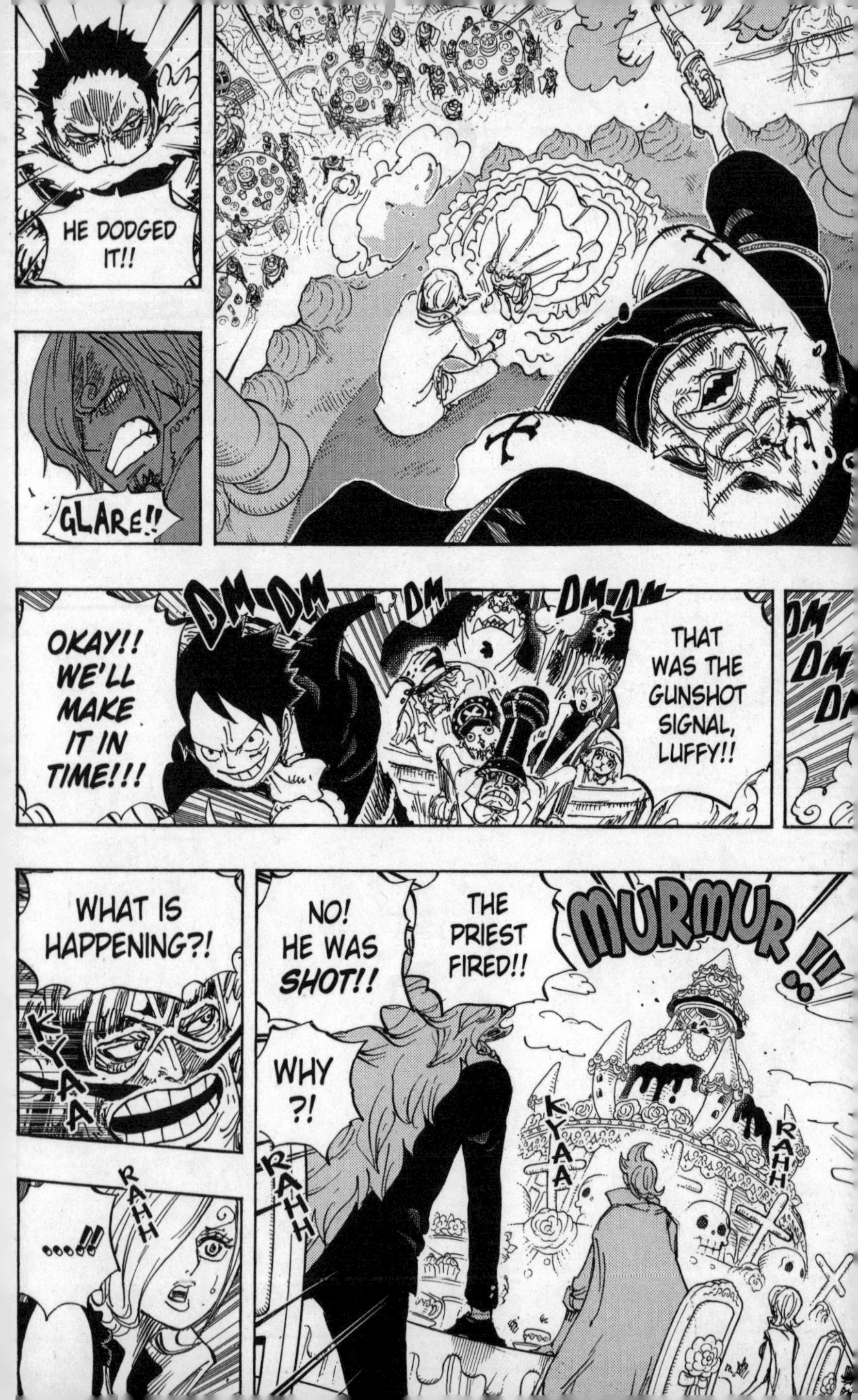
HE DODGED IT!!
GLARE!!
DM DM DM
DM-DM
THAT WAS THE GUNSHOT SIGNAL, LUFFY!!
DM
DM-DM
OKAY!! WE'LL MAKE IT IN TIME!!!
MURMUR!!!
THE PRIEST FIRED!!
NO! HE WAS SHOT!!
KYAA
RAHH
WHY?!
RAHH
WHAT IS HAPPENING?!
KYAA
RAHH
....!!

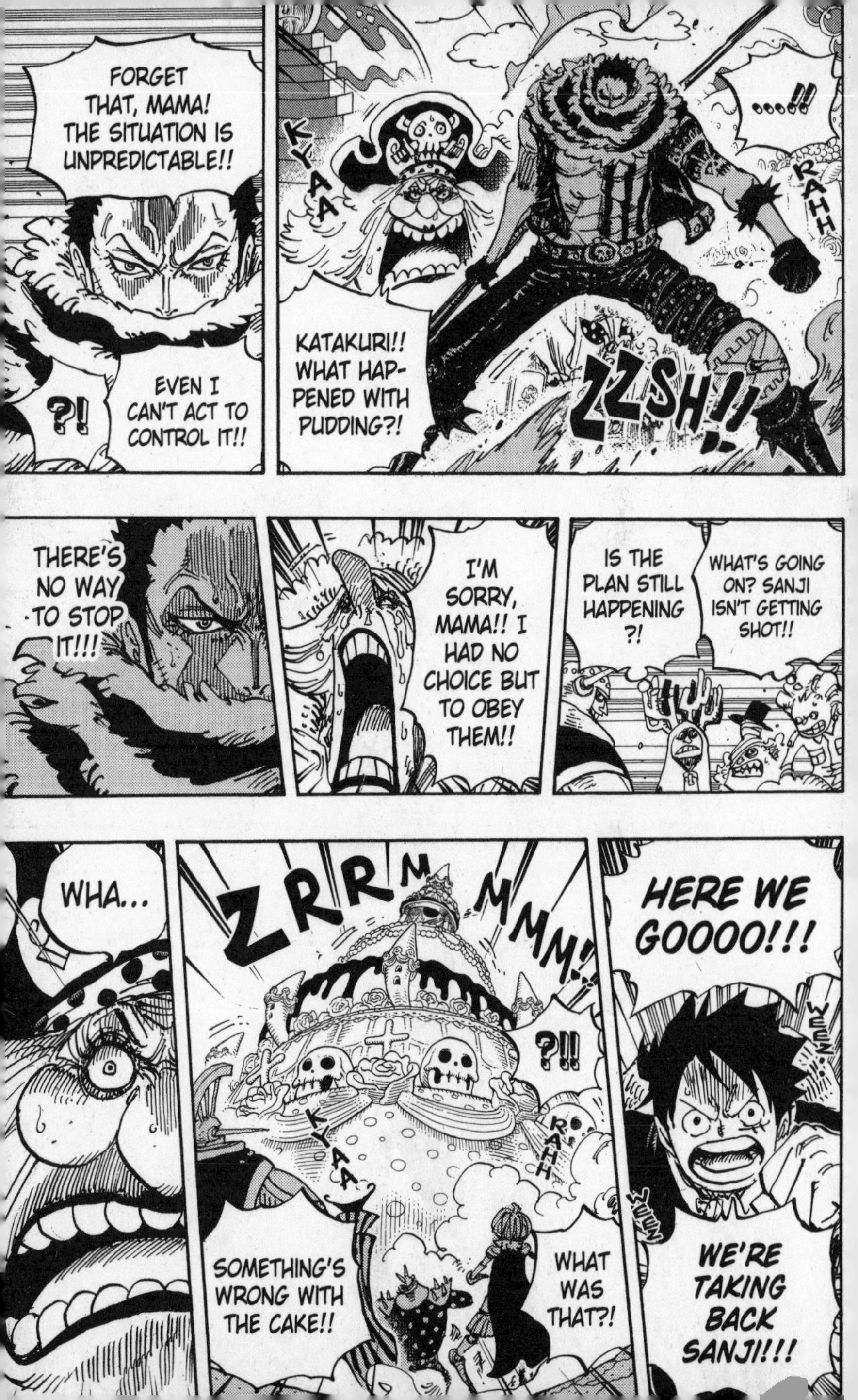
....!!
RAHH
KYAA
KATAKURI!! WHAT HAPPENED WITH PUDDING?!
ZZSH!!
FORGET THAT, MAMA! THE SITUATION IS UNPREDICTABLE!!
?!
EVEN I CAN'T ACT TO CONTROL IT!!
WHAT'S GOING ON? SANJI ISN'T GETTING SHOT!!
IS THE PLAN STILL HAPPENING ?!
I'M SORRY, MAMA!! I HAD NO CHOICE BUT TO OBEY THEM!!
THERE'S NO WAY TO STOP IT!!!
HERE WE GOOOO!!!
WEEZ
WE'RE TAKING BACK SANJI!!!
ZRRRMMMM!!
?!!
RAHH
KYAA
WHAT WAS THAT?!
SOMETHING'S WRONG WITH THE CAKE!!
WHA...

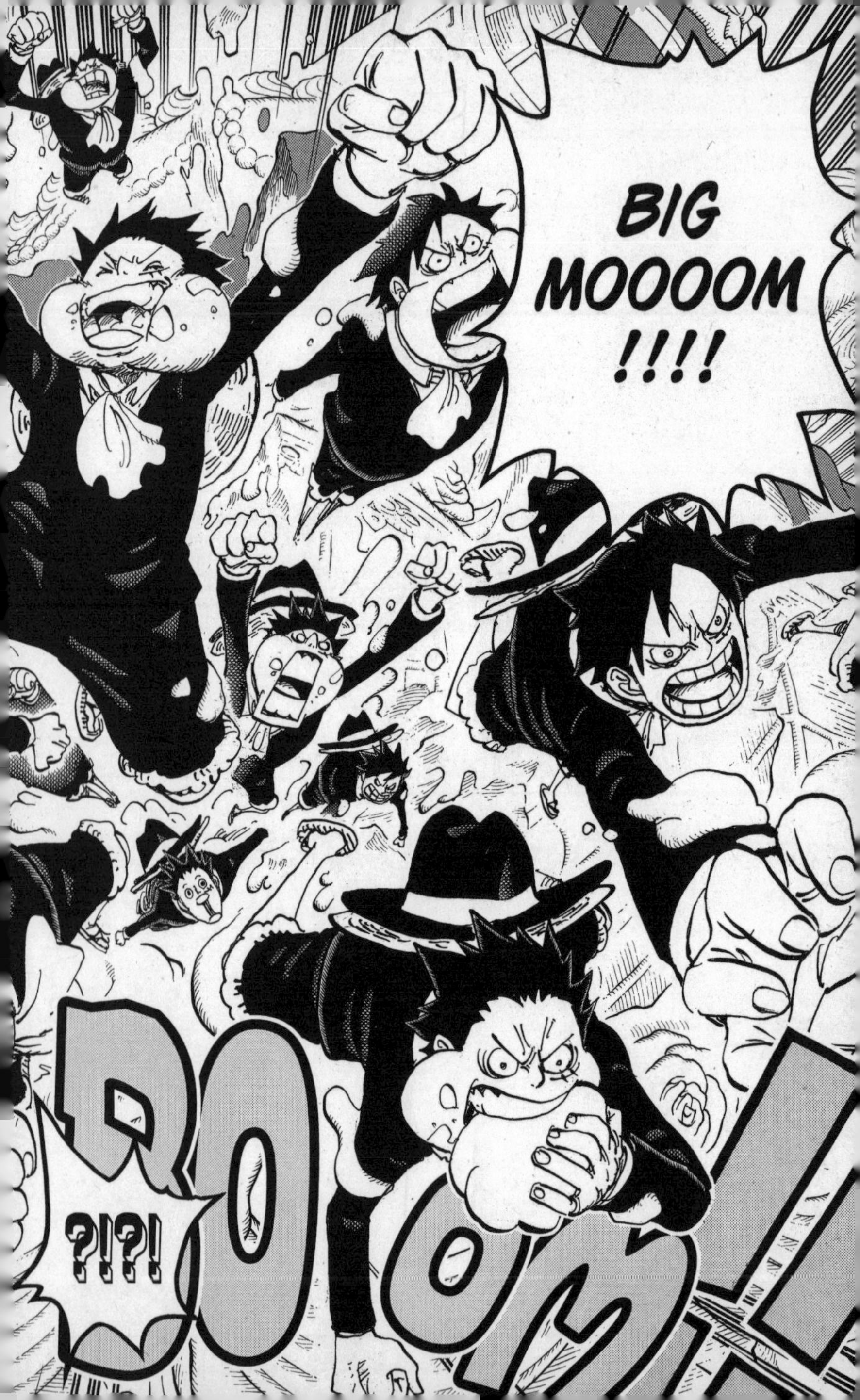
BIG MOOOOM !!!!
?!?!

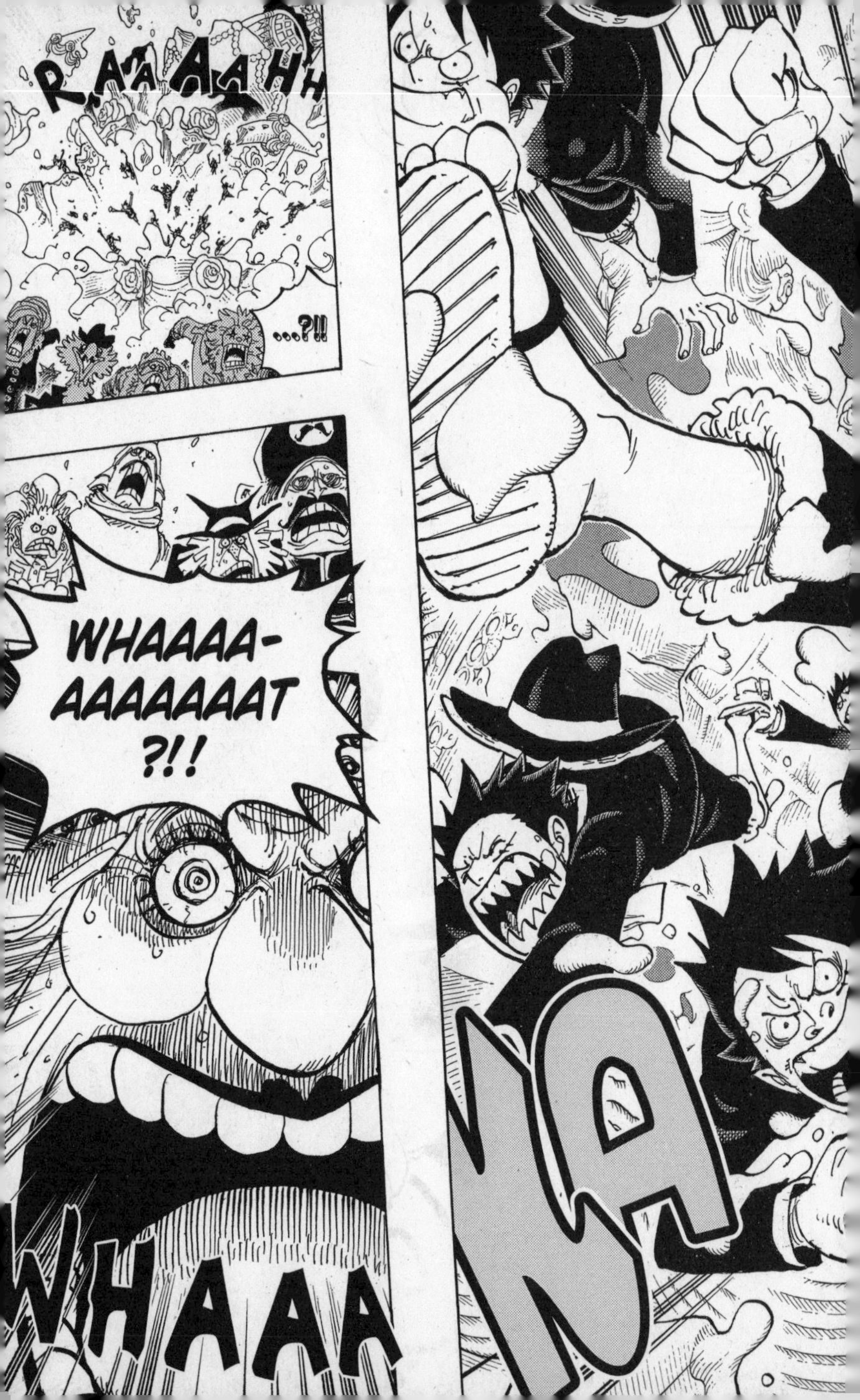
RAAAAHH
...?!!
WHAAAA-AAAAAAAT ?!!
WHAAA

Chapter 863: THE KNIGHT

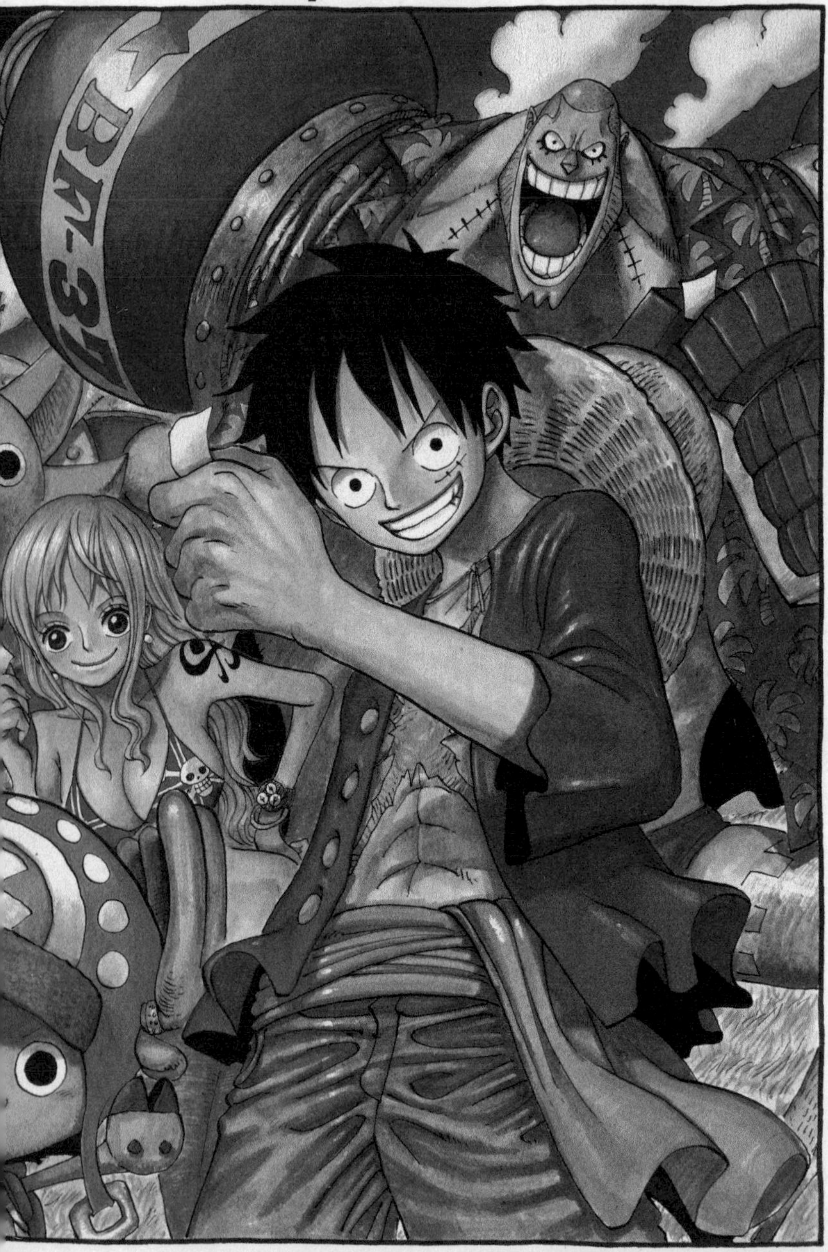
BR7-37

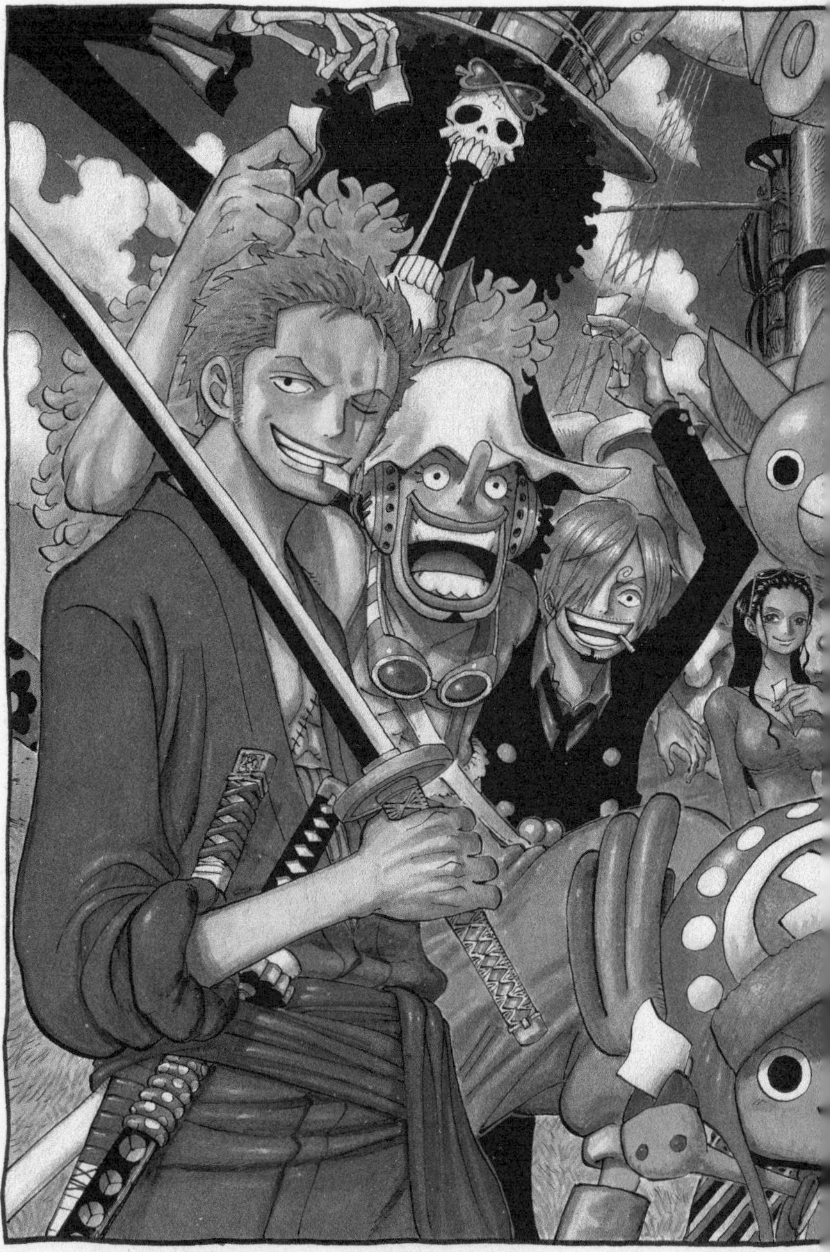

vol.86
ONE PIECE

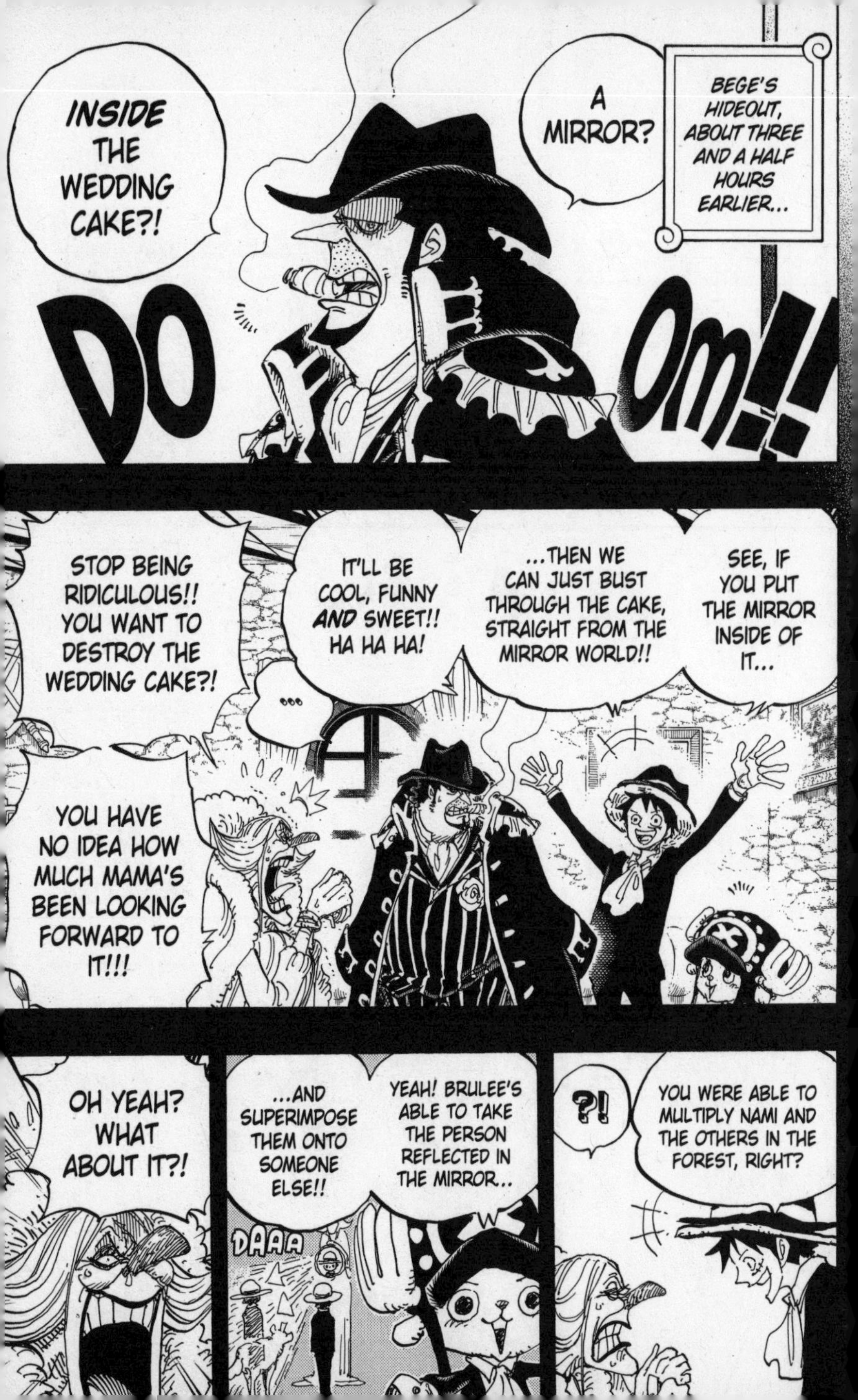
BEGE'S HIDEOUT, ABOUT THREE AND A HALF HOURS EARLIER...
A MIRROR?
INSIDE THE WEDDING CAKE?!
DOOm!!
SEE, IF YOU PUT THE MIRROR INSIDE OF IT...
...THEN WE CAN JUST BUST THROUGH THE CAKE, STRAIGHT FROM THE MIRROR WORLD!!
IT'LL BE COOL, FUNNY AND SWEET!! HA HA HA!
...
STOP BEING RIDICULOUS!! YOU WANT TO DESTROY THE WEDDING CAKE?!
YOU HAVE NO IDEA HOW MUCH MAMA'S BEEN LOOKING FORWARD TO IT!!!
YOU WERE ABLE TO MULTIPLY NAMI AND THE OTHERS IN THE FOREST, RIGHT?
?!
YEAH! BRULEE'S ABLE TO TAKE THE PERSON REFLECTED IN THE MIRROR...
...AND SUPERIMPOSE THEM ONTO SOMEONE ELSE!!
DAAA
OH YEAH? WHAT ABOUT IT?!

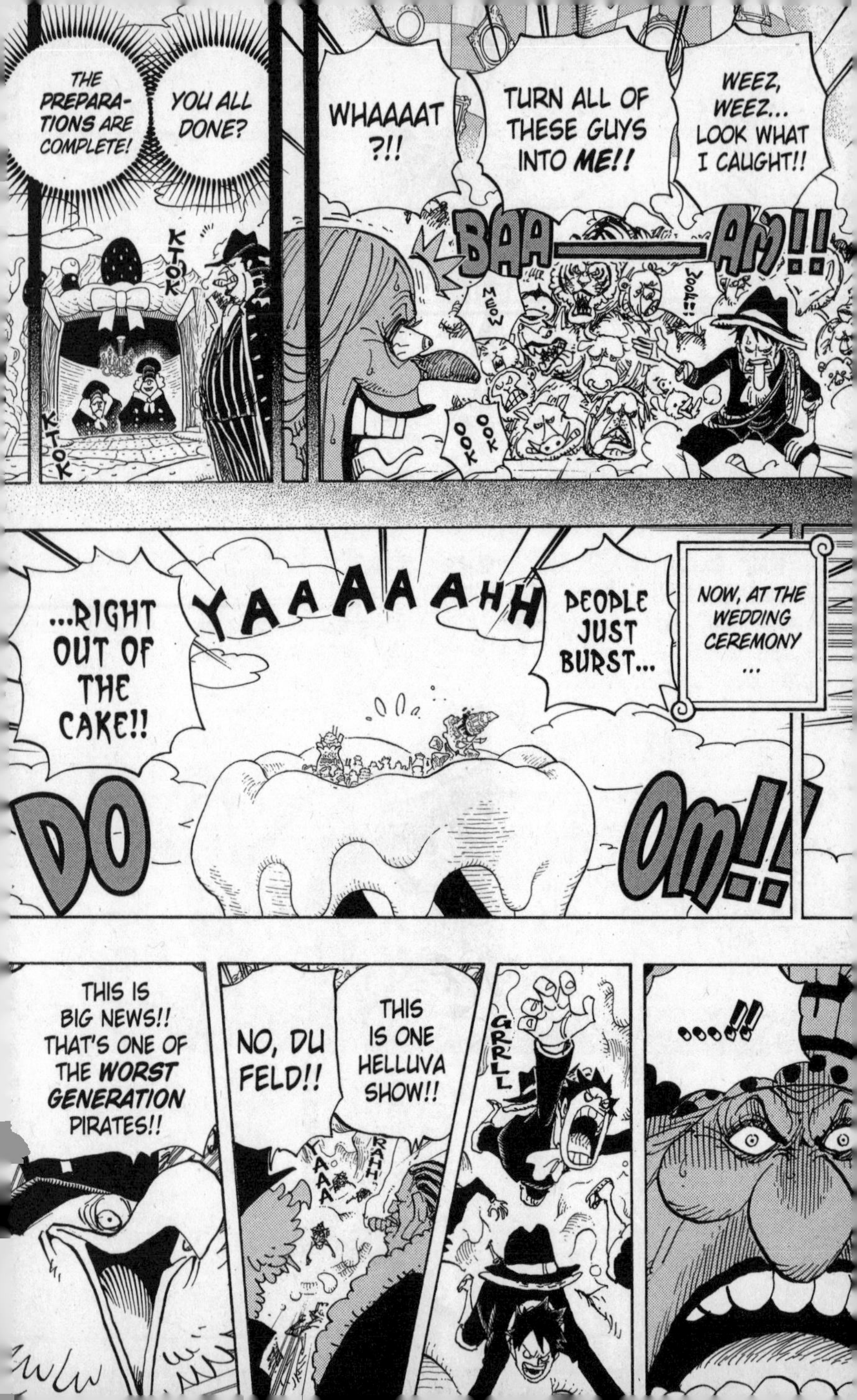
WEEZ, WEEZ... LOOK WHAT I CAUGHT!!
TURN ALL OF THESE GUYS INTO ME!!
WHAAAAT ?!!
BAA——AM!!
WOOF!!
MEOW
OOK OOK OOK
YOU ALL DONE?
THE PREPARATIONS ARE COMPLETE!
KTOK
KTOK
NOW, AT THE WEDDING CEREMONY ...
PEOPLE JUST BURST...
YAAAAAHH
...RIGHT OUT OF THE CAKE!!
DOOM!!
...!!
GRRLL
THIS IS ONE HELLUVA SHOW!!
NO, DU FELD!!
RAHH!
YAAA
THIS IS BIG NEWS!! THAT'S ONE OF THE WORST GENERATION PIRATES!!

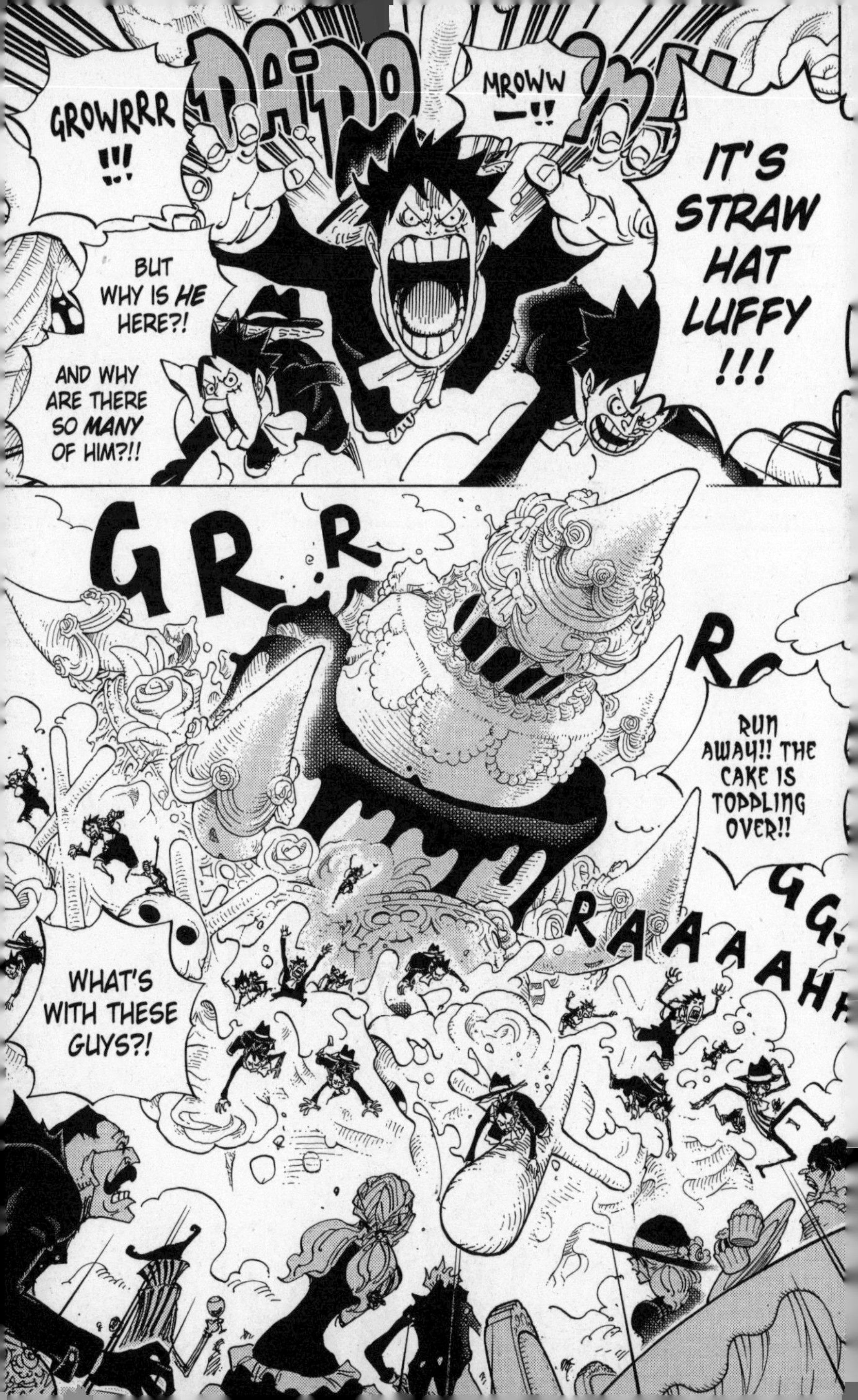
MROWW —!!
IT'S STRAW HAT LUFFY!!!
DA-DO
GROWRRR!!!
BUT WHY IS *HE* HERE?!
AND WHY ARE THERE SO *MANY* OF HIM?!!
GRRR
RUN AWAY!! THE CAKE IS TOPPLING OVER!!
GG
RAAAAAH
WHAT'S WITH THESE GUYS?!

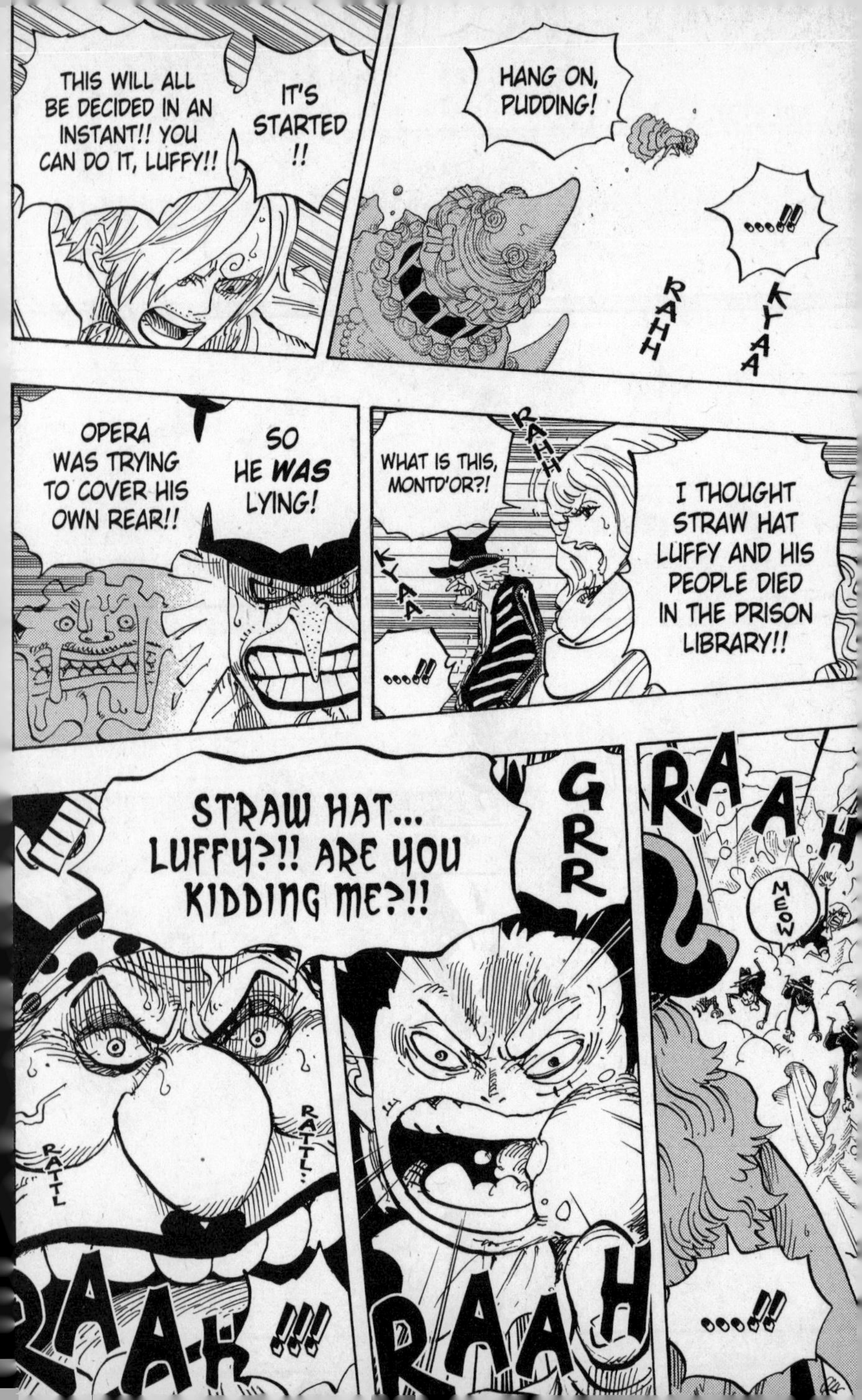
HANG ON, PUDDING!
...!!
RAHH
KYAA
IT'S STARTED!!
THIS WILL ALL BE DECIDED IN AN INSTANT!! YOU CAN DO IT, LUFFY!!
I THOUGHT STRAW HAT LUFFY AND HIS PEOPLE DIED IN THE PRISON LIBRARY!!
RAHH
WHAT IS THIS, MONTD'OR?!
KYAA
...!!
SO HE *WAS* LYING!
OPERA WAS TRYING TO COVER HIS OWN REAR!!
RAAH
MEOW
...!!
GRR
RAAH
STRAW HAT... LUFFY?!! ARE YOU KIDDING ME?!!
RATTL
RATTL
RAA-H!!!

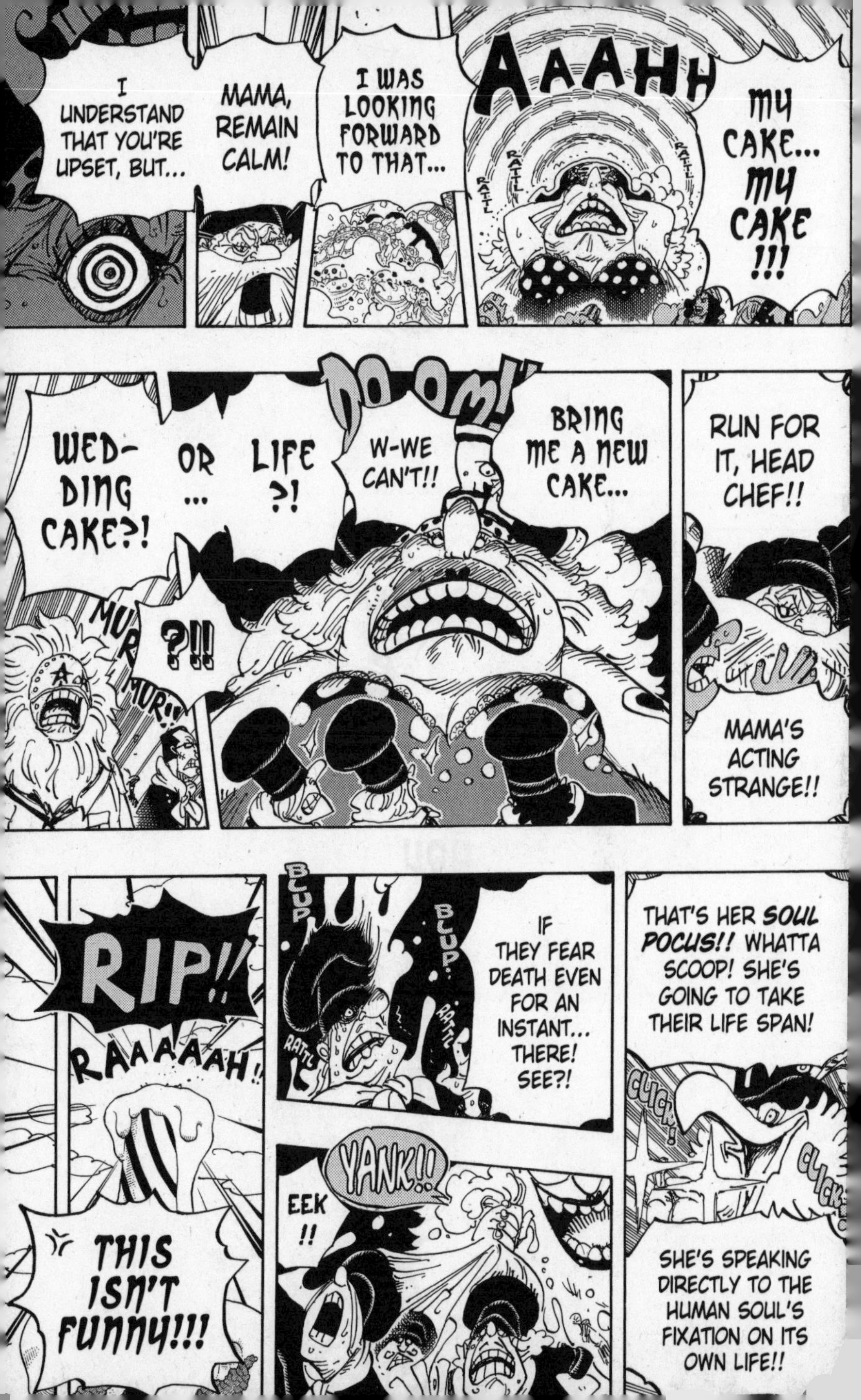
AAAHH
RATTLE RATTLE RATTLE
MY CAKE... MY CAKE!!!
I WAS LOOKING FORWARD TO THAT...
MAMA, REMAIN CALM!
I UNDERSTAND THAT YOU'RE UPSET, BUT...
RUN FOR IT, HEAD CHEF!!
MAMA'S ACTING STRANGE!!
BRING ME A NEW CAKE...
DOOM!!
W-WE CAN'T!!
LIFE?!
OR...
WED-DING CAKE?!
?!!
MUR MUR!!
THAT'S HER SOUL POCUS!! WHATTA SCOOP! SHE'S GOING TO TAKE THEIR LIFE SPAN!
CLICK! CLICK!
SHE'S SPEAKING DIRECTLY TO THE HUMAN SOUL'S FIXATION ON ITS OWN LIFE!!
IF THEY FEAR DEATH EVEN FOR AN INSTANT... THERE! SEE?!
BLUP BLUP
RATTLE RATTLE
YANK!!
EEK!!
RIP!!
RAAAAAH!!
THIS ISN'T FUNNY!!!!

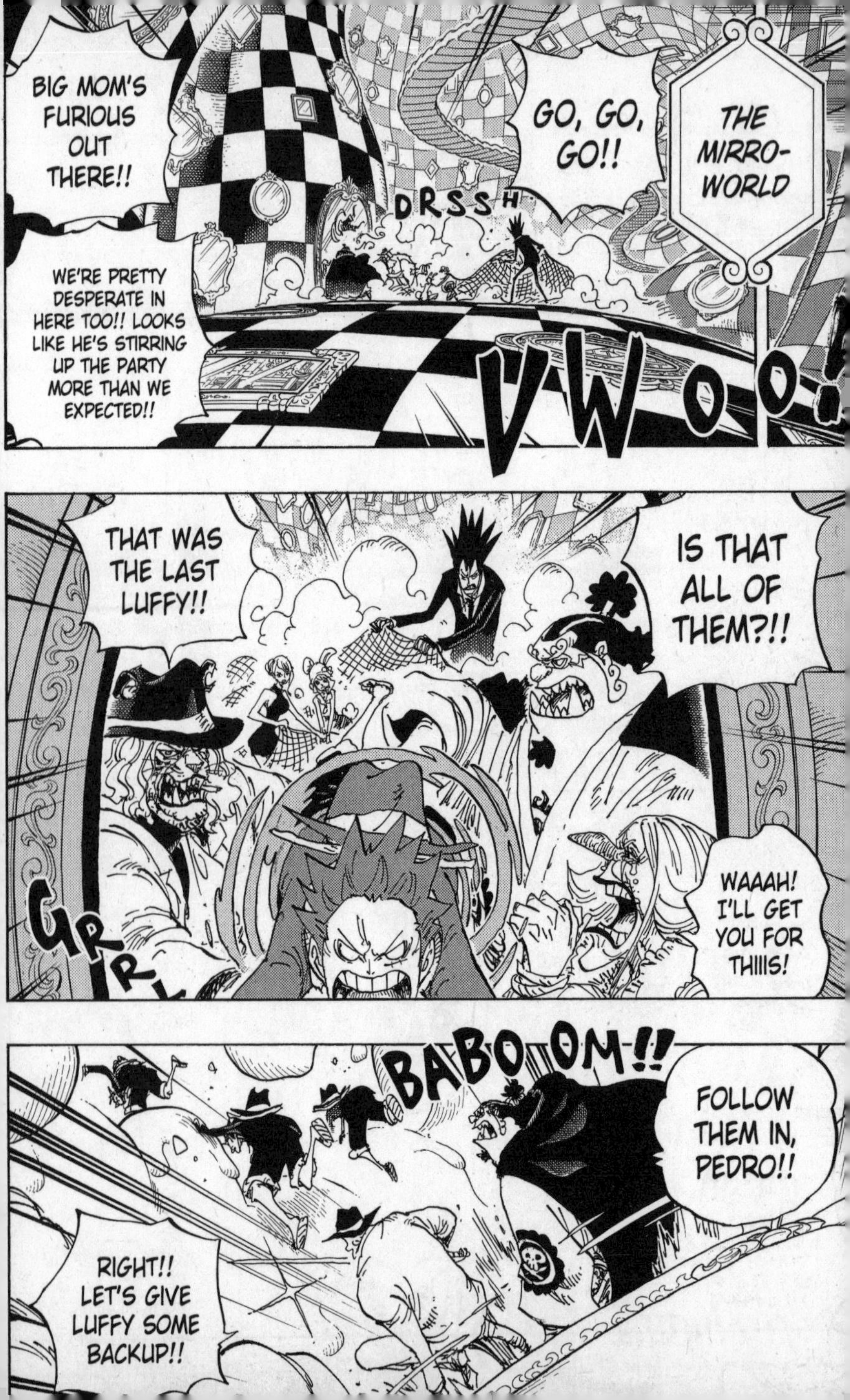
THE MIRRO-WORLD
GO, GO, GO!!
DRSSH
BIG MOM'S FURIOUS OUT THERE!!
VWOO!
WE'RE PRETTY DESPERATE IN HERE TOO!! LOOKS LIKE HE'S STIRRING UP THE PARTY MORE THAN WE EXPECTED!!
IS THAT ALL OF THEM?!!
THAT WAS THE LAST LUFFY!!
WAAAH! I'LL GET YOU FOR THIIIS!
GRR
BABOOM!!
FOLLOW THEM IN, PEDRO!!
RIGHT!! LET'S GIVE LUFFY SOME BACKUP!!

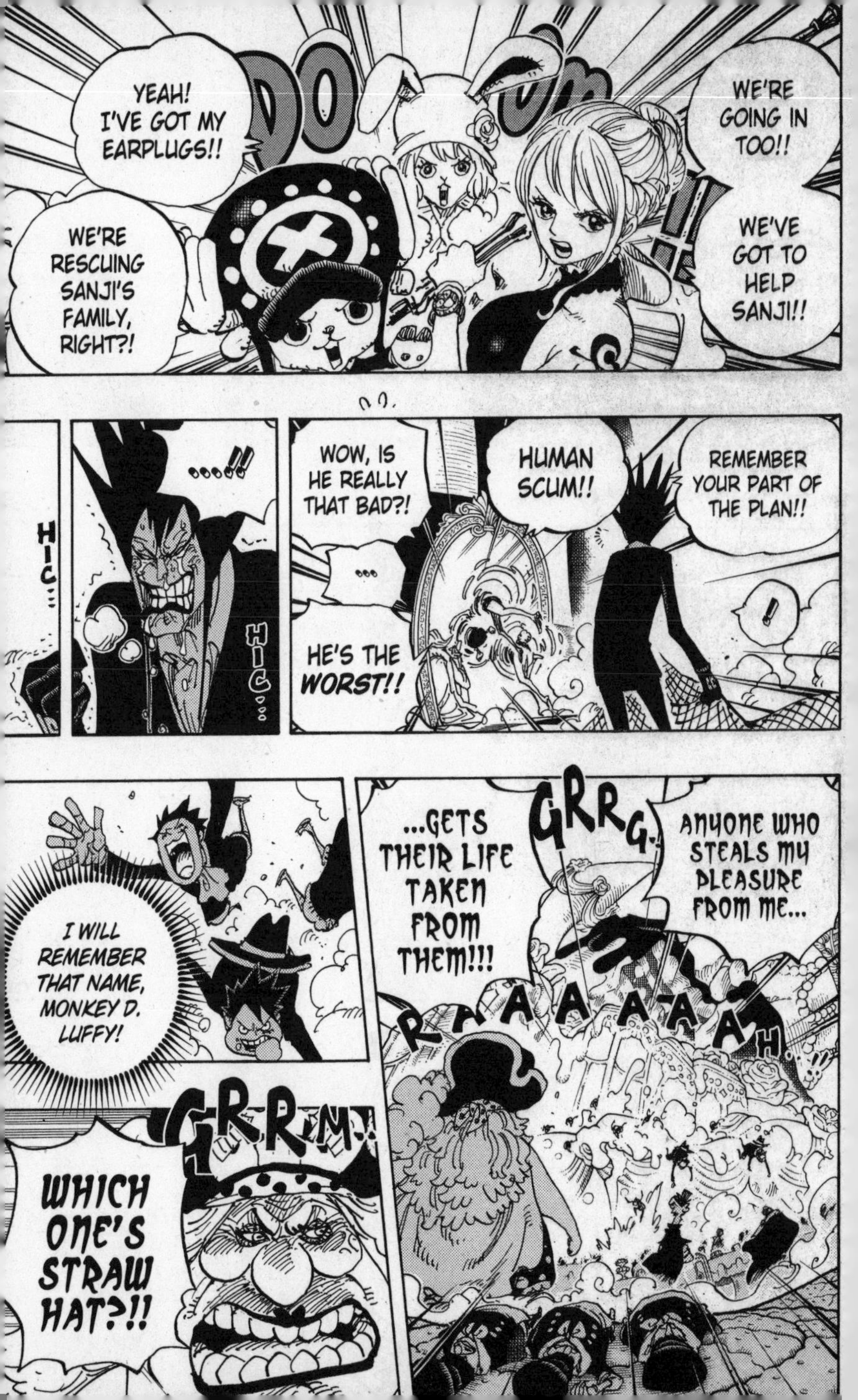
DOOM
WE'RE GOING IN TOO!!
WE'VE GOT TO HELP SANJI!!
YEAH! I'VE GOT MY EARPLUGS!!
WE'RE RESCUING SANJI'S FAMILY, RIGHT?!
REMEMBER YOUR PART OF THE PLAN!!
!
HUMAN SCUM!!
WOW, IS HE REALLY THAT BAD?!
...
HE'S THE WORST!!
....!!
HIC...
HIC...
GRRG..
ANYONE WHO STEALS MY PLEASURE FROM ME...
...GETS THEIR LIFE TAKEN FROM THEM!!!
RAAAAAAH..
I WILL REMEMBER THAT NAME, MONKEY D. LUFFY!
GRRM..
WHICH ONE'S STRAW HAT?!!

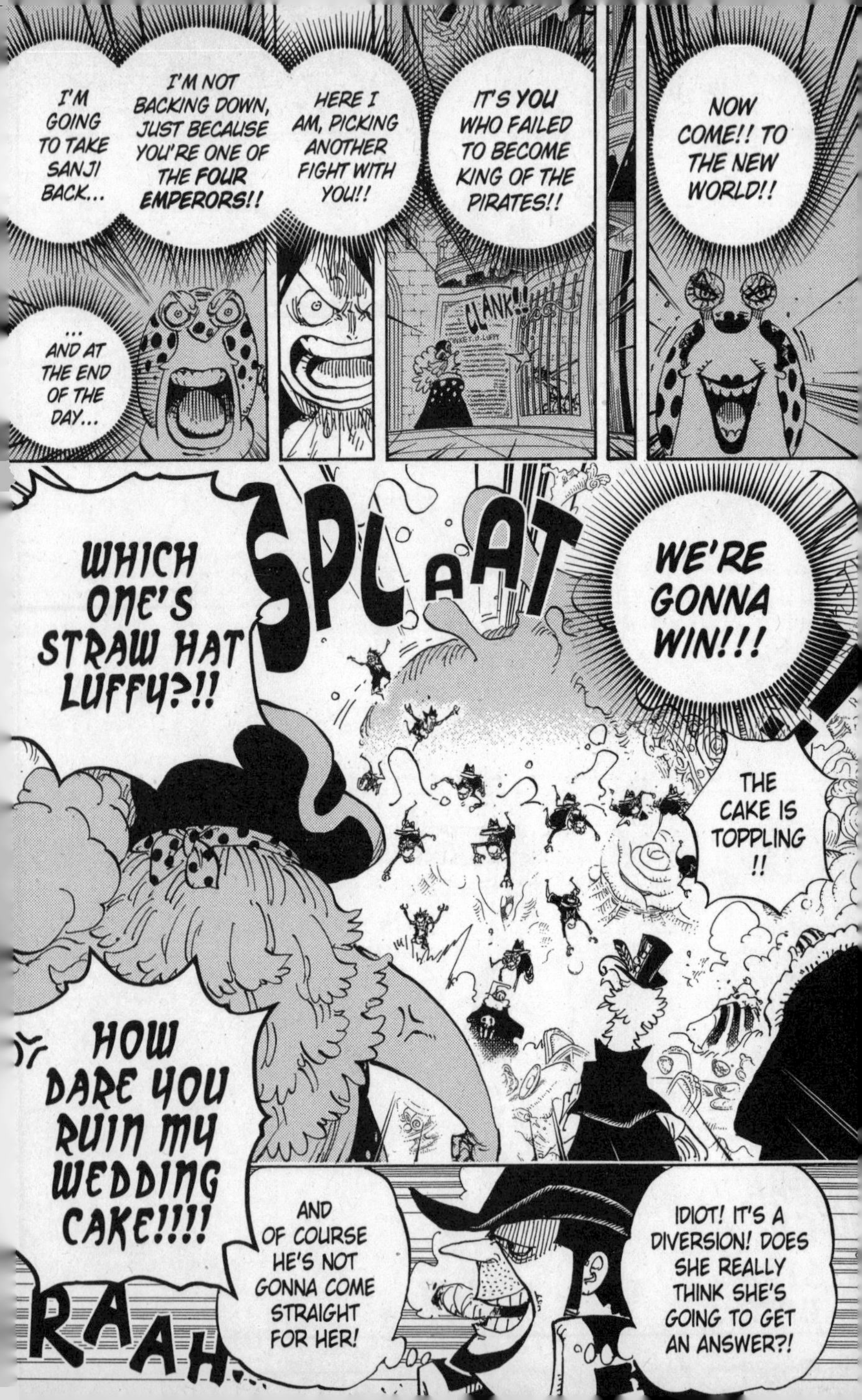
NOW COME!! TO THE NEW WORLD!!
IT'S YOU WHO FAILED TO BECOME KING OF THE PIRATES!!
CLANK!!
HERE I AM, PICKING ANOTHER FIGHT WITH YOU!!
I'M NOT BACKING DOWN, JUST BECAUSE YOU'RE ONE OF THE FOUR EMPERORS!!
I'M GOING TO TAKE SANJI BACK...
...AND AT THE END OF THE DAY...
WE'RE GONNA WIN!!!
SPLAAT
WHICH ONE'S STRAW HAT LUFFY?!!
THE CAKE IS TOPPLING!!
HOW DARE YOU RUIN MY WEDDING CAKE!!!!
IDIOT! IT'S A DIVERSION! DOES SHE REALLY THINK SHE'S GOING TO GET AN ANSWER?!
AND OF COURSE HE'S NOT GONNA COME STRAIGHT FOR HER!
RAAAH...

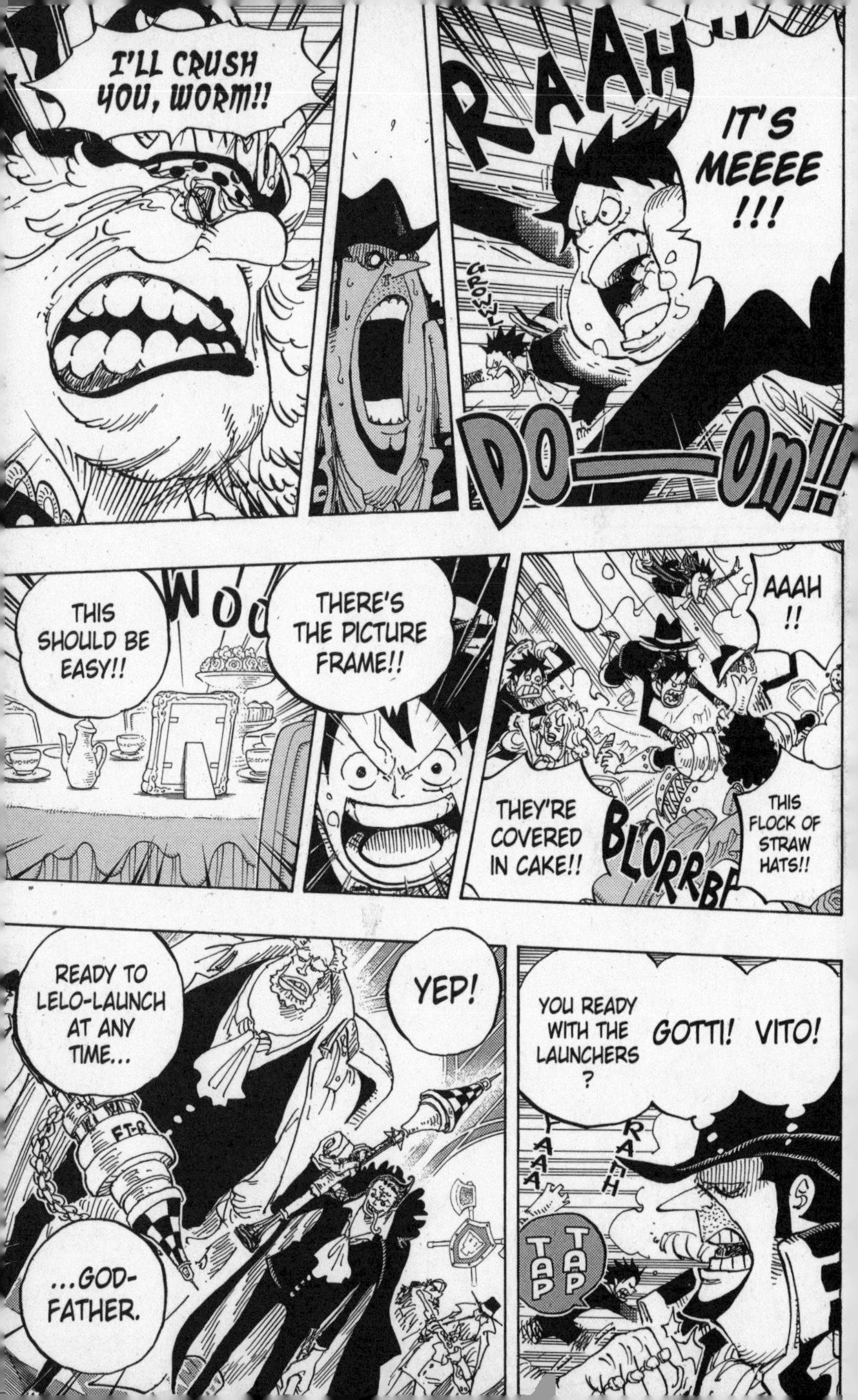
RAAH!!
IT'S MEEEE!!!
GROWL
DO——OM!!
I'LL CRUSH YOU, WORM!!
AAAH!!
THIS FLOCK OF STRAW HATS!!
BLORRB
THEY'RE COVERED IN CAKE!!
THERE'S THE PICTURE FRAME!!
WOO
THIS SHOULD BE EASY!!
GOTTI! VITO!
YOU READY WITH THE LAUNCHERS?
RAAH
AAA
TAP TAP
YEP!
READY TO LELO-LAUNCH AT ANY TIME...
...GOD-FATHER.

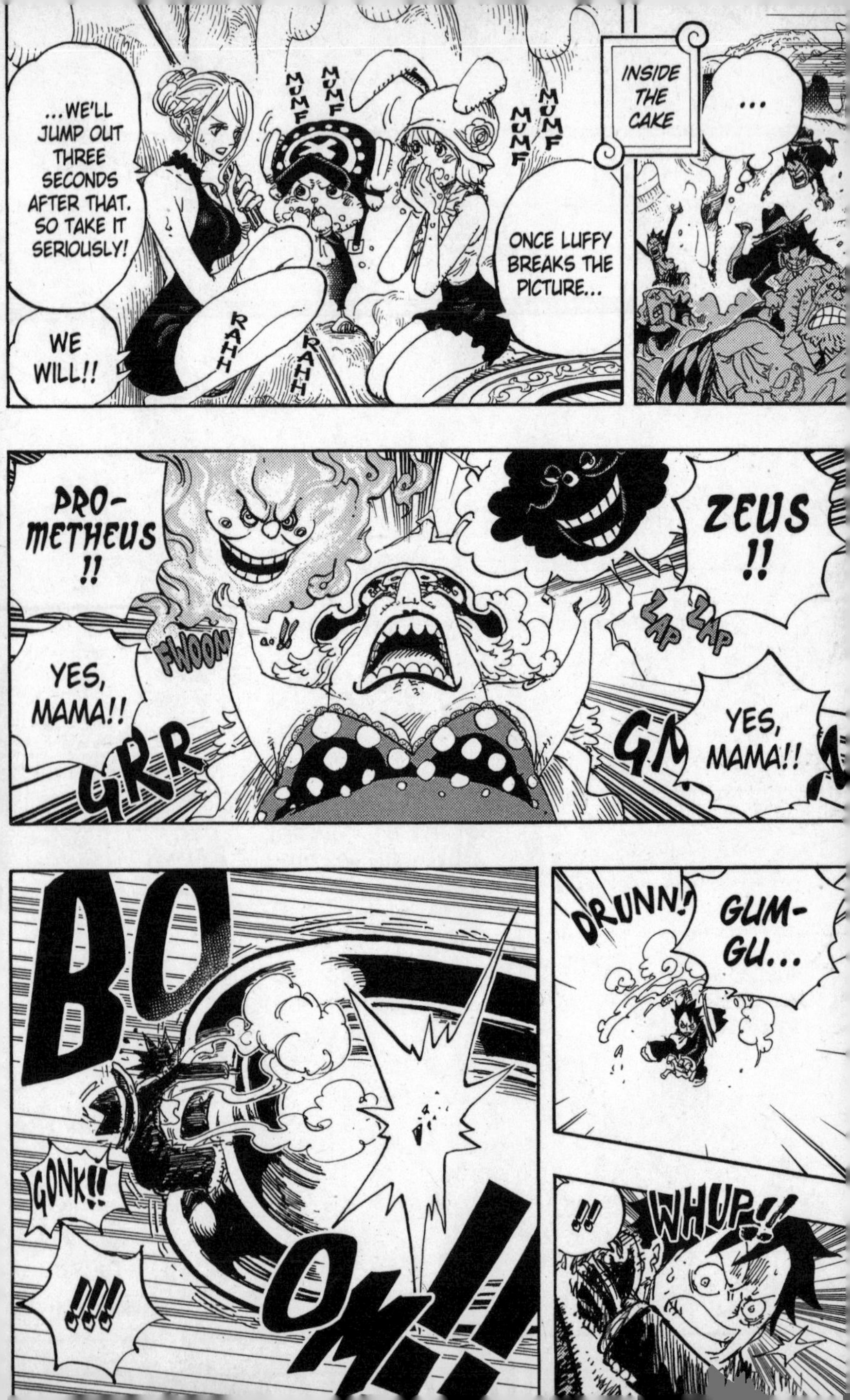

INSIDE THE CAKE
...
ONCE LUFFY BREAKS THE PICTURE...
MUMF MUMF
MUMF MUMF
...WE'LL JUMP OUT THREE SECONDS AFTER THAT. SO TAKE IT SERIOUSLY!
RAHH RAHH
WE WILL!!
ZEUS !!
ZAP ZAP
YES, MAMA!!
PRO-METHEUS !!
FWOOM
YES, MAMA!!
GRR
DRUNN!
GUM-GU...
!!
WHUP!!
BO
OM!!
GONK!!
!!!

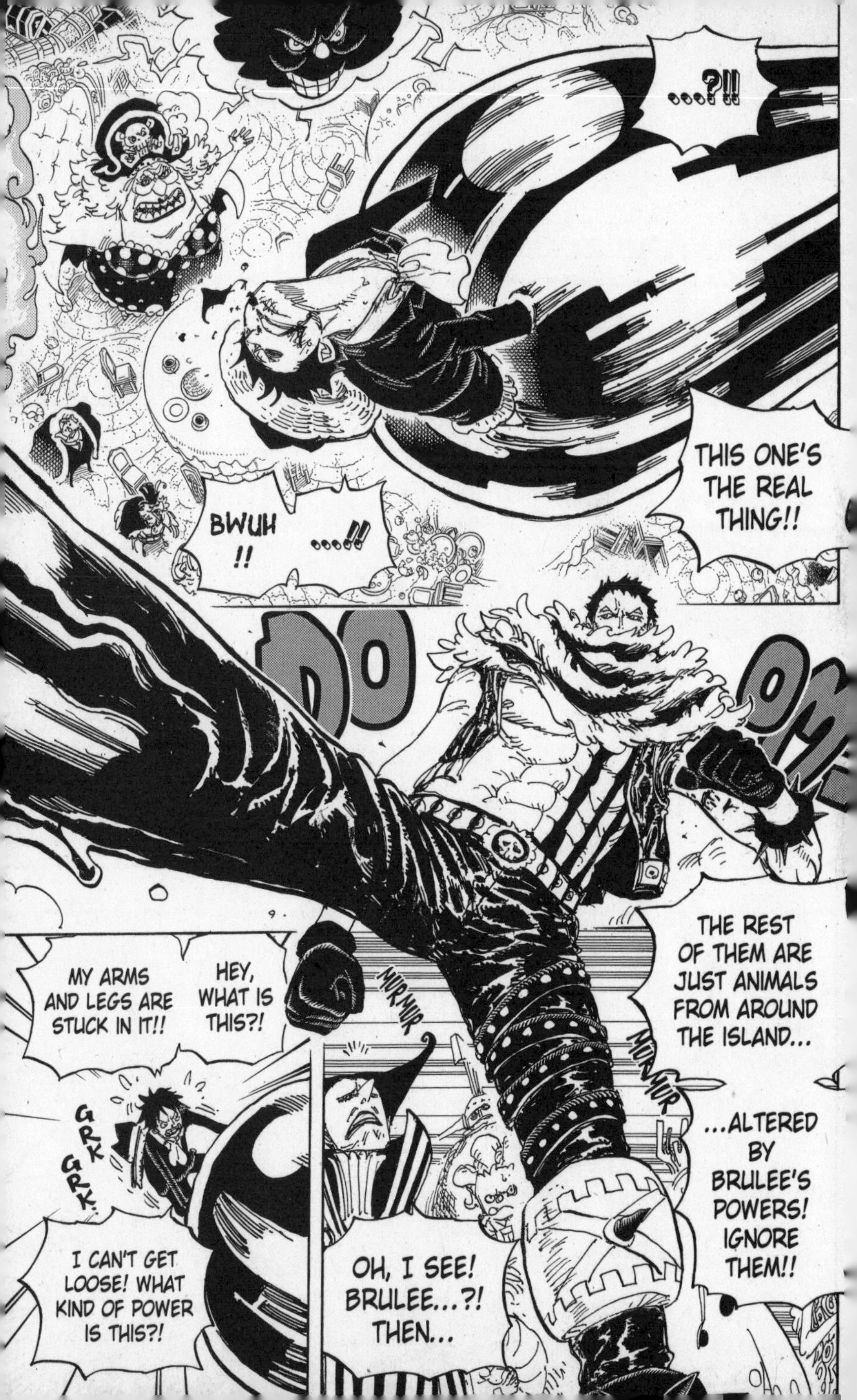
...?!!
THIS ONE'S THE REAL THING!!
...!!
BWUH !!
DO
OM
THE REST OF THEM ARE JUST ANIMALS FROM AROUND THE ISLAND...
...ALTERED BY BRULEE'S POWERS! IGNORE THEM!!
MURMUR
MURMUR
OH, I SEE! BRULEE...?! THEN...
HEY, WHAT IS THIS?!
MY ARMS AND LEGS ARE STUCK IN IT!!
GRK GRK
I CAN'T GET LOOSE! WHAT KIND OF POWER IS THIS?!

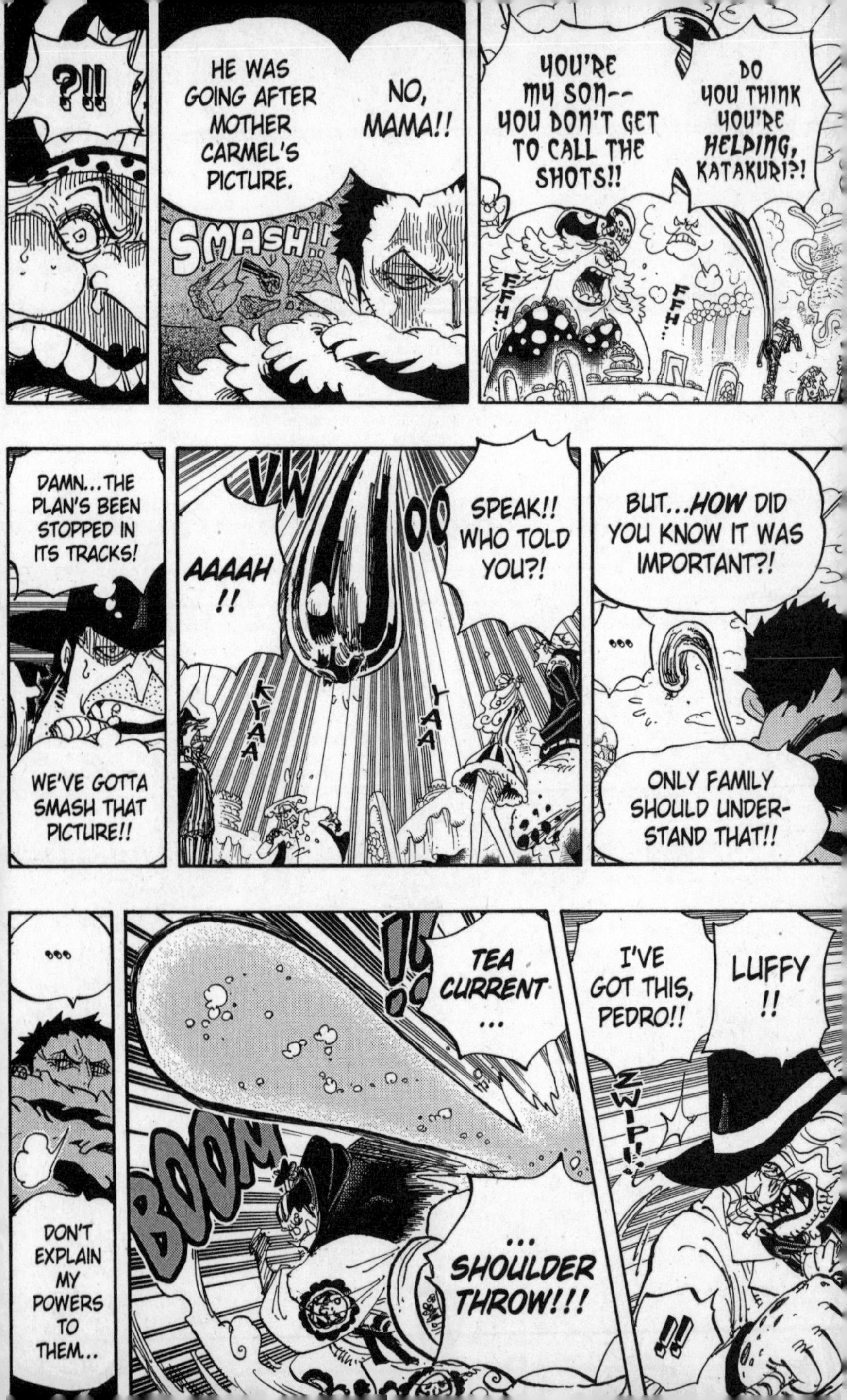
DO YOU THINK YOU'RE HELPING, KATAKURI?!
YOU'RE MY SON-- YOU DON'T GET TO CALL THE SHOTS!!
FFH
FFH
NO, MAMA!!
HE WAS GOING AFTER MOTHER CARMEL'S PICTURE.
SMASH!!
?!!
BUT...HOW DID YOU KNOW IT WAS IMPORTANT?!
...
ONLY FAMILY SHOULD UNDERSTAND THAT!!
SPEAK!! WHO TOLD YOU?!
VWOO
AAAAH!!
KYAA
YAA
DAMN...THE PLAN'S BEEN STOPPED IN ITS TRACKS!
WE'VE GOTTA SMASH THAT PICTURE!!
LUFFY!!
I'VE GOT THIS, PEDRO!!
ZWIP!!
!!
!!
TEA CURRENT...
...SHOULDER THROW!!!
BOOM
...
DON'T EXPLAIN MY POWERS TO THEM...

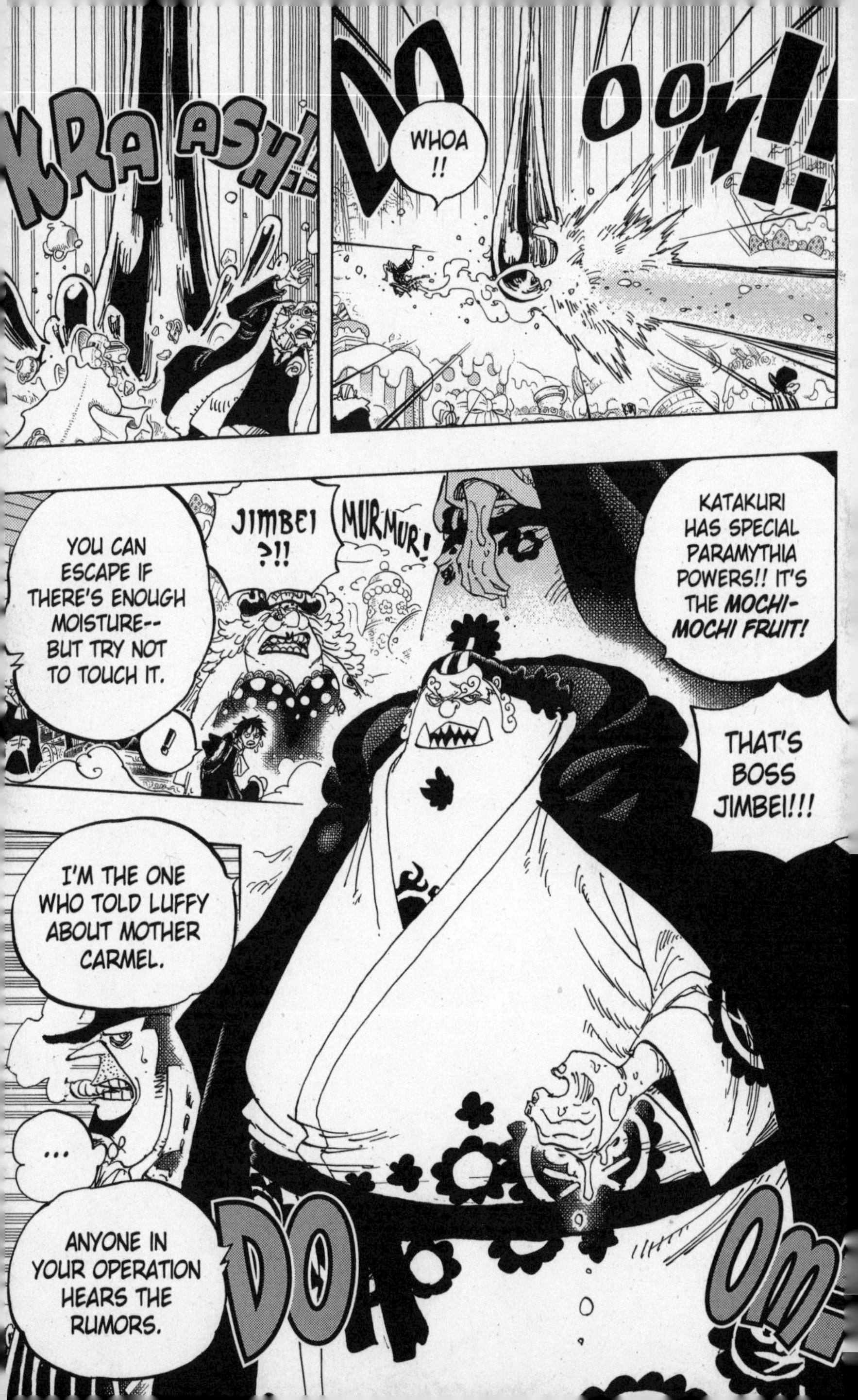
DOOOM!!
WHOA !!
KRAASH!!
KATAKURI HAS SPECIAL PARAMYTHIA POWERS!! IT'S THE *MOCHI-MOCHI FRUIT!*
THAT'S BOSS JIMBEI!!!
DOOM
MURMUR!
JIMBEI ?!!
YOU CAN ESCAPE IF THERE'S ENOUGH MOISTURE-- BUT TRY NOT TO TOUCH IT.
!
I'M THE ONE WHO TOLD LUFFY ABOUT MOTHER CARMEL.
...
ANYONE IN YOUR OPERATION HEARS THE RUMORS.

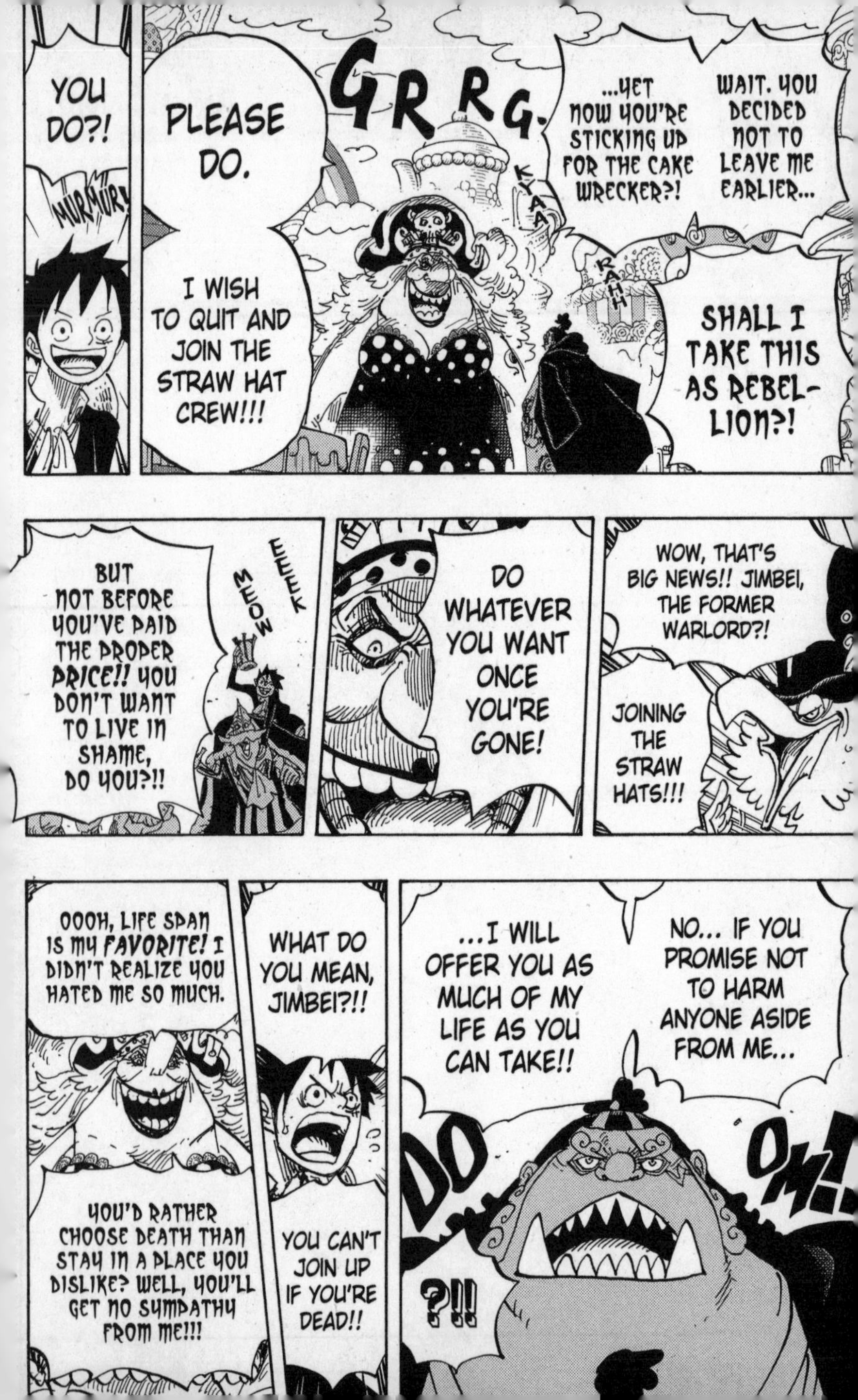
WAIT. YOU DECIDED NOT TO LEAVE ME EARLIER...
...YET NOW YOU'RE STICKING UP FOR THE CAKE WRECKER?!
GRRG.
SHALL I TAKE THIS AS REBELLION?!
KYAA
RAHH
PLEASE DO.
I WISH TO QUIT AND JOIN THE STRAW HAT CREW!!!
YOU DO?!
MURMUR
WOW, THAT'S BIG NEWS!! JIMBEI, THE FORMER WARLORD?!
JOINING THE STRAW HATS!!!
DO WHATEVER YOU WANT ONCE YOU'RE GONE!
BUT NOT BEFORE YOU'VE PAID THE PROPER PRICE!! YOU DON'T WANT TO LIVE IN SHAME, DO YOU?!!
EEEEK
MEOW
NO... IF YOU PROMISE NOT TO HARM ANYONE ASIDE FROM ME...
...I WILL OFFER YOU AS MUCH OF MY LIFE AS YOU CAN TAKE!!
DOOM!!
?!!
WHAT DO YOU MEAN, JIMBEI?!!
YOU CAN'T JOIN UP IF YOU'RE DEAD!!
OOOH, LIFE SPAN IS MY FAVORITE! I DIDN'T REALIZE YOU HATED ME SO MUCH.
YOU'D RATHER CHOOSE DEATH THAN STAY IN A PLACE YOU DISLIKE? WELL, YOU'LL GET NO SYMPATHY FROM ME!!!

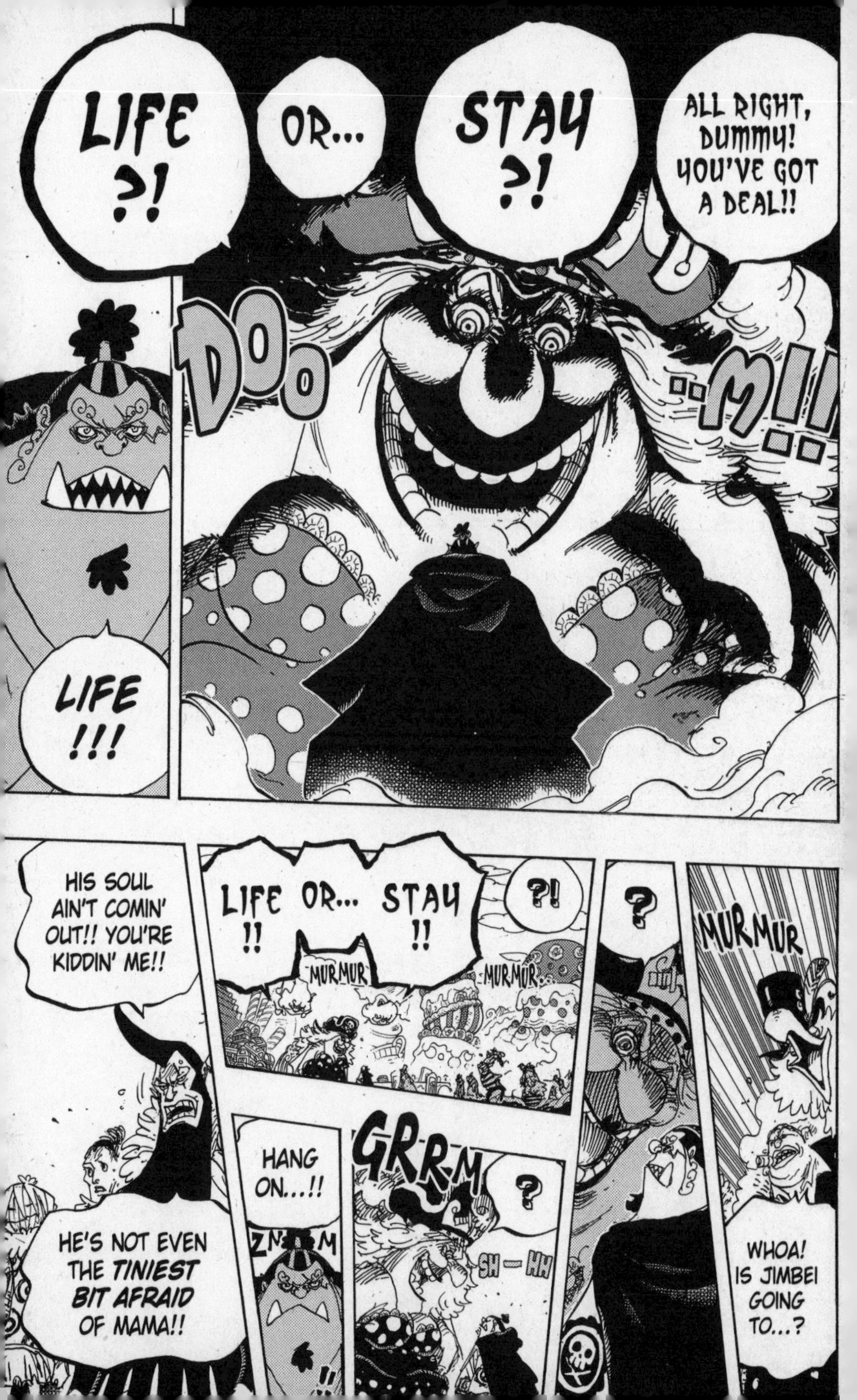
ALL RIGHT, DUMMY! YOU'VE GOT A DEAL!!
LIFE ?!
OR...
STAY ?!
DOOOM!!
LIFE !!!
MURMUR
WHOA! IS JIMBEI GOING TO...?
?
?!
LIFE OR... STAY !! !!
MURMUR
MURMUR
GRRRM
?
SH-HH
HANG ON...!!
ZNM
HIS SOUL AIN'T COMIN' OUT!! YOU'RE KIDDIN' ME!!
HE'S NOT EVEN THE TINIEST BIT AFRAID OF MAMA!!

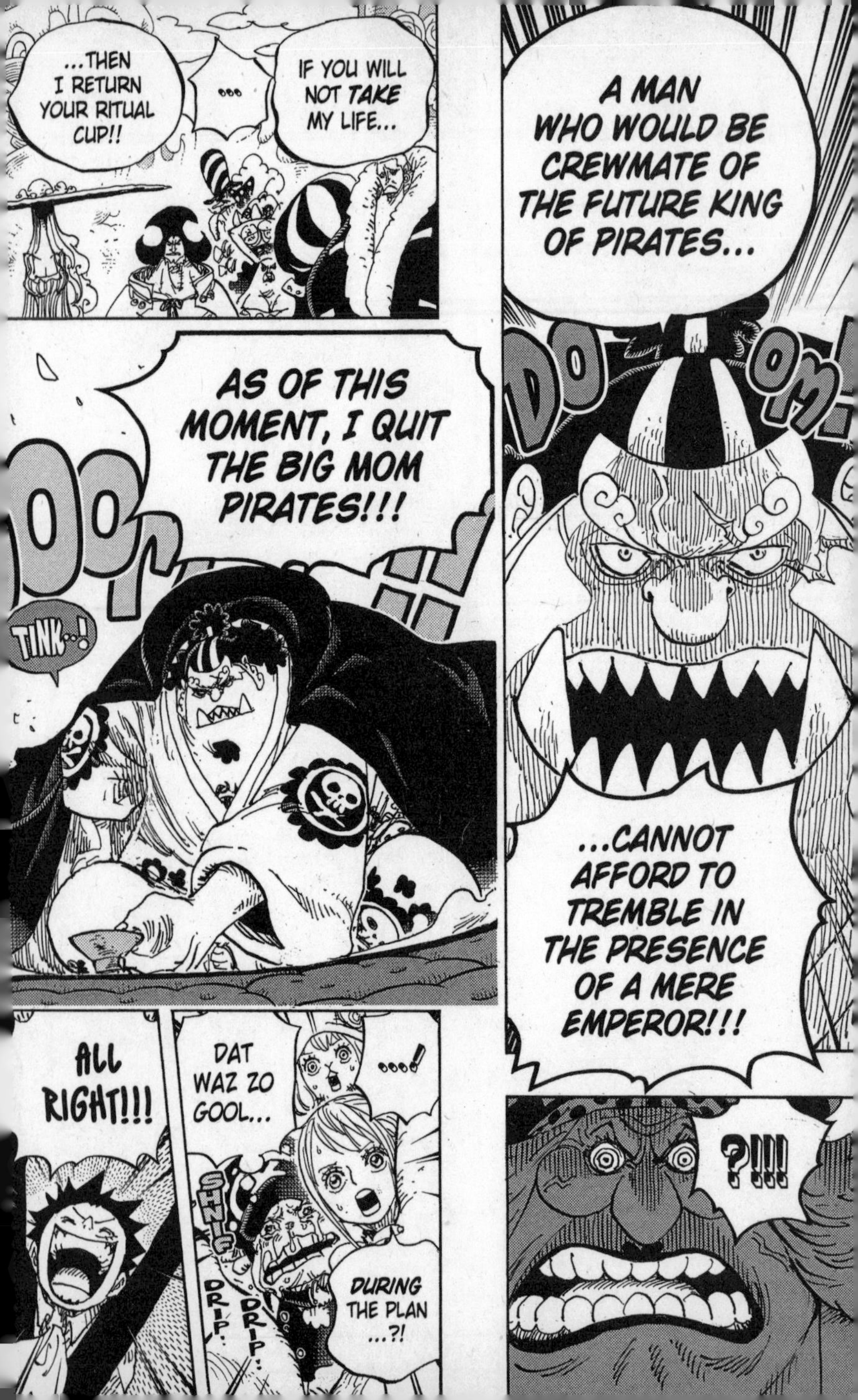
IF YOU WILL NOT TAKE MY LIFE...
...
...THEN I RETURN YOUR RITUAL CUP!!
AS OF THIS MOMENT, I QUIT THE BIG MOM PIRATES!!!
DOOOM
TINK..!
DAT WAZ ZO GOOL...
...!
SHNIFF
DRIP
DRIP
DURING THE PLAN ...?!
ALL RIGHT!!!
A MAN WHO WOULD BE CREWMATE OF THE FUTURE KING OF PIRATES...
DOOM!
...CANNOT AFFORD TO TREMBLE IN THE PRESENCE OF A MERE EMPEROR!!!
?!!!

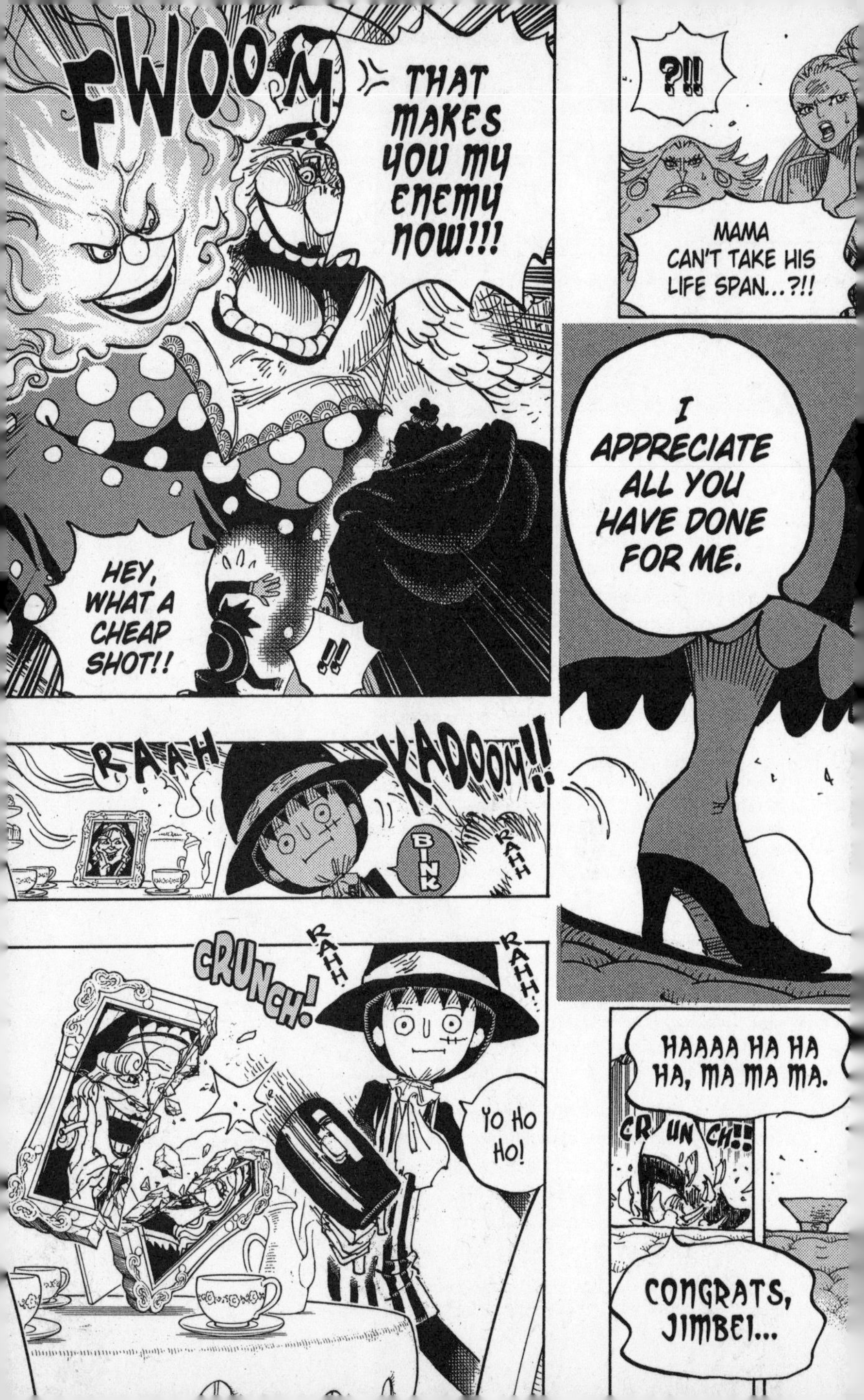
?!!
MAMA CAN'T TAKE HIS LIFE SPAN...?!!
FWOOM
THAT MAKES YOU MY ENEMY NOW!!!
!!
HEY, WHAT A CHEAP SHOT!!
I APPRECIATE ALL YOU HAVE DONE FOR ME.
KADOOM!!
RAAH
RAHH
BINK
HAAAA HA HA HA, MA MA MA.
CRUNCH!!
CONGRATS, JIMBEI...
RAHH
RAHH
CRUNCH!
YO HO HO!

SBS Question Corner

質問コーナー

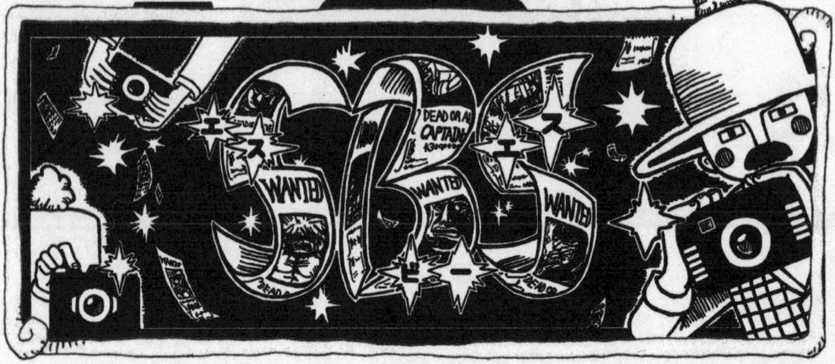
エ
ス
ビ
ー
エ
ス
WANTED
WANTED
WANTED

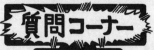

(Fujima, Fukuoka)

Q: On page 28 of volume 85 (chapter 850), you can see the bento lunch that Sanji prepared. When compared to the list of the crew's favorite foods in the SBS section of volume 45, they line up perfectly. However, I just can't figure out what the food is to the left of the sandwich. Is it Brook's favorite, perhaps, since he wasn't in the volume 45 SBS? Can you provide an answer that will swirl my brow?

--OP Girl

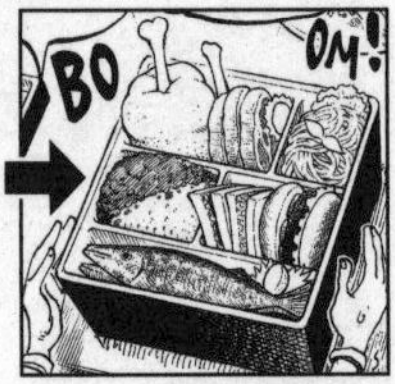
BO
OM!

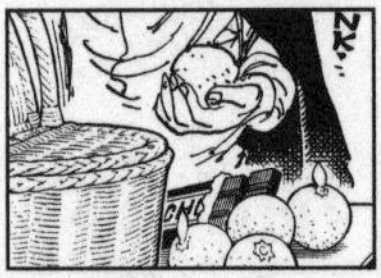

A: Ah, good looking out there. It's supposed to be a scene where Sanji's making a lunch for Pudding, and you wonder, "What are you really thinking about, man?!" You're right, he's made all of the crew's favorite dishes. And look at the amounts. This is not a single meal for one lady, Sanji... Here's the menu:
Meat (Luffy), Rice (Zolo), Seasonal fish (Usopp), Pasta (Sanji), Hamburger (Franky), Sandwich (Robin), Tangerine (Nami), Chocolate (Chopper).
As for the dish you couldn't identify, it is Brook's favorite: curry! Brook loves to eat curry, but he makes an absolute mess of it, so Sanji doesn't normally like to make it for him.

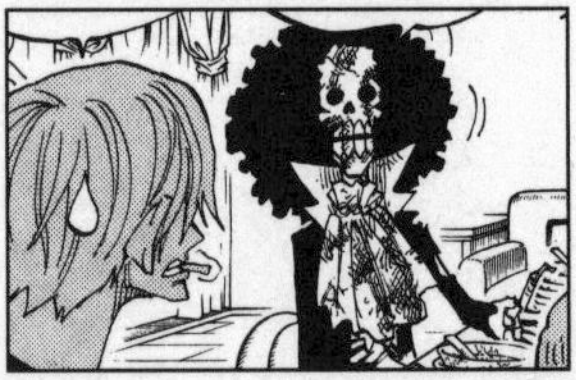

Q: Hello, Oda Sensei. The lunch that Luffy eats at the location of his promise with Sanji looks really gross, but Luffy says it's delicious. Is this because his gratitude is the most delicious seasoning of all? I complained about my wife's cooking, and now she doesn't cook for me anymore.

--I Will Only Eat the Food My Wife Cooks

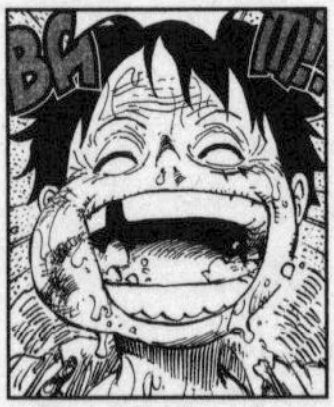

A: That's one of those statements that will cost you your life. You brought it on yourself, buddy.

Chapter 864:
THE VINSMOKE MASSACRE PLOT

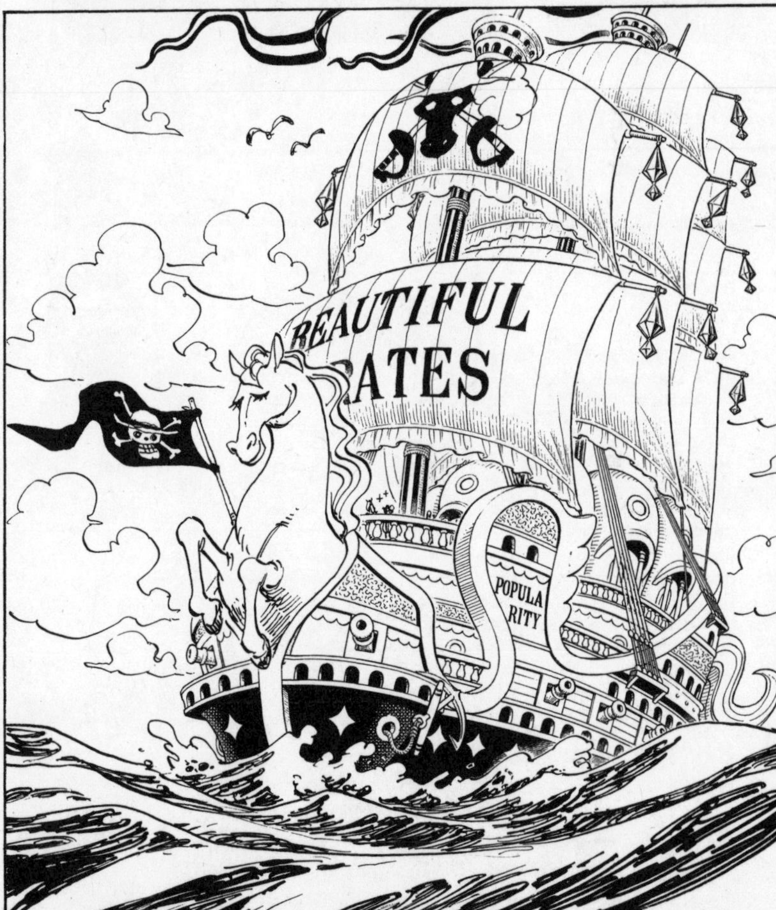
BEAUTIFUL
ATES
POPULA
RITY

LIMITED COVER SERIES, NO. 23 :THE SAGA OF THE SELF-PROCLAIMED STRAW HAT FLEET, VOL. 1: "THE BEAUTIFUL PIRATES BEAUTIFULLY SAIL THE BEAUTIFUL SEAS"

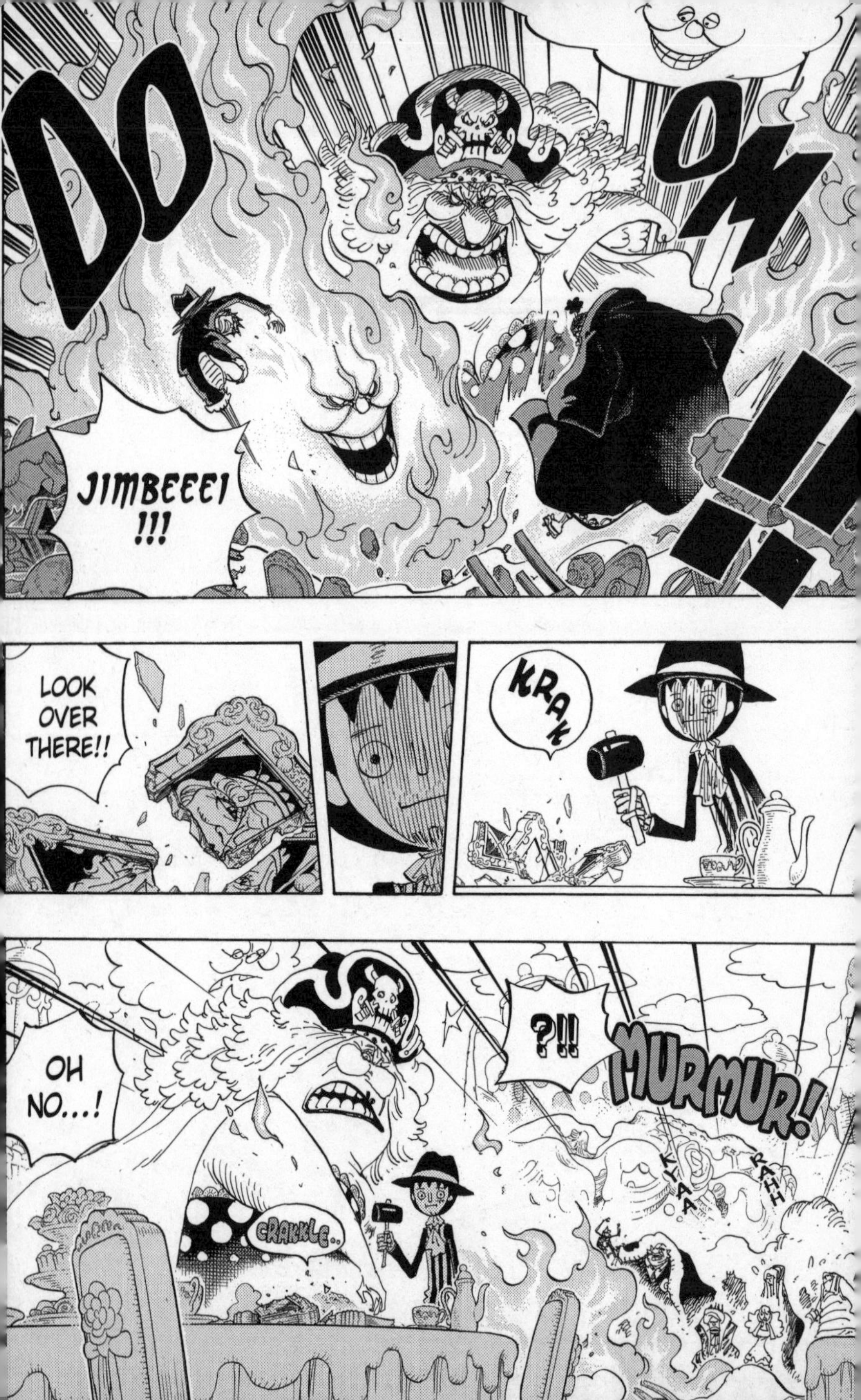
DOOM!!!!
JIMBEEE!!!!
KRAK
LOOK OVER THERE!!
?!!
MURMUR!
KYAA
RAHH
CRAKKLE..
OH NO...!

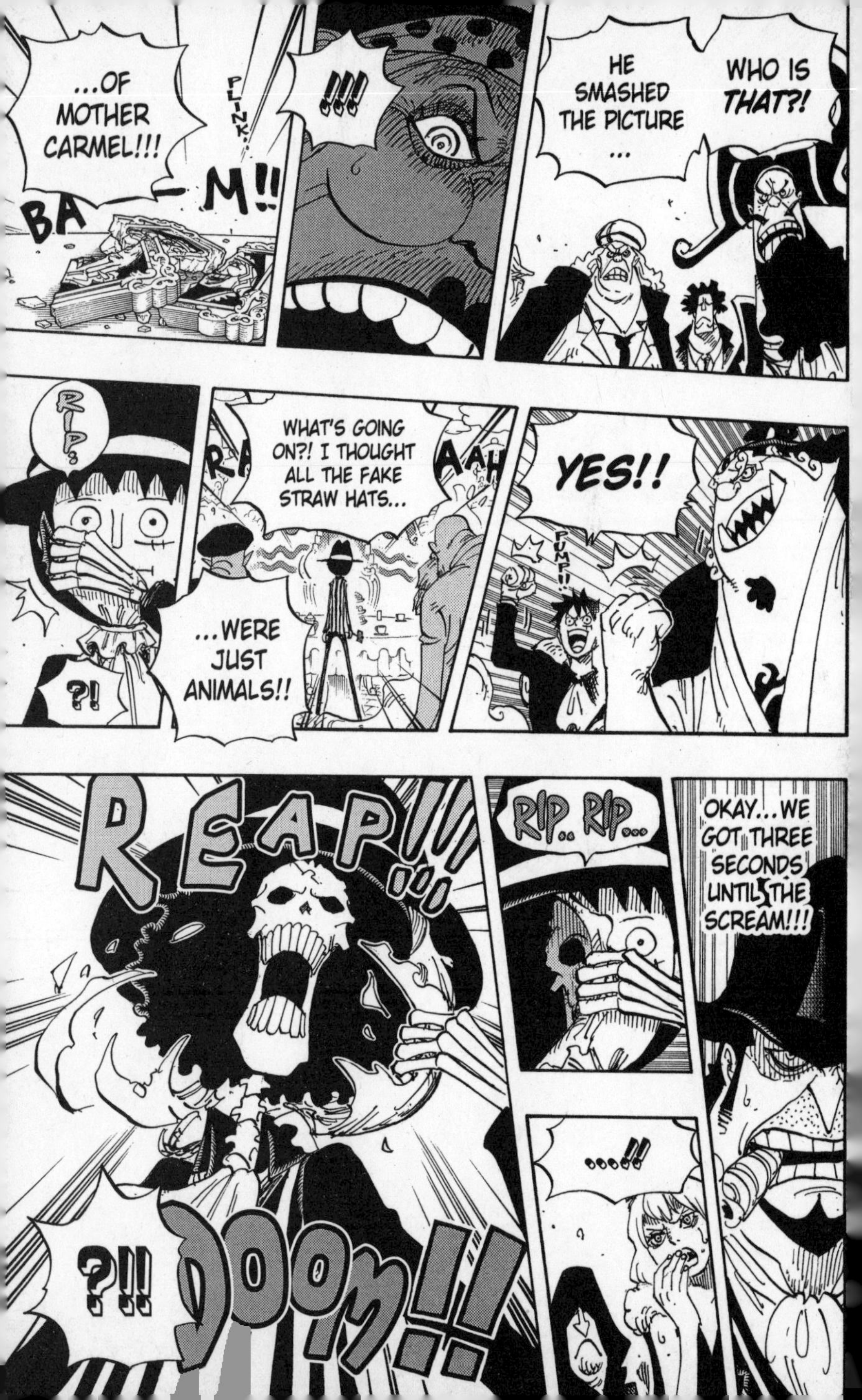
WHO IS THAT?!
HE SMASHED THE PICTURE ...
!!!
...OF MOTHER CARMEL!!!
PLINK
BA-M!!
YES!!
PUMP!!
AAH
WHAT'S GOING ON?! I THOUGHT ALL THE FAKE STRAW HATS...
RA
...WERE JUST ANIMALS!!
RIP
?!
OKAY...WE GOT THREE SECONDS UNTIL THE SCREAM!!!
RIP.. RIP...
....!!
REAP!!
?!!
DOOM!!

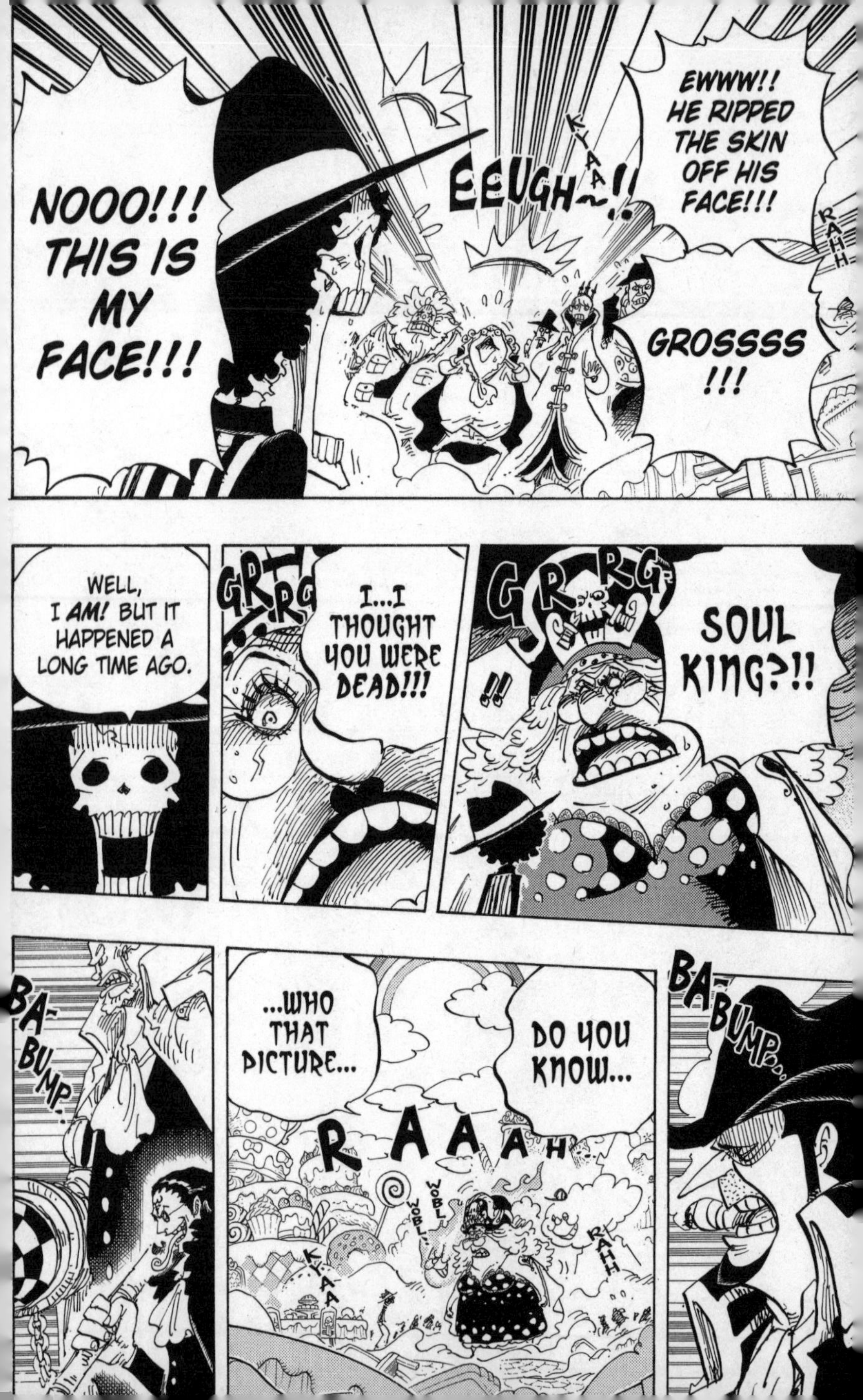
RAHH
EWWW!! HE RIPPED THE SKIN OFF HIS FACE!!!
KYAA~
EEUGH~!!
GROSSSS!!!
NOOO!!! THIS IS MY FACE!!!
GRRG
!!
SOUL KING?!!
GRRG
I...I THOUGHT YOU WERE DEAD!!!
WELL, I AM! BUT IT HAPPENED A LONG TIME AGO.
BA-BUMP...
DO YOU KNOW...
...WHO THAT PICTURE...
RAAAH
WOBL WOBL
RAHH
KYAA
BA-BUMP...

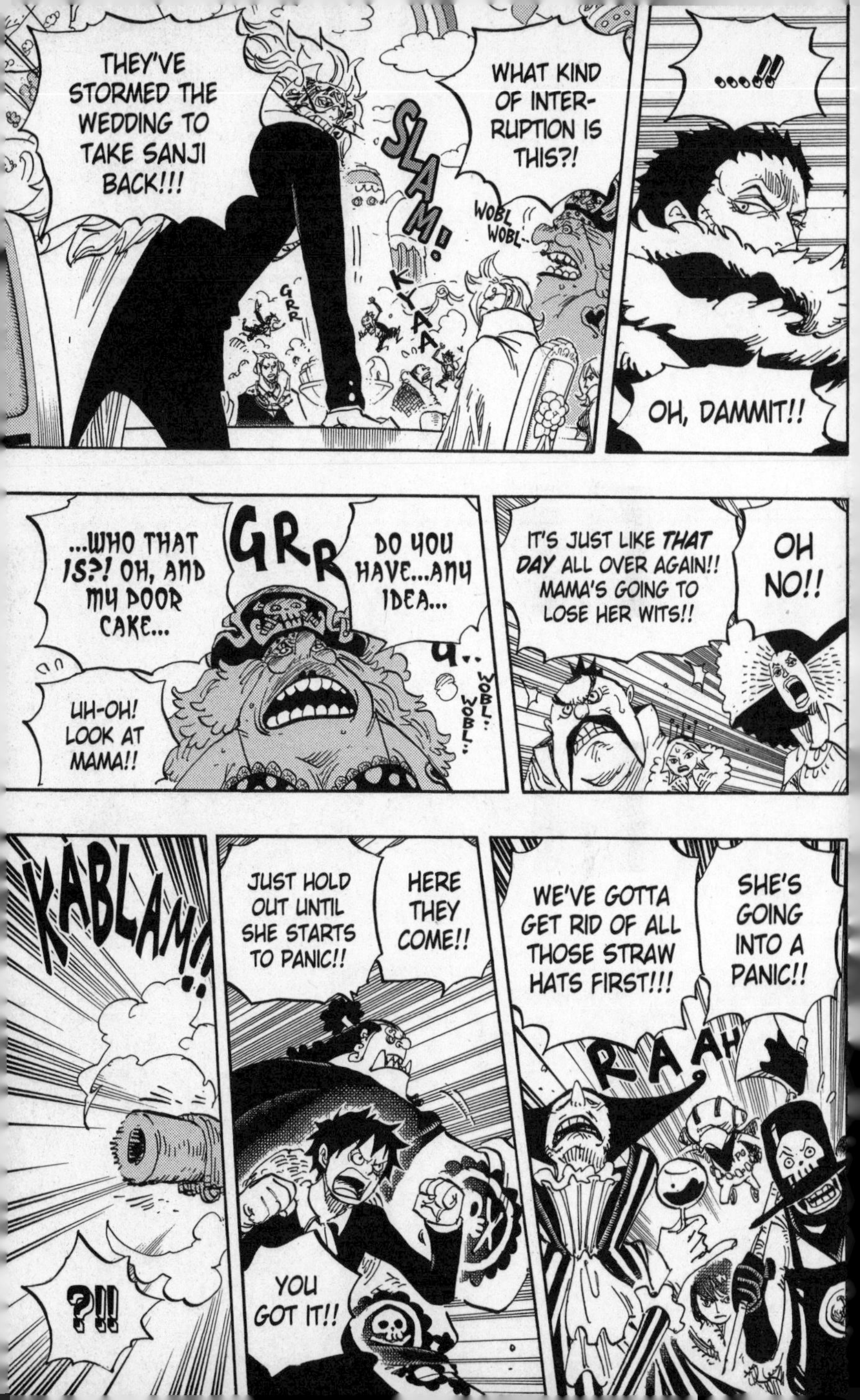
....!!
OH, DAMMIT!!
WHAT KIND OF INTER-RUPTION IS THIS?!
SLAM!
WOBL WOBL
KYAAA
GRR
THEY'VE STORMED THE WEDDING TO TAKE SANJI BACK!!!
OH NO!!
IT'S JUST LIKE THAT DAY ALL OVER AGAIN!! MAMA'S GOING TO LOSE HER WITS!!
DO YOU HAVE...ANY IDEA...
GRR
...WHO THAT IS?! OH, AND MY POOR CAKE...
WOBL WOBL
UH-OH! LOOK AT MAMA!!
SHE'S GOING INTO A PANIC!!
WE'VE GOTTA GET RID OF ALL THOSE STRAW HATS FIRST!!!
RAAAH
HERE THEY COME!!
JUST HOLD OUT UNTIL SHE STARTS TO PANIC!!
YOU GOT IT!!
KABLAM!!
?!!

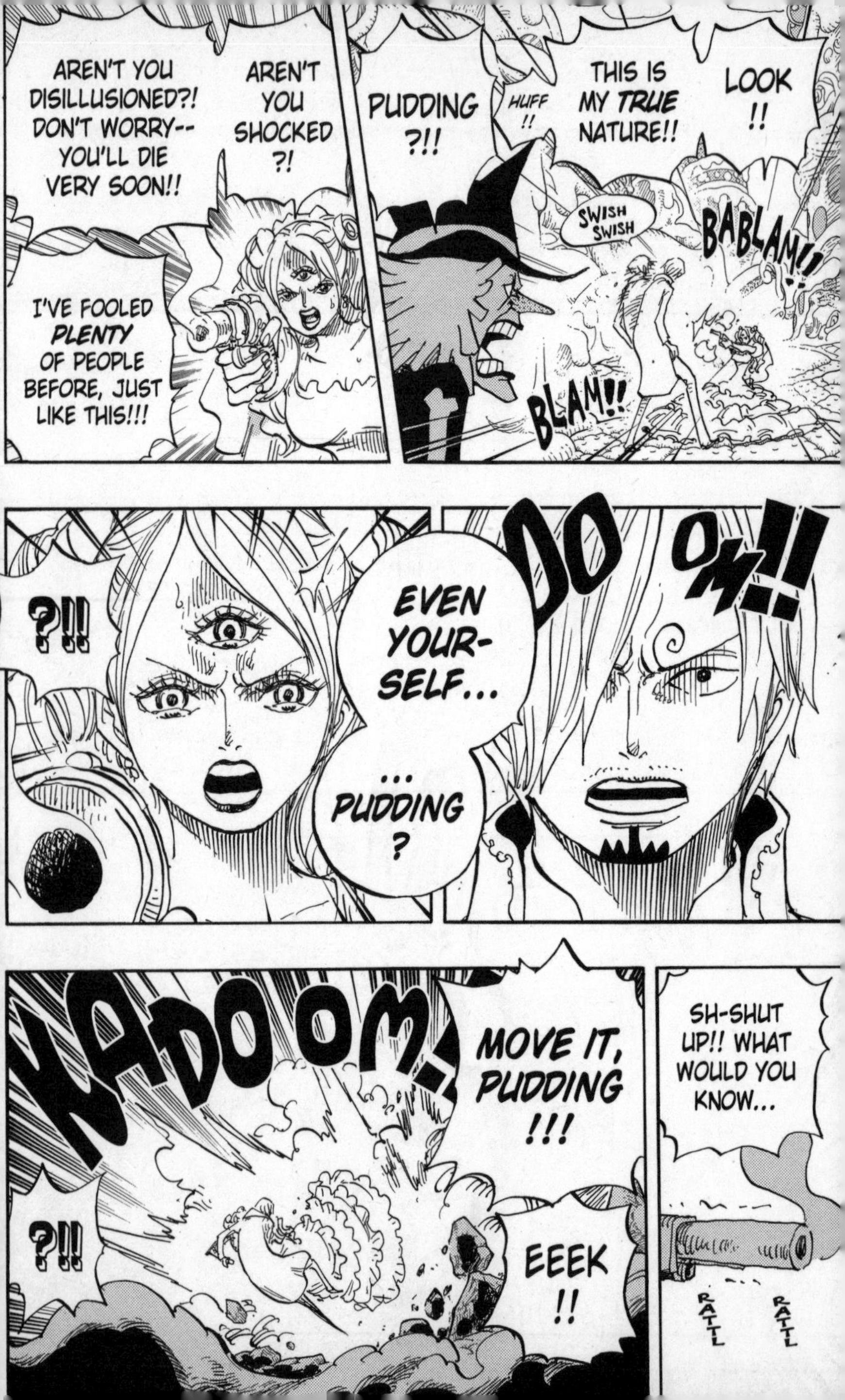
LOOK!!
THIS IS MY TRUE NATURE!!
HUFF!!
PUDDING?!!
SWISH SWISH
BABLAM!!
BLAM!!
AREN'T YOU SHOCKED?!
AREN'T YOU DISILLUSIONED?! DON'T WORRY-- YOU'LL DIE VERY SOON!!
I'VE FOOLED PLENTY OF PEOPLE BEFORE, JUST LIKE THIS!!!
DOOM!!
EVEN YOURSELF...
...PUDDING?
?!!
SH-SHUT UP!! WHAT WOULD YOU KNOW...
RATTL
RATTL
MOVE IT, PUDDING!!!
KADOOM!!
EEEK!!
?!!

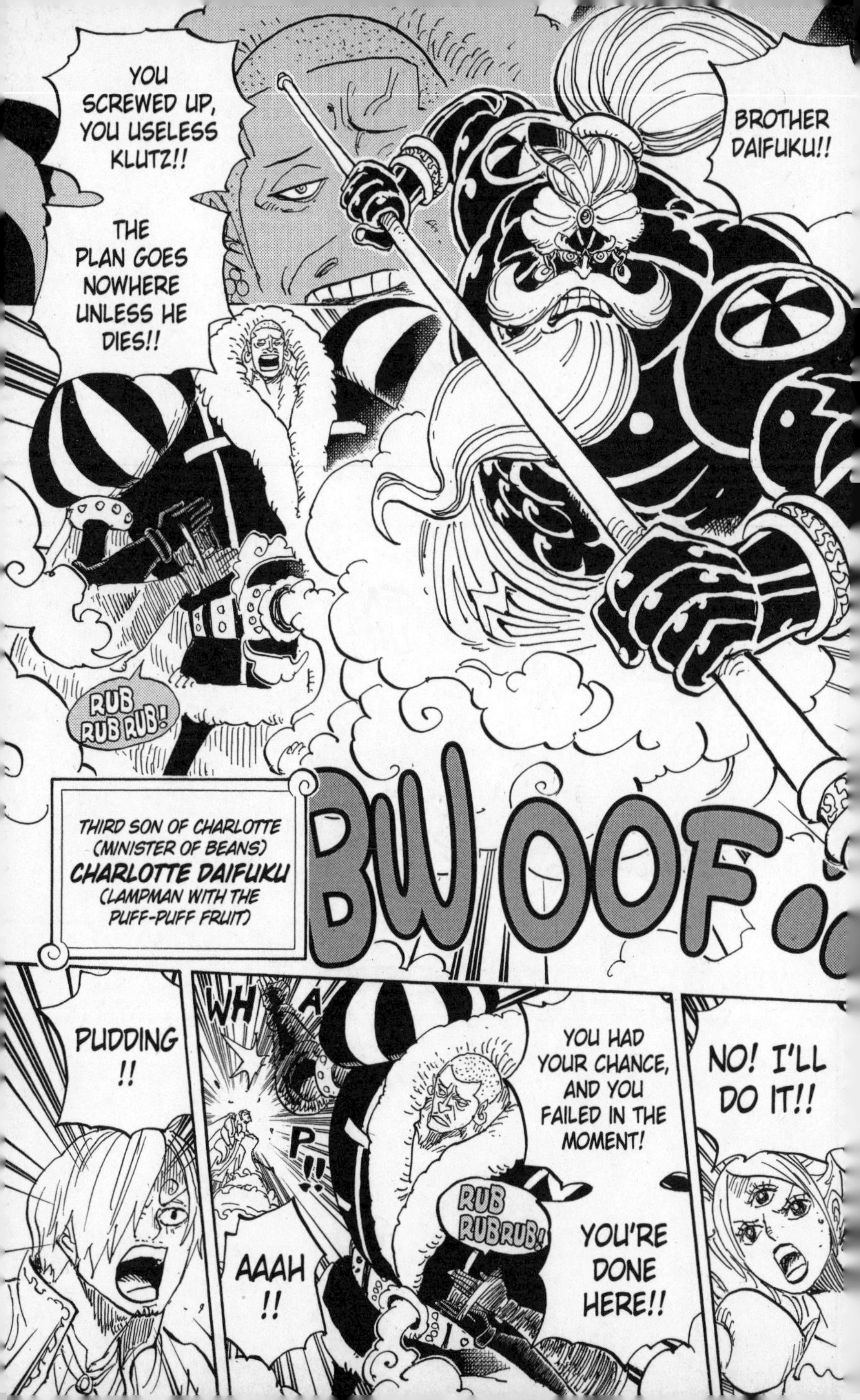
BROTHER DAIFUKU!!
YOU SCREWED UP, YOU USELESS KLUTZ!!
THE PLAN GOES NOWHERE UNLESS HE DIES!!
RUB RUB RUB!
THIRD SON OF CHARLOTTE (MINISTER OF BEANS) CHARLOTTE DAIFUKU (LAMPMAN WITH THE PUFF-PUFF FRUIT)
BWOOF...
NO! I'LL DO IT!!
YOU HAD YOUR CHANCE, AND YOU FAILED IN THE MOMENT!
RUB RUB RUB!
YOU'RE DONE HERE!!
WHAP!!
AAAH!!
PUDDING!!

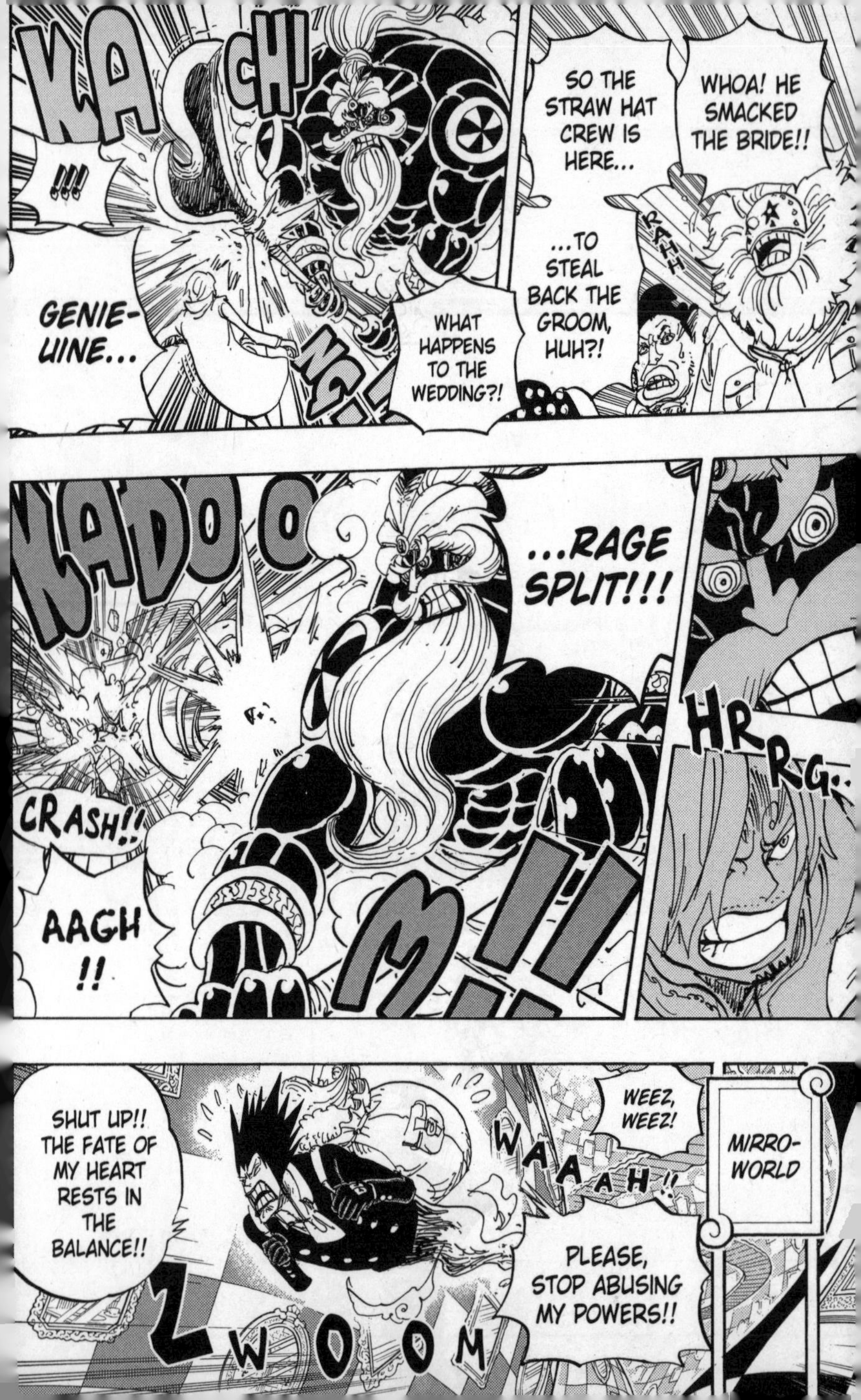
WHOA! HE SMACKED THE BRIDE!!
RAHH
SO THE STRAW HAT CREW IS HERE...
...TO STEAL BACK THE GROOM, HUH?!
WHAT HAPPENS TO THE WEDDING?!
KACHI
!!!
GENIE-UINE...
HRRG..
...RAGE SPLIT!!!
KADOOO
CRASH!!
AAGH !!
MIRRO-WORLD
WEEZ, WEEZ!
WAAAH!!
SHUT UP!! THE FATE OF MY HEART RESTS IN THE BALANCE!!
PLEASE, STOP ABUSING MY POWERS!!
ZWOOOM

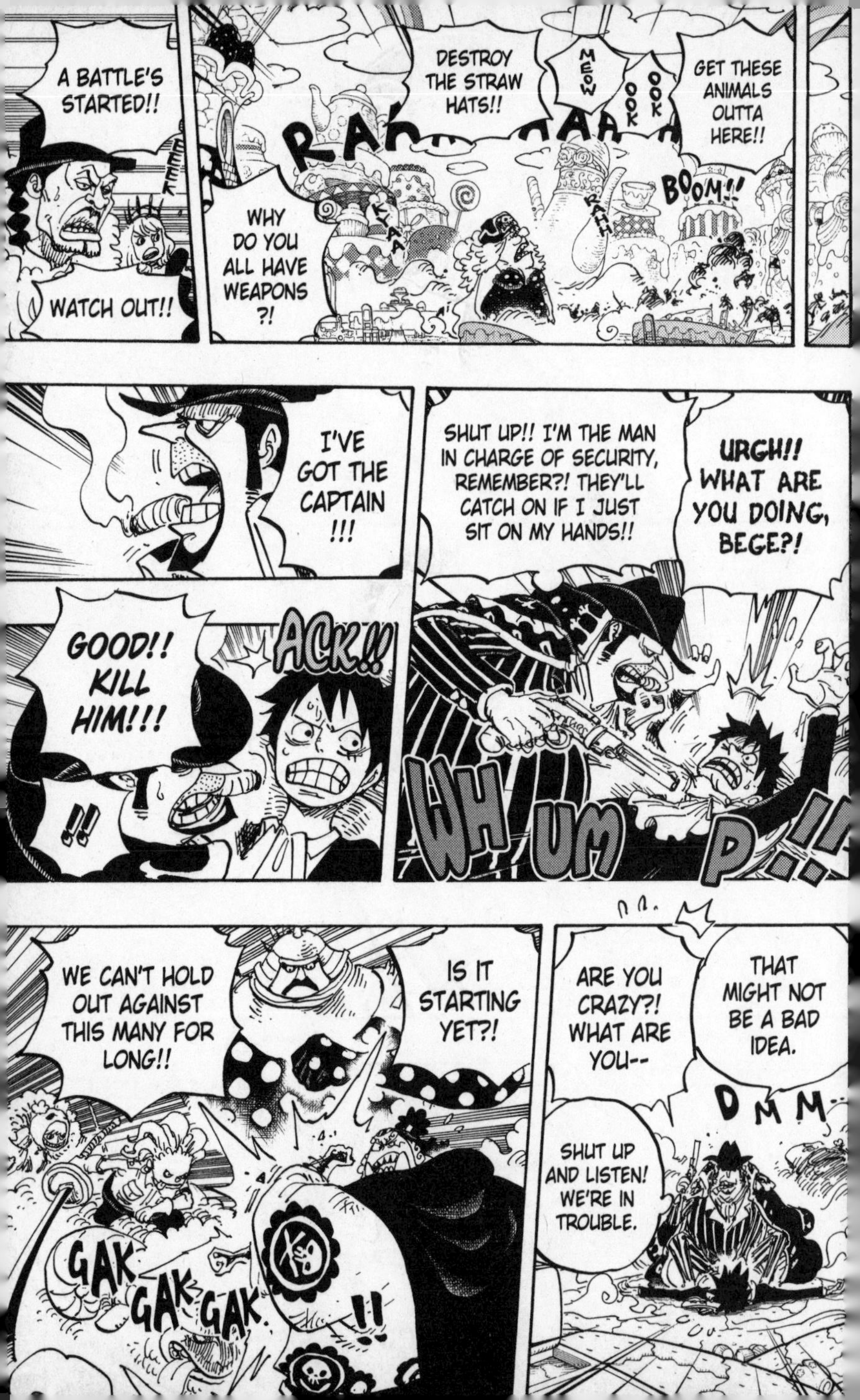
GET THESE ANIMALS OUTTA HERE!!
OOK OOK
MEOW
DESTROY THE STRAW HATS!!
BOOM!!
RAHH
KYAA
WHY DO YOU ALL HAVE WEAPONS ?!
A BATTLE'S STARTED!!
WATCH OUT!!
URGH!! WHAT ARE YOU DOING, BEGE?!
SHUT UP!! I'M THE MAN IN CHARGE OF SECURITY, REMEMBER?! THEY'LL CATCH ON IF I JUST SIT ON MY HANDS!!
WH UM P!!
I'VE GOT THE CAPTAIN !!!
ACK!!
GOOD!! KILL HIM!!!
!!
THAT MIGHT NOT BE A BAD IDEA.
ARE YOU CRAZY?! WHAT ARE YOU--
DMM..
SHUT UP AND LISTEN! WE'RE IN TROUBLE.
IS IT STARTING YET?!
WE CAN'T HOLD OUT AGAINST THIS MANY FOR LONG!!
GAK GAK GAK
!!

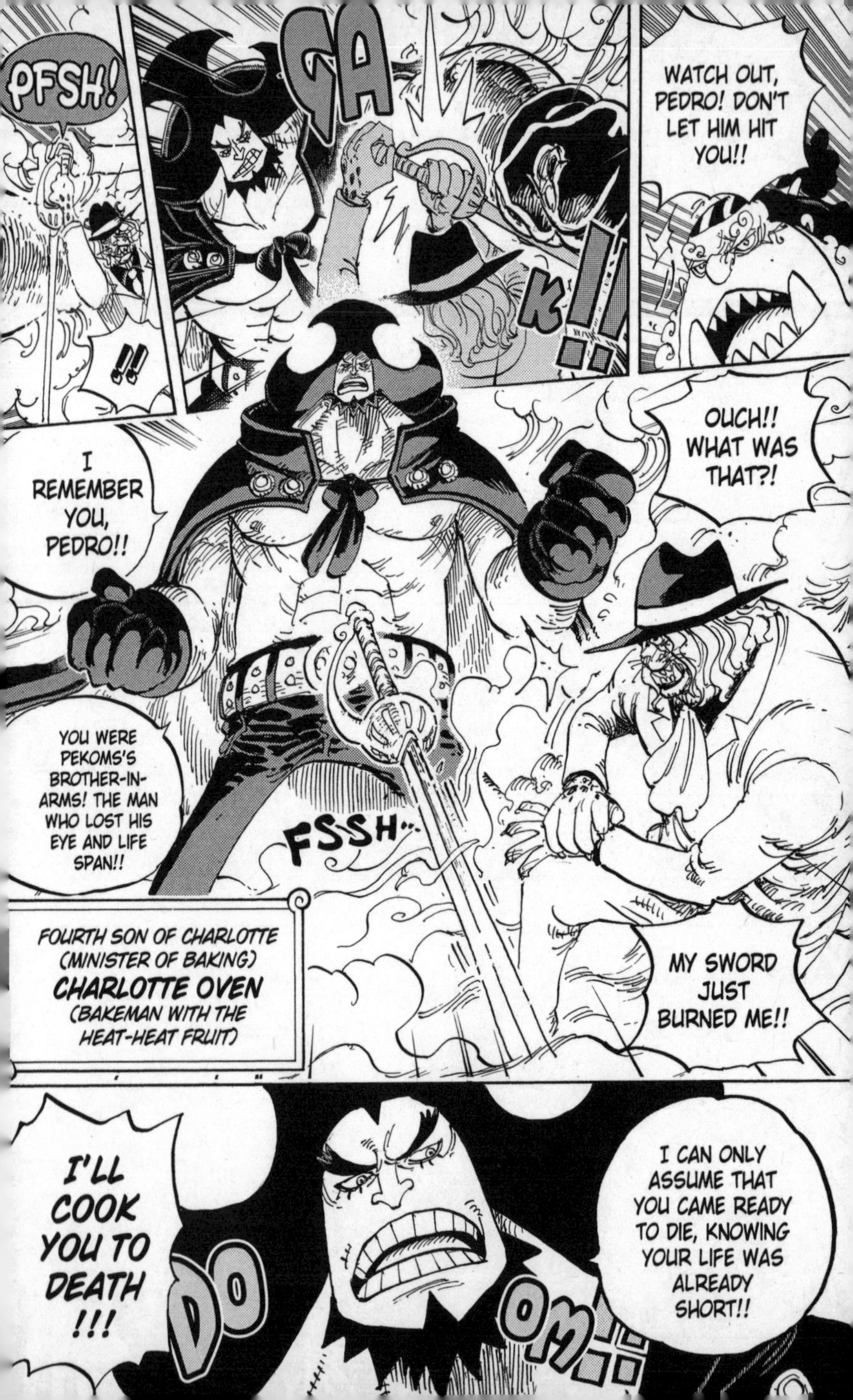

WATCH OUT, PEDRO! DON'T LET HIM HIT YOU!!
GA
K!!
PFSH!
!!
OUCH!! WHAT WAS THAT?!
I REMEMBER YOU, PEDRO!!
YOU WERE PEKOMS'S BROTHER-IN-ARMS! THE MAN WHO LOST HIS EYE AND LIFE SPAN!!
FSSH..
MY SWORD JUST BURNED ME!!
FOURTH SON OF CHARLOTTE (MINISTER OF BAKING) CHARLOTTE OVEN (BAKEMAN WITH THE HEAT-HEAT FRUIT)
I CAN ONLY ASSUME THAT YOU CAME READY TO DIE, KNOWING YOUR LIFE WAS ALREADY SHORT!!
DOOM!!
I'LL COOK YOU TO DEATH!!!

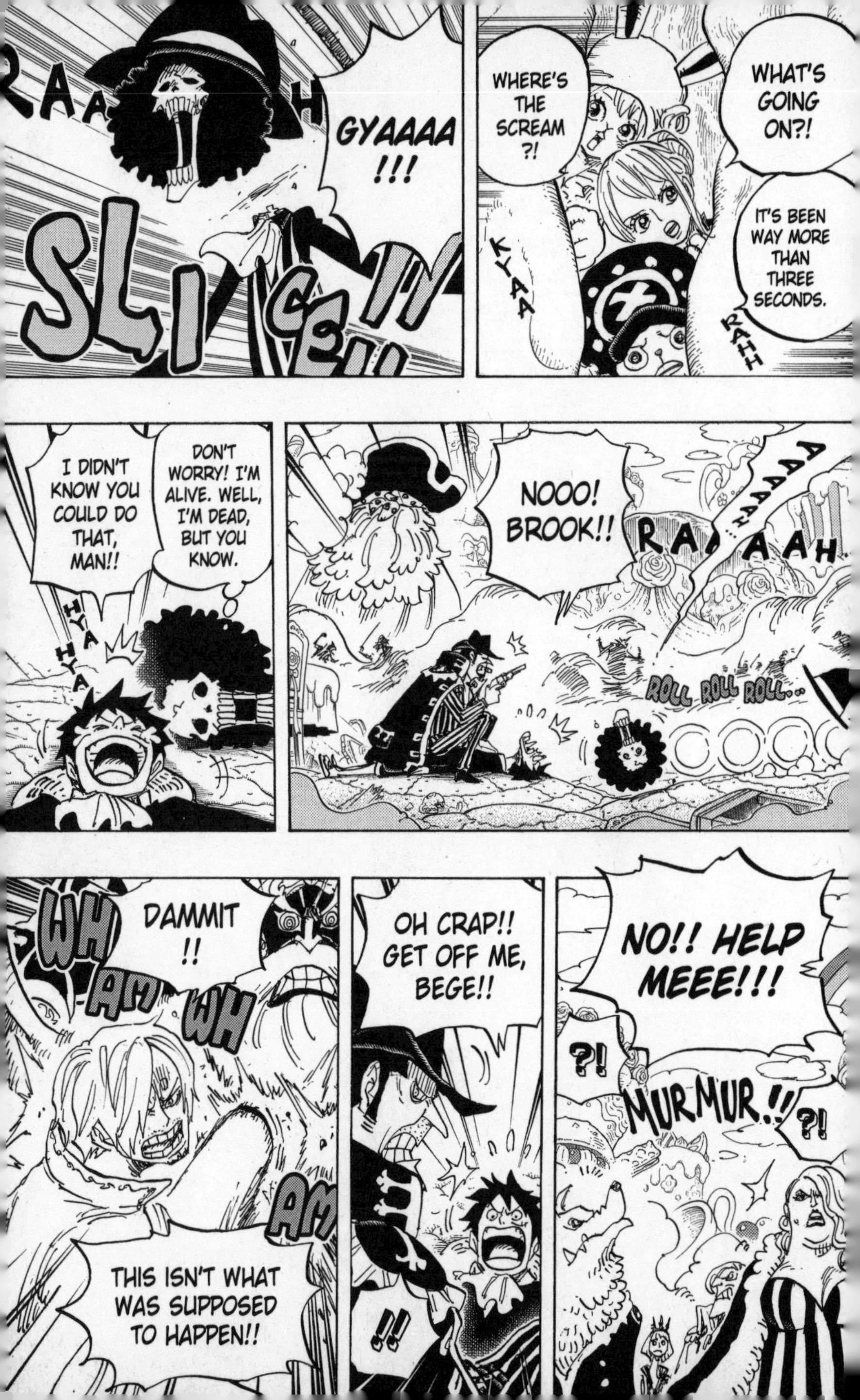
WHAT'S GOING ON?!
IT'S BEEN WAY MORE THAN THREE SECONDS.
RAHH
WHERE'S THE SCREAM ?!
KYAA
GYAAAA !!!
NOOO! BROOK!!
ROLL ROLL ROLL...
I DIDN'T KNOW YOU COULD DO THAT, MAN!!
DON'T WORRY! I'M ALIVE. WELL, I'M DEAD, BUT YOU KNOW.
HYA HYA
NO!! HELP MEEE!!!
?!
MURMUR!!
?!
OH CRAP!! GET OFF ME, BEGE!!
!!
DAMMIT !!
THIS ISN'T WHAT WAS SUPPOSED TO HAPPEN!!

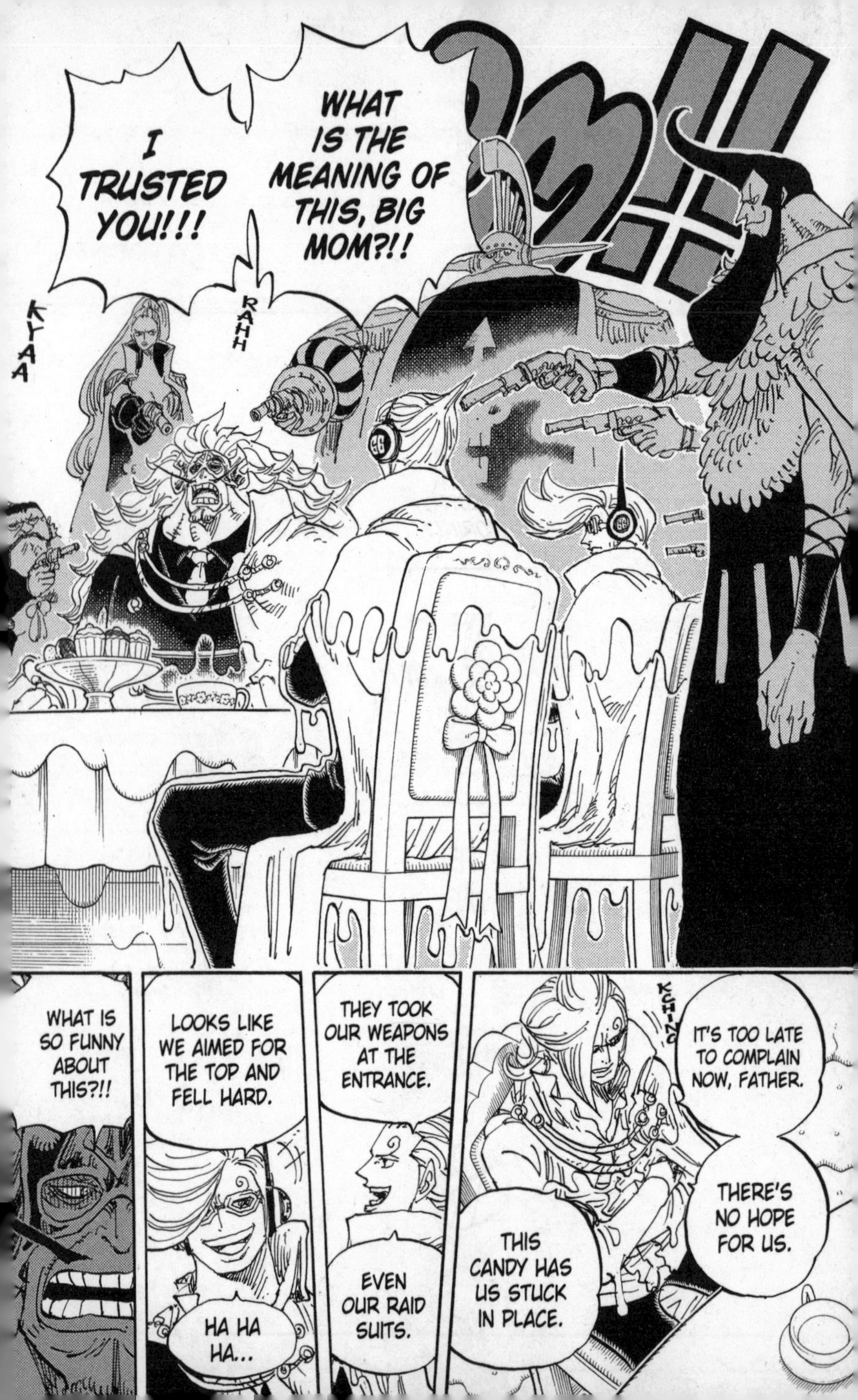
WHAT IS THE MEANING OF THIS, BIG MOM?!!
RAHH
I TRUSTED YOU!!!
KYAA
KCHING
IT'S TOO LATE TO COMPLAIN NOW, FATHER.
THERE'S NO HOPE FOR US.
THIS CANDY HAS US STUCK IN PLACE.
THEY TOOK OUR WEAPONS AT THE ENTRANCE.
EVEN OUR RAID SUITS.
LOOKS LIKE WE AIMED FOR THE TOP AND FELL HARD.
HA HA HA...
WHAT IS SO FUNNY ABOUT THIS?!!

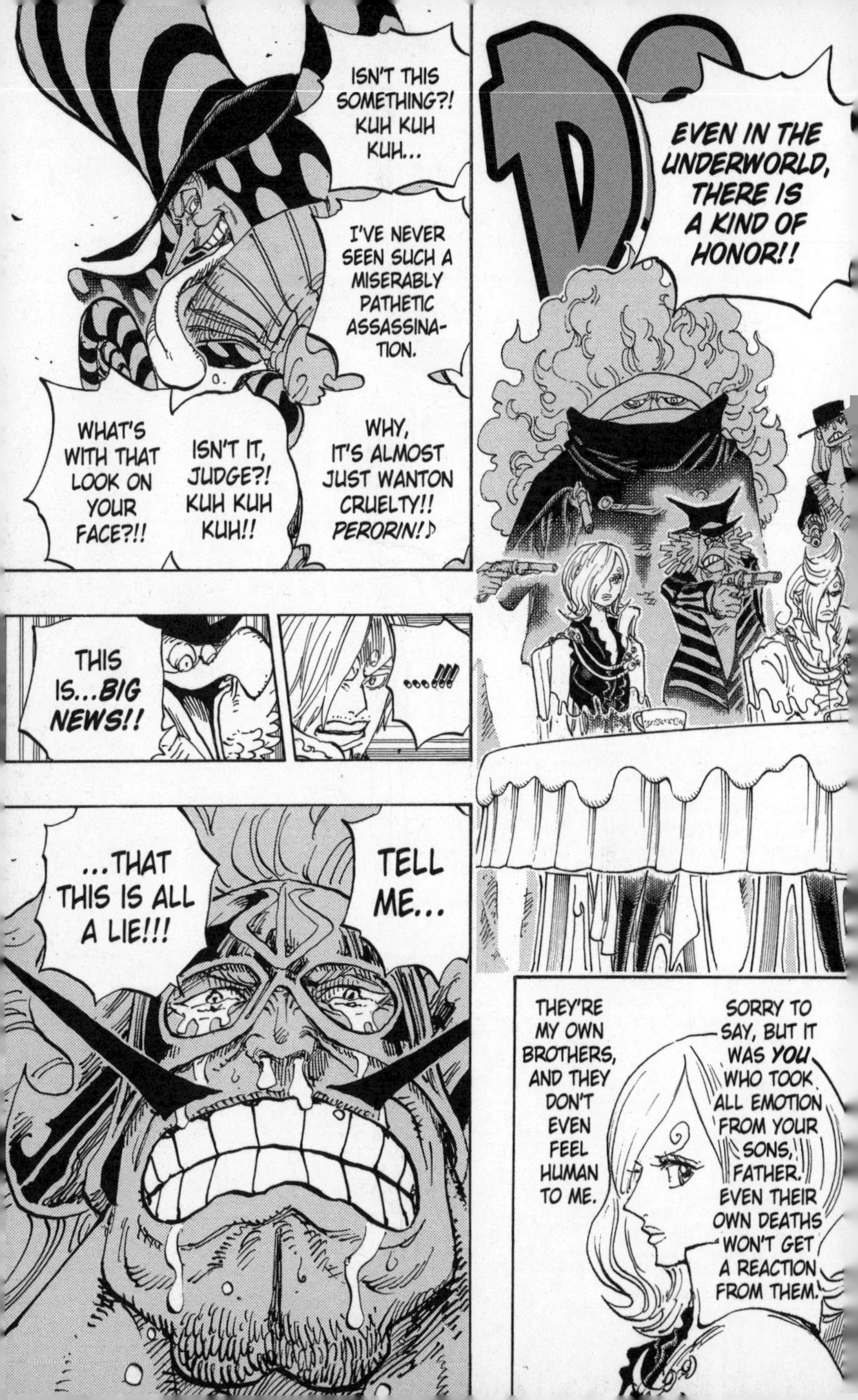
DO
EVEN IN THE UNDERWORLD, THERE IS A KIND OF HONOR!!
SORRY TO SAY, BUT IT WAS YOU WHO TOOK ALL EMOTION FROM YOUR SONS, FATHER. EVEN THEIR OWN DEATHS WON'T GET A REACTION FROM THEM.
THEY'RE MY OWN BROTHERS, AND THEY DON'T EVEN FEEL HUMAN TO ME.
ISN'T THIS SOMETHING?! KUH KUH KUH...
I'VE NEVER SEEN SUCH A MISERABLY PATHETIC ASSASSINATION.
WHY, IT'S ALMOST JUST WANTON CRUELTY!! PERORIN!♪
ISN'T IT, JUDGE?! KUH KUH KUH!!
WHAT'S WITH THAT LOOK ON YOUR FACE?!!
...!!!
THIS IS...BIG NEWS!!
TELL ME...
...THAT THIS IS ALL A LIE!!!

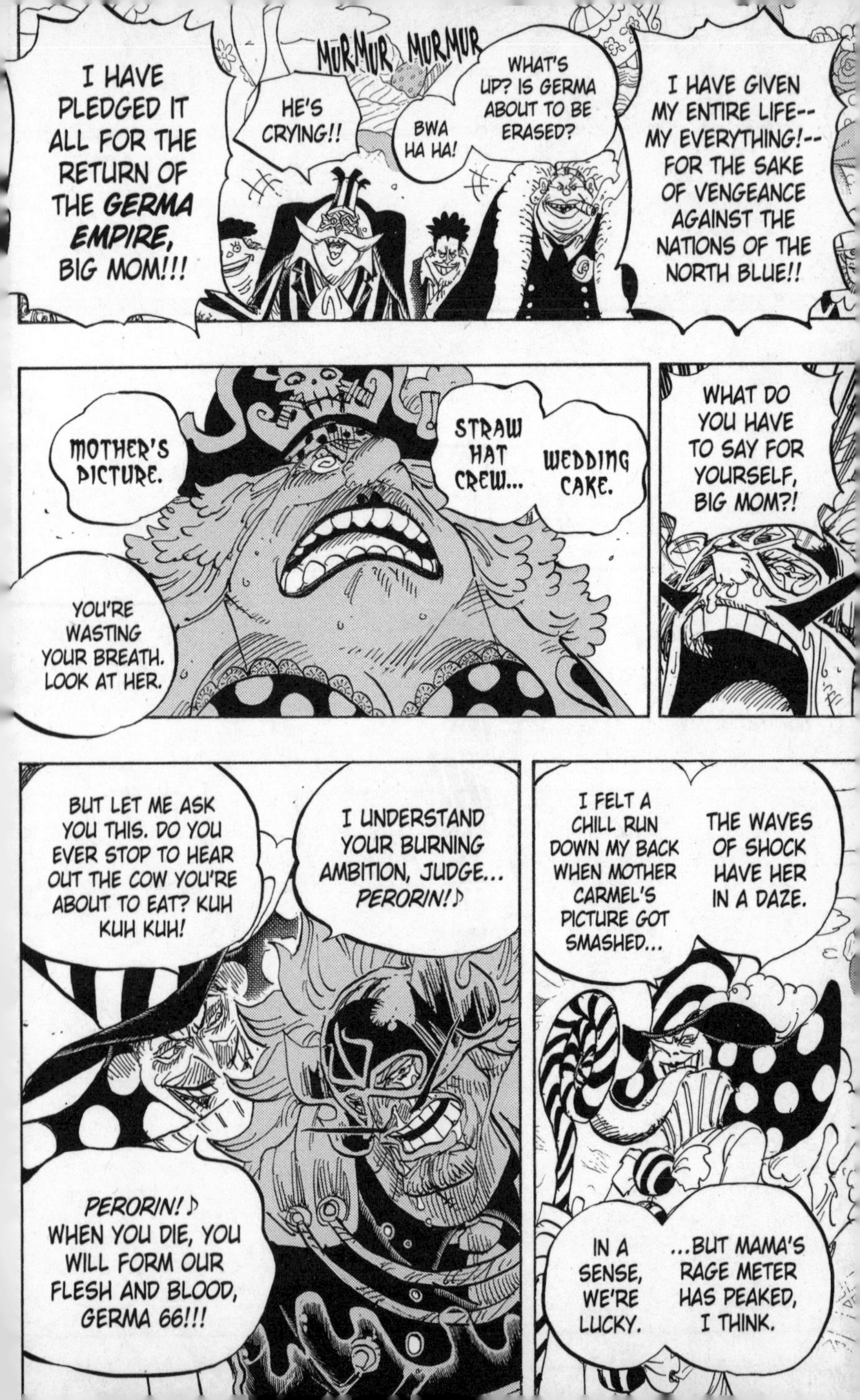
I HAVE GIVEN MY ENTIRE LIFE--MY EVERYTHING!--FOR THE SAKE OF VENGEANCE AGAINST THE NATIONS OF THE NORTH BLUE!!
WHAT'S UP? IS GERMA ABOUT TO BE ERASED?
BWA HA HA!
HE'S CRYING!!
MURMUR MURMUR
I HAVE PLEDGED IT ALL FOR THE RETURN OF THE GERMA EMPIRE, BIG MOM!!!
WHAT DO YOU HAVE TO SAY FOR YOURSELF, BIG MOM?!
WEDDING CAKE.
STRAW HAT CREW...
MOTHER'S PICTURE.
YOU'RE WASTING YOUR BREATH. LOOK AT HER.
THE WAVES OF SHOCK HAVE HER IN A DAZE.
I FELT A CHILL RUN DOWN MY BACK WHEN MOTHER CARMEL'S PICTURE GOT SMASHED...
...BUT MAMA'S RAGE METER HAS PEAKED, I THINK.
IN A SENSE, WE'RE LUCKY.
I UNDERSTAND YOUR BURNING AMBITION, JUDGE... PERORIN!♪
BUT LET ME ASK YOU THIS. DO YOU EVER STOP TO HEAR OUT THE COW YOU'RE ABOUT TO EAT? KUH KUH KUH!
PERORIN!♪ WHEN YOU DIE, YOU WILL FORM OUR FLESH AND BLOOD, GERMA 66!!!

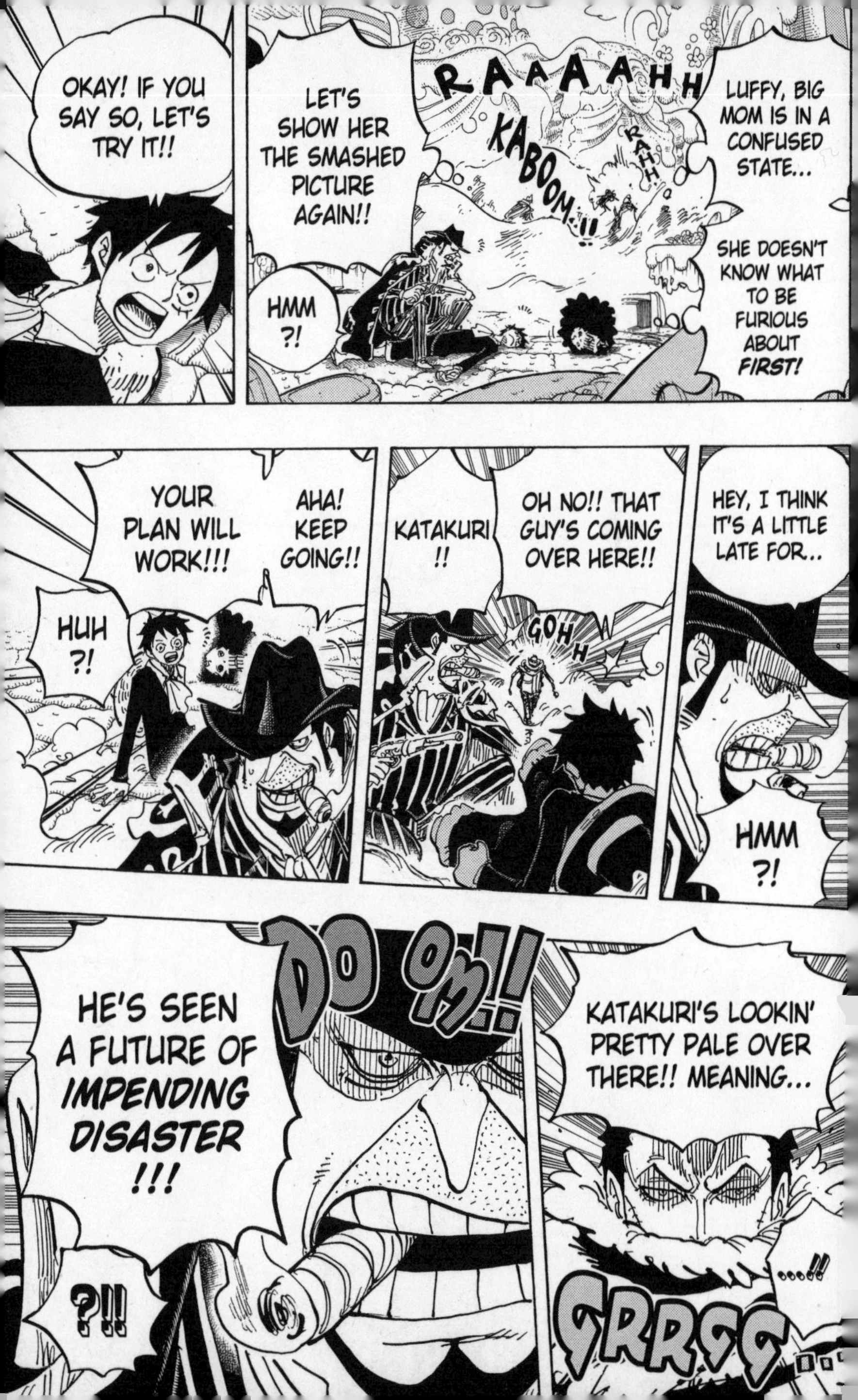
LUFFY, BIG MOM IS IN A CONFUSED STATE...
SHE DOESN'T KNOW WHAT TO BE FURIOUS ABOUT *FIRST!*
RAAAAHH
RAHH
KABOOM!!
LET'S SHOW HER THE SMASHED PICTURE AGAIN!!
HMM?!
OKAY! IF YOU SAY SO, LET'S TRY IT!!
HEY, I THINK IT'S A LITTLE LATE FOR...
HMM?!
OH NO!! THAT GUY'S COMING OVER HERE!!
KATAKURI!!
GOHH
AHA! KEEP GOING!!
YOUR PLAN WILL WORK!!!
HUH?!
KATAKURI'S LOOKIN' PRETTY PALE OVER THERE!! MEANING...
...!!
GRRGG
DOOM!!
HE'S SEEN A FUTURE OF *IMPENDING DISASTER* !!!
?!!

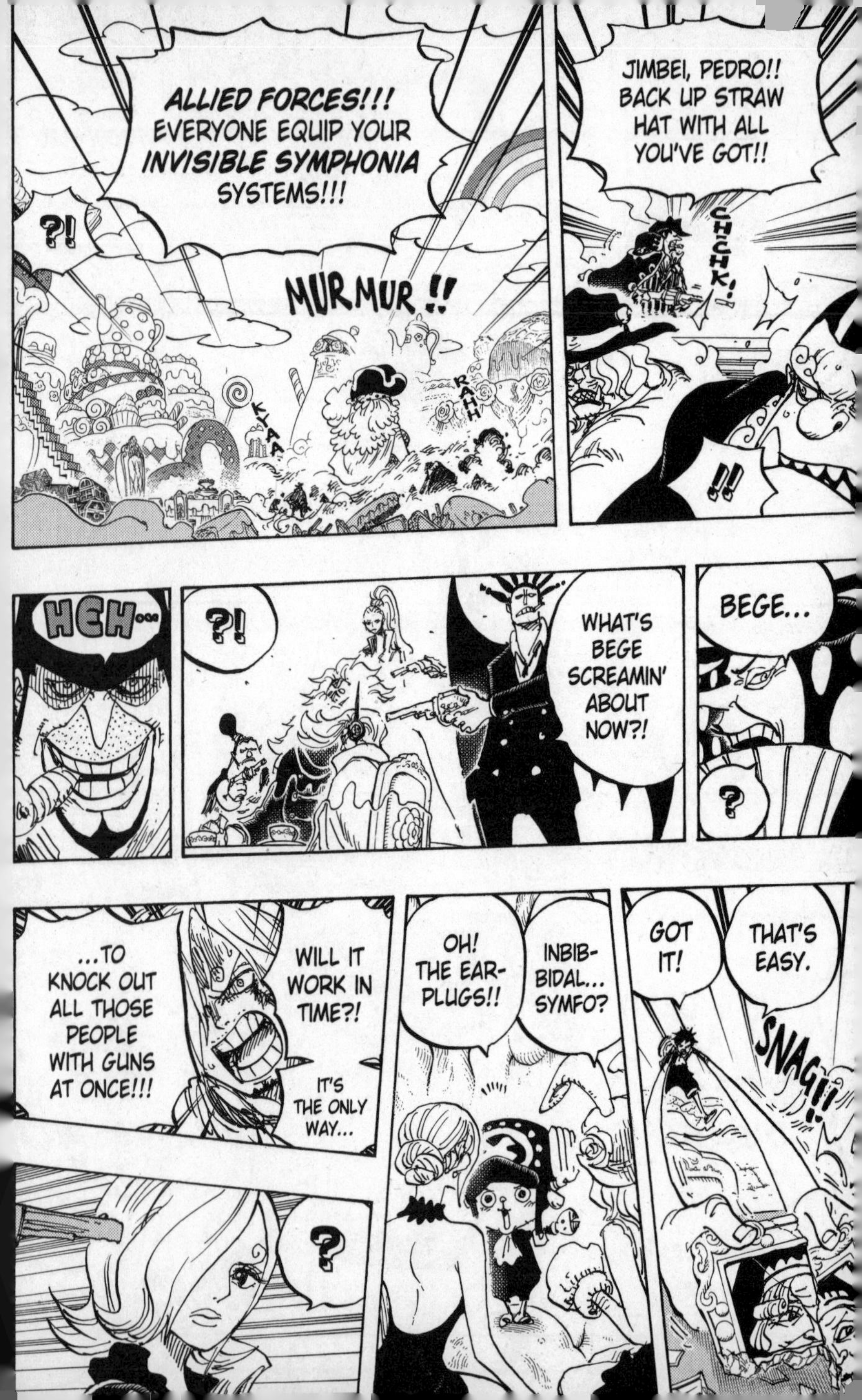
JIMBEI, PEDRO!! BACK UP STRAW HAT WITH ALL YOU'VE GOT!!
CHCHK!
!!
ALLIED FORCES!!! EVERYONE EQUIP YOUR INVISIBLE SYMPHONIA SYSTEMS!!!
?!
MURMUR!!
RAHH
KYAA
BEGE...
?
WHAT'S BEGE SCREAMIN' ABOUT NOW?!
?!
HEH...
THAT'S EASY.
GOT IT!
SNAG!!
INBIB-BIDAL... SYMFO?
OH! THE EAR-PLUGS!!
WILL IT WORK IN TIME?!
...TO KNOCK OUT ALL THOSE PEOPLE WITH GUNS AT ONCE!!!
IT'S THE ONLY WAY...
?

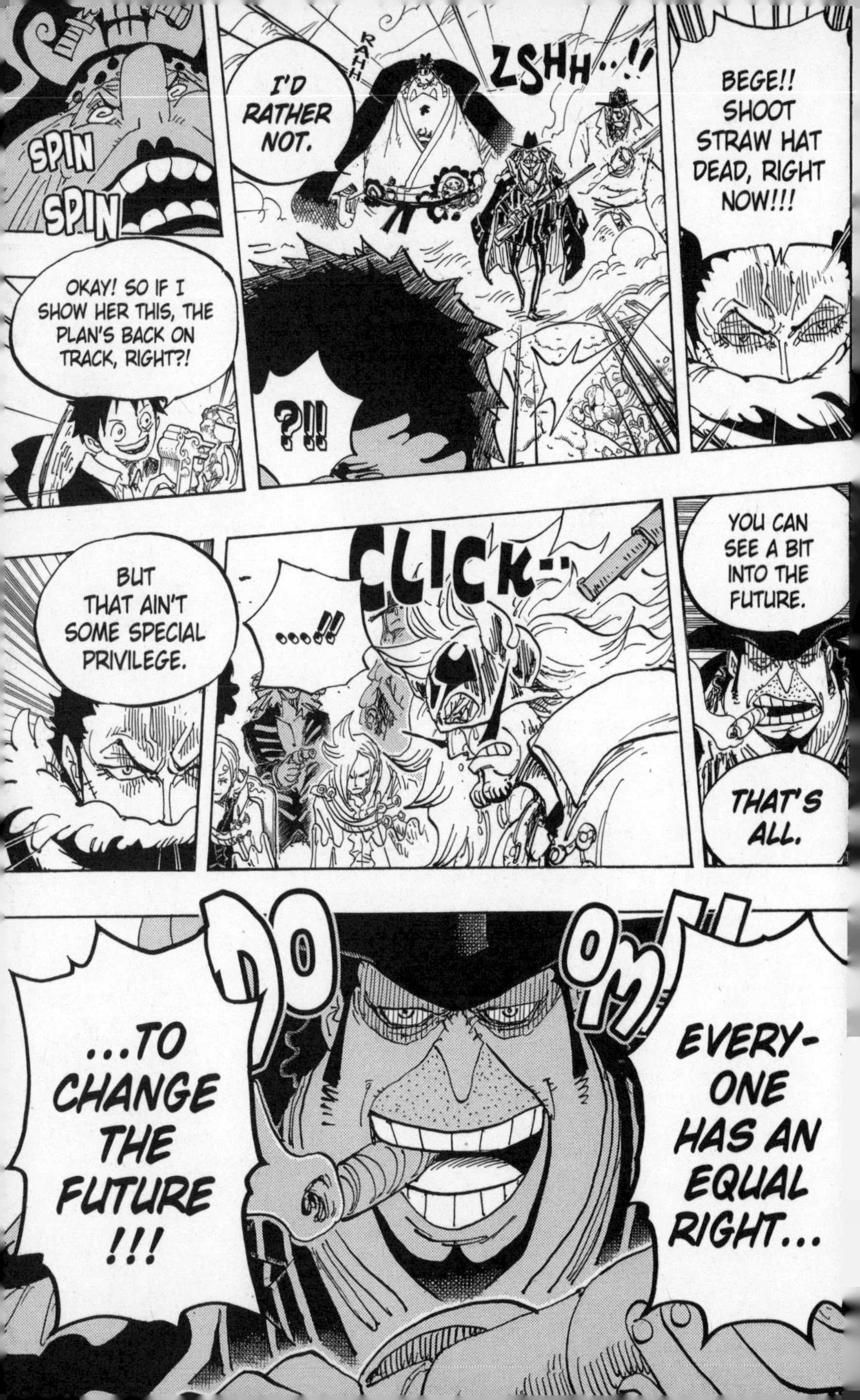
BEGE!! SHOOT STRAW HAT DEAD, RIGHT NOW!!!
ZSHH..!!
RAHH
I'D RATHER NOT.
?!!
SPIN
SPIN
OKAY! SO IF I SHOW HER THIS, THE PLAN'S BACK ON TRACK, RIGHT?!
YOU CAN SEE A BIT INTO THE FUTURE.
THAT'S ALL.
CLICK..
...!!
BUT THAT AIN'T SOME SPECIAL PRIVILEGE.
DOOM..
EVERY-ONE HAS AN EQUAL RIGHT...
...TO CHANGE THE FUTURE!!!

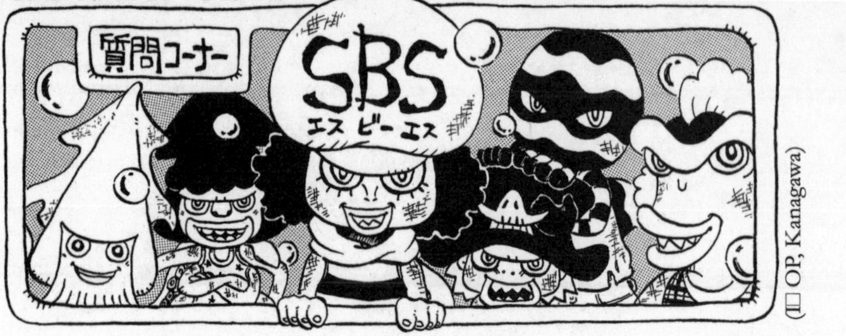
質問コーナー
SBS
エス ビー エス

(☐ OP, Kanagawa)

Q: Hi there, Odacchi! I've been a reader since volume 1, and I was noticing that pretty much all the characters of *One Piece,* no matter how they speak, express their gratitude in a straightforward way, with "thank you" or "thanks," but not with alternate sayings like "appreciate it" or "much obliged." Is this an intentional choice on your part?

--Luna

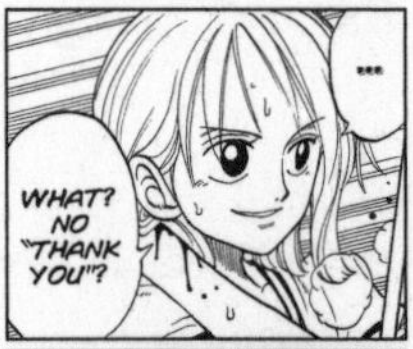
...
WHAT? NO "THANK YOU"?

A: Ooh. That's quite an observation to make in the 20th year of the series (laughs). This is indeed an intention of mine. Some of the characters are rather shy about openly admitting their feelings or being polite, like Zolo. From my perspective, people who have to hide it or act cool by twisting their words are actually pretty uncool. So as long as it doesn't totally mess up the flow of dialogue, I always have them just say "Thanks." It's direct and honest. Sometimes the scriptwriters for the anime version will throw in other words and I'll think, "Oh no..." But really, it's not like the people watching would notice, and I don't think it's so important to impose on everyone. It's basically just a personal thing for me. Thanks for noticing!!

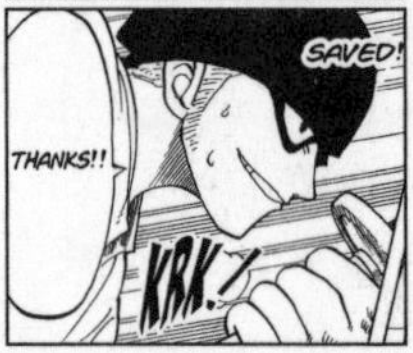
SAVED!
THANKS!!
KRK!

Q: Hello, Odacchi! Do the transponder snails have a silent mode? I mean, everyone's got times where they really don't want their phone going off… Can they change the volume on them?

--Uzura

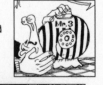

A: Well, transponder snails are living creatures, so it really comes down to training. If you tell it, "Shhh!" and it obeys, then you're in silent mode. As far as volume goes, it's just how well you train and feed them.

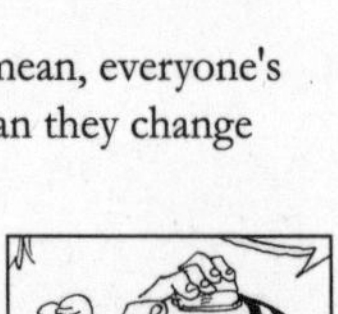
Mr. 3

Q: I have something to say to my dad.

"Everyone has an equal right to change the channel!!!"

--Naotsu

A: You're still living at home with your parents. I don't know if dependents are strictly equal with grown adults...

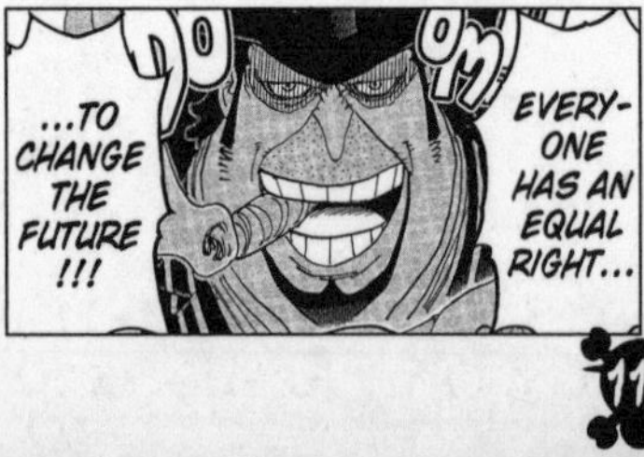
EVERYONE HAS AN EQUAL RIGHT...
...TO CHANGE THE FUTURE!!!

Chapter 865:
HEY, MOTHER

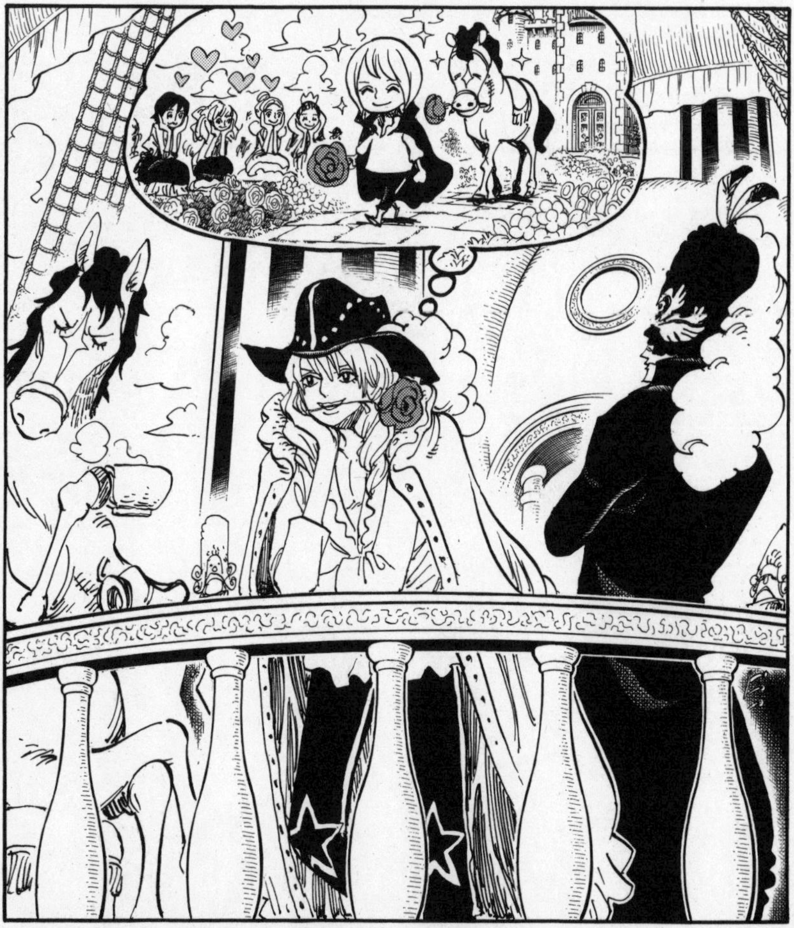

THE SAGA OF THE SELF-PROCLAIMED STRAW HAT FLEET, VOL. 2, CAVENDISH: "AS YOU PROBABLY KNOW, YEARS AGO..."

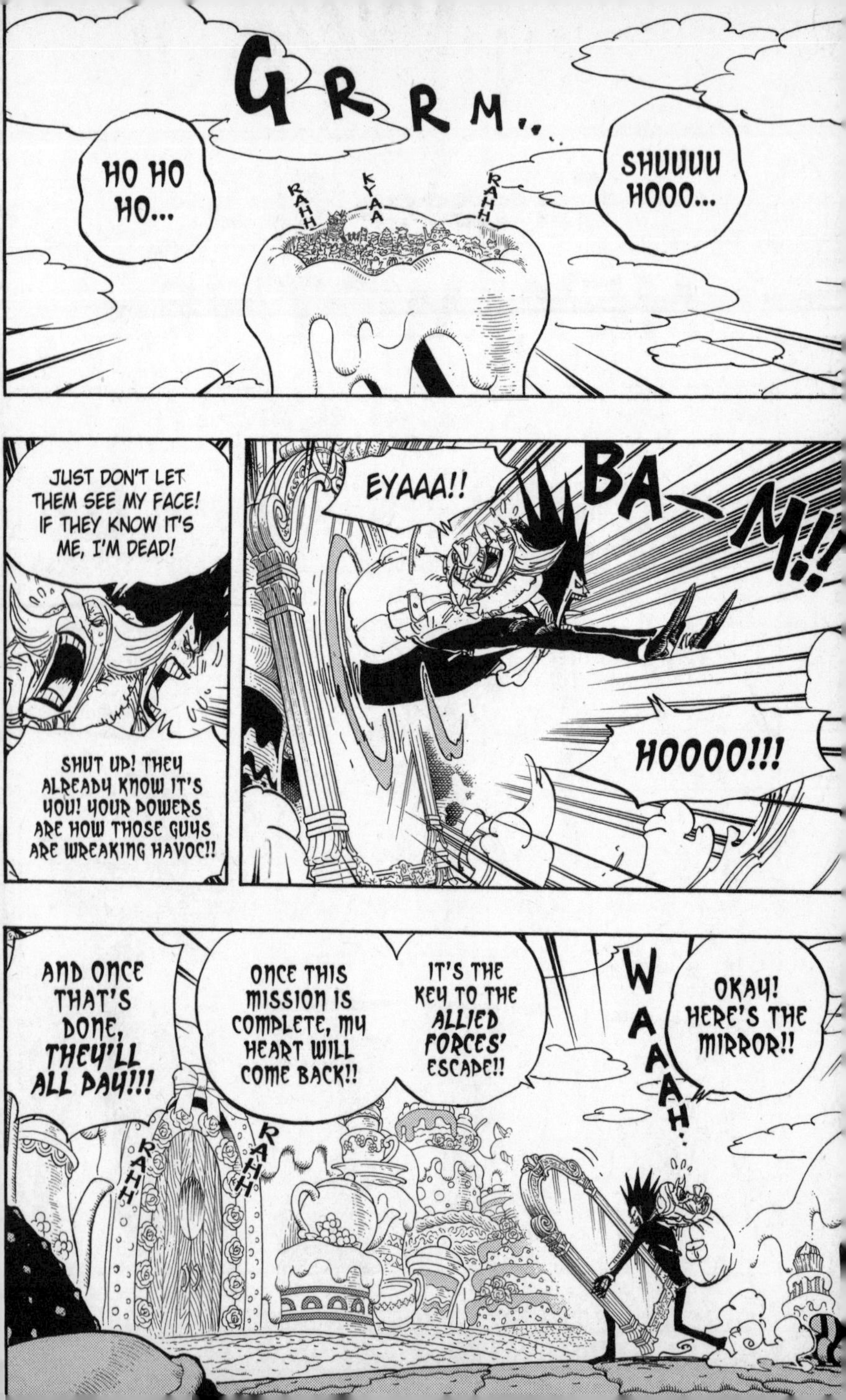
GRRRM...
SHUUUU HOOO...
RAHH
KYAA
RAHH
HO HO HO...
BA-M!!
EYAAA!!
HOOOO!!!
JUST DON'T LET THEM SEE MY FACE! IF THEY KNOW IT'S ME, I'M DEAD!
SHUT UP! THEY ALREADY KNOW IT'S YOU! YOUR POWERS ARE HOW THOSE GUYS ARE WREAKING HAVOC!!
OKAY! HERE'S THE MIRROR!!
WAAAH..
IT'S THE KEY TO THE **ALLIED FORCES'** ESCAPE!!
ONCE THIS MISSION IS COMPLETE, MY HEART WILL COME BACK!!
AND ONCE THAT'S DONE, **THEY'LL ALL PAY!!!**
RAHH
RAHH

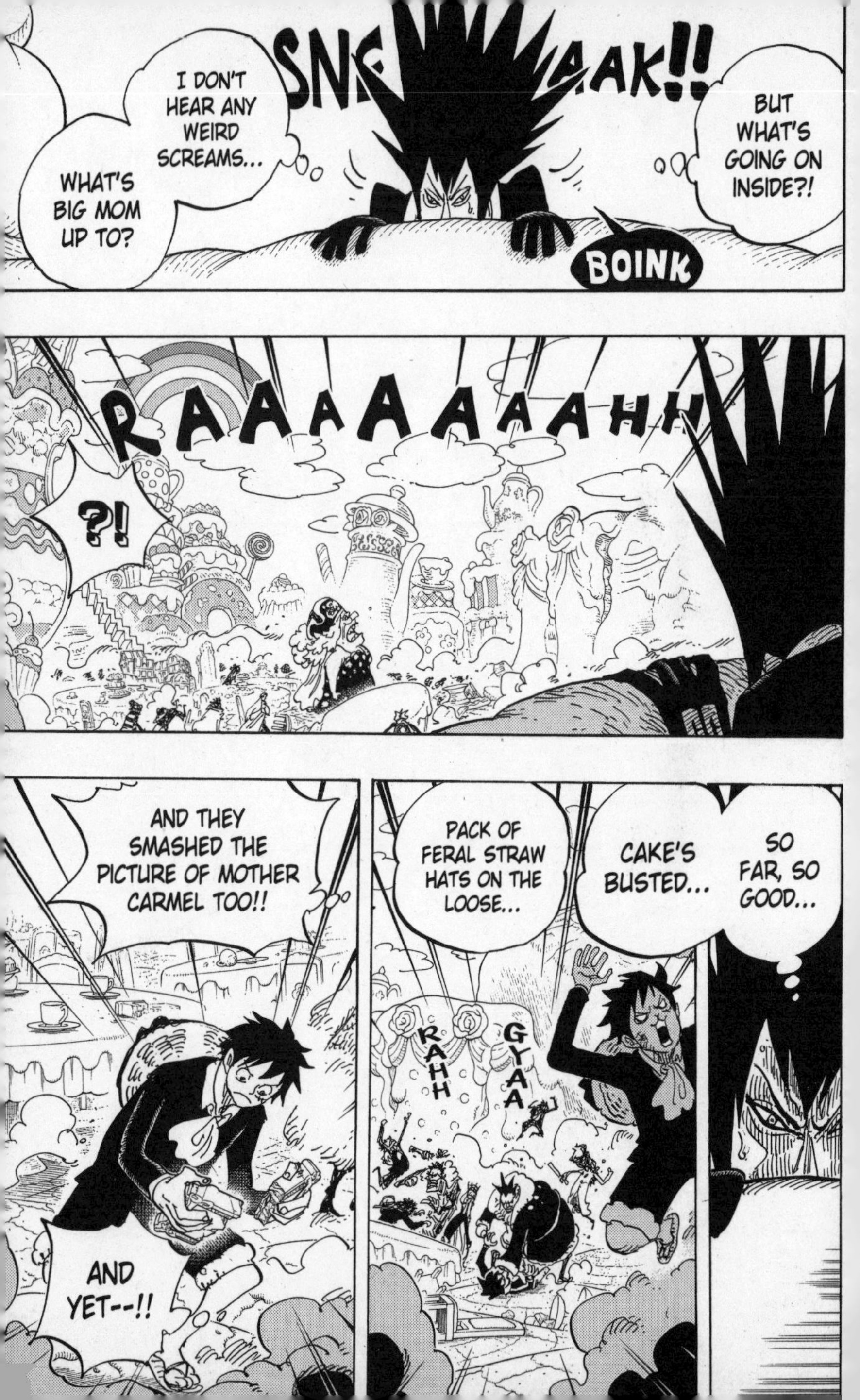

BUT WHAT'S GOING ON INSIDE?!
I DON'T HEAR ANY WEIRD SCREAMS...
BOINK
WHAT'S BIG MOM UP TO?
RAAAAAAAAHH
?!
SO FAR, SO GOOD...
CAKE'S BUSTED...
PACK OF FERAL STRAW HATS ON THE LOOSE...
GYAA
RAHH
AND THEY SMASHED THE PICTURE OF MOTHER CARMEL TOO!!
AND YET--!!

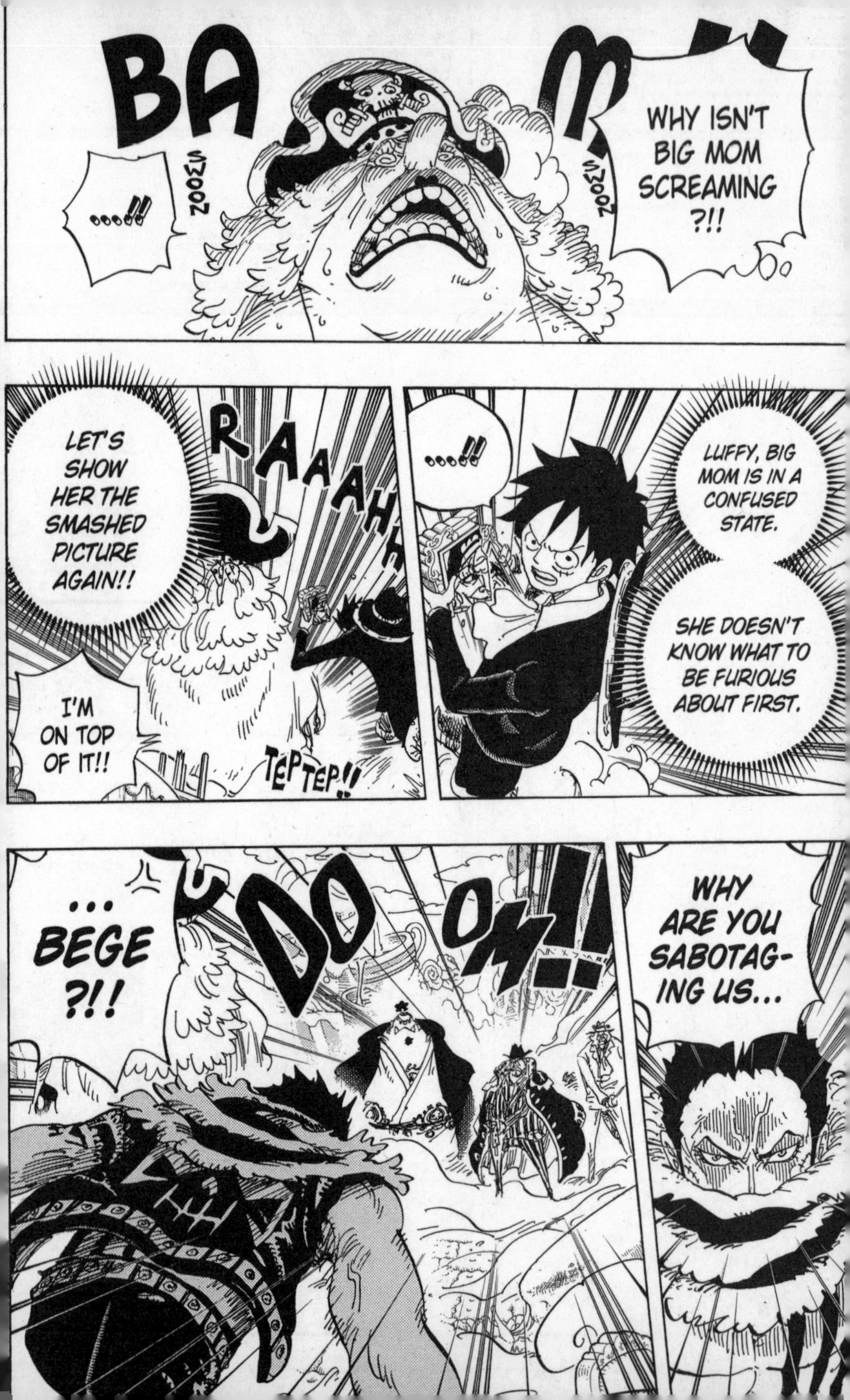
BAM
WHY ISN'T BIG MOM SCREAMING ?!!
SWOON
SWOON
....!!
LUFFY, BIG MOM IS IN A CONFUSED STATE.
SHE DOESN'T KNOW WHAT TO BE FURIOUS ABOUT FIRST.
....!!
RAAAHH
LET'S SHOW HER THE SMASHED PICTURE AGAIN!!
I'M ON TOP OF IT!!
TEP TEP!!
WHY ARE YOU SABOTAG-ING US...
DOOM!!
... BEGE ?!!

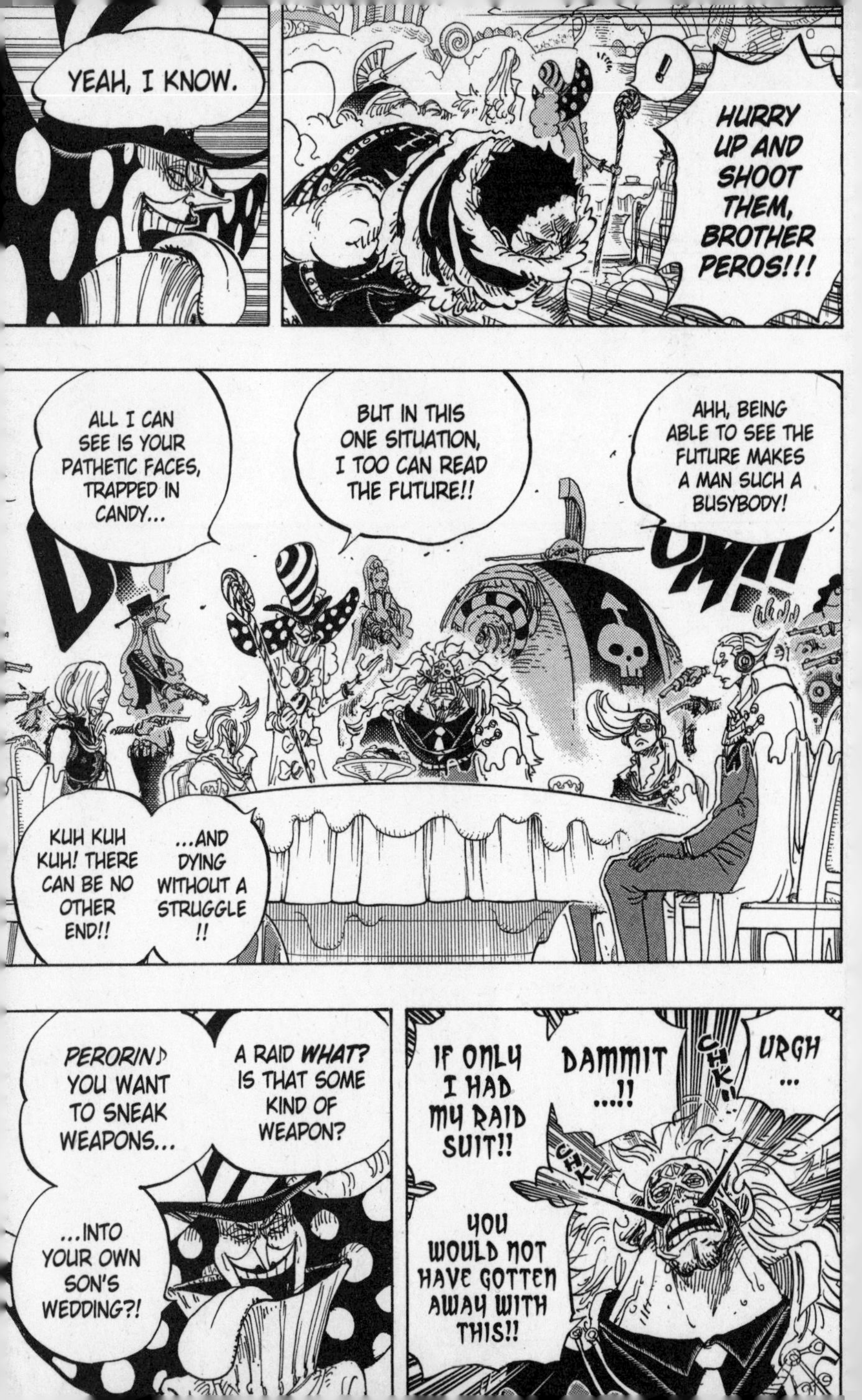
!
HURRY UP AND SHOOT THEM, BROTHER PEROS!!!
YEAH, I KNOW.
AHH, BEING ABLE TO SEE THE FUTURE MAKES A MAN SUCH A BUSYBODY!
BUT IN THIS ONE SITUATION, I TOO CAN READ THE FUTURE!!
ALL I CAN SEE IS YOUR PATHETIC FACES, TRAPPED IN CANDY...
...AND DYING WITHOUT A STRUGGLE!!
KUH KUH KUH! THERE CAN BE NO OTHER END!!
URGH ...
DAMMIT ...!!
IF ONLY I HAD MY RAID SUIT!!
YOU WOULD NOT HAVE GOTTEN AWAY WITH THIS!!
A RAID WHAT? IS THAT SOME KIND OF WEAPON?
PERORIN♪ YOU WANT TO SNEAK WEAPONS...
...INTO YOUR OWN SON'S WEDDING?!

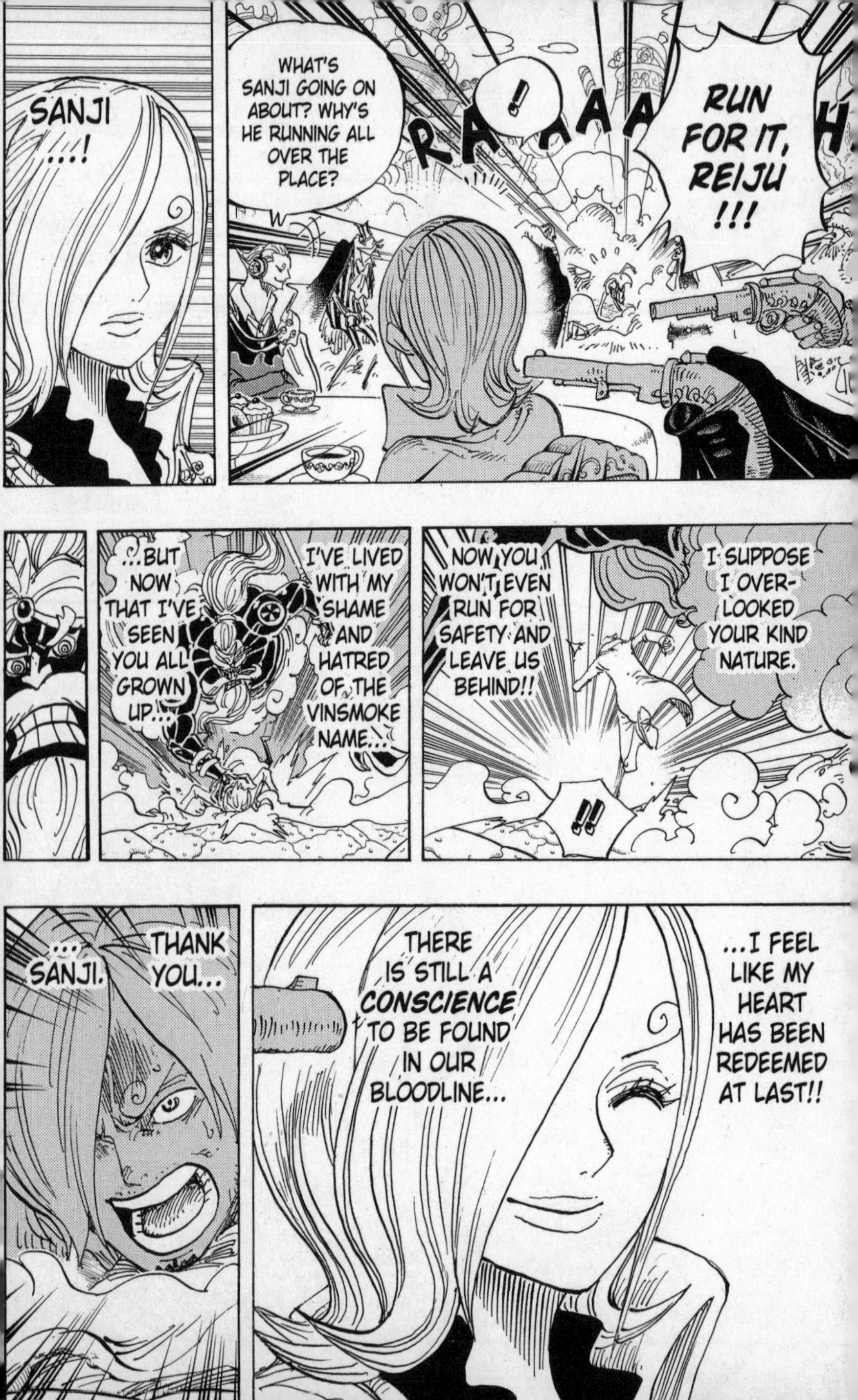
RUN FOR IT, REIJU!!!
RAAAA
!
WHAT'S SANJI GOING ON ABOUT? WHY'S HE RUNNING ALL OVER THE PLACE?
SANJI ...!
I SUPPOSE I OVERLOOKED YOUR KIND NATURE.
NOW YOU WON'T EVEN RUN FOR SAFETY AND LEAVE US BEHIND!!
!!
I'VE LIVED WITH MY SHAME AND HATRED OF THE VINSMOKE NAME...
...BUT NOW THAT I'VE SEEN YOU ALL GROWN UP...
...I FEEL LIKE MY HEART HAS BEEN REDEEMED AT LAST!!
THERE IS STILL A CONSCIENCE TO BE FOUND IN OUR BLOODLINE...
THANK YOU...
...SANJI.

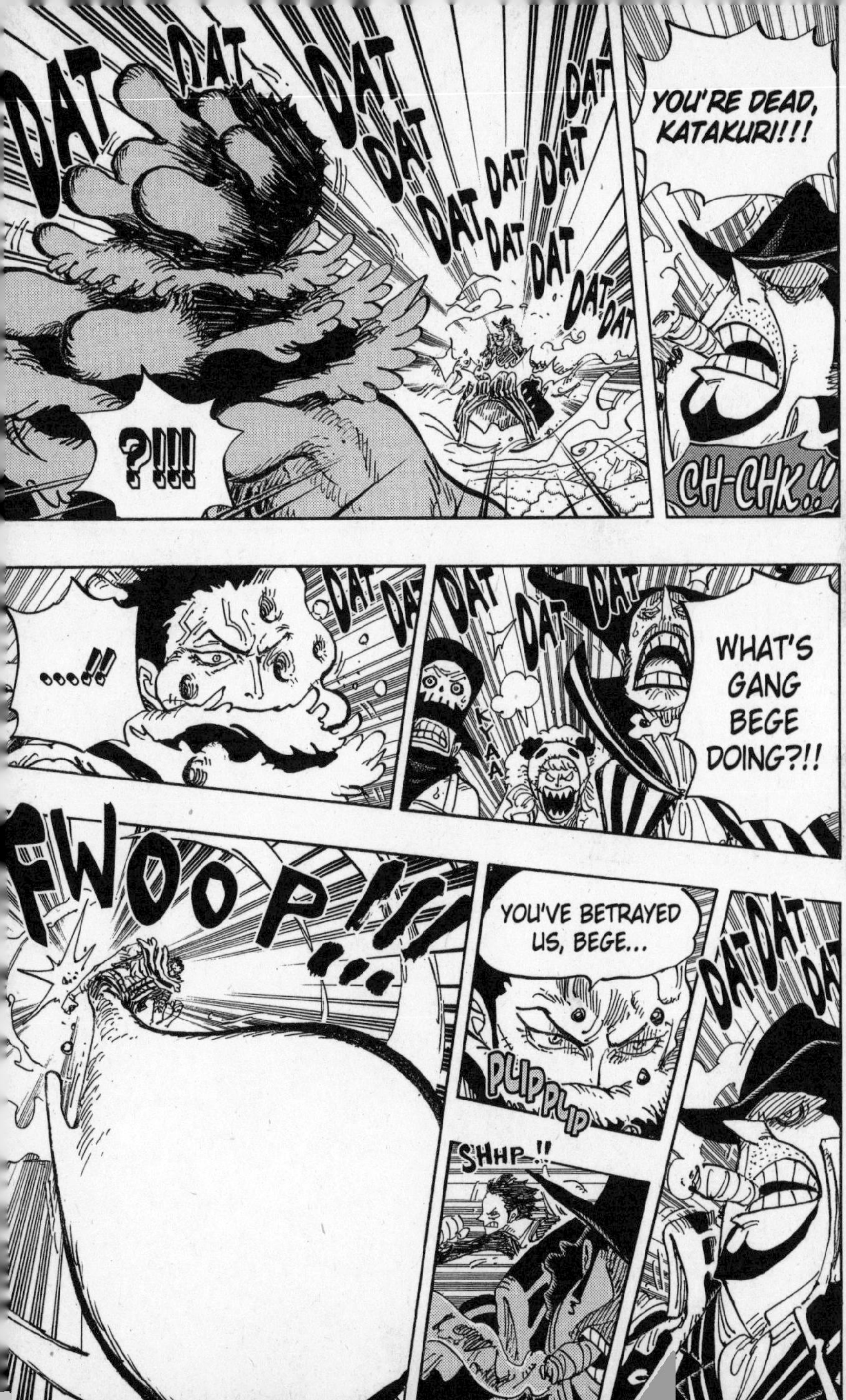
YOU'RE DEAD, KATAKURI!!!
CH-CHK!!
DAT DAT DAT DAT DAT DAT DAT DAT DAT DAT DAT DAT DAT DAT
?!!!
WHAT'S GANG BEGE DOING?!!
DAT DAT DAT
KYAA
DAT DAT
...!!
DAT DAT DA
YOU'VE BETRAYED US, BEGE...
PLIP PLIP
SHHP!!
FWOOP!!!
...

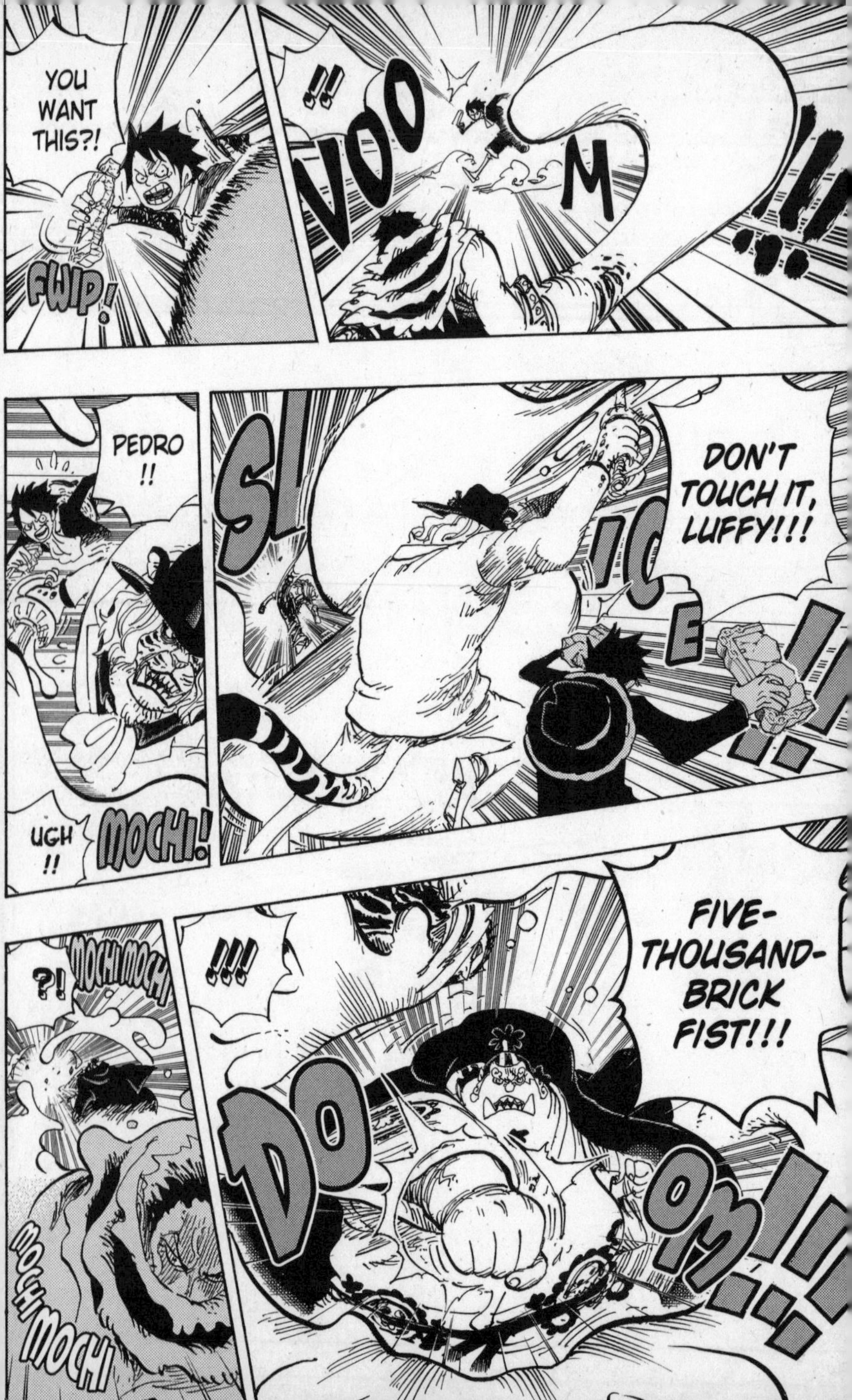
!!
VOOM!!!
YOU WANT THIS?!
FWIP!
DON'T TOUCH IT, LUFFY!!!
SLICE!!
PEDRO !!
UGH !!
MOCHI!
FIVE-THOUSAND-BRICK FIST!!!
!!!
DOOM!!!
?!
MOCHI MOCHI
MOCHI MOCHI

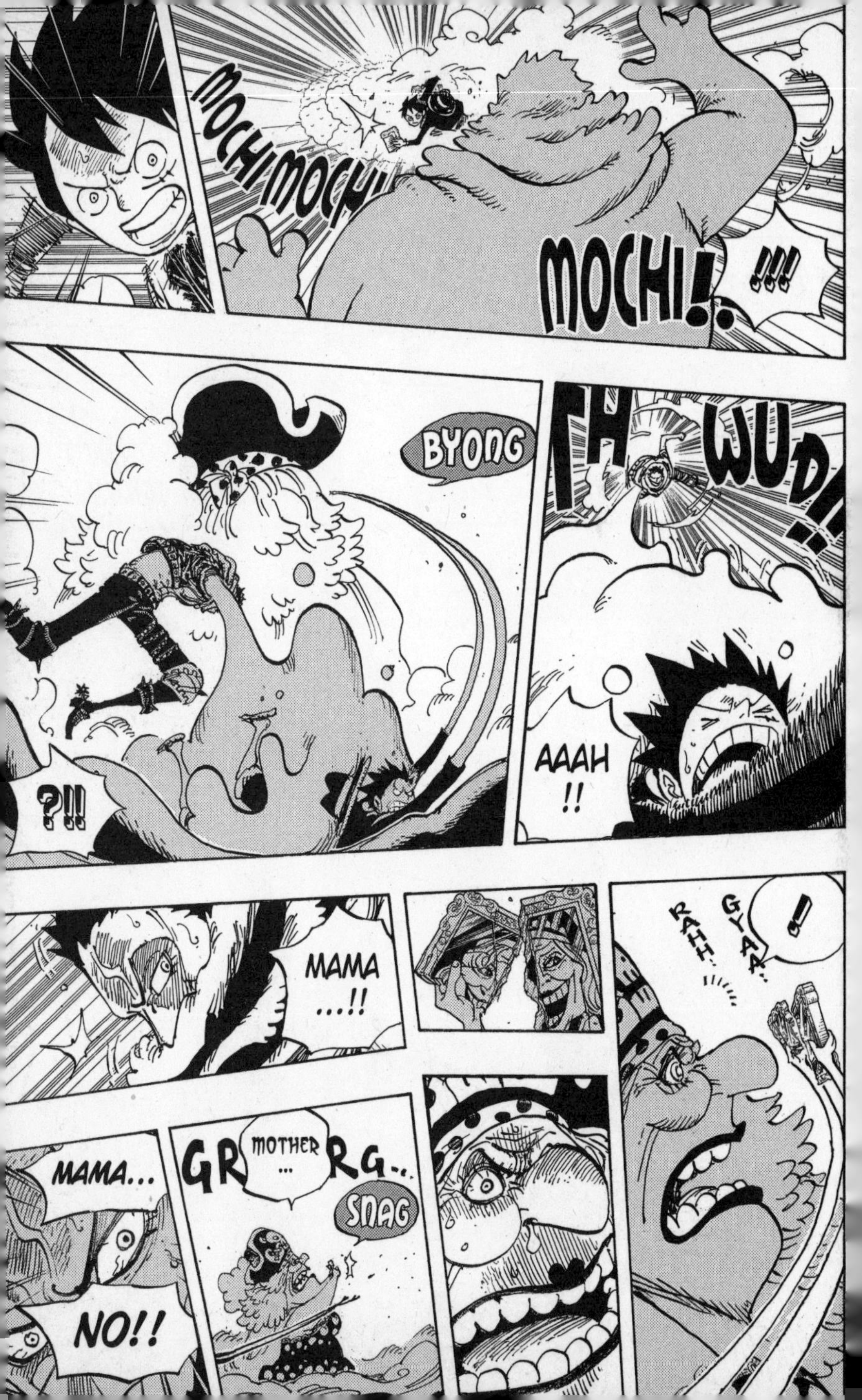
MOCHI MOCHI
MOCHI!!
!!!
THWUD!!
AAAH !!
BYONG
?!!
!
GYAA..
RAHH..
MAMA ...!!
GR
MOTHER ...
RG..
SNAG
MAMA...
NO!!

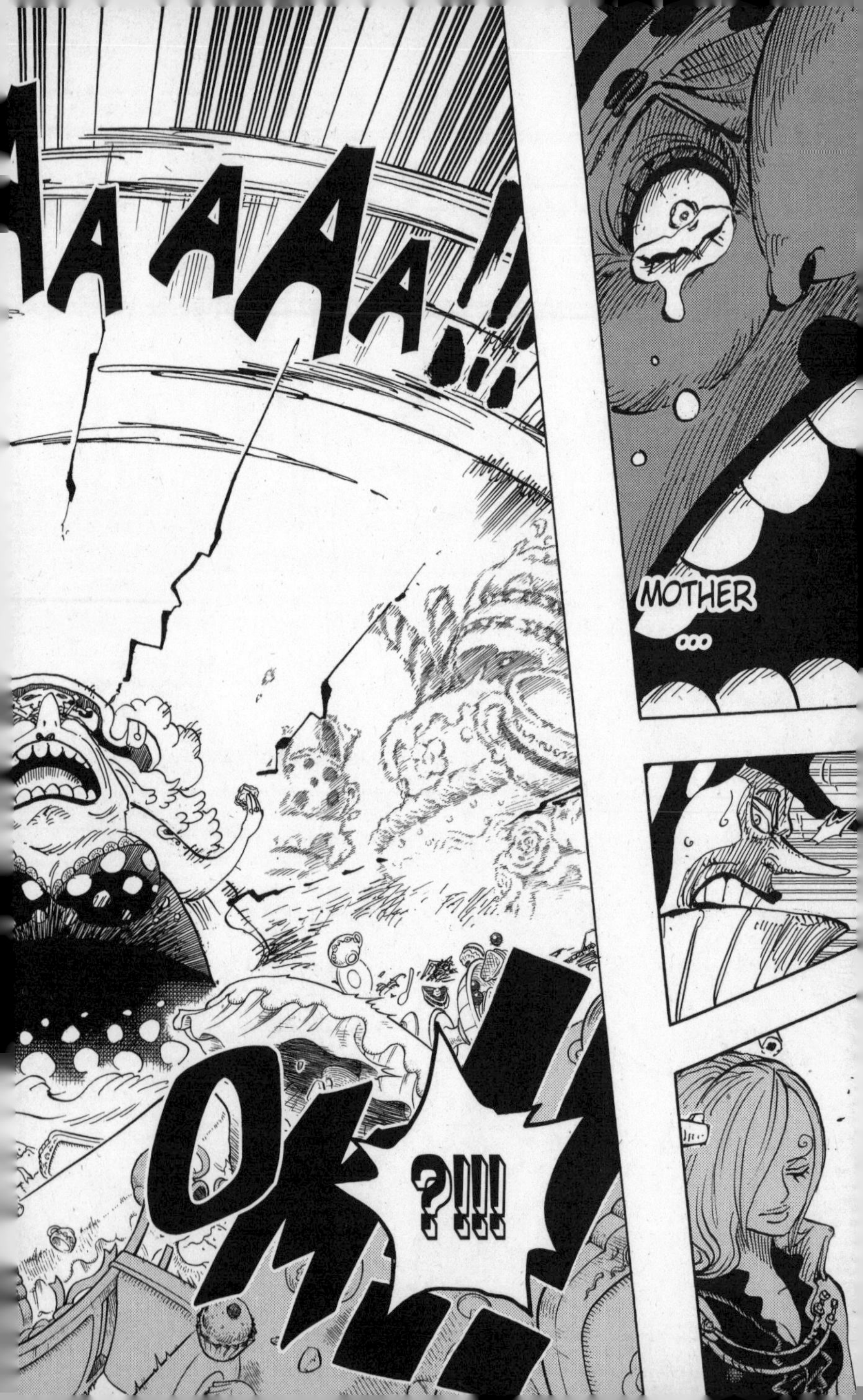

MOTHER...
AAAAA!!!
?!!!

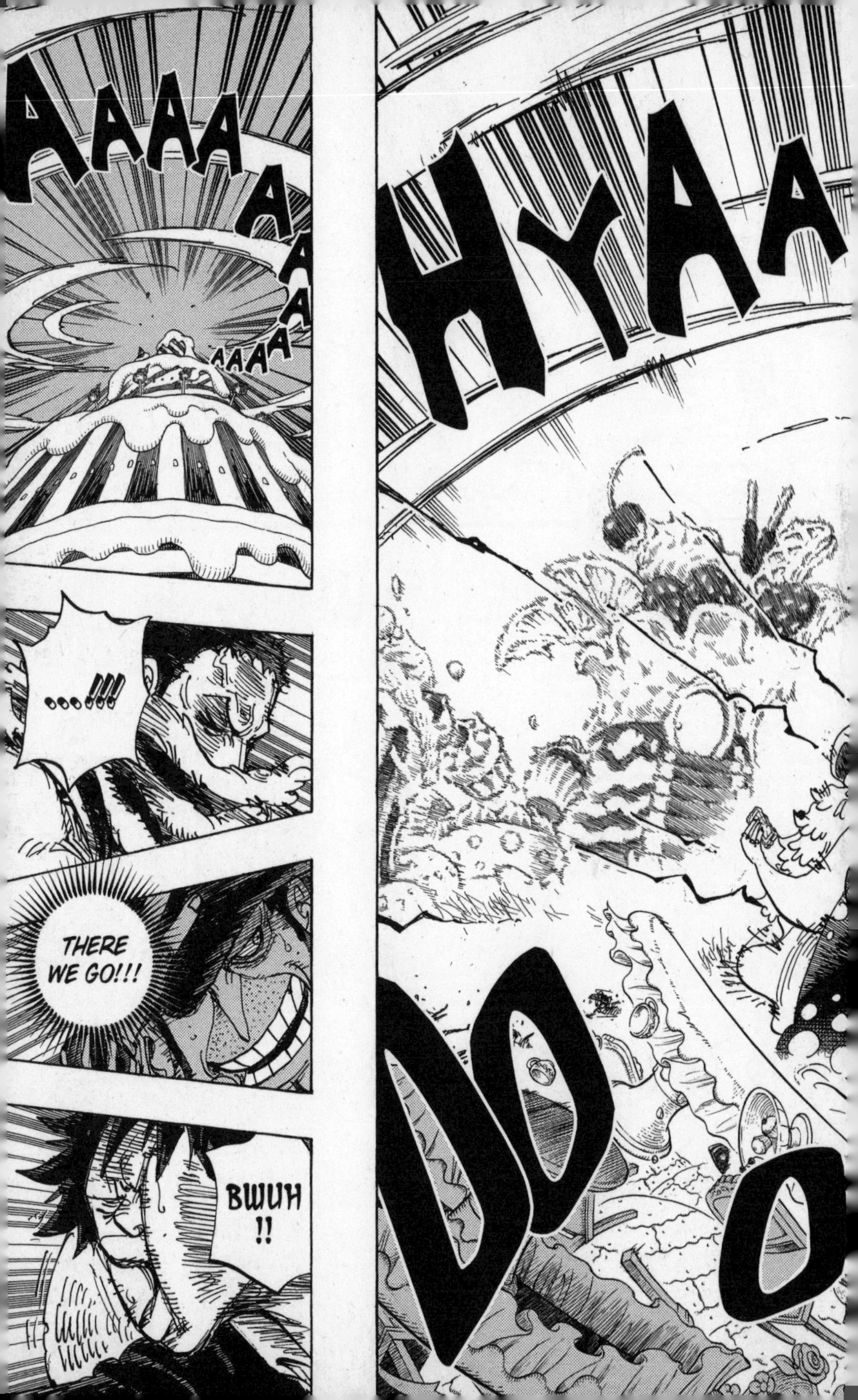
HYAA
DOO
AAAAAAAAAAA
...!!!
THERE WE GO!!!
BWUH !!

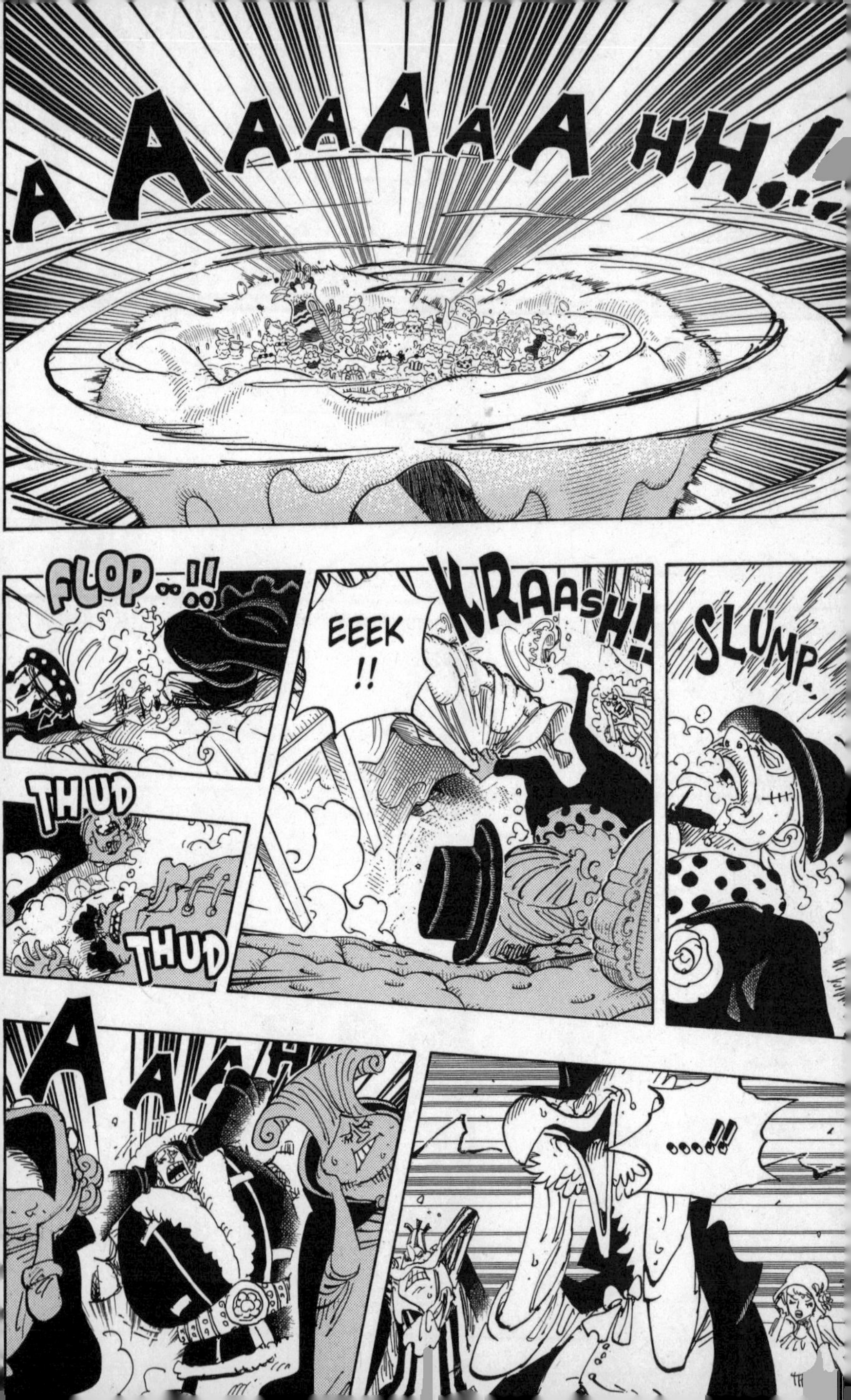
AAAAAAAHH!!
SLUMP
KRAASH!!
EEEK !!
FLOP..!!
THUD
THUD
....!!
AAAH

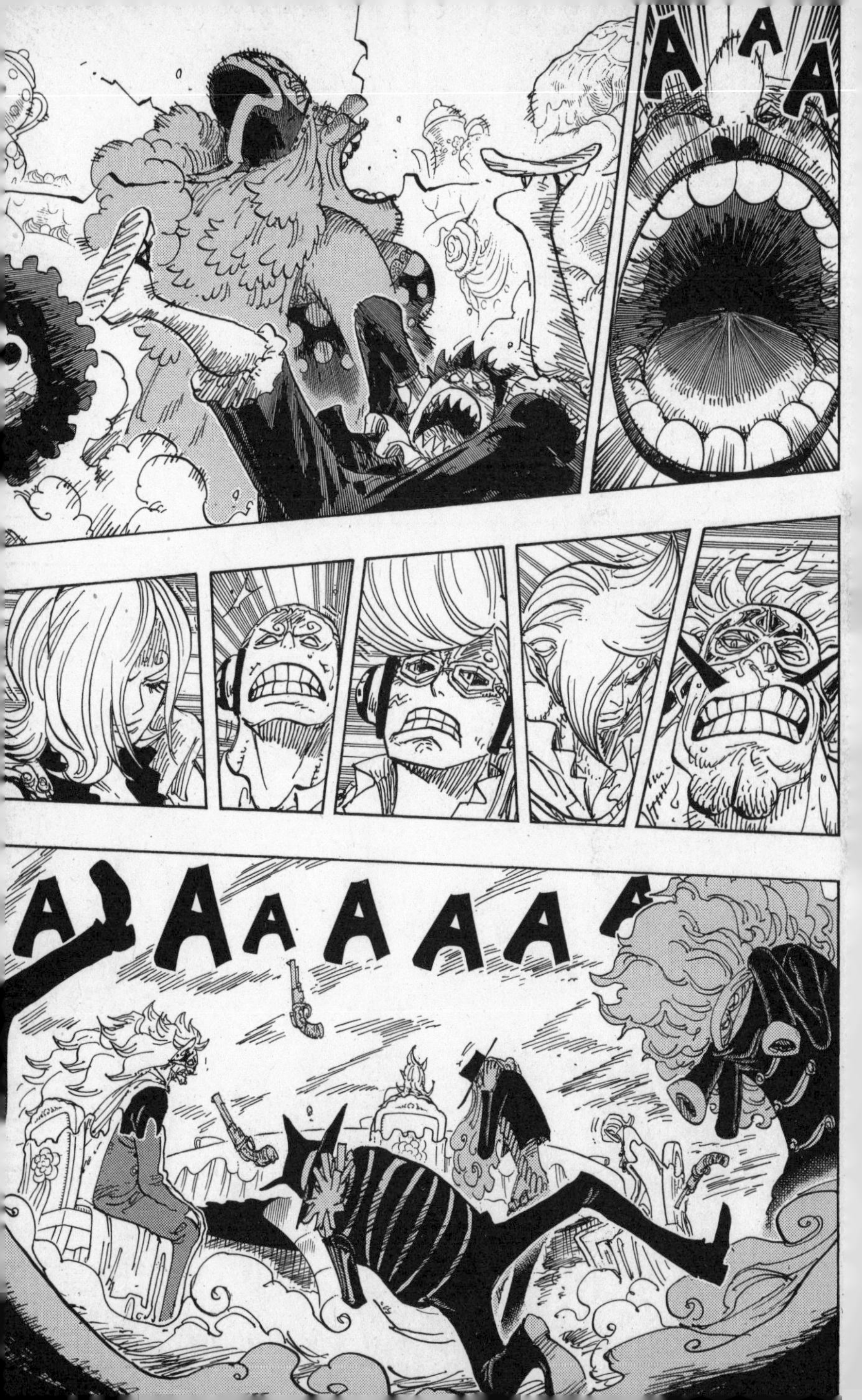
AAA
AAAAAAA

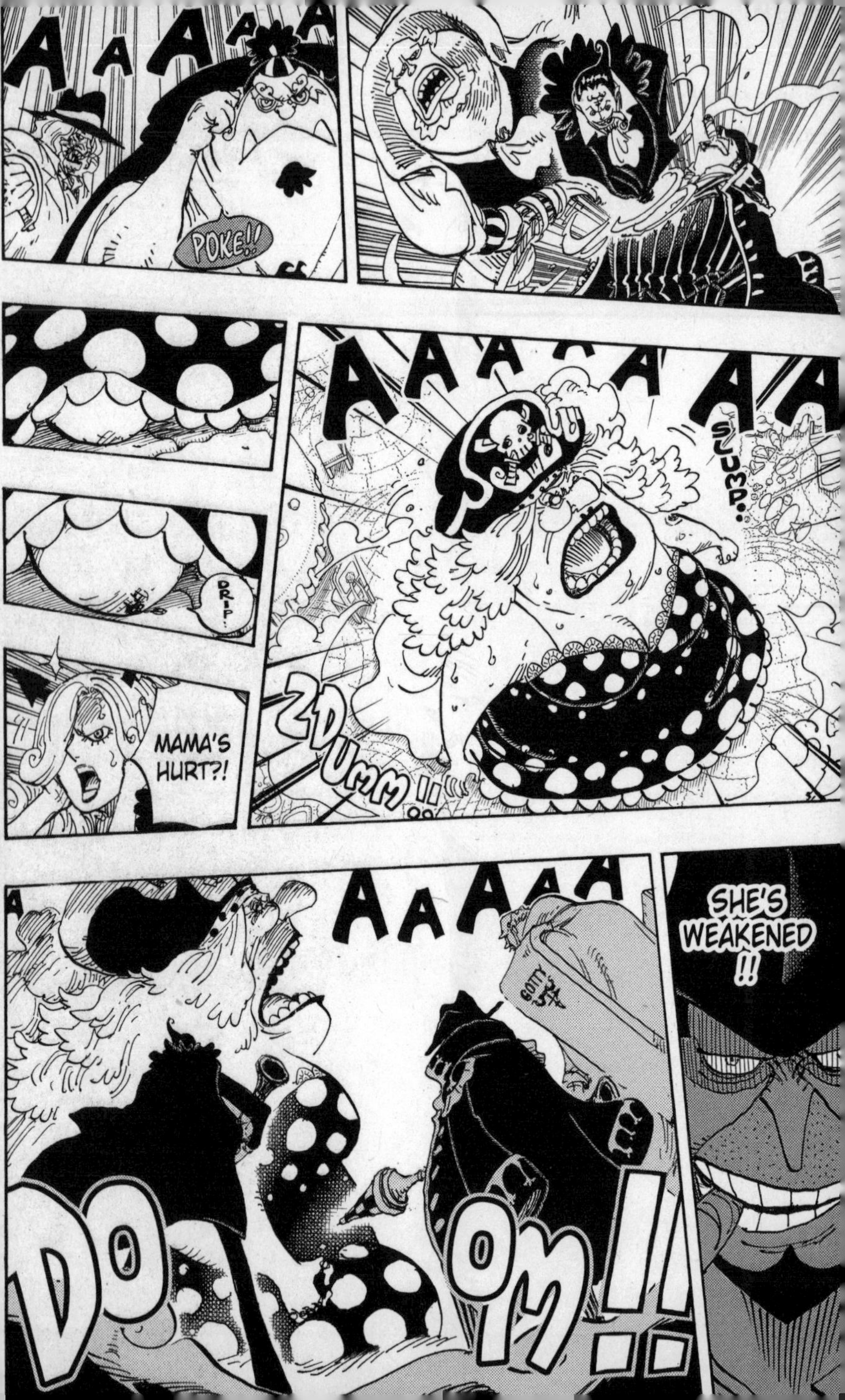

AAAAA
POKE!!
AAAAAAA
SLUMP..
ZDUMM!!
DRIP!
MAMA'S HURT?!
SHE'S WEAKENED!!
AAAAA
DOOM!!

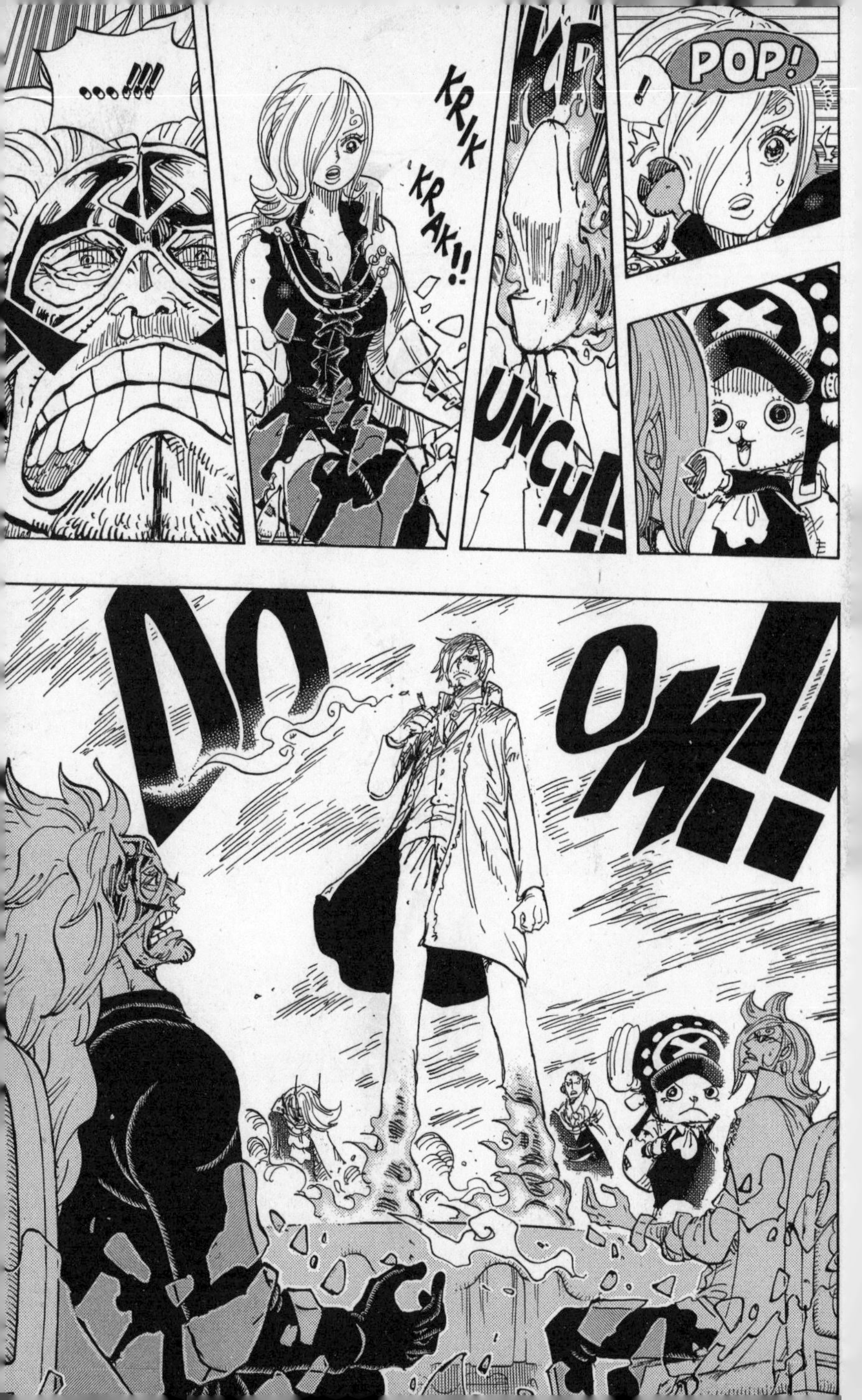
POP!
!
UNCH!!
KRIK
KRAK!!
...!!!
DO
OM!!

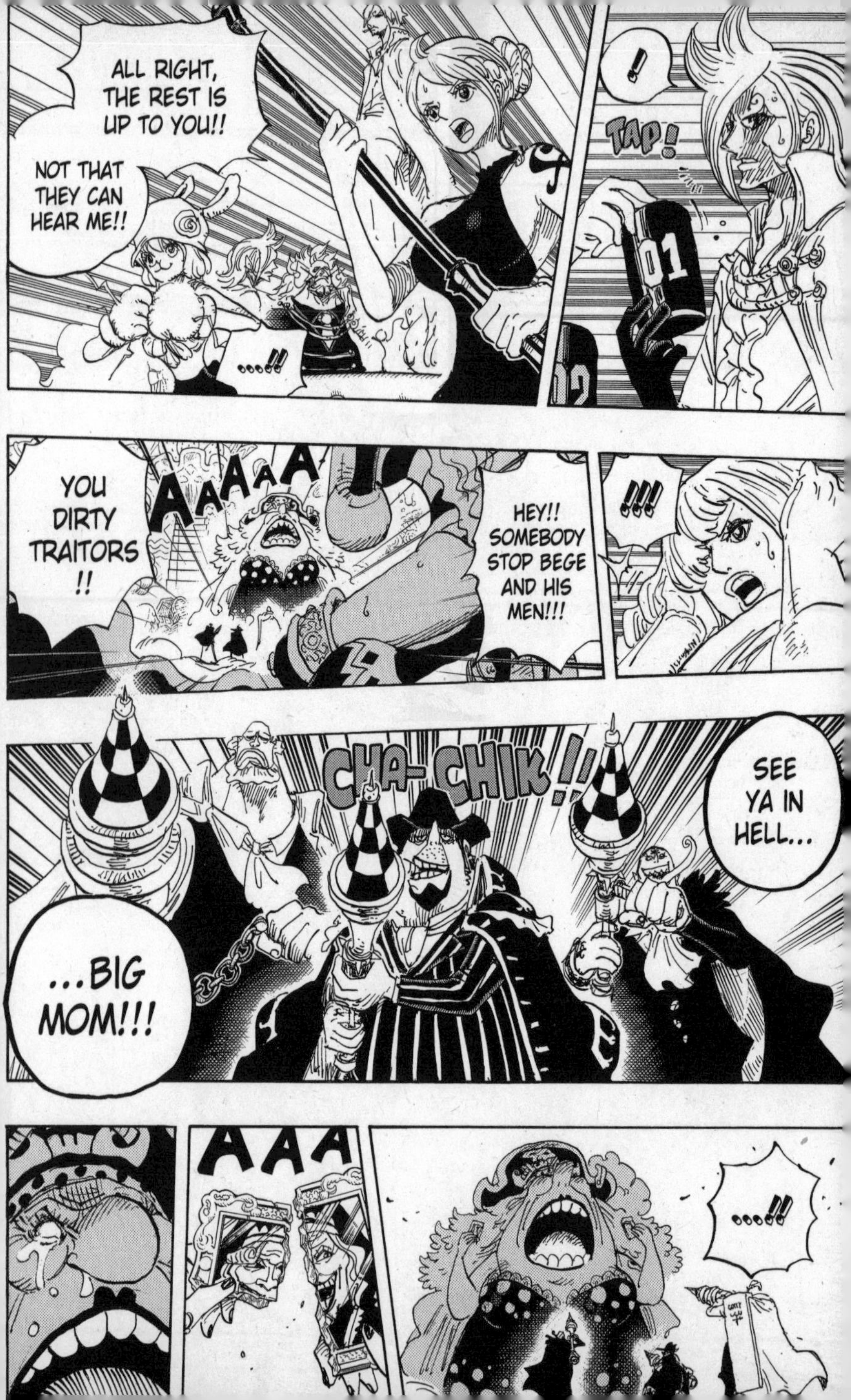
!
TAP!
ALL RIGHT, THE REST IS UP TO YOU!!
NOT THAT THEY CAN HEAR ME!!
...!!
!!!
HEY!! SOMEBODY STOP BEGE AND HIS MEN!!!
AAAAA
YOU DIRTY TRAITORS !!
SEE YA IN HELL...
CHA-CHIK!!
...BIG MOM!!!
...!!
AAA

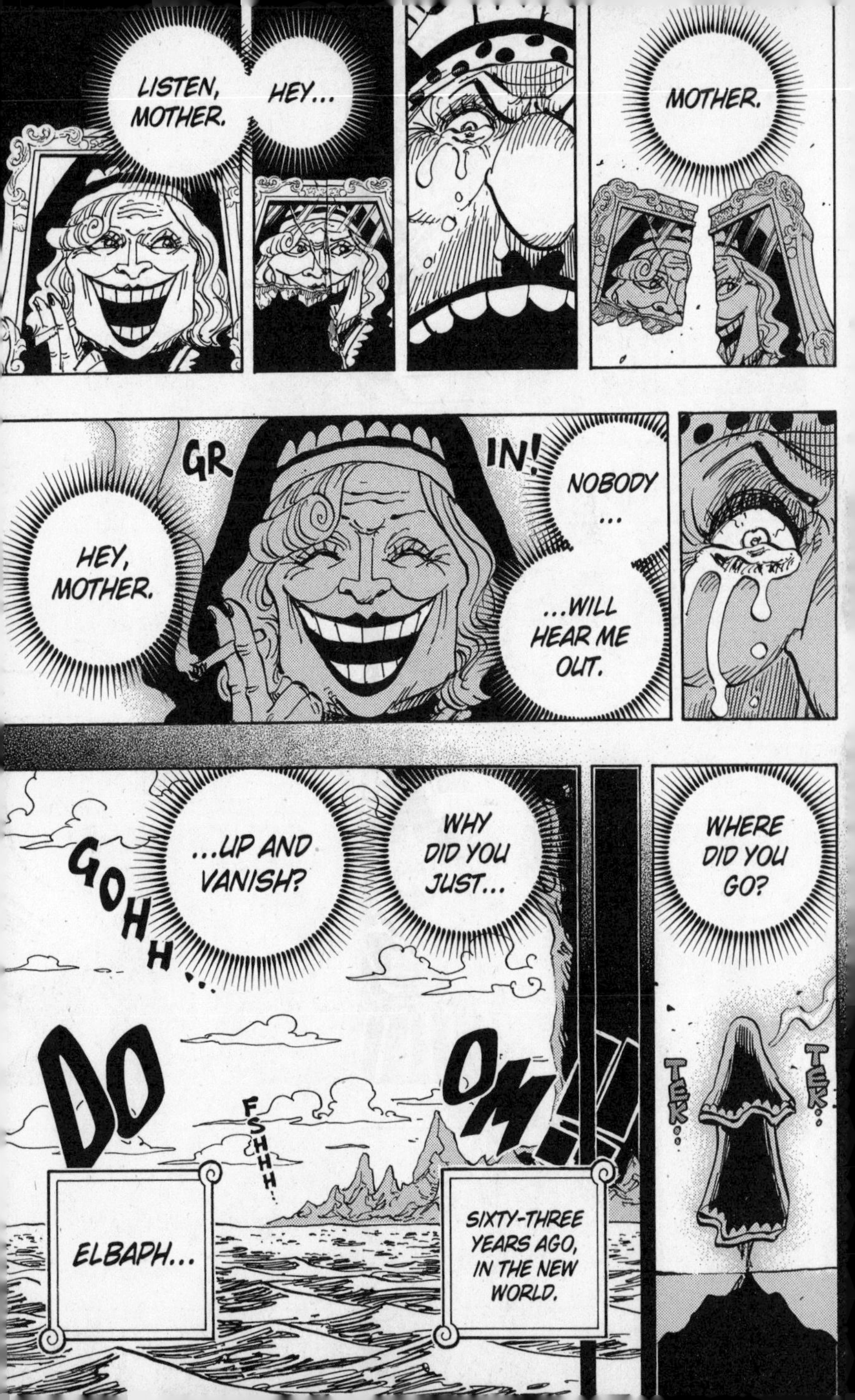
MOTHER.
HEY...
LISTEN, MOTHER.
NOBODY ...
...WILL HEAR ME OUT.
GR IN!
HEY, MOTHER.
WHERE DID YOU GO?
TEK TEK
WHY DID YOU JUST...
...UP AND VANISH?
GOHH
DO OM!!
FSHHH
SIXTY-THREE YEARS AGO, IN THE NEW WORLD.
ELBAPH...

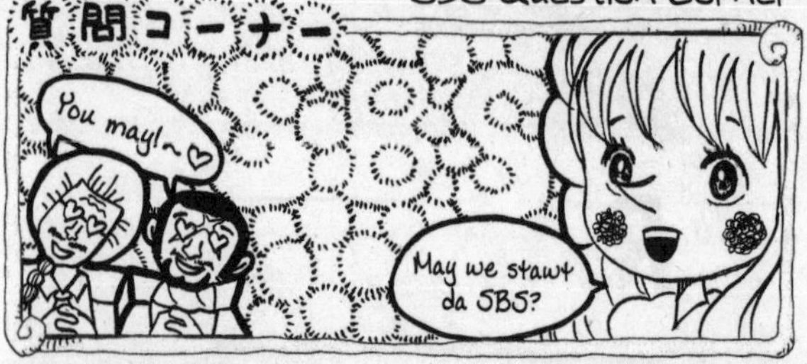
質問コーナー
You may!~♡
May we stawt da SBS?
(Yuko Honda, Saitama)

A: Spot the differences! Thank you for this one, Yucchan's Papa!! Find the answers on page 188!

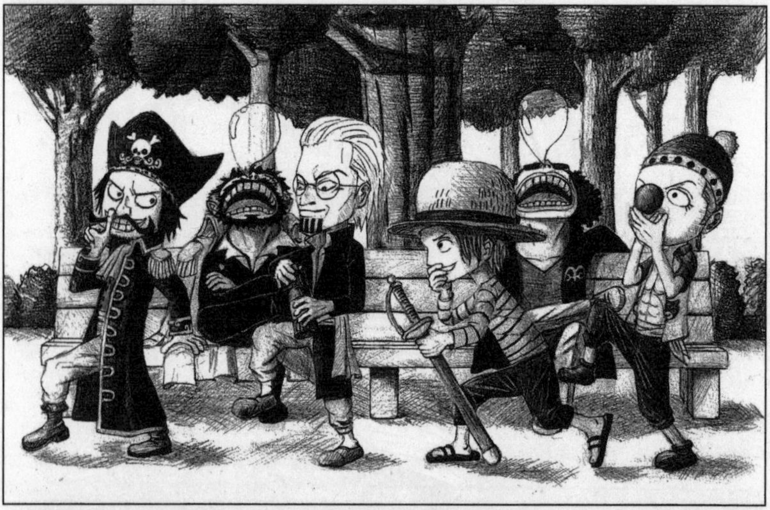

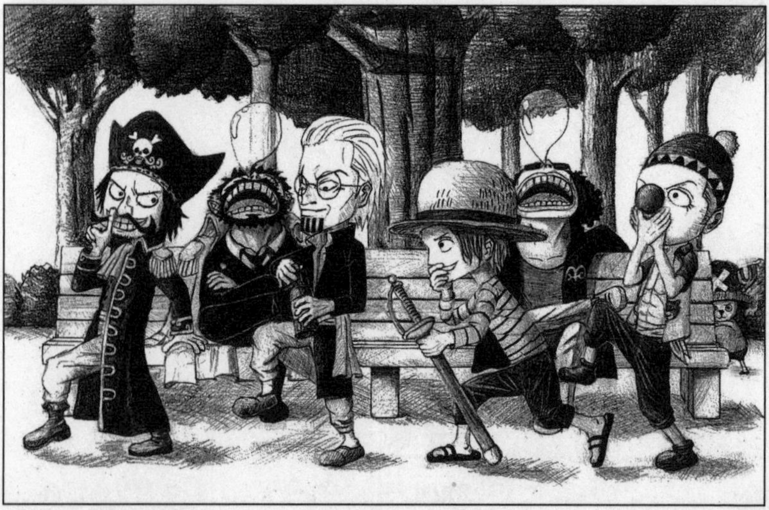
(Yucchan's Papa, Saitama)

Chapter 866:
NATURAL BORN DESTROYER

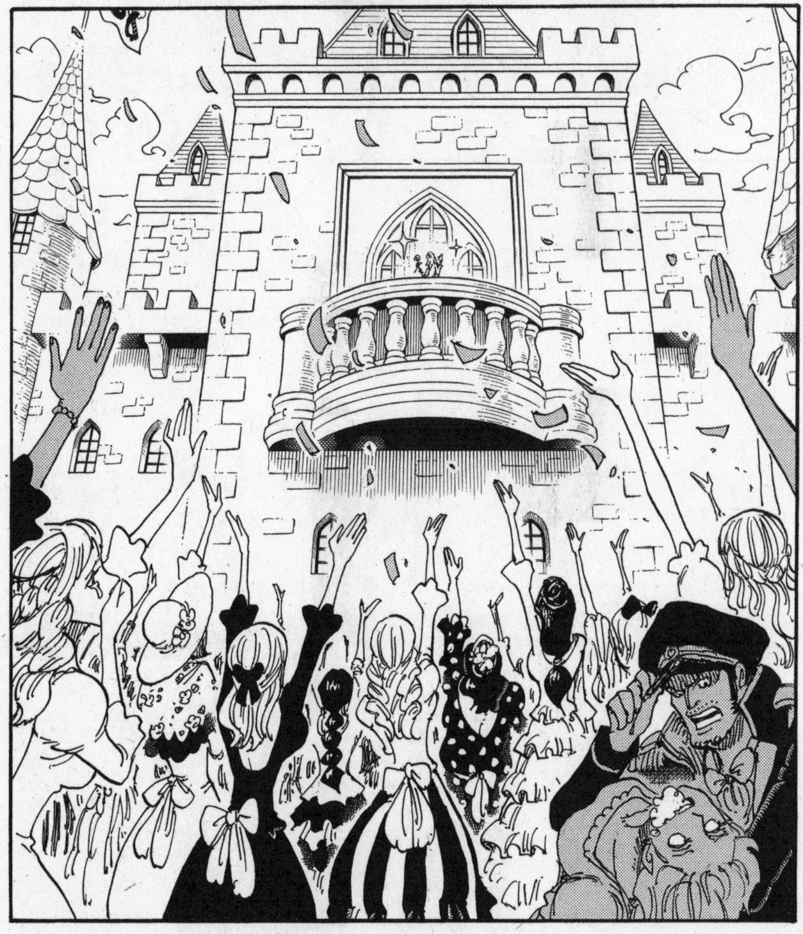

THE SAGA OF THE SELF-PROCLAIMED STRAW HAT FLEET, VOL. 3, CAVENDISH: "PRINCE CAVENDISH OF BOURGEOIS KINGDOM IS SO POPULAR NO YOUNG LADIES ARE GETTING MARRIED"

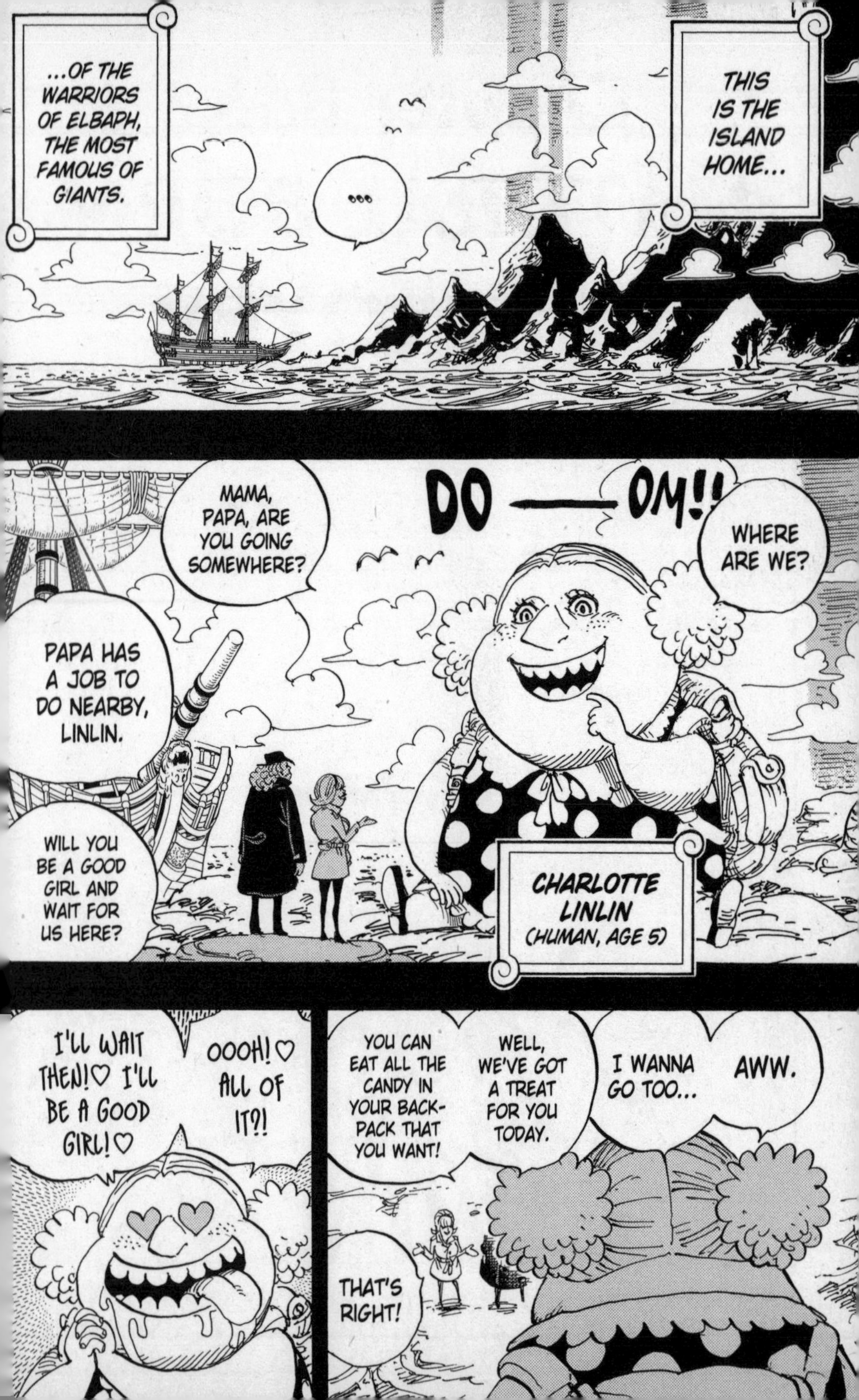
THIS IS THE ISLAND HOME...
...
...OF THE WARRIORS OF ELBAPH, THE MOST FAMOUS OF GIANTS.
DO——OM!!
WHERE ARE WE?
CHARLOTTE LINLIN (HUMAN, AGE 5)
MAMA, PAPA, ARE YOU GOING SOMEWHERE?
PAPA HAS A JOB TO DO NEARBY, LINLIN.
WILL YOU BE A GOOD GIRL AND WAIT FOR US HERE?
AWW.
I WANNA GO TOO...
WELL, WE'VE GOT A TREAT FOR YOU TODAY.
YOU CAN EAT ALL THE CANDY IN YOUR BACKPACK THAT YOU WANT!
THAT'S RIGHT!
OOOH! ♡ ALL OF IT?!
I'LL WAIT THEN! ♡ I'LL BE A GOOD GIRL! ♡

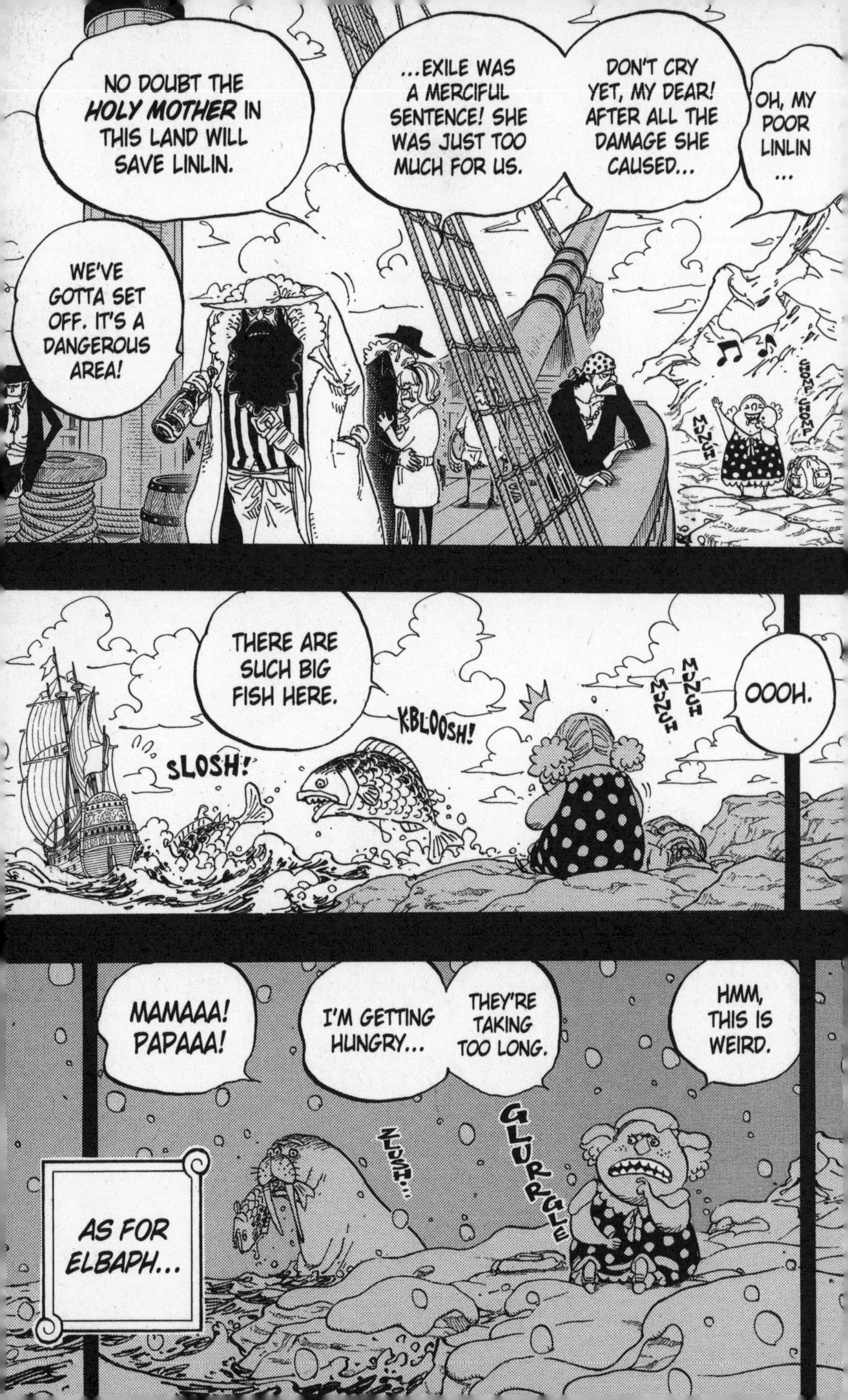
OH, MY POOR LINLIN ...
DON'T CRY YET, MY DEAR! AFTER ALL THE DAMAGE SHE CAUSED...
...EXILE WAS A MERCIFUL SENTENCE! SHE WAS JUST TOO MUCH FOR US.
NO DOUBT THE HOLY MOTHER IN THIS LAND WILL SAVE LINLIN.
WE'VE GOTTA SET OFF. IT'S A DANGEROUS AREA!
CHOMP CHOMP
MUNCH
OOOH.
MUNCH MUNCH
KBLOOSH!
THERE ARE SUCH BIG FISH HERE.
SLOSH!
HMM, THIS IS WEIRD.
THEY'RE TAKING TOO LONG.
I'M GETTING HUNGRY...
MAMAAA! PAPAAA!
GLURRGLE
ZLUSH...
AS FOR ELBAPH...

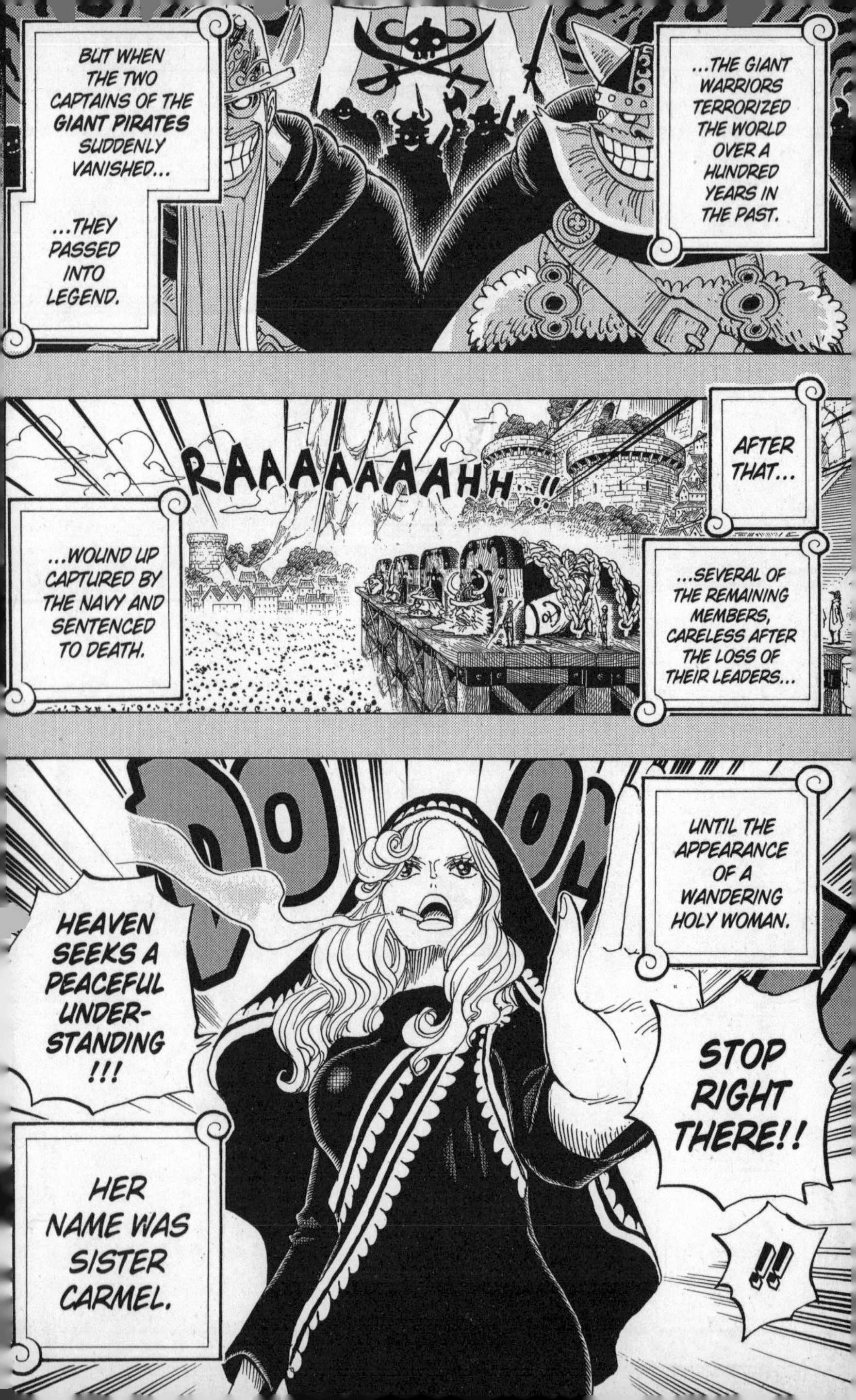
...THE GIANT WARRIORS TERRORIZED THE WORLD OVER A HUNDRED YEARS IN THE PAST.
BUT WHEN THE TWO CAPTAINS OF THE GIANT PIRATES SUDDENLY VANISHED...
...THEY PASSED INTO LEGEND.
AFTER THAT...
...SEVERAL OF THE REMAINING MEMBERS, CARELESS AFTER THE LOSS OF THEIR LEADERS...
RAAAAAAAHH!!
...WOUND UP CAPTURED BY THE NAVY AND SENTENCED TO DEATH.
UNTIL THE APPEARANCE OF A WANDERING HOLY WOMAN.
STOP RIGHT THERE!!
!!
HEAVEN SEEKS A PEACEFUL UNDER-STANDING!!!
HER NAME WAS SISTER CARMEL.

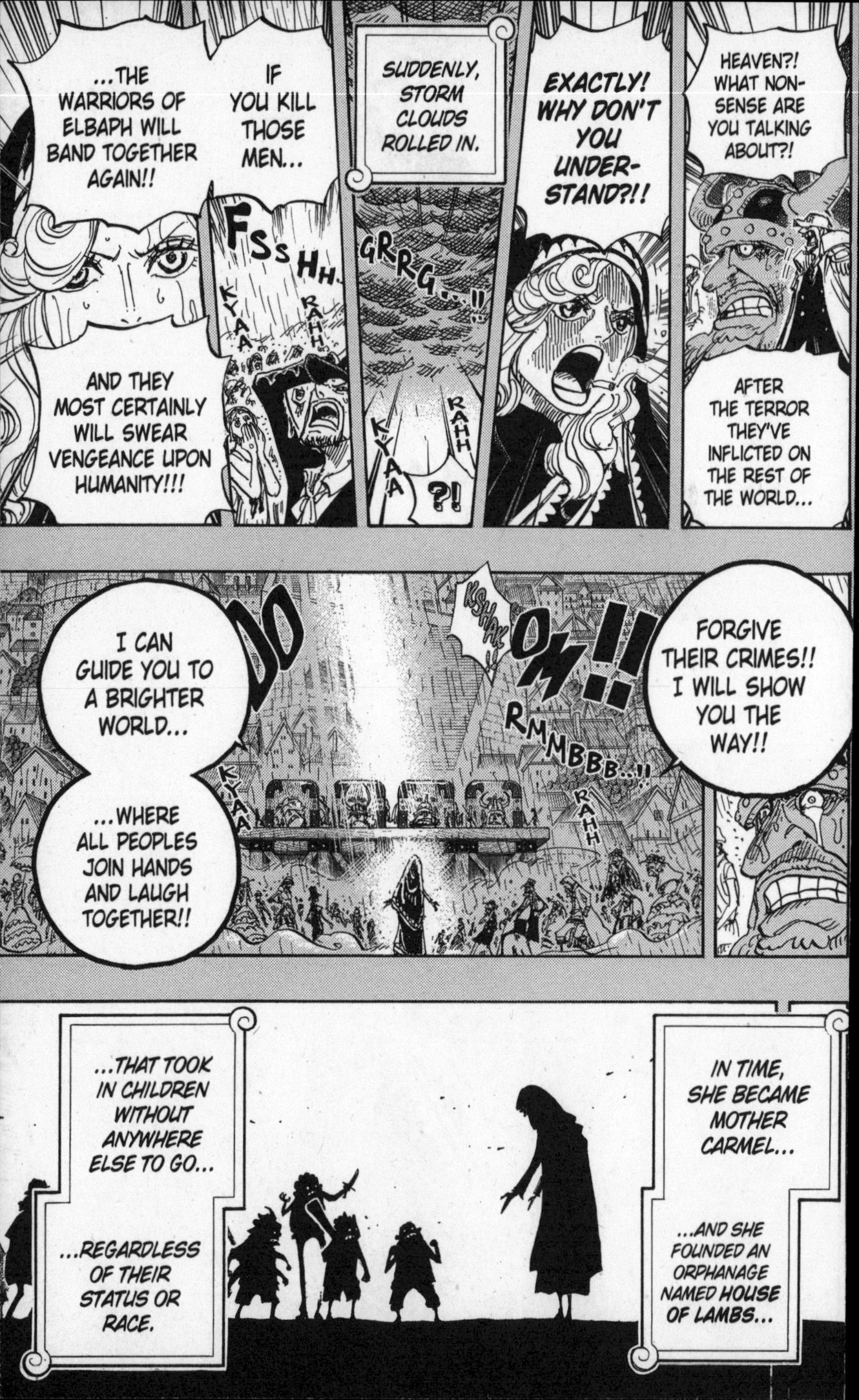
HEAVEN?! WHAT NON-SENSE ARE YOU TALKING ABOUT?!
AFTER THE TERROR THEY'VE INFLICTED ON THE REST OF THE WORLD...
EXACTLY! WHY DON'T YOU UNDER-STAND?!!
SUDDENLY, STORM CLOUDS ROLLED IN.
GRRRG...!!
KYAA
RAHH
?!
IF YOU KILL THOSE MEN...
FSSHH
KYAA
RAHH
...THE WARRIORS OF ELBAPH WILL BAND TOGETHER AGAIN!!
AND THEY MOST CERTAINLY WILL SWEAR VENGEANCE UPON HUMANITY!!!
FORGIVE THEIR CRIMES!! I WILL SHOW YOU THE WAY!!
KSHAK
DOOM!!
RMMBBB..!!
RAHH
KYAA
I CAN GUIDE YOU TO A BRIGHTER WORLD...
...WHERE ALL PEOPLES JOIN HANDS AND LAUGH TOGETHER!!
IN TIME, SHE BECAME MOTHER CARMEL...
...AND SHE FOUNDED AN ORPHANAGE NAMED HOUSE OF LAMBS...
...THAT TOOK IN CHILDREN WITHOUT ANYWHERE ELSE TO GO...
...REGARDLESS OF THEIR STATUS OR RACE.

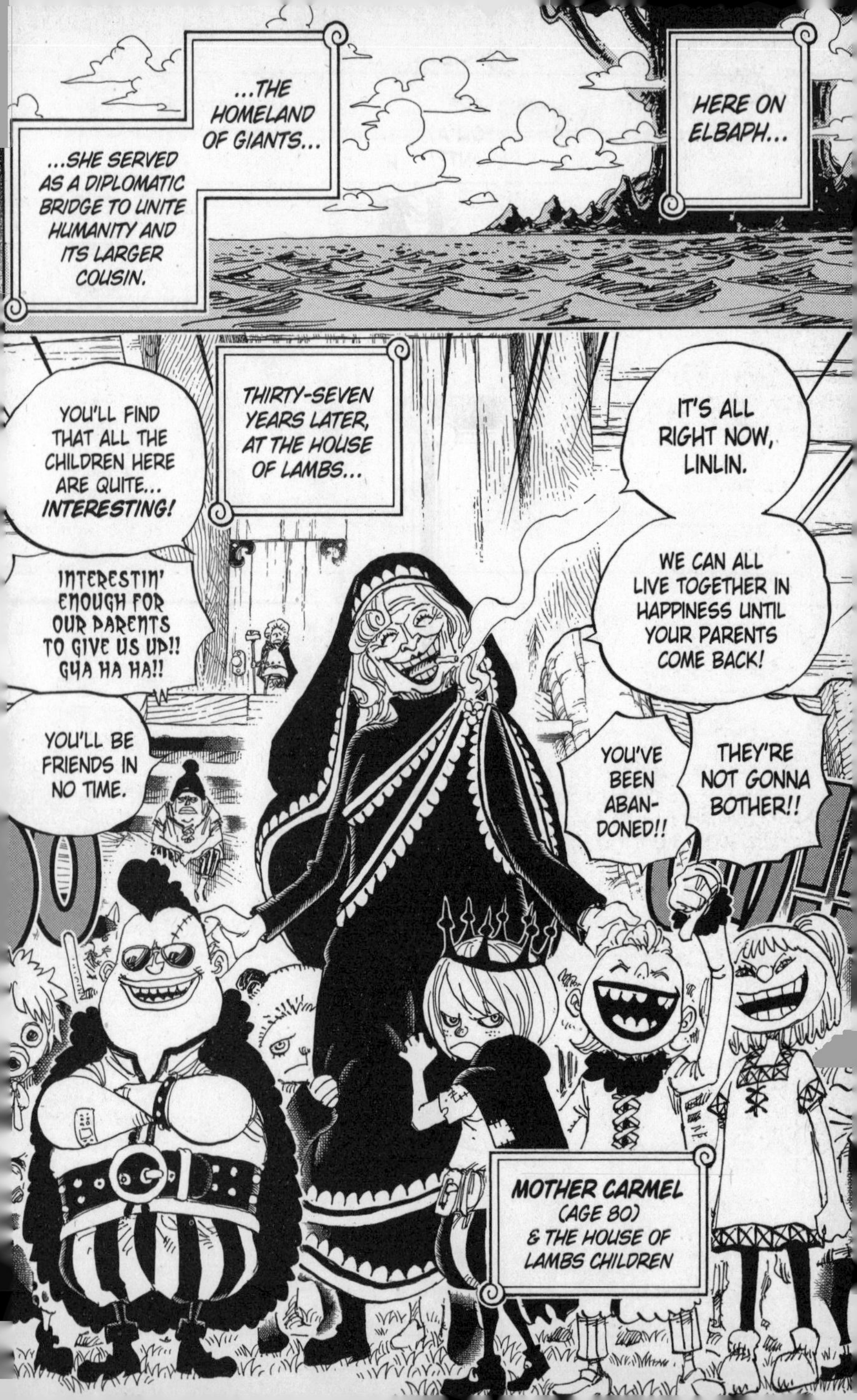
HERE ON ELBAPH...
...THE HOMELAND OF GIANTS...
...SHE SERVED AS A DIPLOMATIC BRIDGE TO UNITE HUMANITY AND ITS LARGER COUSIN.
THIRTY-SEVEN YEARS LATER, AT THE HOUSE OF LAMBS...
IT'S ALL RIGHT NOW, LINLIN.
WE CAN ALL LIVE TOGETHER IN HAPPINESS UNTIL YOUR PARENTS COME BACK!
YOU'LL FIND THAT ALL THE CHILDREN HERE ARE QUITE... INTERESTING!
INTERESTIN' ENOUGH FOR OUR PARENTS TO GIVE US UP!! GYA HA HA!!
THEY'RE NOT GONNA BOTHER!!
YOU'VE BEEN ABAN-DONED!!
YOU'LL BE FRIENDS IN NO TIME.
MOTHER CARMEL (AGE 80) & THE HOUSE OF LAMBS CHILDREN

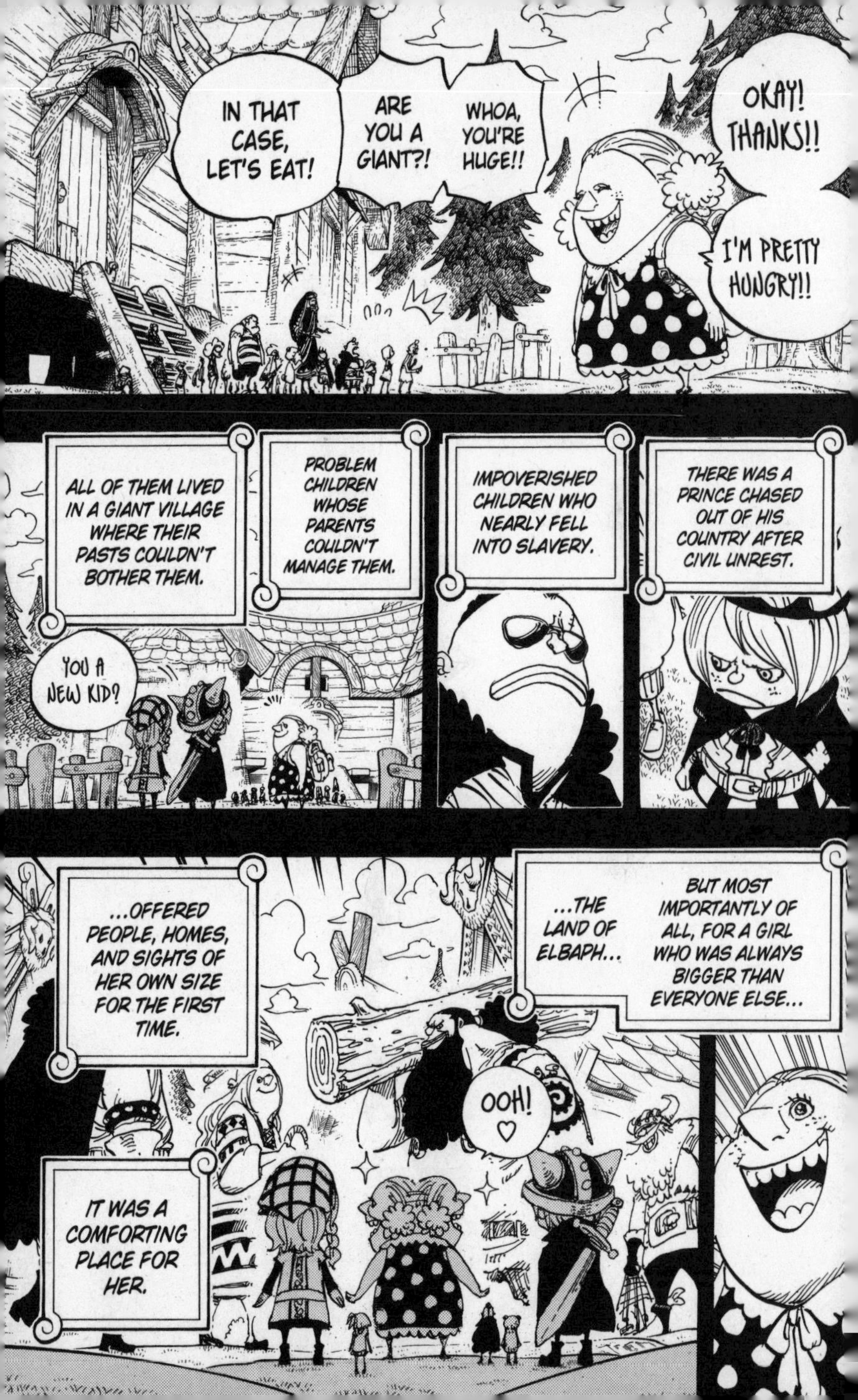
OKAY! THANKS!!
I'M PRETTY HUNGRY!!
WHOA, YOU'RE HUGE!!
ARE YOU A GIANT?!
IN THAT CASE, LET'S EAT!
THERE WAS A PRINCE CHASED OUT OF HIS COUNTRY AFTER CIVIL UNREST.
IMPOVERISHED CHILDREN WHO NEARLY FELL INTO SLAVERY.
PROBLEM CHILDREN WHOSE PARENTS COULDN'T MANAGE THEM.
ALL OF THEM LIVED IN A GIANT VILLAGE WHERE THEIR PASTS COULDN'T BOTHER THEM.
YOU A NEW KID?
BUT MOST IMPORTANTLY OF ALL, FOR A GIRL WHO WAS ALWAYS BIGGER THAN EVERYONE ELSE...
...THE LAND OF ELBAPH...
...OFFERED PEOPLE, HOMES, AND SIGHTS OF HER OWN SIZE FOR THE FIRST TIME.
OOH! ♡
IT WAS A COMFORTING PLACE FOR HER.

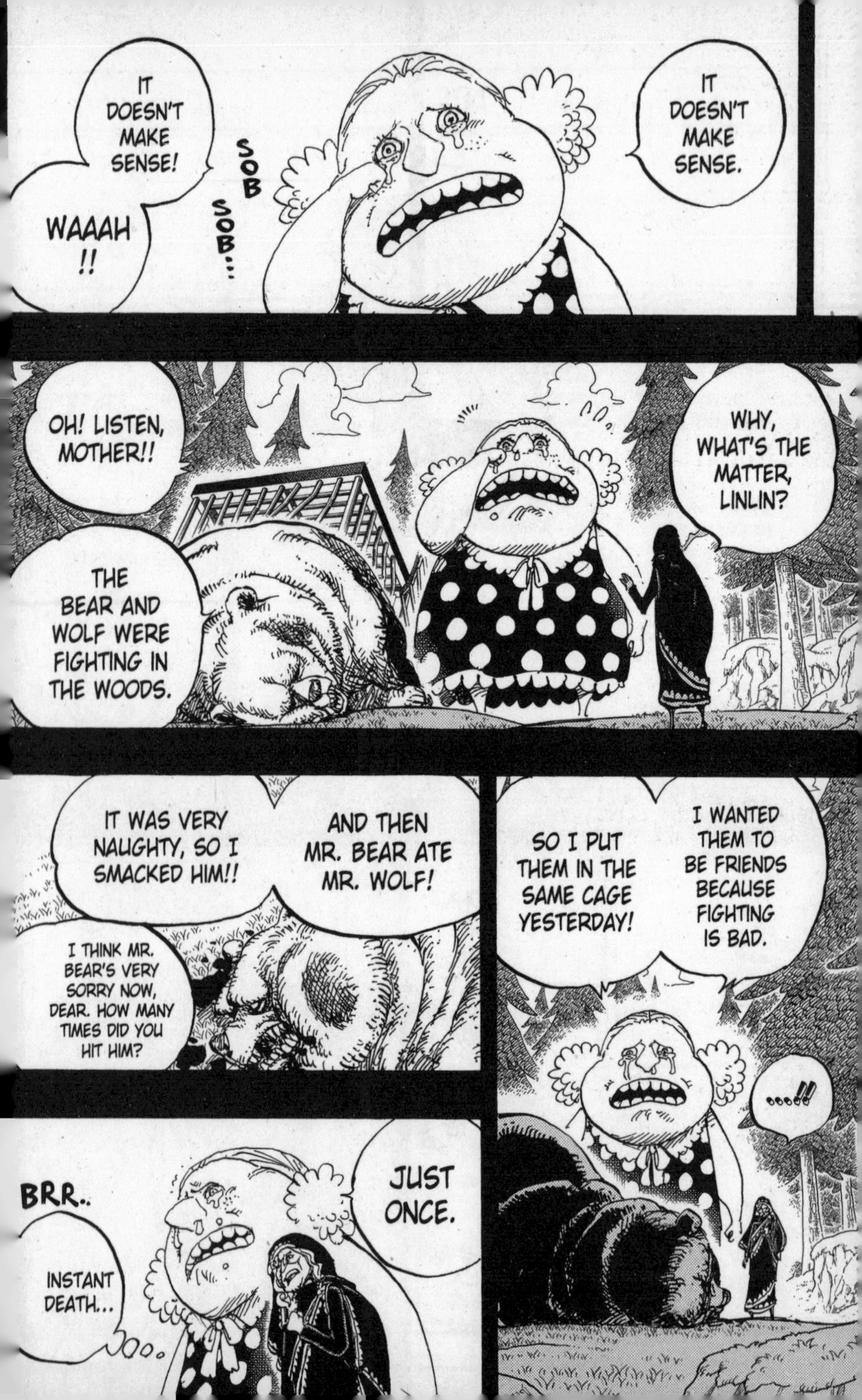
IT DOESN'T MAKE SENSE.
IT DOESN'T MAKE SENSE!
WAAAH!!
SOB SOB...
WHY, WHAT'S THE MATTER, LINLIN?
OH! LISTEN, MOTHER!!
THE BEAR AND WOLF WERE FIGHTING IN THE WOODS.
I WANTED THEM TO BE FRIENDS BECAUSE FIGHTING IS BAD.
SO I PUT THEM IN THE SAME CAGE YESTERDAY!
...!!
AND THEN MR. BEAR ATE MR. WOLF!
IT WAS VERY NAUGHTY, SO I SMACKED HIM!!
I THINK MR. BEAR'S VERY SORRY NOW, DEAR. HOW MANY TIMES DID YOU HIT HIM?
JUST ONCE.
BRR..
INSTANT DEATH...

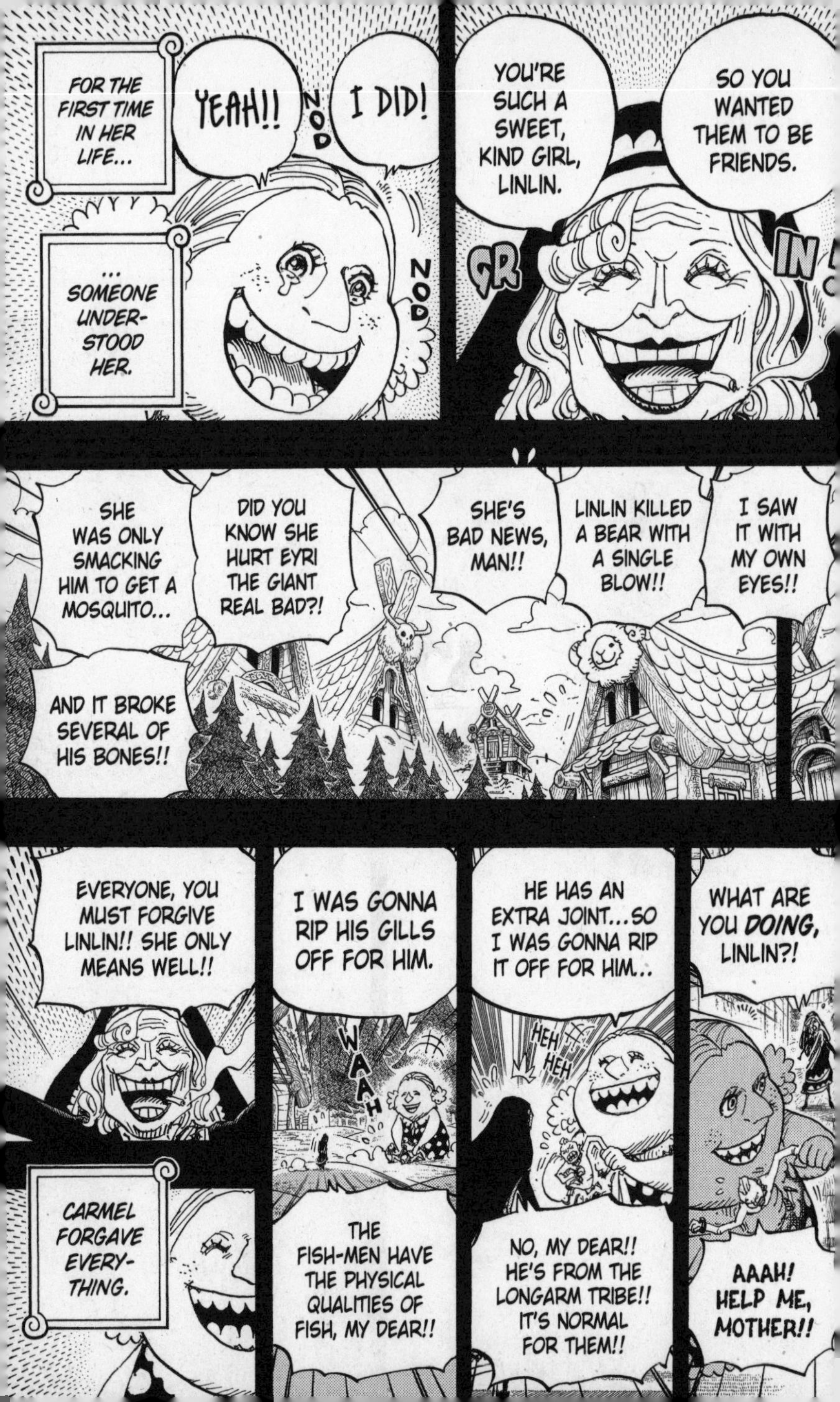
SO YOU WANTED THEM TO BE FRIENDS.
YOU'RE SUCH A SWEET, KIND GIRL, LINLIN.
GR
IN
I DID!
NOD
YEAH!!
NOD
FOR THE FIRST TIME IN HER LIFE...
... SOMEONE UNDER-STOOD HER.
I SAW IT WITH MY OWN EYES!!
LINLIN KILLED A BEAR WITH A SINGLE BLOW!!
SHE'S BAD NEWS, MAN!!
DID YOU KNOW SHE HURT EYRI THE GIANT REAL BAD?!
SHE WAS ONLY SMACKING HIM TO GET A MOSQUITO...
AND IT BROKE SEVERAL OF HIS BONES!!
WHAT ARE YOU *DOING*, LINLIN?!
AAAH! HELP ME, MOTHER!!
HE HAS AN EXTRA JOINT...SO I WAS GONNA RIP IT OFF FOR HIM..
HEH HEH
NO, MY DEAR!! HE'S FROM THE LONGARM TRIBE!! IT'S NORMAL FOR THEM!!
I WAS GONNA RIP HIS GILLS OFF FOR HIM.
WAAH
THE FISH-MEN HAVE THE PHYSICAL QUALITIES OF FISH, MY DEAR!!
EVERYONE, YOU MUST FORGIVE LINLIN!! SHE ONLY MEANS WELL!!
CARMEL FORGAVE EVERY-THING.

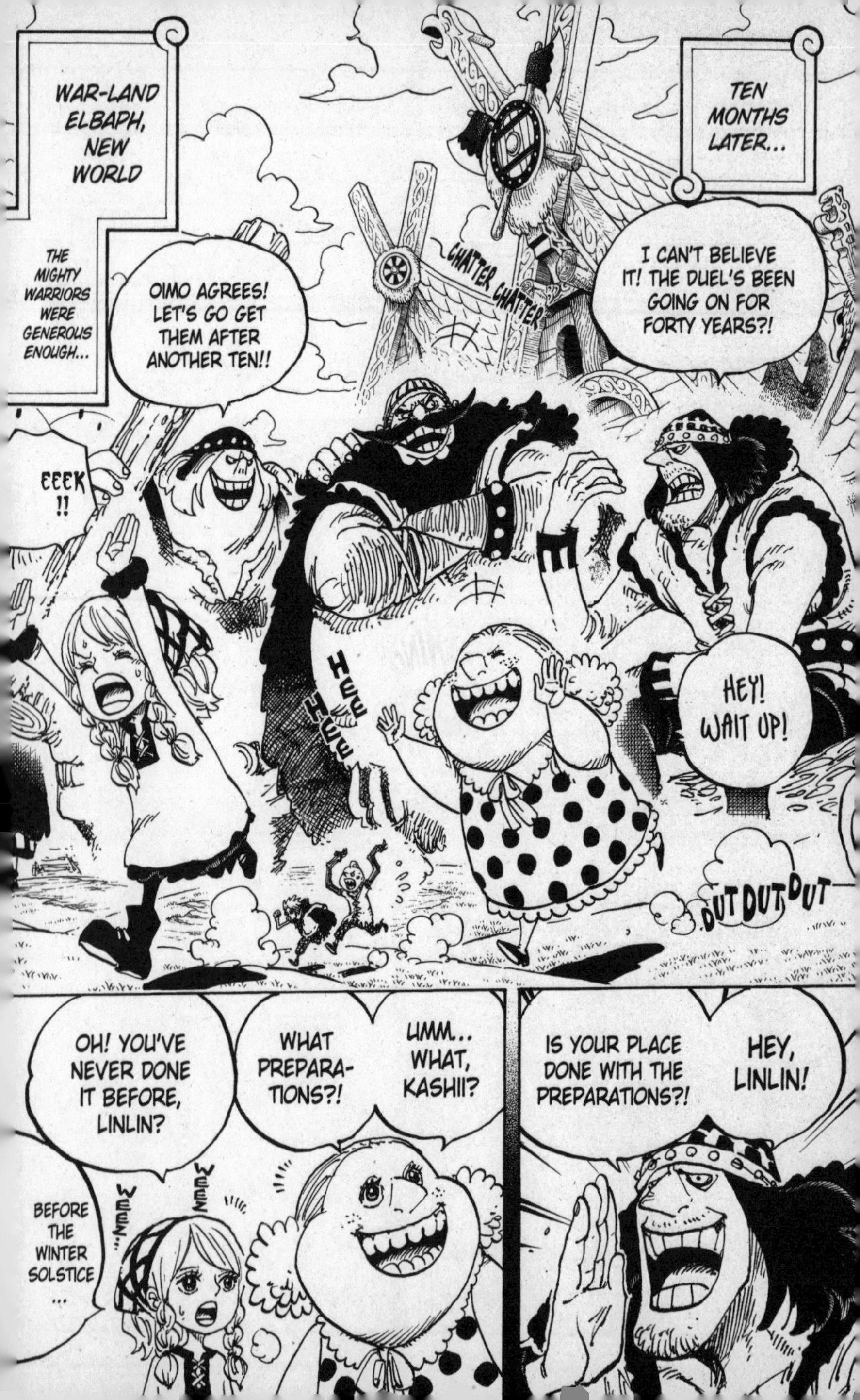
TEN MONTHS LATER...
WAR-LAND ELBAPH, NEW WORLD
I CAN'T BELIEVE IT! THE DUEL'S BEEN GOING ON FOR FORTY YEARS?!
CHATTER CHATTER
OIMO AGREES! LET'S GO GET THEM AFTER ANOTHER TEN!!
THE MIGHTY WARRIORS WERE GENEROUS ENOUGH...
EEEK !!
HEY! WAIT UP!
HEE HEE
DUT DUT DUT
HEY, LINLIN!
IS YOUR PLACE DONE WITH THE PREPARATIONS?!
UMM... WHAT, KASHII?
WHAT PREPARA-TIONS?!
OH! YOU'VE NEVER DONE IT BEFORE, LINLIN?
WEEN
WEEN...
BEFORE THE WINTER SOLSTICE ...

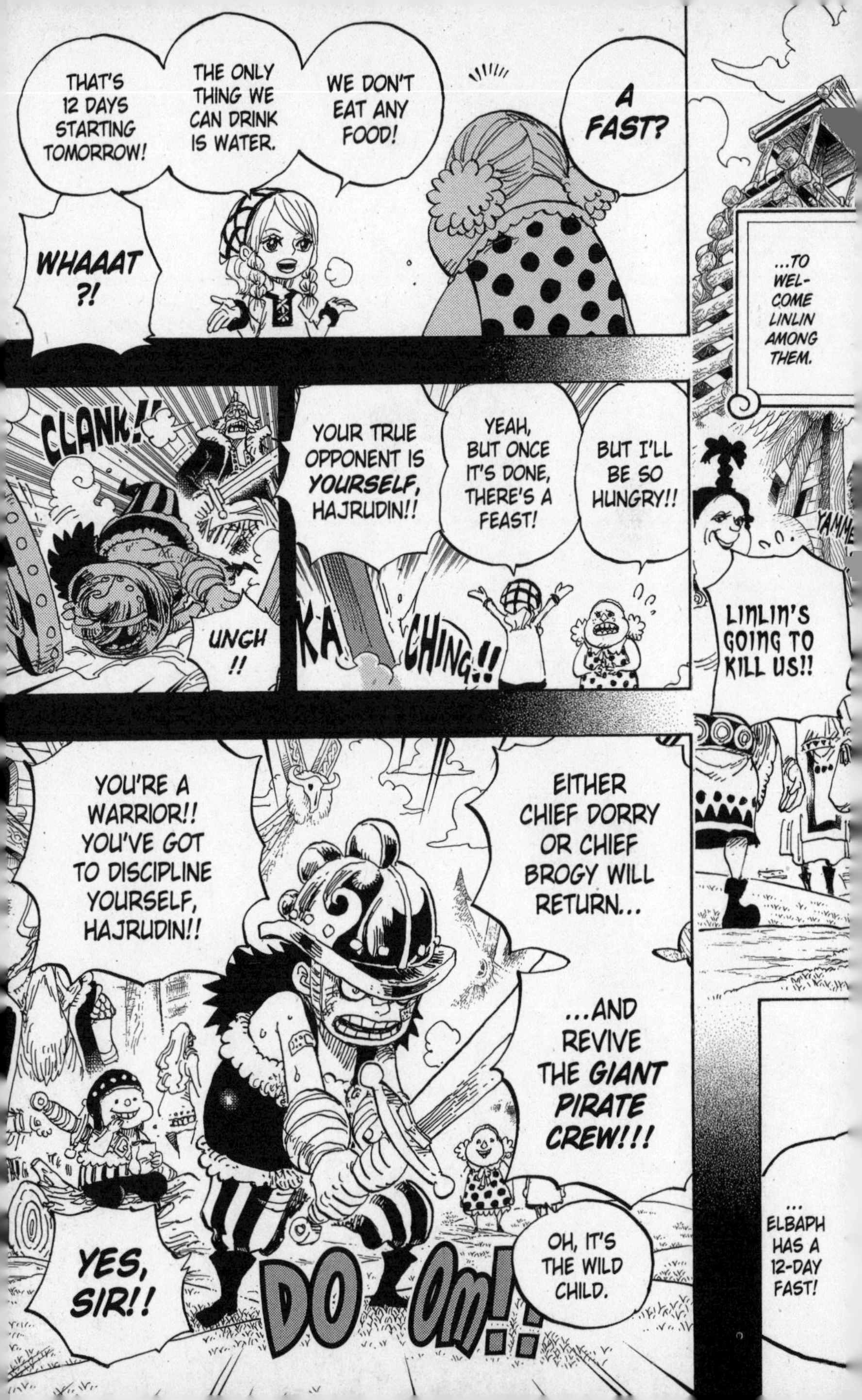
...TO WELCOME LINLIN AMONG THEM.
LINLIN'S GOING TO KILL US!!
... ELBAPH HAS A 12-DAY FAST!
A FAST?
WE DON'T EAT ANY FOOD!
THE ONLY THING WE CAN DRINK IS WATER.
THAT'S 12 DAYS STARTING TOMORROW!
WHAAAT?!
BUT I'LL BE SO HUNGRY!!
YEAH, BUT ONCE IT'S DONE, THERE'S A FEAST!
YOUR TRUE OPPONENT IS YOURSELF, HAJRUDIN!!
KA CHING!!
CLANK!!
UNGH!!
EITHER CHIEF DORRY OR CHIEF BROGY WILL RETURN...
...AND REVIVE THE GIANT PIRATE CREW!!!
OH, IT'S THE WILD CHILD.
YOU'RE A WARRIOR!! YOU'VE GOT TO DISCIPLINE YOURSELF, HAJRUDIN!!
DOOM!!
YES, SIR!!

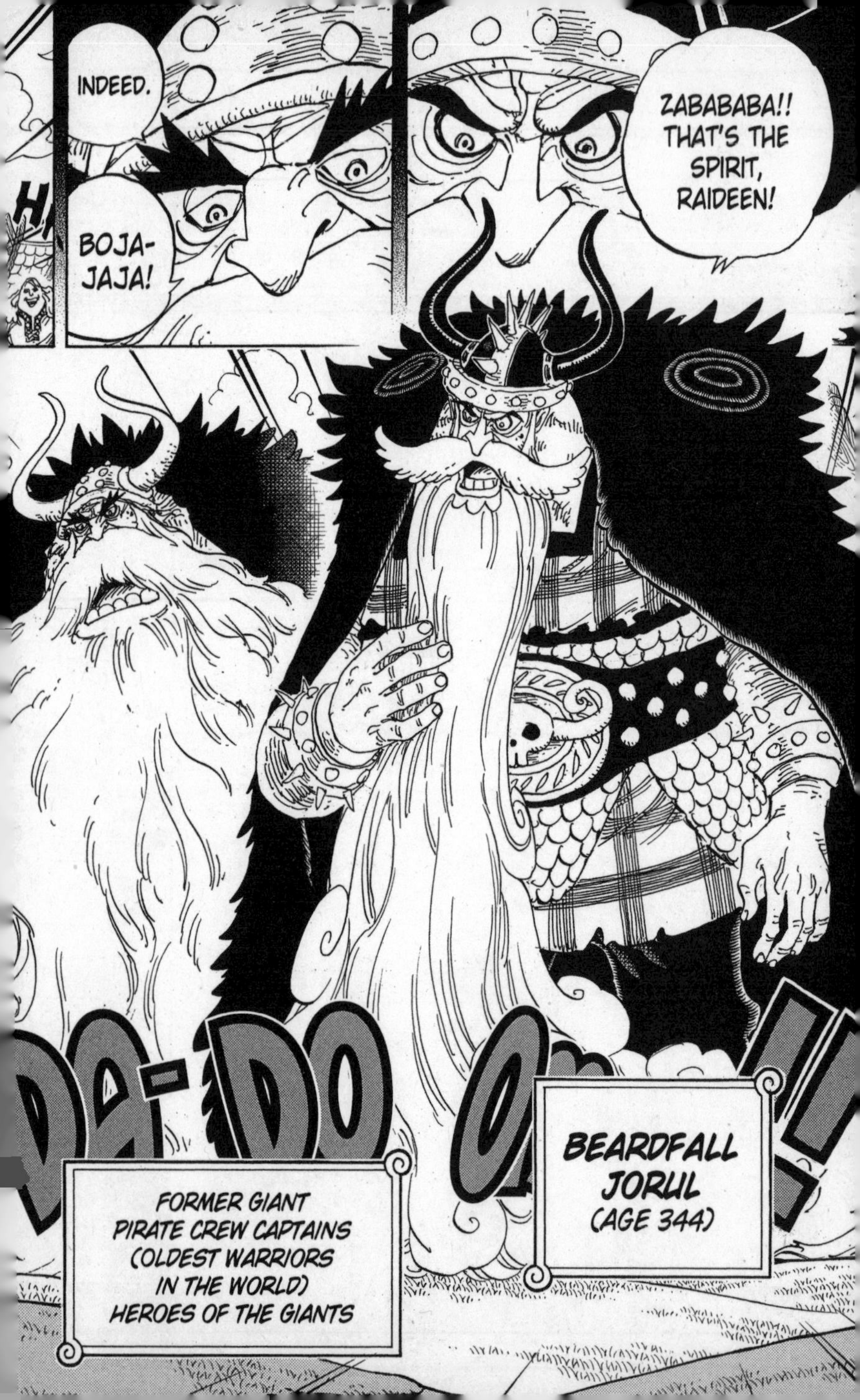
ZABABABA!! THAT'S THE SPIRIT, RAIDEEN!
INDEED.
BOJA-JAJA!
BEARDFALL JORUL (AGE 344)
FORMER GIANT PIRATE CREW CAPTAINS (OLDEST WARRIORS IN THE WORLD) HEROES OF THE GIANTS

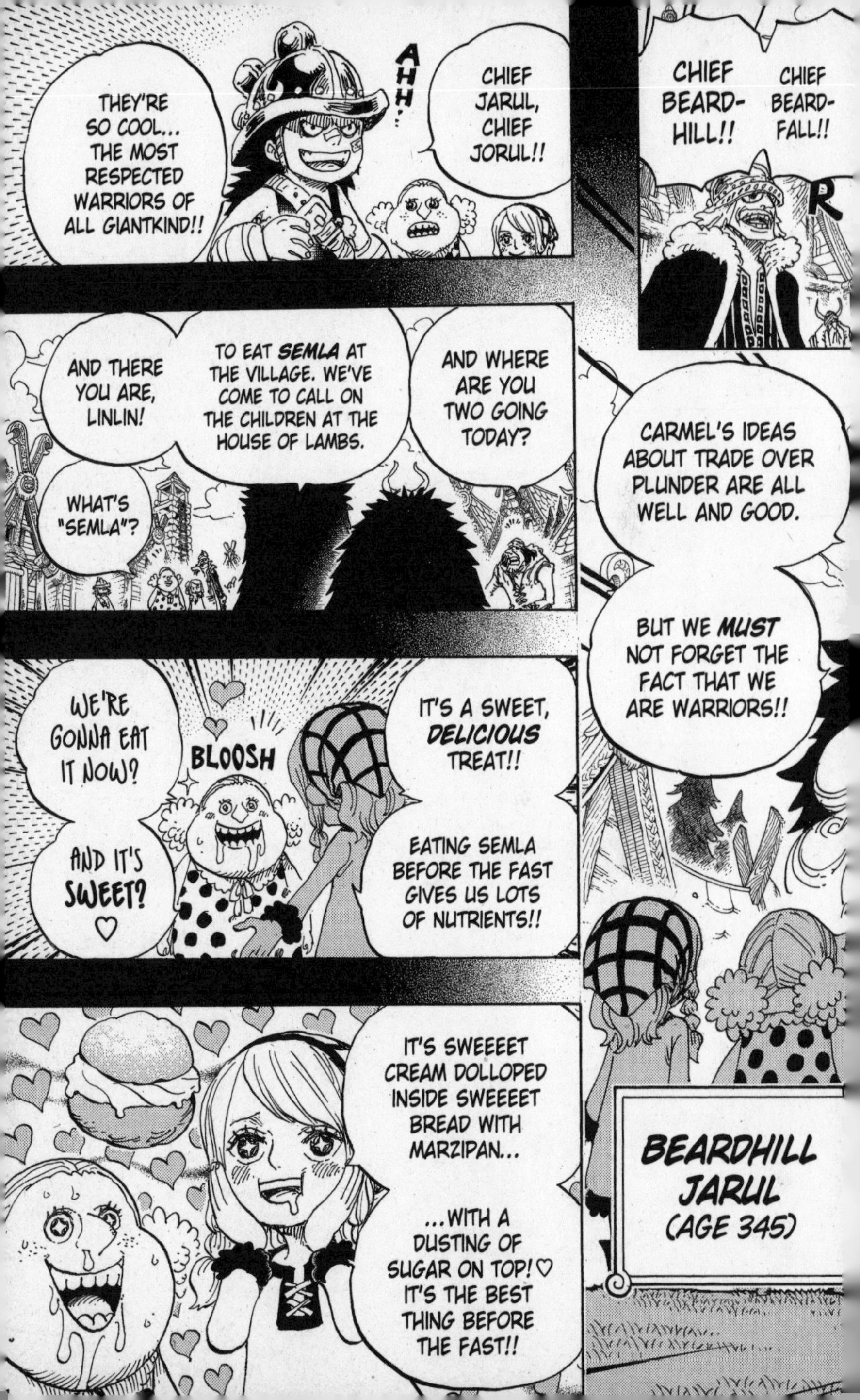
CHIEF BEARD-HILL!!
CHIEF BEARD-FALL!!
R
CHIEF JARUL, CHIEF JORUL!!
AHH
THEY'RE SO COOL... THE MOST RESPECTED WARRIORS OF ALL GIANTKIND!!
CARMEL'S IDEAS ABOUT TRADE OVER PLUNDER ARE ALL WELL AND GOOD.
BUT WE MUST NOT FORGET THE FACT THAT WE ARE WARRIORS!!
BEARDHILL JARUL (AGE 345)
AND WHERE ARE YOU TWO GOING TODAY?
TO EAT SEMLA AT THE VILLAGE. WE'VE COME TO CALL ON THE CHILDREN AT THE HOUSE OF LAMBS.
AND THERE YOU ARE, LINLIN!
WHAT'S "SEMLA"?
IT'S A SWEET, DELICIOUS TREAT!!
EATING SEMLA BEFORE THE FAST GIVES US LOTS OF NUTRIENTS!!
BLOOSH
WE'RE GONNA EAT IT NOW?
AND IT'S SWEET? ♡
IT'S SWEEEET CREAM DOLLOPED INSIDE SWEEEET BREAD WITH MARZIPAN...
...WITH A DUSTING OF SUGAR ON TOP! ♡ IT'S THE BEST THING BEFORE THE FAST!!

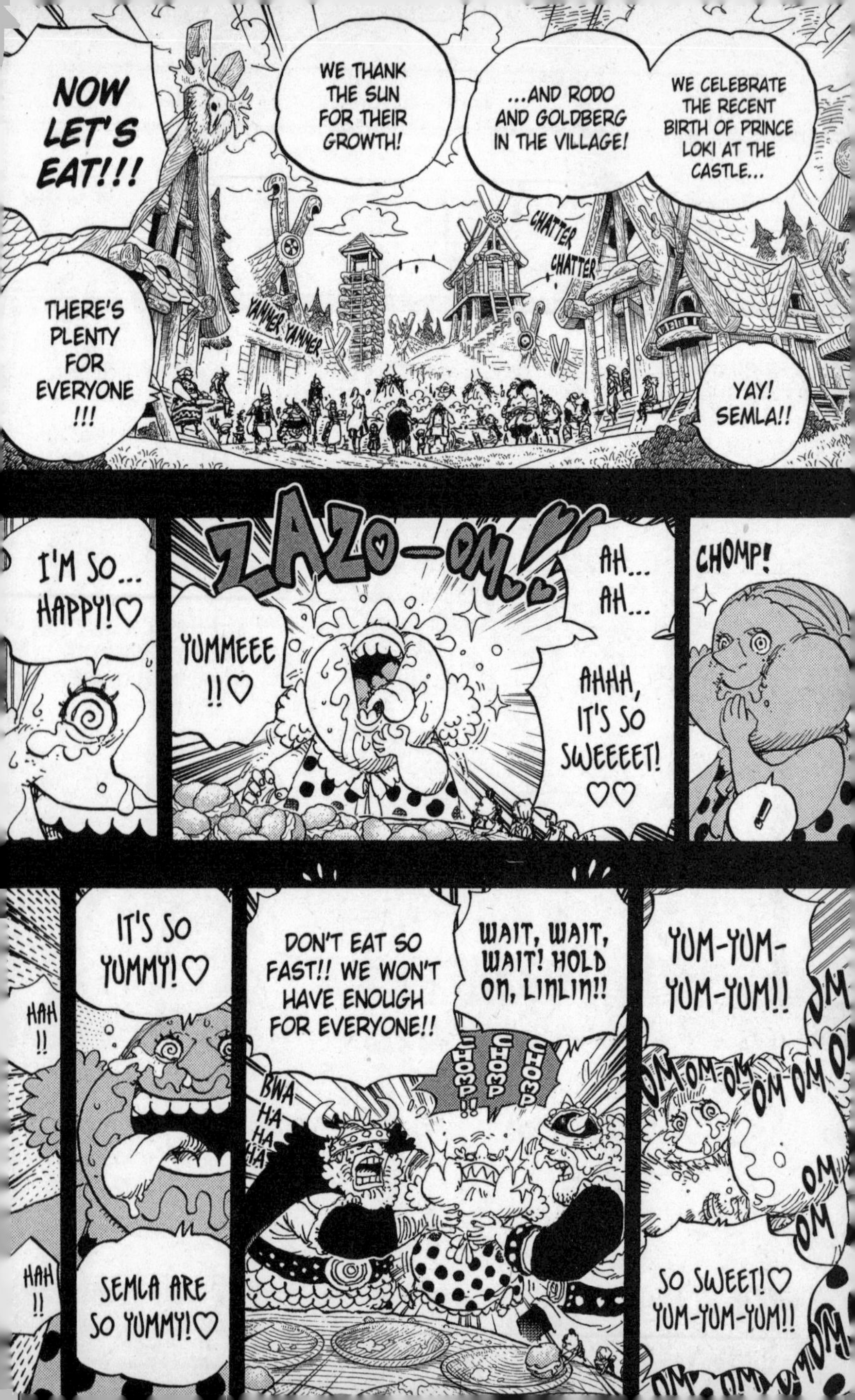
WE CELEBRATE THE RECENT BIRTH OF PRINCE LOKI AT THE CASTLE...
...AND RODO AND GOLDBERG IN THE VILLAGE!
WE THANK THE SUN FOR THEIR GROWTH!
NOW LET'S EAT!!!
CHATTER CHATTER
YAY! SEMLA!!
YAMMER YAMMER
THERE'S PLENTY FOR EVERYONE!!!
CHOMP!
!
ZAZO-OM!!
AH... AH...
AHHH, IT'S SO SWEEEET! ♡♡
YUMMEEE!!♡
I'M SO... HAPPY!♡
YUM-YUM-YUM-YUM!!
OM OM OM OM OM OM
SO SWEET!♡ YUM-YUM-YUM!!
WAIT, WAIT, WAIT! HOLD ON, LINLIN!!
DON'T EAT SO FAST!! WE WON'T HAVE ENOUGH FOR EVERYONE!!
CHOMP CHOMP CHOMP!!
BWA HA HA HA
IT'S SO YUMMY!♡
HAH!!
SEMLA ARE SO YUMMY!♡
HAH!!

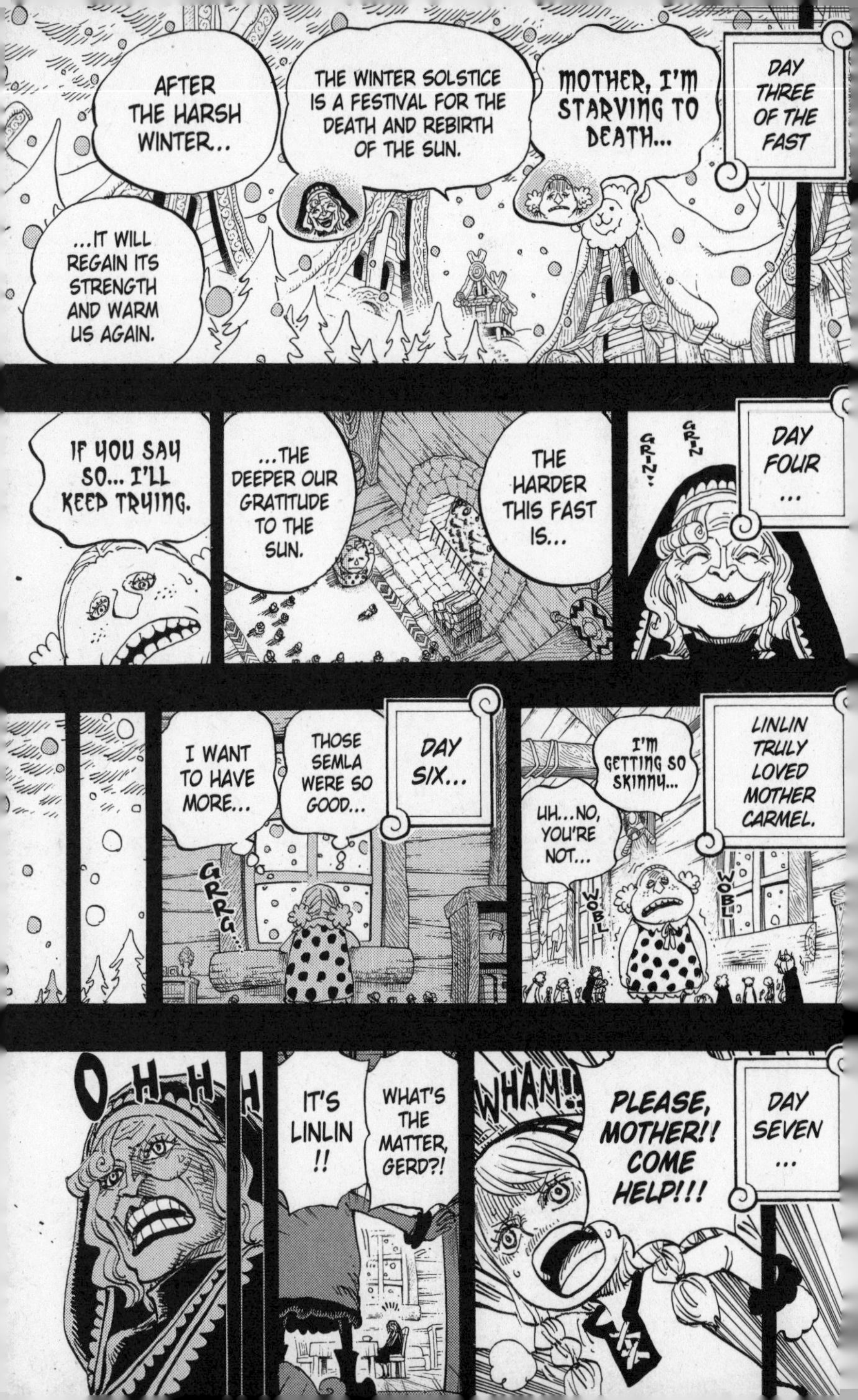
DAY THREE OF THE FAST
MOTHER, I'M STARVING TO DEATH...
THE WINTER SOLSTICE IS A FESTIVAL FOR THE DEATH AND REBIRTH OF THE SUN.
AFTER THE HARSH WINTER...
...IT WILL REGAIN ITS STRENGTH AND WARM US AGAIN.
DAY FOUR ...
GRIN
GRIN
THE HARDER THIS FAST IS...
...THE DEEPER OUR GRATITUDE TO THE SUN.
IF YOU SAY SO... I'LL KEEP TRYING.
LINLIN TRULY LOVED MOTHER CARMEL.
I'M GETTING SO SKINNY...
UH...NO, YOU'RE NOT...
WOBL
WOBL
DAY SIX...
THOSE SEMLA WERE SO GOOD...
I WANT TO HAVE MORE...
GRRG...
DAY SEVEN ...
PLEASE, MOTHER!! COME HELP!!!
WHAM!!
WHAT'S THE MATTER, GERD?!
IT'S LINLIN !!
OHHHH

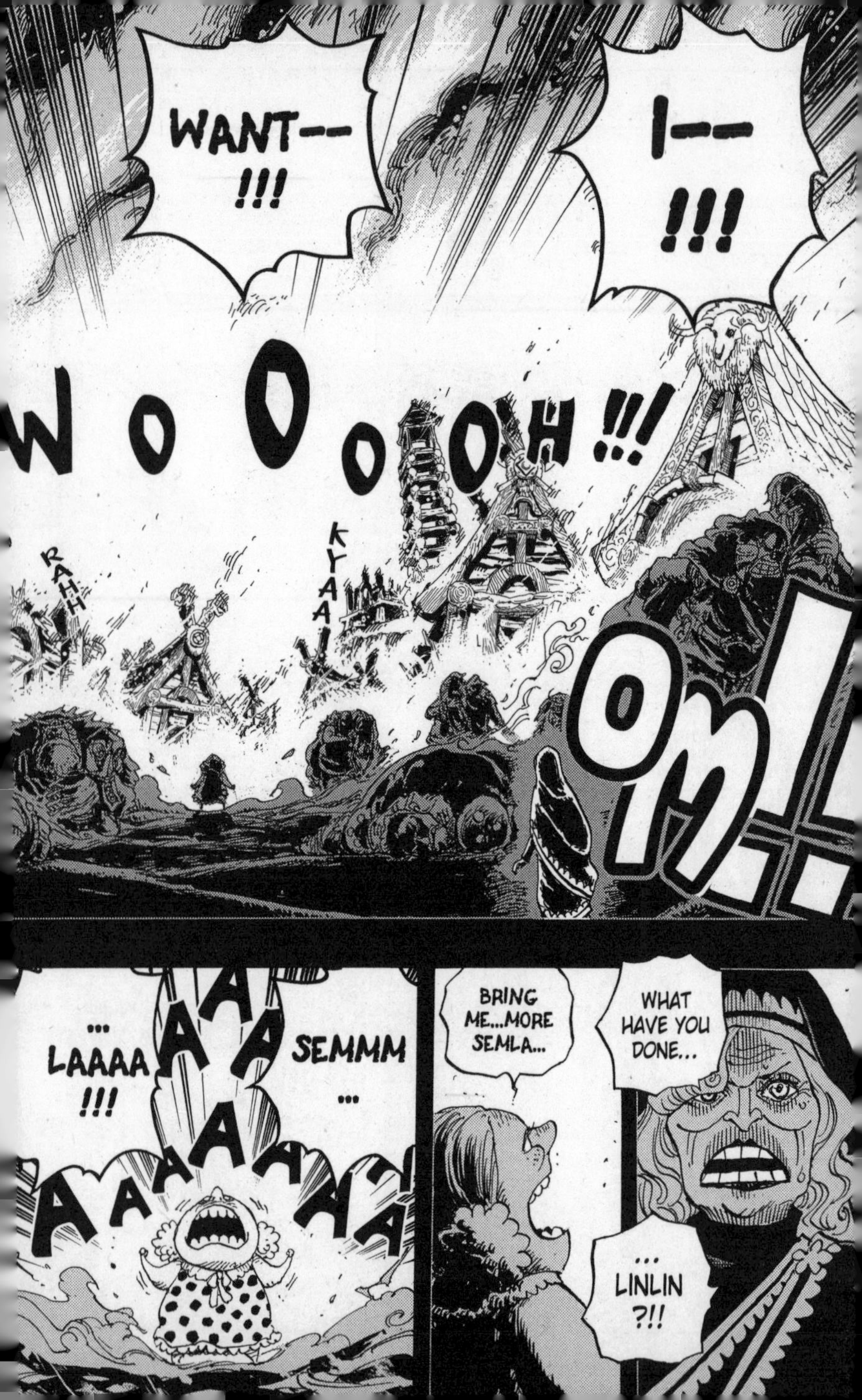

I-- !!!
WANT-- !!!
WOOOOH!!!
KYAAA
RAHHH
WHAT HAVE YOU DONE...
BRING ME...MORE SEMLA...
... LINLIN ?!!
SEMMM ...
AAAAA
... LAAAA !!!
AAAAAAA

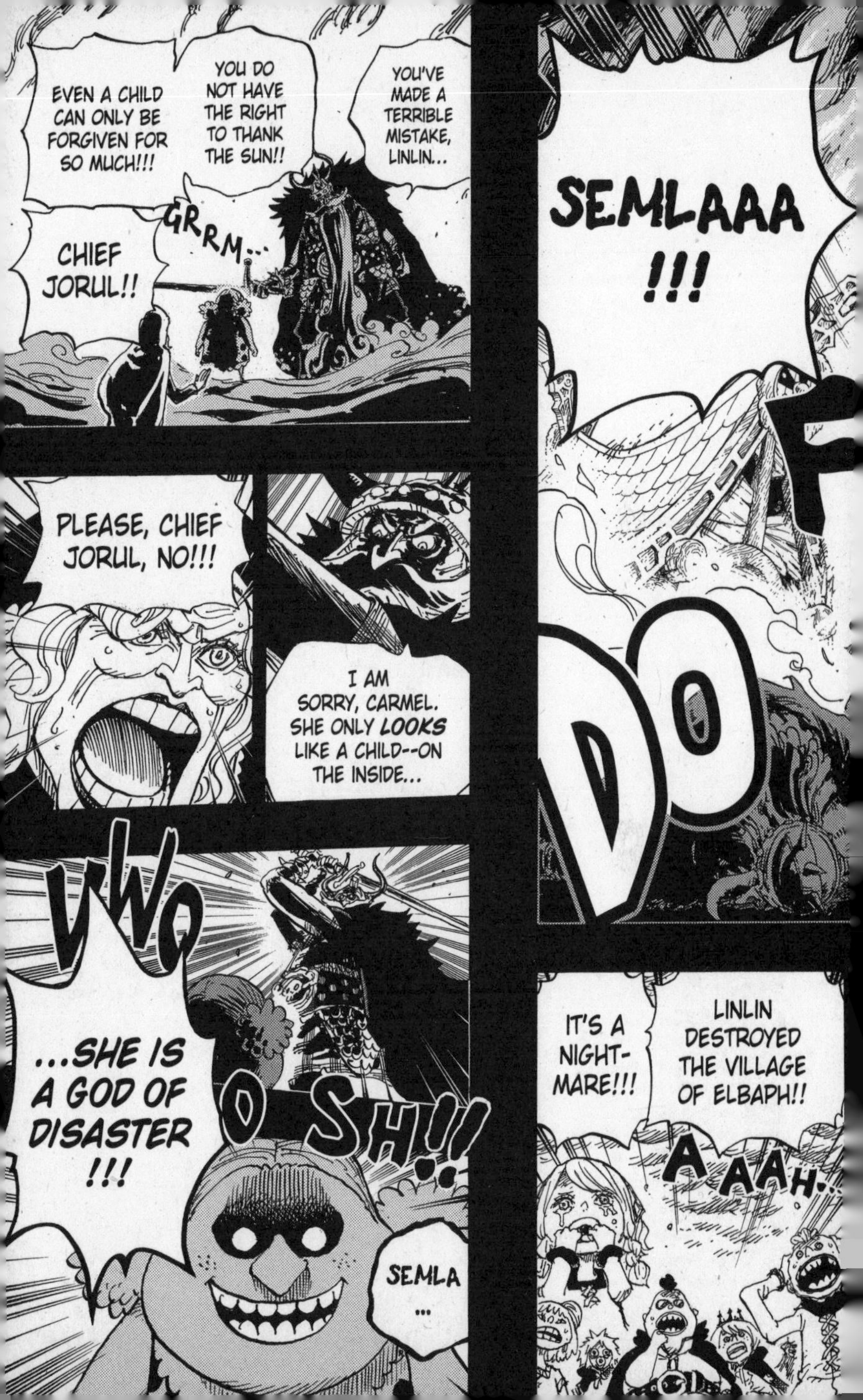
SEMLAAA!!!
DO
LINLIN DESTROYED THE VILLAGE OF ELBAPH!!
IT'S A NIGHT-MARE!!!
AAAH...
YOU'VE MADE A TERRIBLE MISTAKE, LINLIN...
YOU DO NOT HAVE THE RIGHT TO THANK THE SUN!!
EVEN A CHILD CAN ONLY BE FORGIVEN FOR SO MUCH!!!
GRRRM...
CHIEF JORUL!!
I AM SORRY, CARMEL. SHE ONLY *LOOKS* LIKE A CHILD--ON THE INSIDE...
PLEASE, CHIEF JORUL, NO!!!
VWOOSH!!
...SHE IS A GOD OF DISASTER!!!
SEMLA...

SBS Question Corner

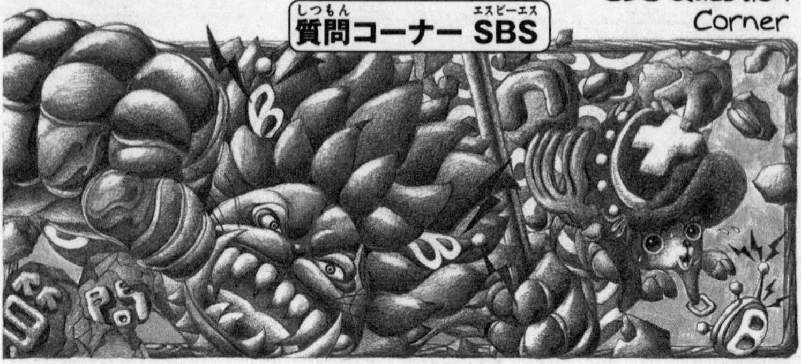
質問コーナー SBS

(Takahisa Fujimoto, Nara)

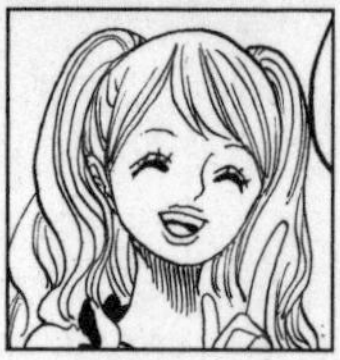

Q: Heso, Odacchi!! Apparently the 25th of every month is "Pudding Day." How about if Charlotte Pudding's birthday is June (*roku* from "Charlotte") 25?

--Dori

A: How about? You want to just "how about" this question? You think you can simply decide the day a person is born that way?! Okay, sure.

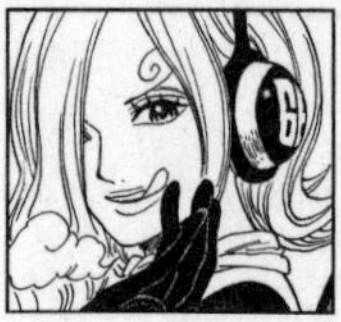

Q: I have a matter to discuss with you, Oda Sensei. Can Reiju's birthday be November 30? That would be 11 (*i-i* onna = pretty woman) 3 (*San*-ji's sister) 0 (*Rei*-ju). Let's just assume that it's settled! Thank you very much for agreeing with me!

--The Morio

A: What?! Hang on a second!! Now you listen to me! That's cool.

Q: Hello, Odacchi! I've been trying to come up with very obscure dates for character birthdays, to help fill in the calendar. Sorry that there are so many.

--Charlotte Senbei

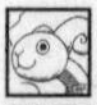
Merry: January 22
(*hi-tsu-ji* = sheep)

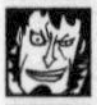
Kin'emon: January 29
(*i-fu-ku* = clothes)

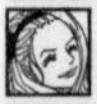
Nojiko: July 25
(*no-ji-ko sounds like "7-2-5"*)

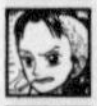
Bellemere: December 3
(Tangerine Day)

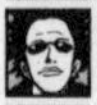
Mr. 5: July 26
(*No-se* = Fancy *Bo-mu* = Nez-Palm)

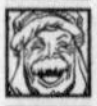
Toh-Toh: June 17
(World Day to Combat Desertification and Drought)

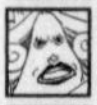
Terracotta: September 25
(*kyu-ji-cho* = stewardess Terra-*ko*-*tta*)

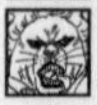
Pekoms: April 11
(Fist Pump Day)

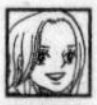
Kaya: August 24
(*Ka-ya jo-i* = Doctor Kaya)

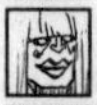
Kanjuro: July 21
(*natsu-no-i-sha* = "summer doctor" rakugo story)

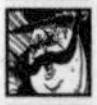
Baron Tamago: May 14
(egg = 5-7-7 in the alphabet)

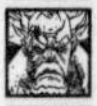
King Riku: June 27
(Speech Day)

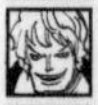
Blue Gilly: November 27
(Bruce Lee's birthday)

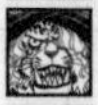
Pedro: June 16 (*ki* = tree, "Treetop" = *ka* before *ki* is the 6th character in hiragana, plus Pe-*do*-*ro* = 16)

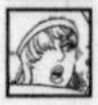
Smoothie: October 12
(*Ju*-ice *dai-jin* = minister)

A: Whoaaaaa!! Hang on, hang on, hang on!! You can't just throw a whole pile of birthdays at me...and just expect me...to decline them!

Chapter 867:

HAPPY BIRTHDAY

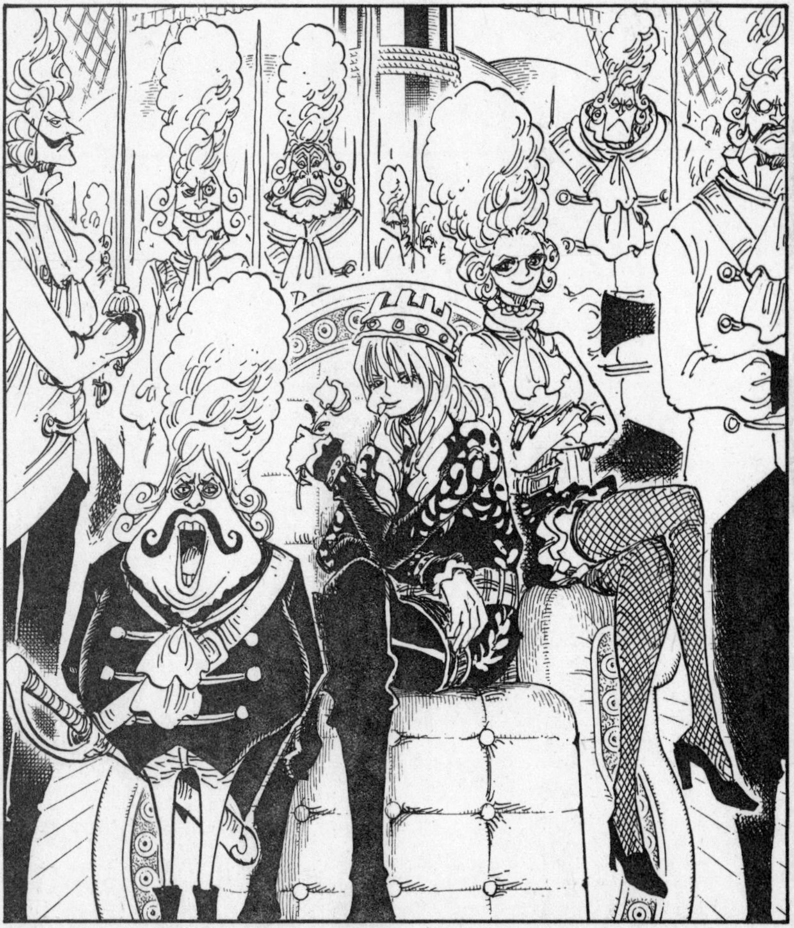

THE SAGA OF THE SELF-PROCLAIMED STRAW HAT FLEET,
VOL. 4, CAVENDISH: "A LIFE OF MISERY IN EXILE FOR BEING TOO POPULAR, WITH ONLY 74 SERVANTS AND 500 MILLION BERRIES"

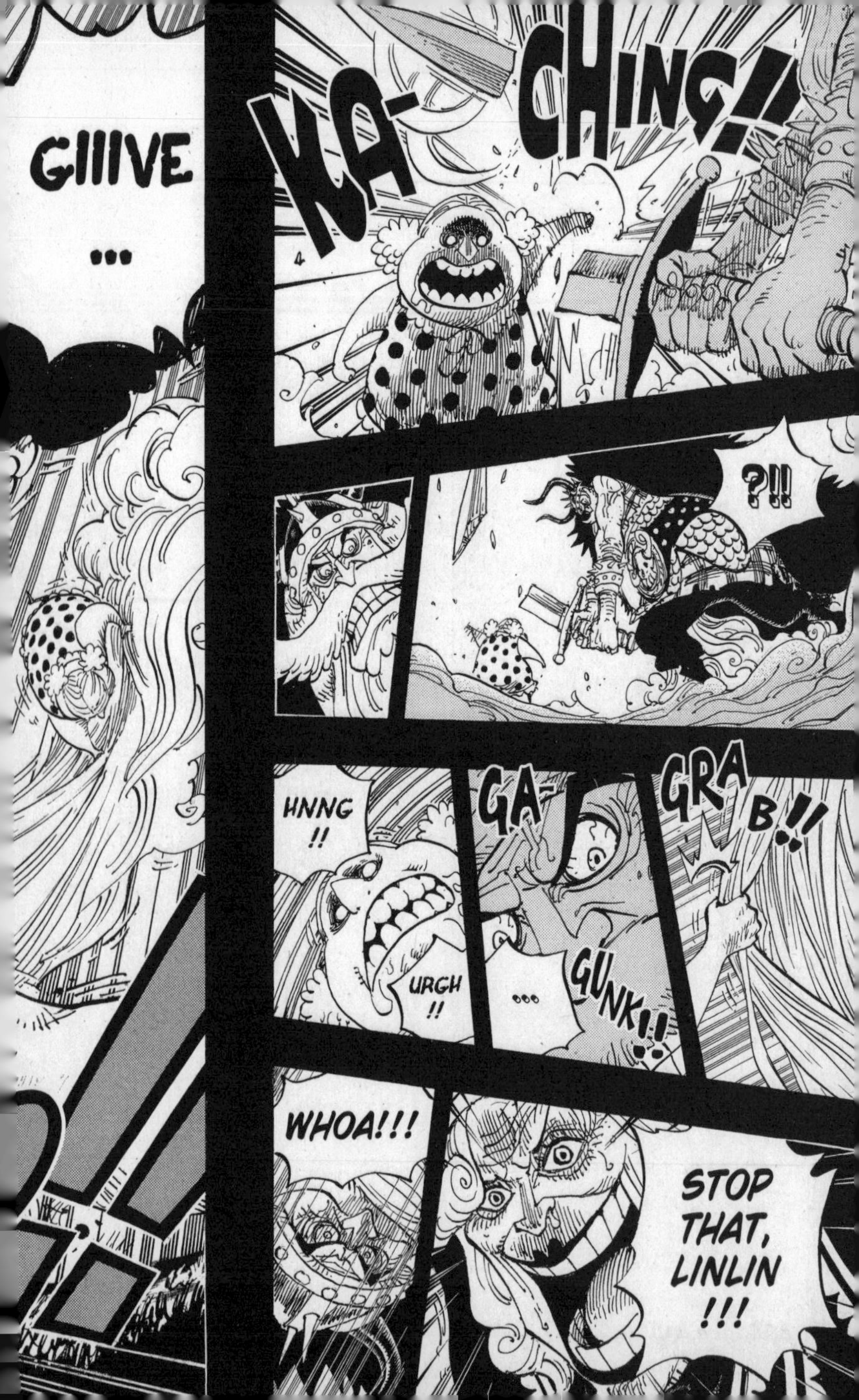
KA-CHING!!
?!!
GRAB!!
GA-GUNK!!
...
HNNG!!
URGH!!
STOP THAT, LINLIN!!!
WHOA!!!
GIIIVE ...

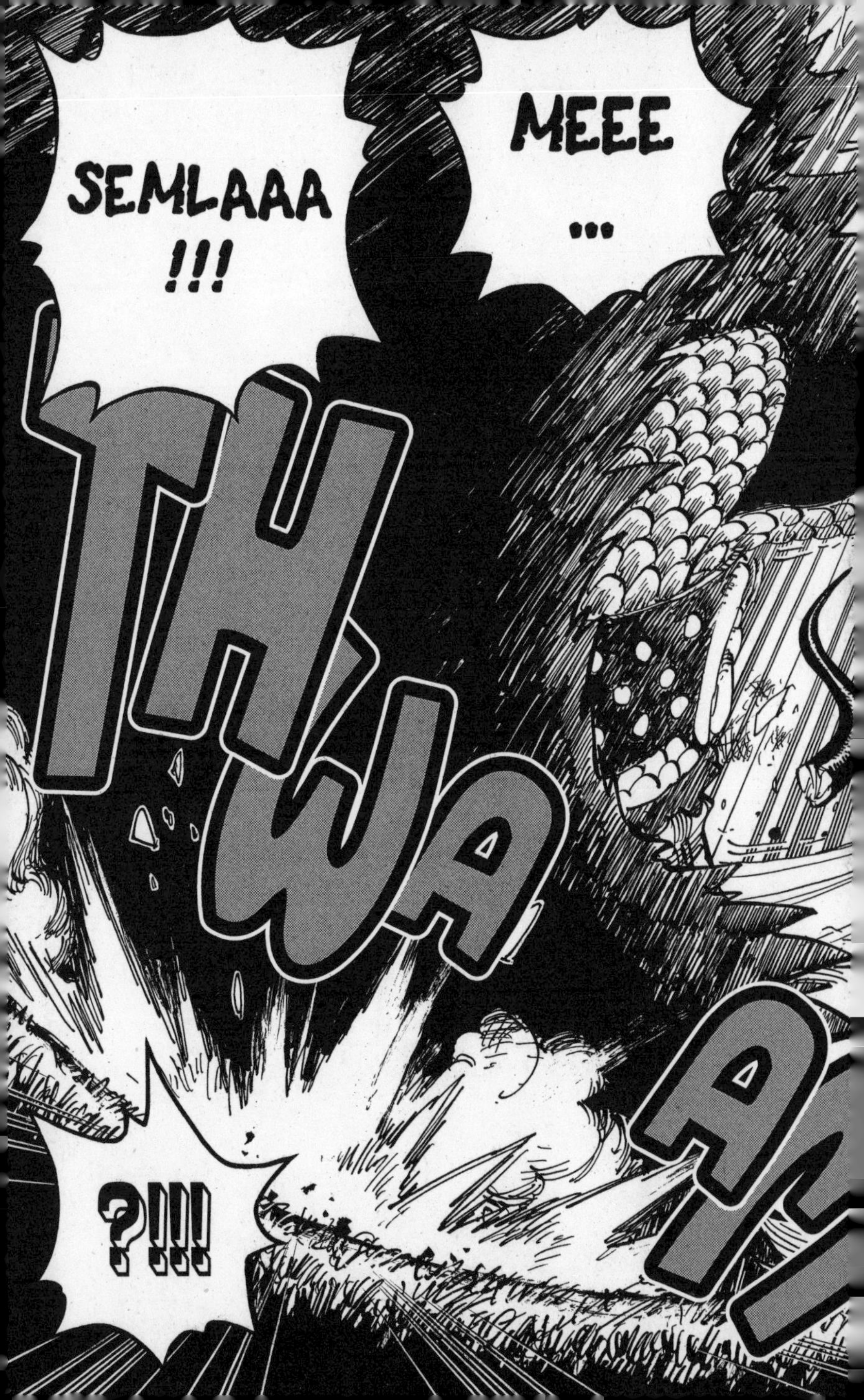
MEEE ...
SEMLAAA !!!
THWAA
?!!!

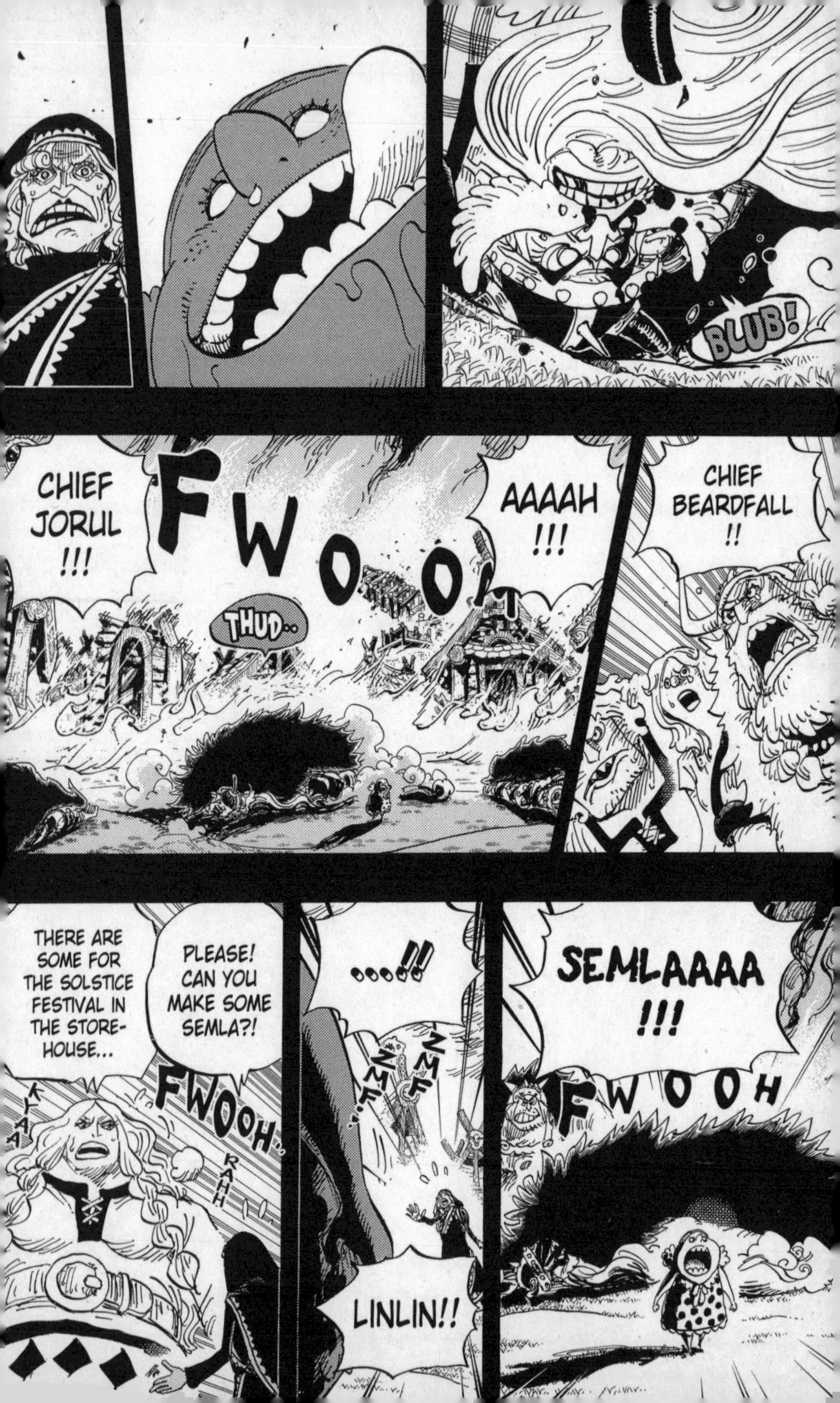
BLUB!
CHIEF BEARDFALL !!
AAAAH !!!
FWOOM
CHIEF JORUL !!!
THUD..
SEMLAAAA !!!
FWOOH
...!!
ZMF
ZMF
LINLIN!!
PLEASE! CAN YOU MAKE SOME SEMLA?!
THERE ARE SOME FOR THE SOLSTICE FESTIVAL IN THE STORE-HOUSE...
FWOOH..
KYAA
RAHH

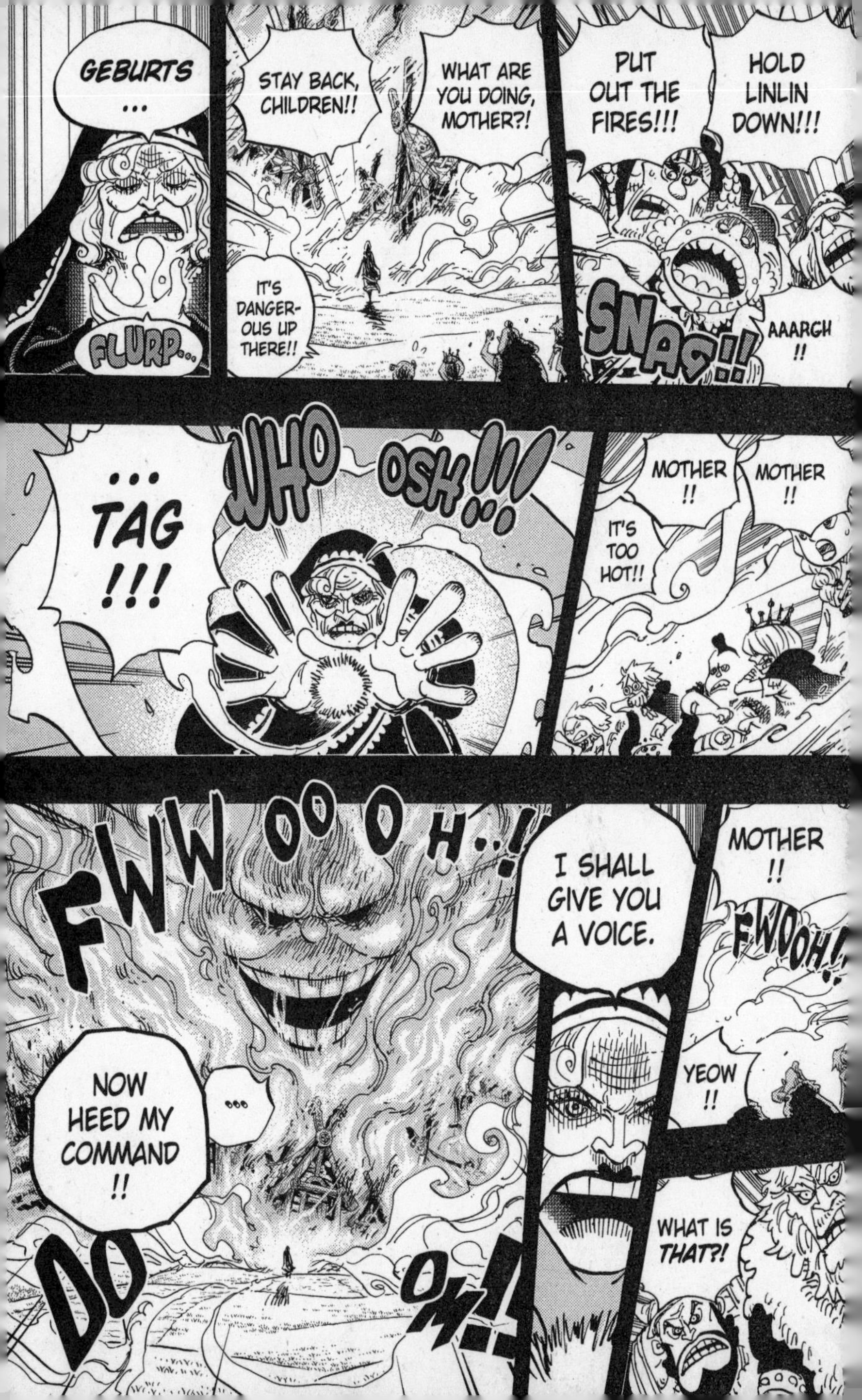
HOLD LINLIN DOWN!!!
PUT OUT THE FIRES!!!
AAARGH!!
SNAG!!
WHAT ARE YOU DOING, MOTHER?!
STAY BACK, CHILDREN!!
IT'S DANGER-OUS UP THERE!!
GEBURTS...
FLURP...
MOTHER!!
MOTHER!!
IT'S TOO HOT!!
WHOOSH!!!
...TAG!!!
MOTHER!!
FWOOH!!
YEOW!!
WHAT IS THAT?!
I SHALL GIVE YOU A VOICE.
FWWOOOH..!!
...
NOW HEED MY COMMAND!!
DOOM!!

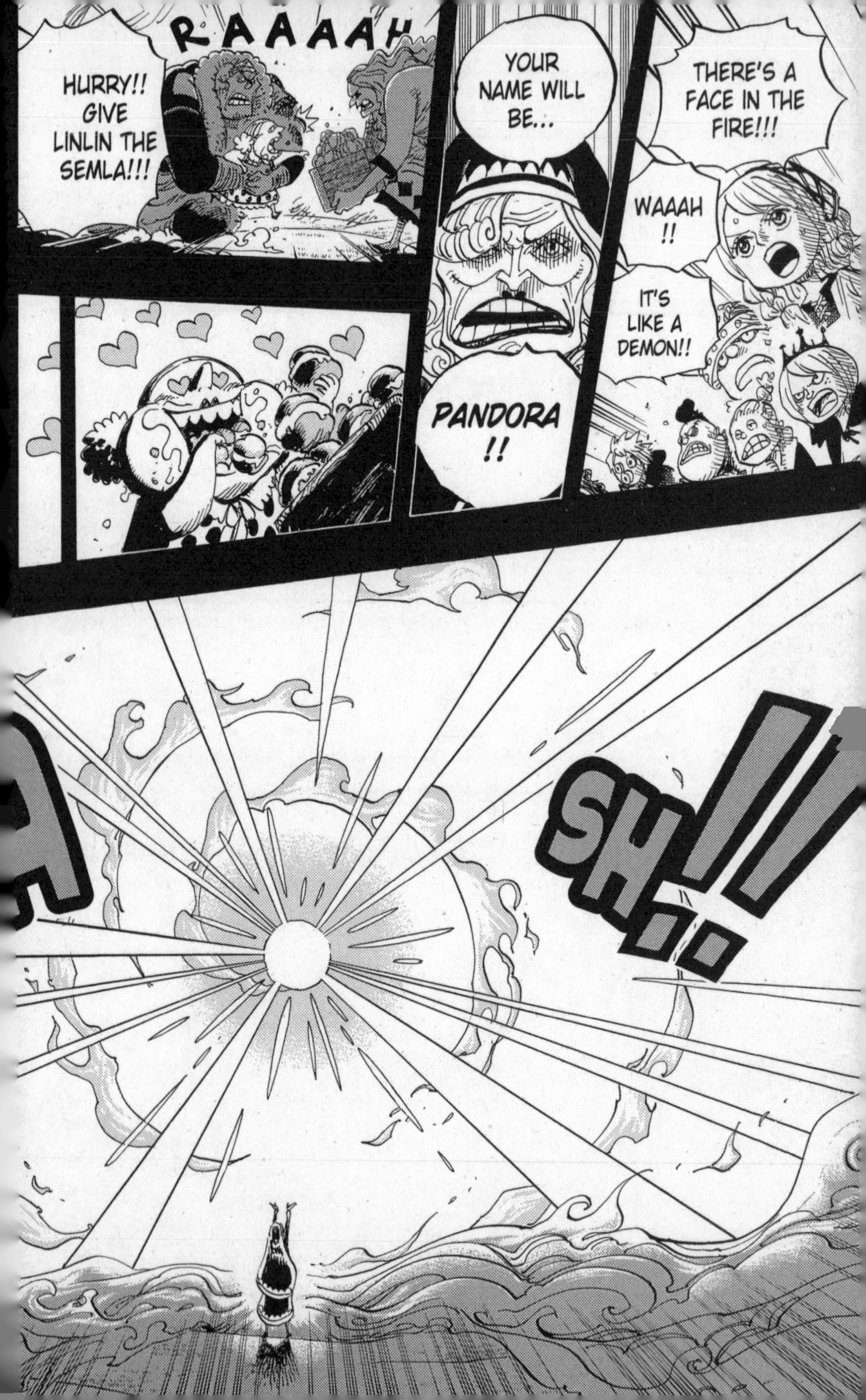
THERE'S A FACE IN THE FIRE!!!
WAAAH !!
IT'S LIKE A DEMON!!
YOUR NAME WILL BE...
PANDORA !!
RAAAAH
HURRY!! GIVE LINLIN THE SEMLA!!!
SH..!!

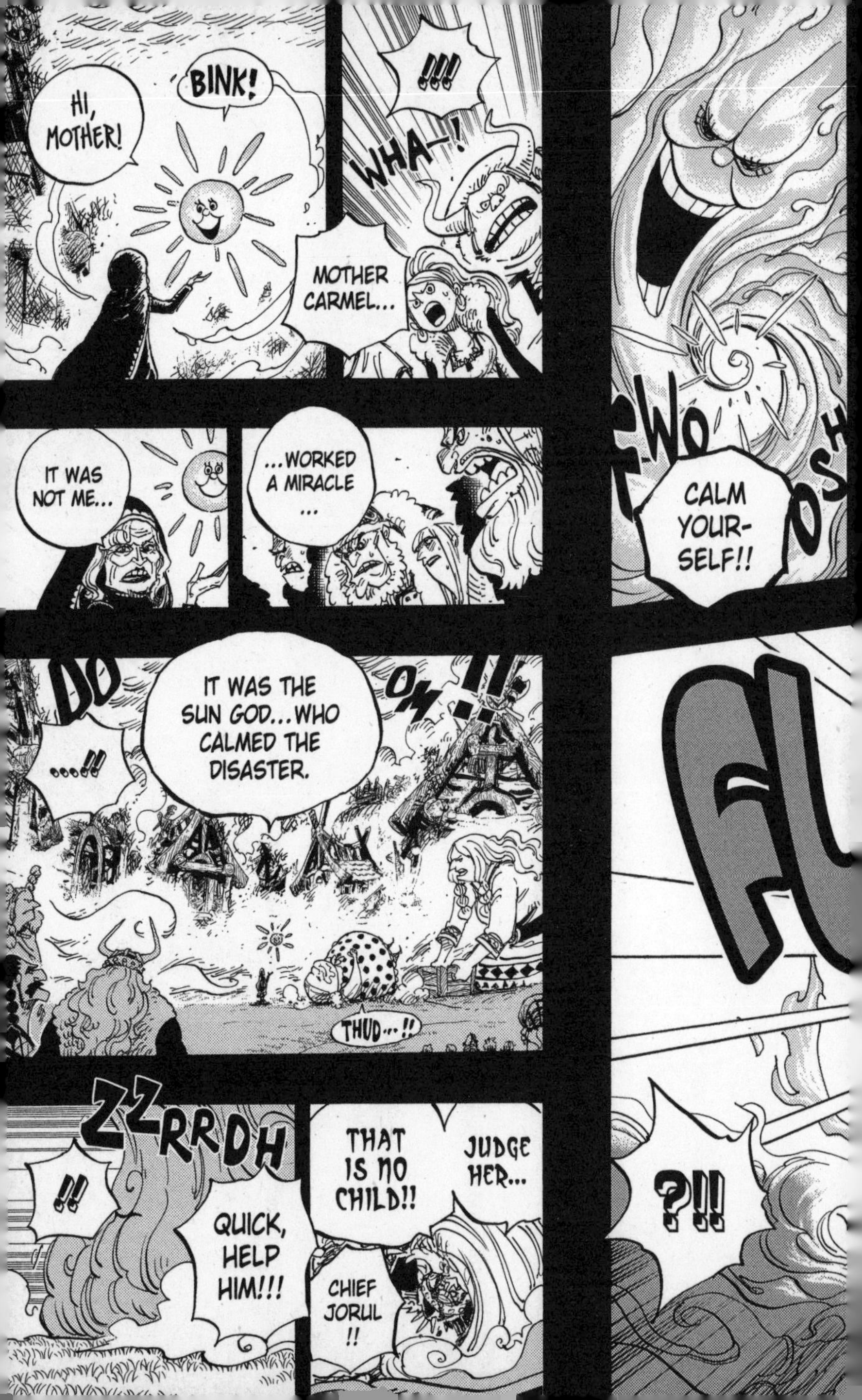
WOOSH
CALM YOURSELF!!
FU
?!!
!!!
WHA—!
MOTHER CARMEL...
BINK!
HI, MOTHER!
...WORKED A MIRACLE ...
IT WAS NOT ME...
DOOM!!
...!!
IT WAS THE SUN GOD...WHO CALMED THE DISASTER.
THUD...!!
JUDGE HER...
THAT IS NO CHILD!!
CHIEF JORUL!!
ZZRRRDH
!!
QUICK, HELP HIM!!!

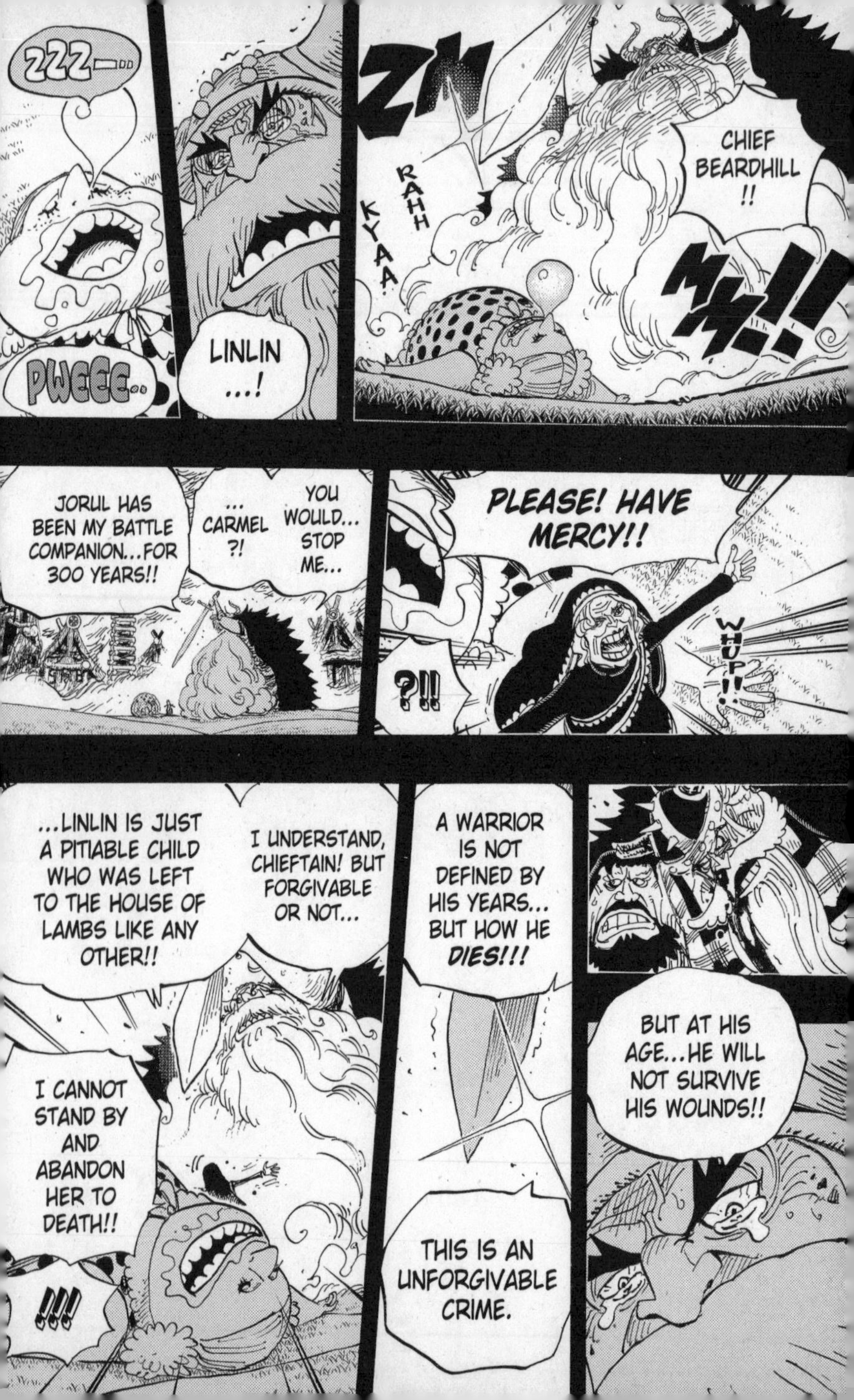

ZN
CHIEF BEARDHILL !!
RAHH
KYAA
LINLIN ...!
ZZZ—...
PWEEE...
PLEASE! HAVE MERCY!!
WHUP!!
?!!
YOU WOULD... STOP ME...
... CARMEL ?!
JORUL HAS BEEN MY BATTLE COMPANION...FOR 300 YEARS!!
BUT AT HIS AGE...HE WILL NOT SURVIVE HIS WOUNDS!!
A WARRIOR IS NOT DEFINED BY HIS YEARS... BUT HOW HE DIES!!!
THIS IS AN UNFORGIVABLE CRIME.
I UNDERSTAND, CHIEFTAIN! BUT FORGIVABLE OR NOT...
...LINLIN IS JUST A PITIABLE CHILD WHO WAS LEFT TO THE HOUSE OF LAMBS LIKE ANY OTHER!!
I CANNOT STAND BY AND ABANDON HER TO DEATH!!
!!!

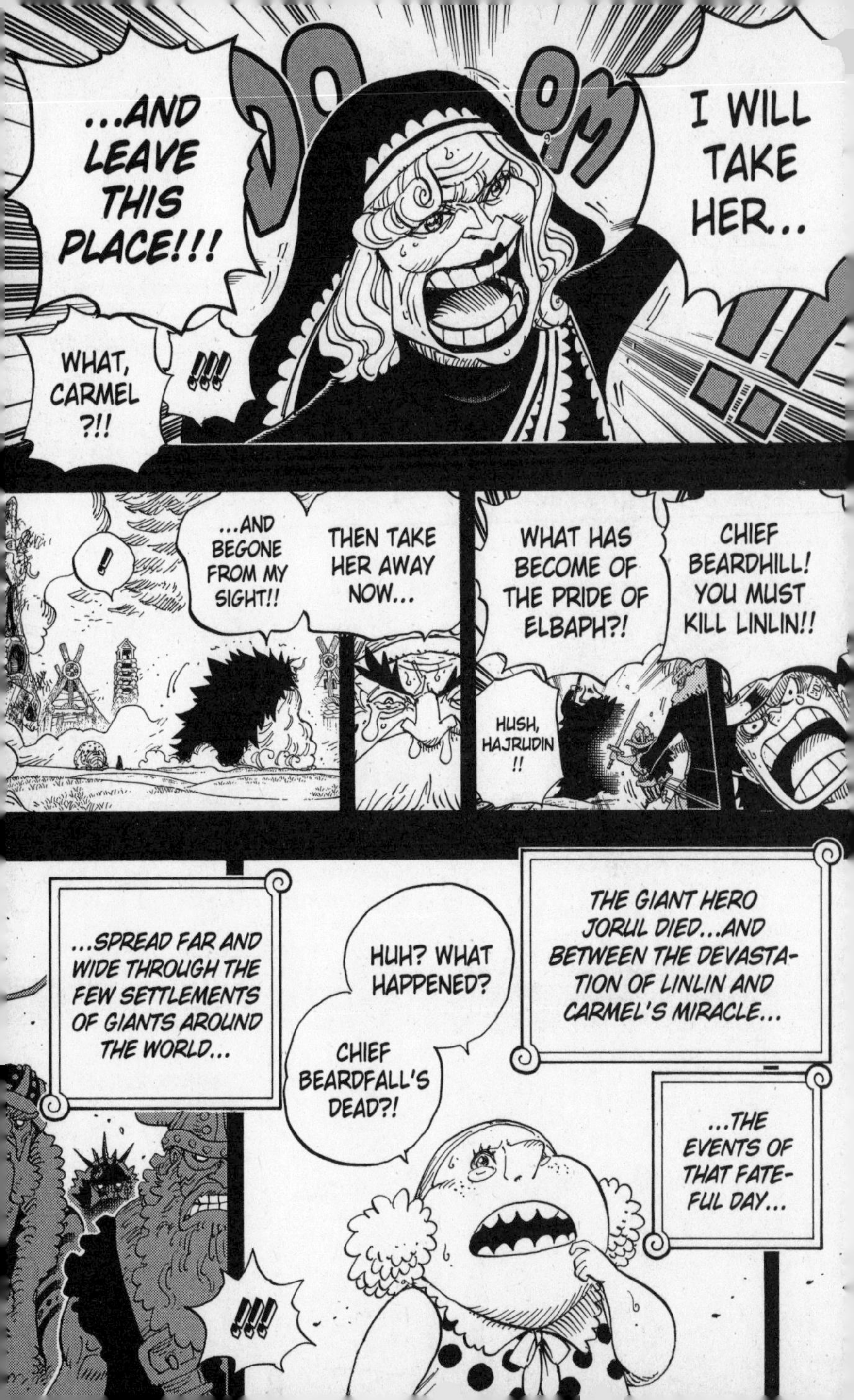
I WILL TAKE HER...
...AND LEAVE THIS PLACE!!!
!!!
WHAT, CARMEL?!!
CHIEF BEARDHILL! YOU MUST KILL LINLIN!!
WHAT HAS BECOME OF THE PRIDE OF ELBAPH?!
HUSH, HAJRUDIN!!
THEN TAKE HER AWAY NOW...
...AND BEGONE FROM MY SIGHT!!
!
THE GIANT HERO JORUL DIED...AND BETWEEN THE DEVASTATION OF LINLIN AND CARMEL'S MIRACLE...
...THE EVENTS OF THAT FATEFUL DAY...
HUH? WHAT HAPPENED?
CHIEF BEARDFALL'S DEAD?!
...SPREAD FAR AND WIDE THROUGH THE FEW SETTLEMENTS OF GIANTS AROUND THE WORLD...
!!!

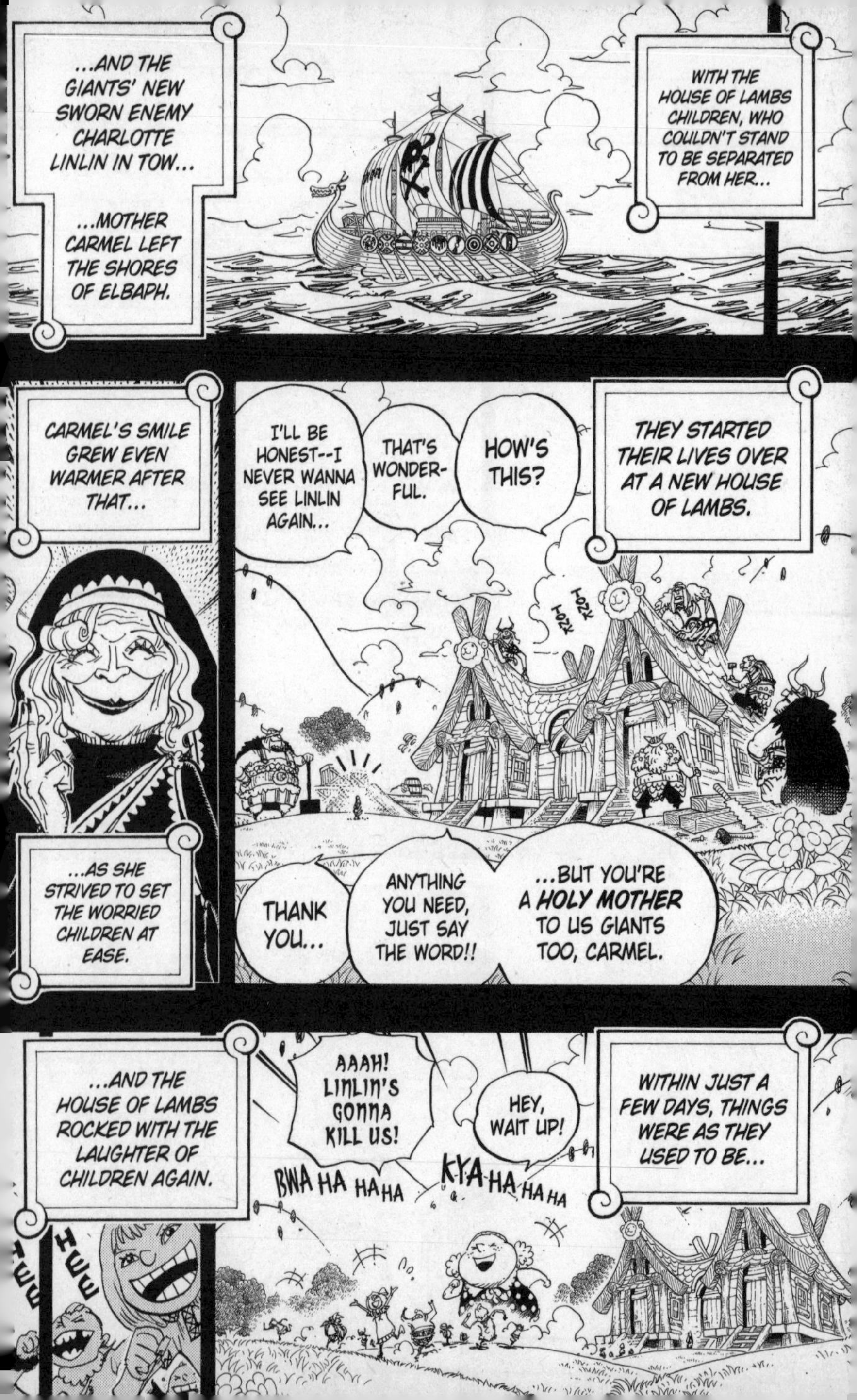
WITH THE HOUSE OF LAMBS CHILDREN, WHO COULDN'T STAND TO BE SEPARATED FROM HER...
...AND THE GIANTS' NEW SWORN ENEMY CHARLOTTE LINLIN IN TOW...
...MOTHER CARMEL LEFT THE SHORES OF ELBAPH.
THEY STARTED THEIR LIVES OVER AT A NEW HOUSE OF LAMBS.
HOW'S THIS?
THAT'S WONDERFUL.
I'LL BE HONEST--I NEVER WANNA SEE LINLIN AGAIN...
TONK TONK
...BUT YOU'RE A **HOLY MOTHER** TO US GIANTS TOO, CARMEL.
ANYTHING YOU NEED, JUST SAY THE WORD!!
THANK YOU...
CARMEL'S SMILE GREW EVEN WARMER AFTER THAT...
...AS SHE STRIVED TO SET THE WORRIED CHILDREN AT EASE.
WITHIN JUST A FEW DAYS, THINGS WERE AS THEY USED TO BE...
HEY, WAIT UP!
AAAH! LINLIN'S GONNA KILL US!
KYA HA HA HA
BWA HA HA HA
...AND THE HOUSE OF LAMBS ROCKED WITH THE LAUGHTER OF CHILDREN AGAIN.

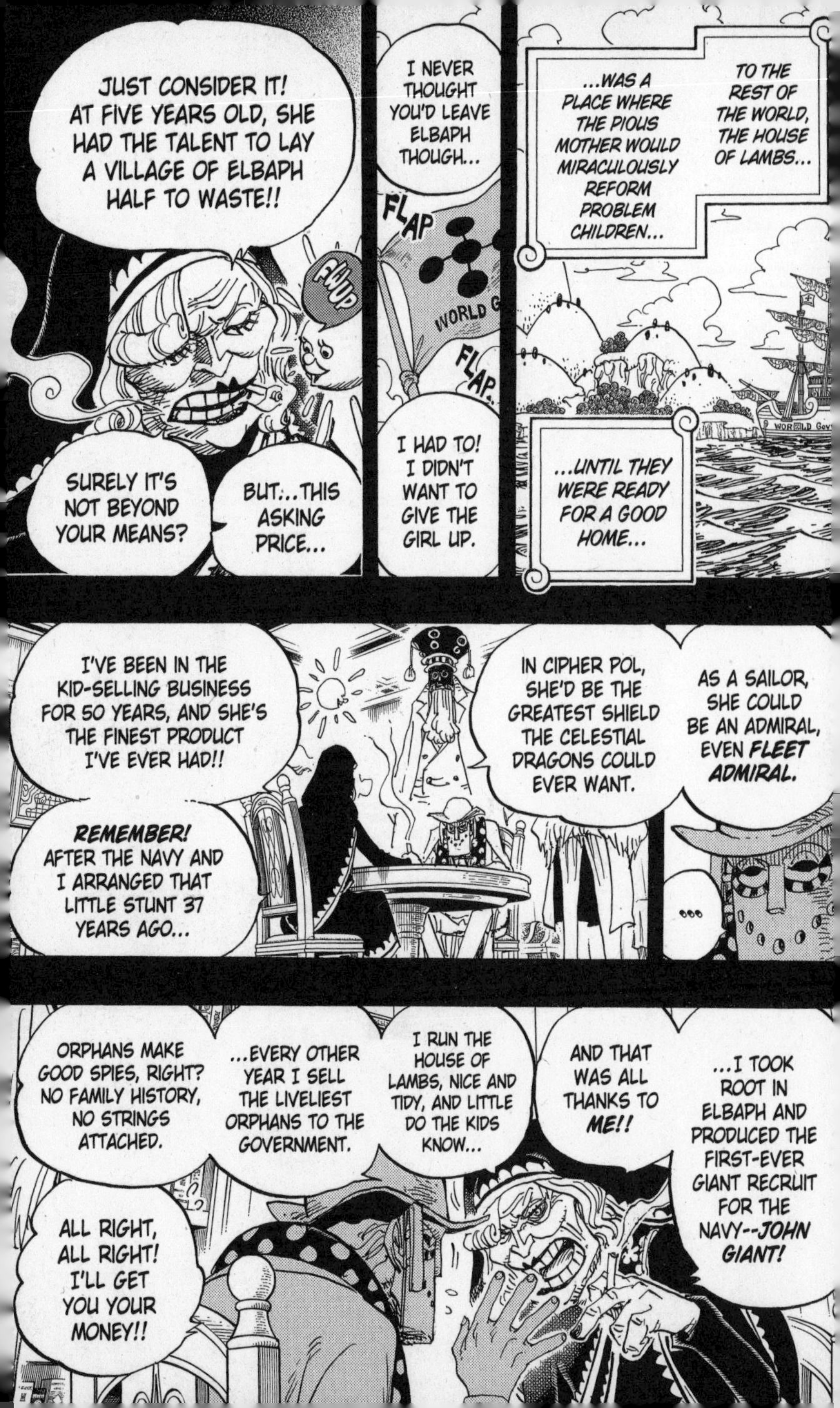
TO THE REST OF THE WORLD, THE HOUSE OF LAMBS...
...WAS A PLACE WHERE THE PIOUS MOTHER WOULD MIRACULOUSLY REFORM PROBLEM CHILDREN...
...UNTIL THEY WERE READY FOR A GOOD HOME...
I NEVER THOUGHT YOU'D LEAVE ELBAPH THOUGH...
FLAP
WORLD G
FLAP
I HAD TO! I DIDN'T WANT TO GIVE THE GIRL UP.
JUST CONSIDER IT! AT FIVE YEARS OLD, SHE HAD THE TALENT TO LAY A VILLAGE OF ELBAPH HALF TO WASTE!!
FWUP
BUT...THIS ASKING PRICE...
SURELY IT'S NOT BEYOND YOUR MEANS?
AS A SAILOR, SHE COULD BE AN ADMIRAL, EVEN ***FLEET ADMIRAL.***
...
IN CIPHER POL, SHE'D BE THE GREATEST SHIELD THE CELESTIAL DRAGONS COULD EVER WANT.
I'VE BEEN IN THE KID-SELLING BUSINESS FOR 50 YEARS, AND SHE'S THE FINEST PRODUCT I'VE EVER HAD!!
REMEMBER! AFTER THE NAVY AND I ARRANGED THAT LITTLE STUNT 37 YEARS AGO...
...I TOOK ROOT IN ELBAPH AND PRODUCED THE FIRST-EVER GIANT RECRUIT FOR THE NAVY--***JOHN GIANT!***
AND THAT WAS ALL THANKS TO ***ME!!***
I RUN THE HOUSE OF LAMBS, NICE AND TIDY, AND LITTLE DO THE KIDS KNOW...
...EVERY OTHER YEAR I SELL THE LIVELIEST ORPHANS TO THE GOVERNMENT.
ORPHANS MAKE GOOD SPIES, RIGHT? NO FAMILY HISTORY, NO STRINGS ATTACHED.
ALL RIGHT, ALL RIGHT! I'LL GET YOU YOUR MONEY!!

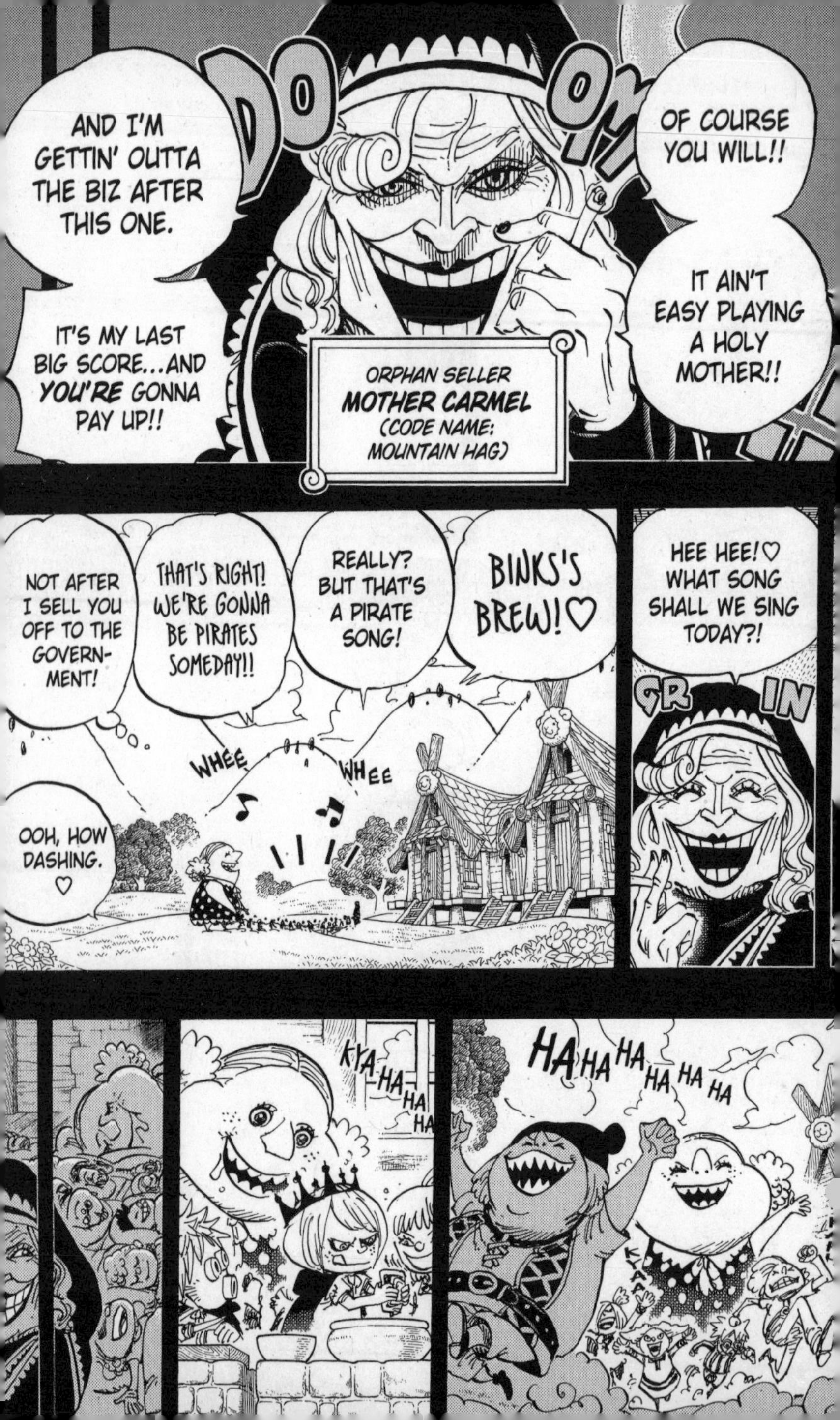

OF COURSE YOU WILL!!
DOOM
AND I'M GETTIN' OUTTA THE BIZ AFTER THIS ONE.
IT AIN'T EASY PLAYING A HOLY MOTHER!!
ORPHAN SELLER
MOTHER CARMEL
(CODE NAME: MOUNTAIN HAG)
IT'S MY LAST BIG SCORE...AND ***YOU'RE*** GONNA PAY UP!!
HEE HEE!♡ WHAT SONG SHALL WE SING TODAY?!
GRIN
BINKS'S BREW!♡
REALLY? BUT THAT'S A PIRATE SONG!
THAT'S RIGHT! WE'RE GONNA BE PIRATES SOMEDAY!!
NOT AFTER I SELL YOU OFF TO THE GOVERN-MENT!
WHEE
WHEE
OOH, HOW DASHING. ♡
HA HA HA HA HA HA HA
KYAA
KYA-HA-HA-HA

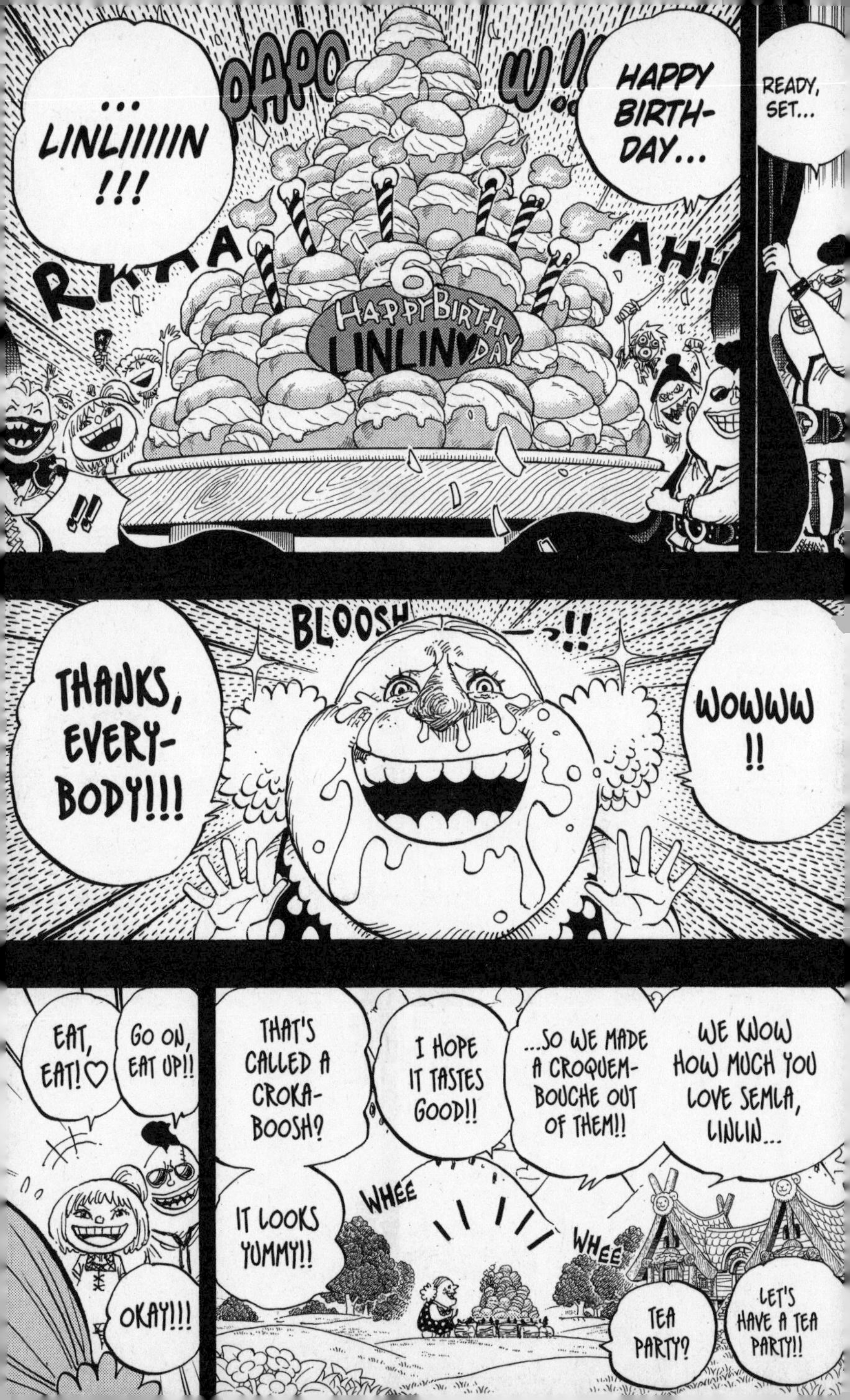
READY, SET...
HAPPY BIRTH-DAY...
AHH
6
HAPPY BIRTH DAY LINLIN♥
...LINLIIIIIN!!!
WOWWW!!
BLOOSH—!!
THANKS, EVERY-BODY!!!!
WE KNOW HOW MUCH YOU LOVE SEMLA, LINLIN...
...SO WE MADE A CROQUEM-BOUCHE OUT OF THEM!!
I HOPE IT TASTES GOOD!!
THAT'S CALLED A CROKA-BOOSH?
LET'S HAVE A TEA PARTY!!
TEA PARTY?
WHEE
WHEE
IT LOOKS YUMMY!!
GO ON, EAT UP!!
EAT, EAT!♡
OKAY!!!

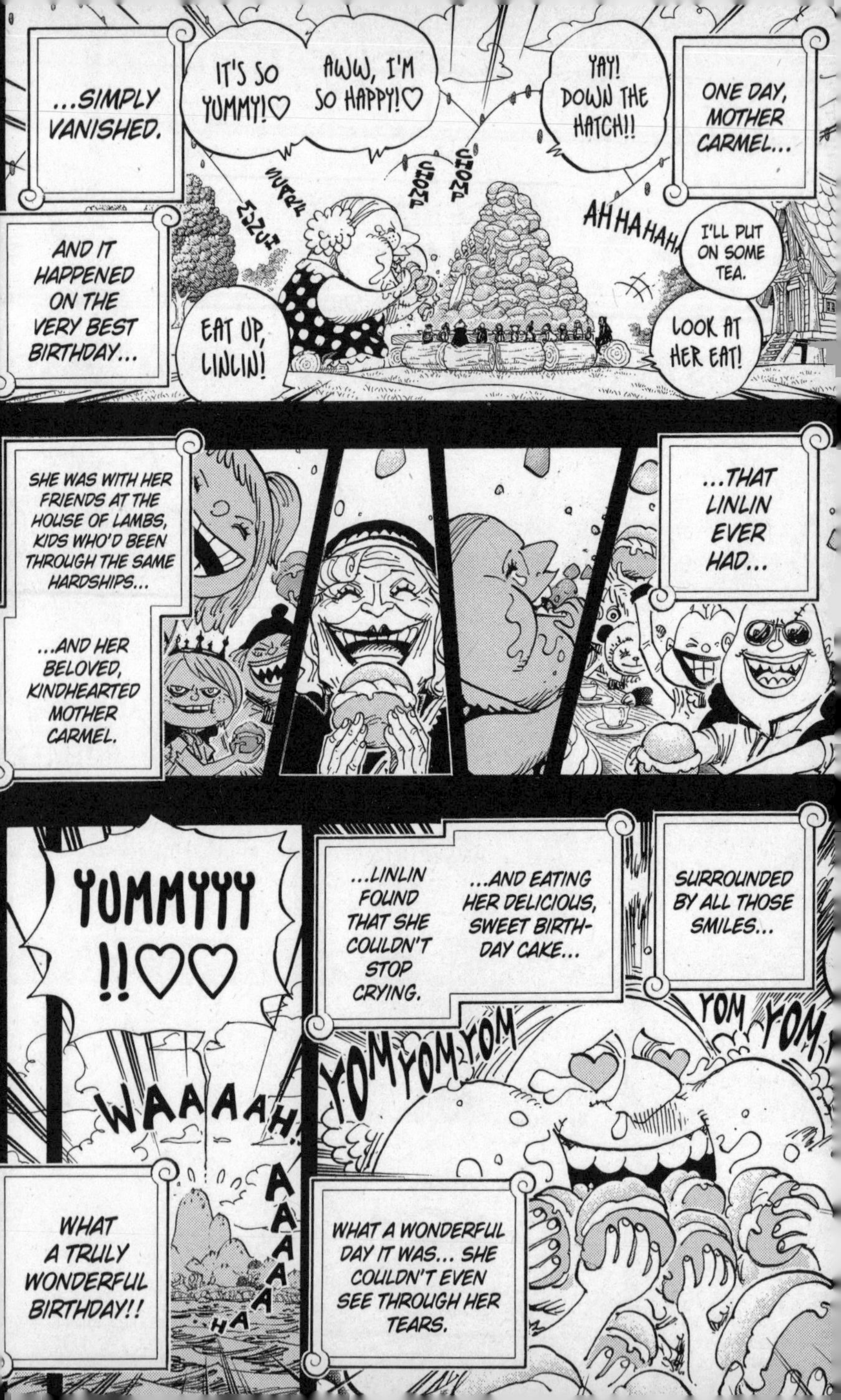
ONE DAY, MOTHER CARMEL...
YAY! DOWN THE HATCH!!
CHOMP
CHOMP
AWW, I'M SO HAPPY!♡
IT'S SO YUMMY!♡
...SIMPLY VANISHED.
AH HA HA HA
I'LL PUT ON SOME TEA.
LOOK AT HER EAT!
EAT UP, LINLIN!
AND IT HAPPENED ON THE VERY BEST BIRTHDAY...
...THAT LINLIN EVER HAD...
SHE WAS WITH HER FRIENDS AT THE HOUSE OF LAMBS, KIDS WHO'D BEEN THROUGH THE SAME HARDSHIPS...
...AND HER BELOVED, KINDHEARTED MOTHER CARMEL.
SURROUNDED BY ALL THOSE SMILES...
...AND EATING HER DELICIOUS, SWEET BIRTHDAY CAKE...
...LINLIN FOUND THAT SHE COULDN'T STOP CRYING.
YOM YOM
YOM YOM YOM
WHAT A WONDERFUL DAY IT WAS... SHE COULDN'T EVEN SEE THROUGH HER TEARS.
YUMMYYY!!♡♡
WAAAAAH!!
AAAAAHA
WHAT A TRULY WONDERFUL BIRTHDAY!!

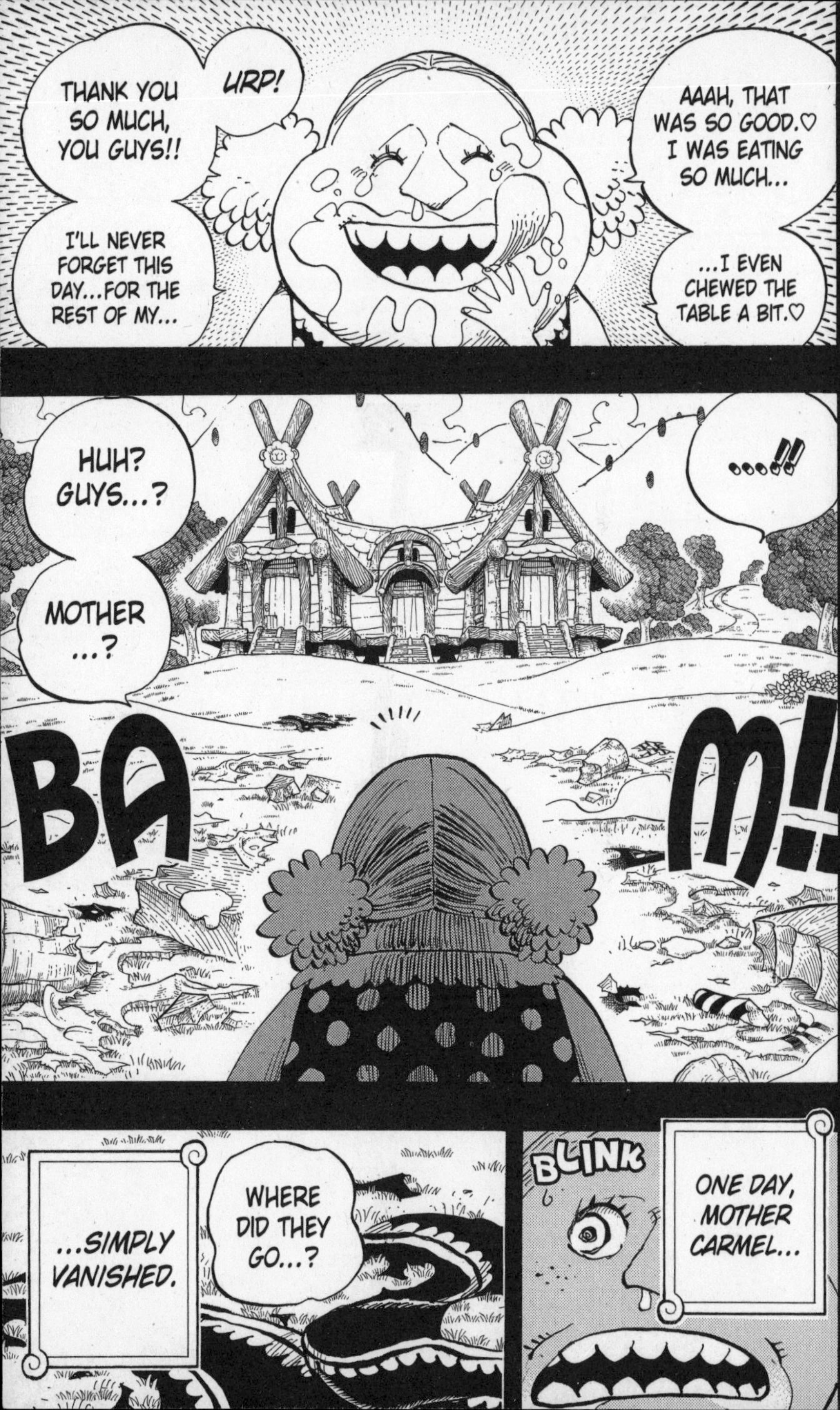
AAAH, THAT WAS SO GOOD.♡ I WAS EATING SO MUCH...
...I EVEN CHEWED THE TABLE A BIT.♡
URP!
THANK YOU SO MUCH, YOU GUYS!!
I'LL NEVER FORGET THIS DAY...FOR THE REST OF MY...
....!!
HUH? GUYS...?
MOTHER ...?
BAM!!
BLINK
ONE DAY, MOTHER CARMEL...
WHERE DID THEY GO...?
...SIMPLY VANISHED.

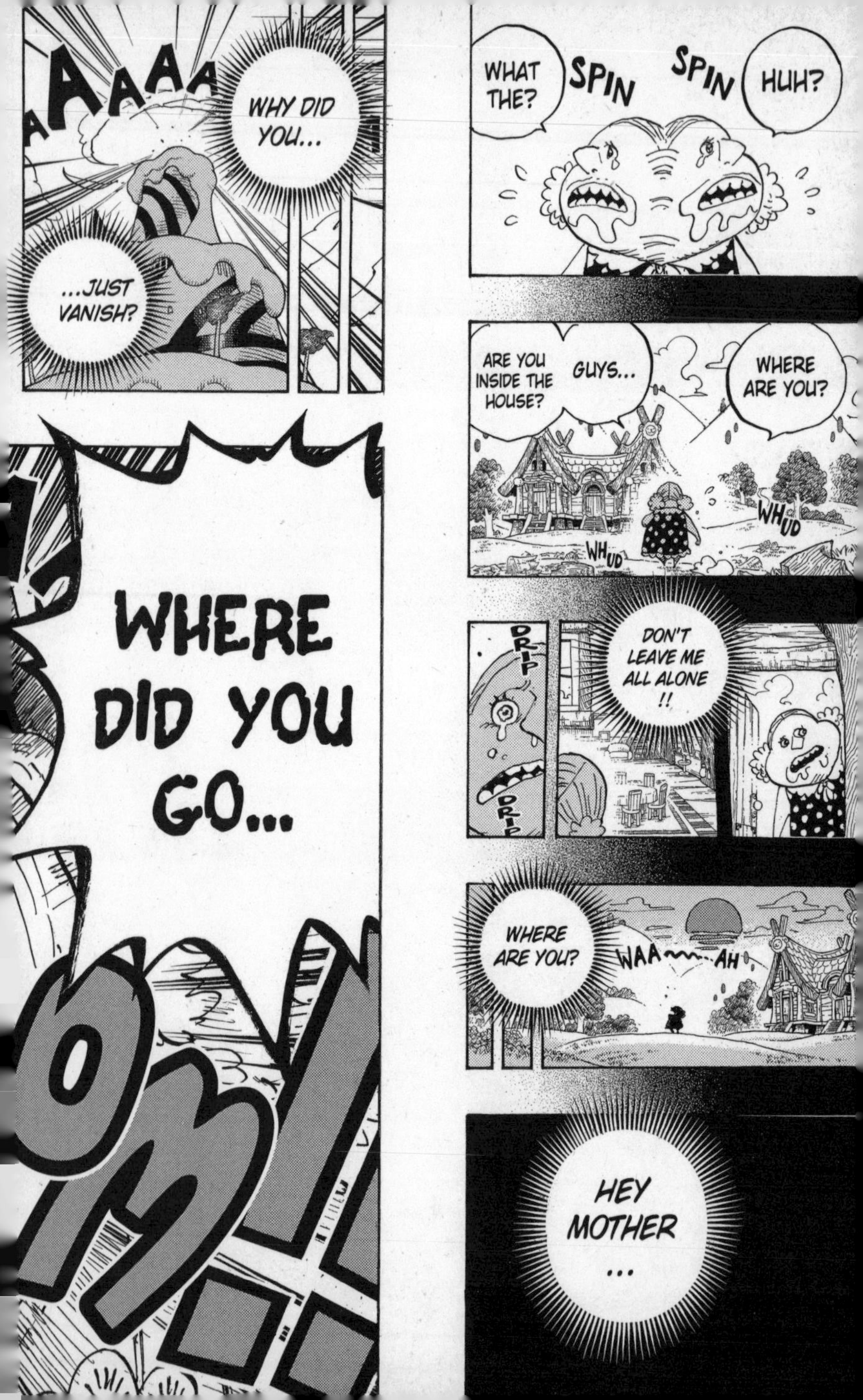
HUH?
SPIN
SPIN
WHAT THE?
WHERE ARE YOU?
GUYS...
ARE YOU INSIDE THE HOUSE?
WHUD
WHUD
DON'T LEAVE ME ALL ALONE !!
DRIP
DRIP
WAA~~~AH
WHERE ARE YOU?
HEY MOTHER ...
AAAAA
WHY DID YOU...
...JUST VANISH?
WHERE DID YOU GO...

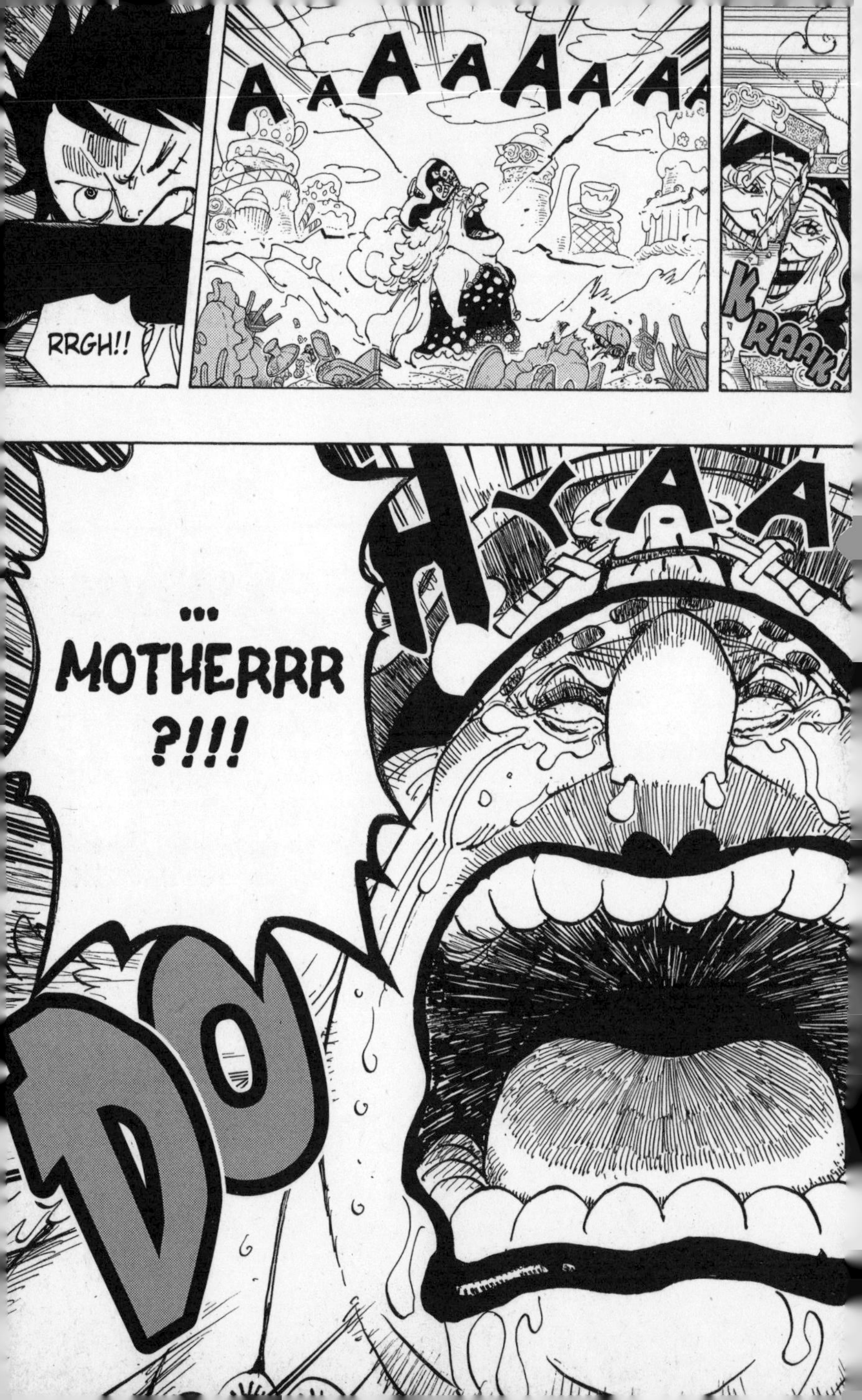
KRAAK!
AAAAAAAA
RRGH!!
HYAA
...MOTHERRR ?!!!
DO

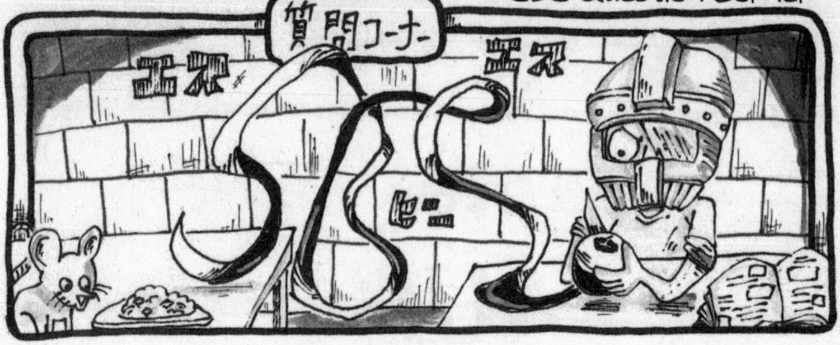
質問コーナー
SBS

(Hayato Asami, Kanagawa)

Q: Hi, Oda Sensei! My question is about Bepo's distant brother that you mentioned in volume 84's SBS segment. Is that the Zepo who appeared in chapter 850? Or is it just an un-bear-able coincidence?

--Haru Mihashi

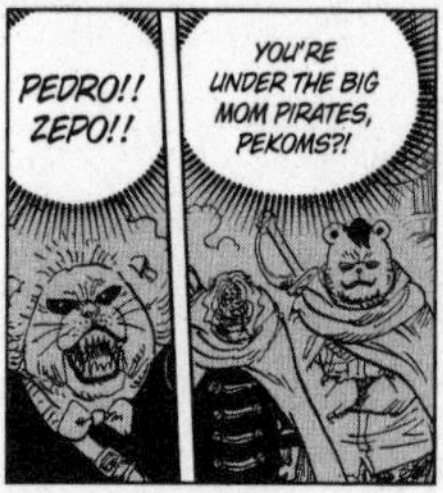
YOU'RE UNDER THE BIG MOM PIRATES, PEKOMS?!
PEDRO!! ZEPO!!

A: They do look alike! You're correct. Pedro's Nox Explorers were pursued by the government for searching for Poneglyphs, which turned them into the Nox Pirates. That was about 15 years ago. Bepo loved and admired his older brother Zepo. He descended the elephant to gaze at the sea, and ended up getting washed over to the North Blue, where he met Law. Meanwhile, Pekoms took all the Nox Pirates who were unable to continue due to injury or lack of will, leaving just Pedro and Zepo at sea. Pekoms' group wound up in Big Mom's territory, which saved their lives and gave them a new master to serve. Pedro and Zepo ultimately set their sights on Big Mom's Poneglyphs after five years of searching, which led to their reunion with Pekoms.

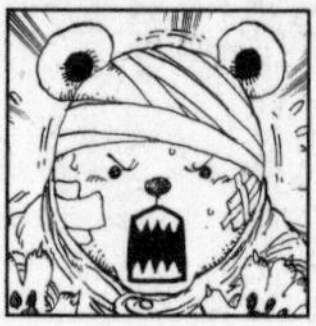

Q: I really want to see Charlotte Linlin at ages 28 and 48. Can you help with that?

--M Natsuo

A: Here you go.

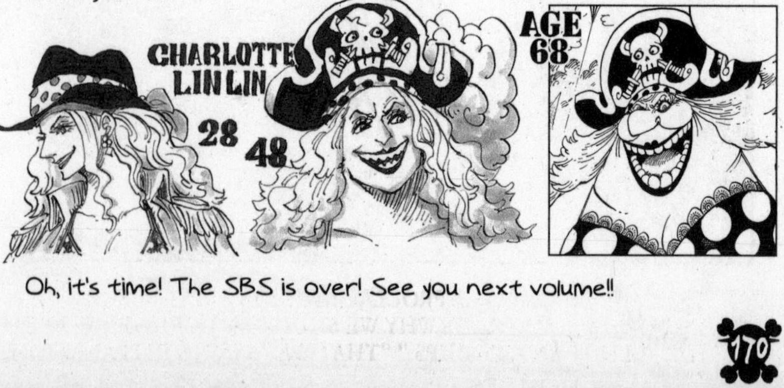
CHARLOTTE LINLIN
28
48
AGE 68

Oh, it's time! The SBS is over! See you next volume!!

Chapter 868:

KX LAUNCHER

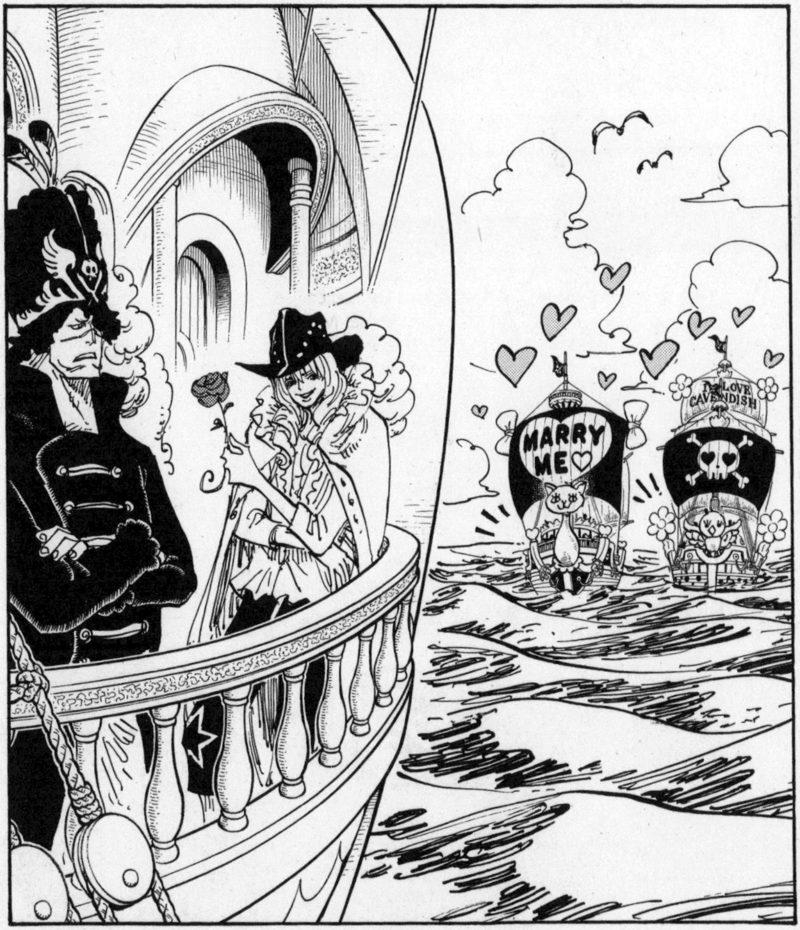

MARRY ME♡
I♡LOVE CAVENDISH

THE SAGA OF THE SELF-PROCLAIMED STRAW HAT FLEET, VOL. 5, CAVENDISH: "...AND THAT'S WHY WE SHOULDN'T OPEN FIRE, BECAUSE THEY'RE NOT ENEMY SHIPS." "THAT WAS A LONG EXPLANATION."

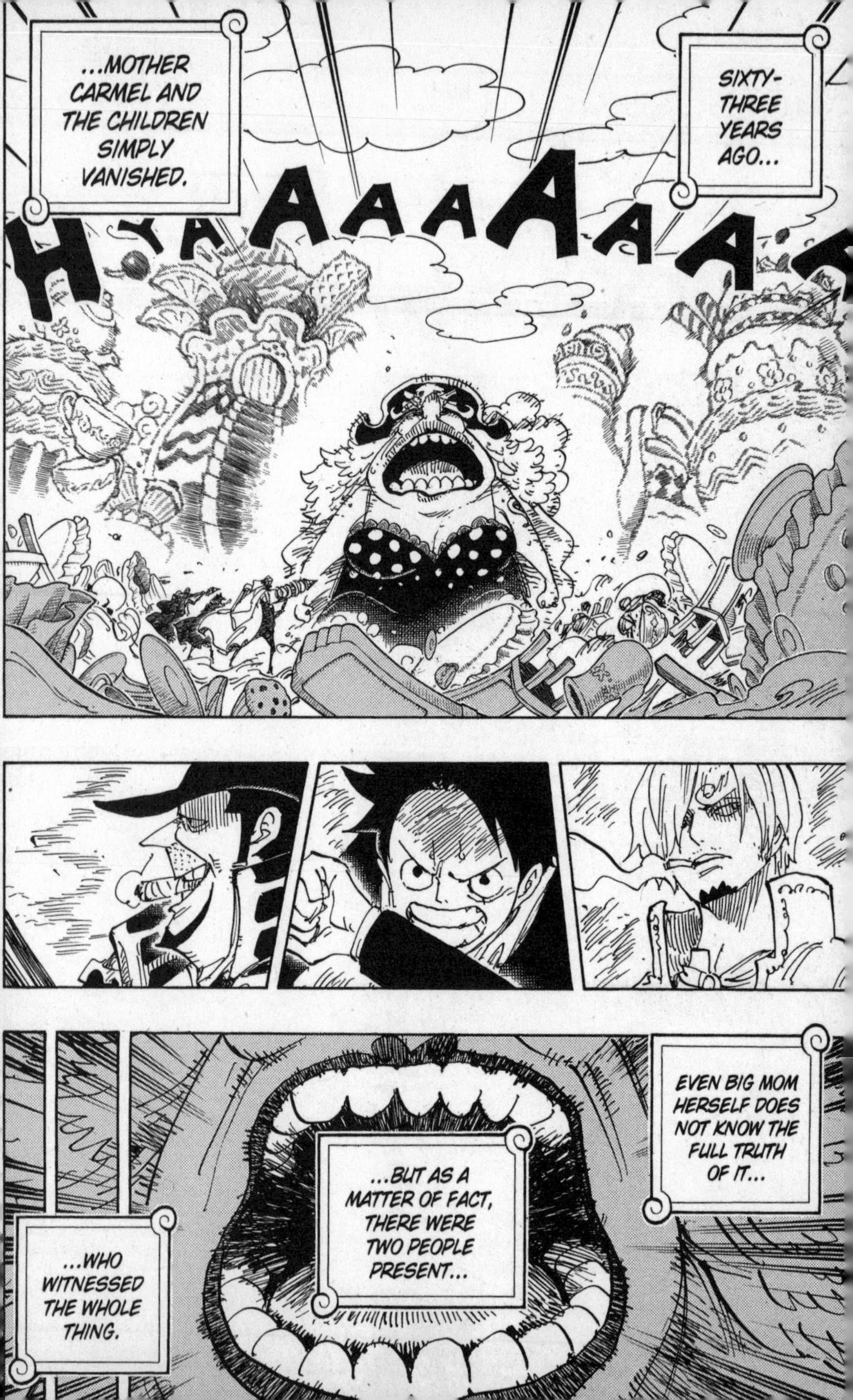
SIXTY-THREE YEARS AGO...
...MOTHER CARMEL AND THE CHILDREN SIMPLY VANISHED.
HYAAAAAAAA
EVEN BIG MOM HERSELF DOES NOT KNOW THE FULL TRUTH OF IT...
...BUT AS A MATTER OF FACT, THERE WERE TWO PEOPLE PRESENT...
...WHO WITNESSED THE WHOLE THING.

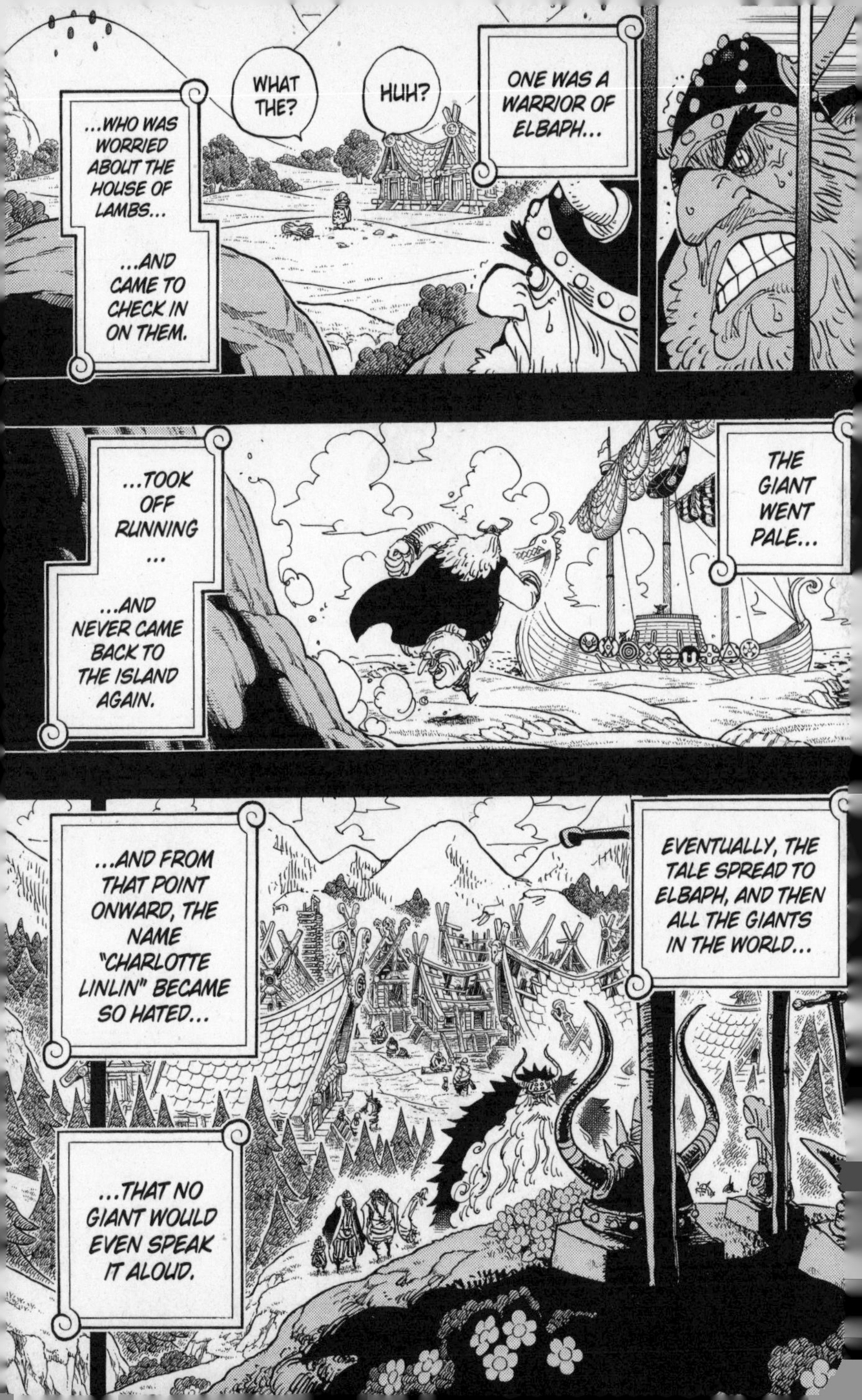
ONE WAS A WARRIOR OF ELBAPH...
HUH?
WHAT THE?
...WHO WAS WORRIED ABOUT THE HOUSE OF LAMBS...
...AND CAME TO CHECK IN ON THEM.
THE GIANT WENT PALE...
...TOOK OFF RUNNING...
...AND NEVER CAME BACK TO THE ISLAND AGAIN.
EVENTUALLY, THE TALE SPREAD TO ELBAPH, AND THEN ALL THE GIANTS IN THE WORLD...
...AND FROM THAT POINT ONWARD, THE NAME "CHARLOTTE LINLIN" BECAME SO HATED...
...THAT NO GIANT WOULD EVEN SPEAK IT ALOUD.

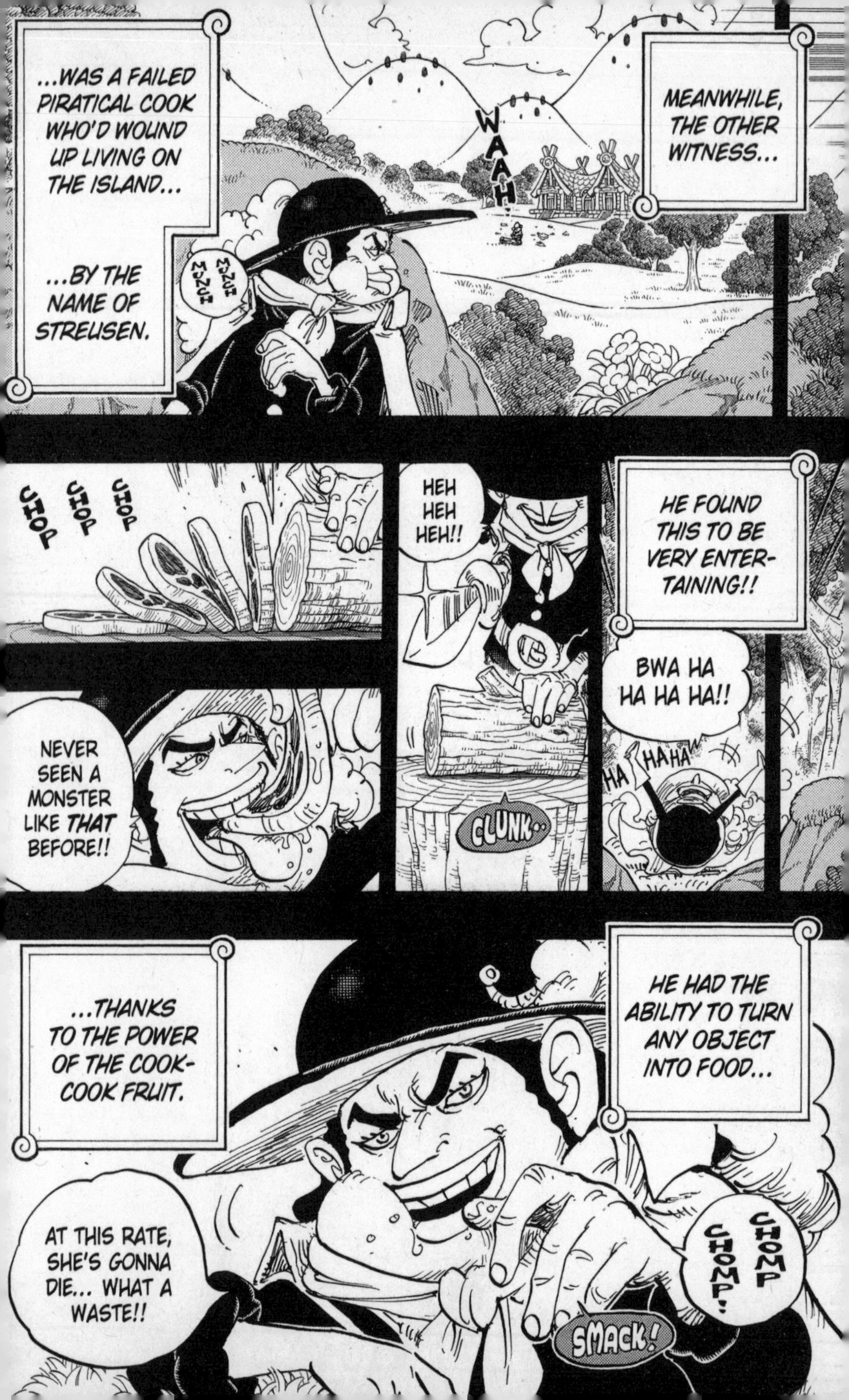
MEANWHILE, THE OTHER WITNESS...
WAAH
...WAS A FAILED PIRATICAL COOK WHO'D WOUND UP LIVING ON THE ISLAND...
MUNCH MUNCH
...BY THE NAME OF STREUSEN.
HE FOUND THIS TO BE VERY ENTERTAINING!!
BWA HA HA HA HA!!
HA HA HA
HEH HEH HEH!!
CLUNK
CHOP CHOP CHOP
NEVER SEEN A MONSTER LIKE THAT BEFORE!!
HE HAD THE ABILITY TO TURN ANY OBJECT INTO FOOD...
...THANKS TO THE POWER OF THE COOK-COOK FRUIT.
CHOMP CHOMP
SMACK!
AT THIS RATE, SHE'S GONNA DIE... WHAT A WASTE!!

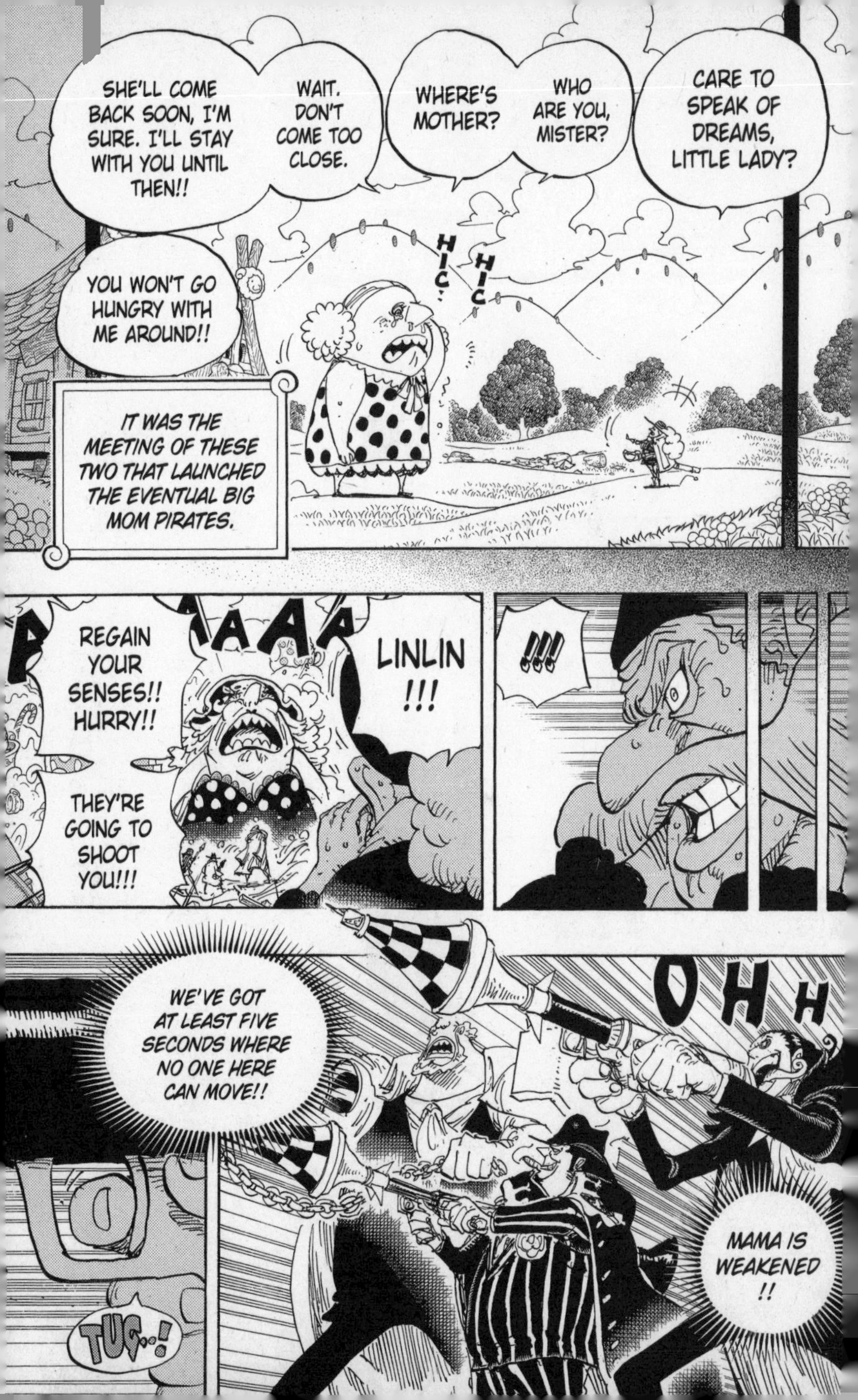
CARE TO SPEAK OF DREAMS, LITTLE LADY?
WHO ARE YOU, MISTER?
WHERE'S MOTHER?
WAIT. DON'T COME TOO CLOSE.
SHE'LL COME BACK SOON, I'M SURE. I'LL STAY WITH YOU UNTIL THEN!!
HIC HIC
YOU WON'T GO HUNGRY WITH ME AROUND!!
IT WAS THE MEETING OF THESE TWO THAT LAUNCHED THE EVENTUAL BIG MOM PIRATES.
!!!
AAAA
LINLIN !!!
REGAIN YOUR SENSES!! HURRY!!
THEY'RE GOING TO SHOOT YOU!!!
OHH
MAMA IS WEAKENED !!
WE'VE GOT AT LEAST FIVE SECONDS WHERE NO ONE HERE CAN MOVE!!
TUG..!

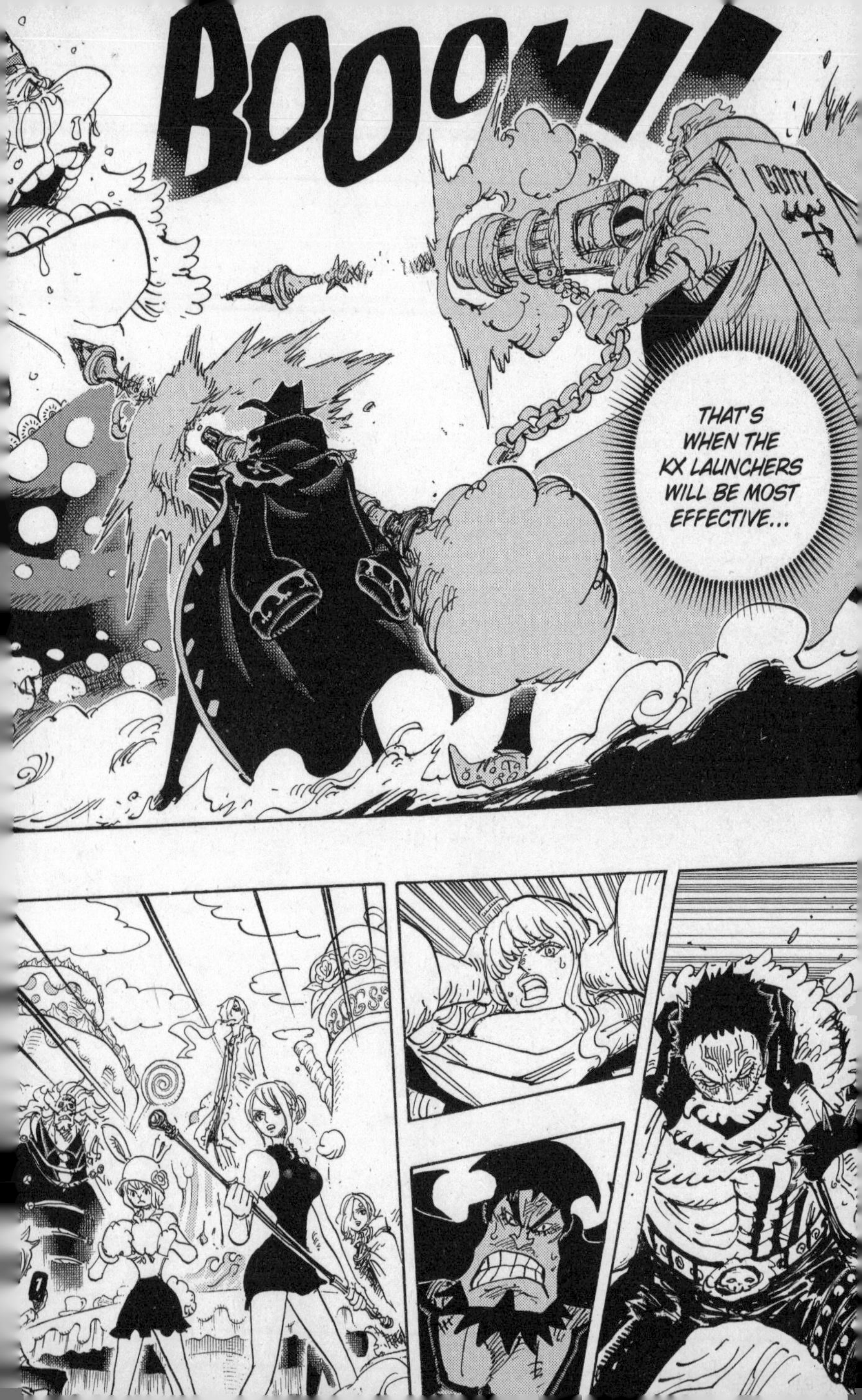
BOOOM!!
THAT'S WHEN THE KX LAUNCHERS WILL BE MOST EFFECTIVE...
GOTTY

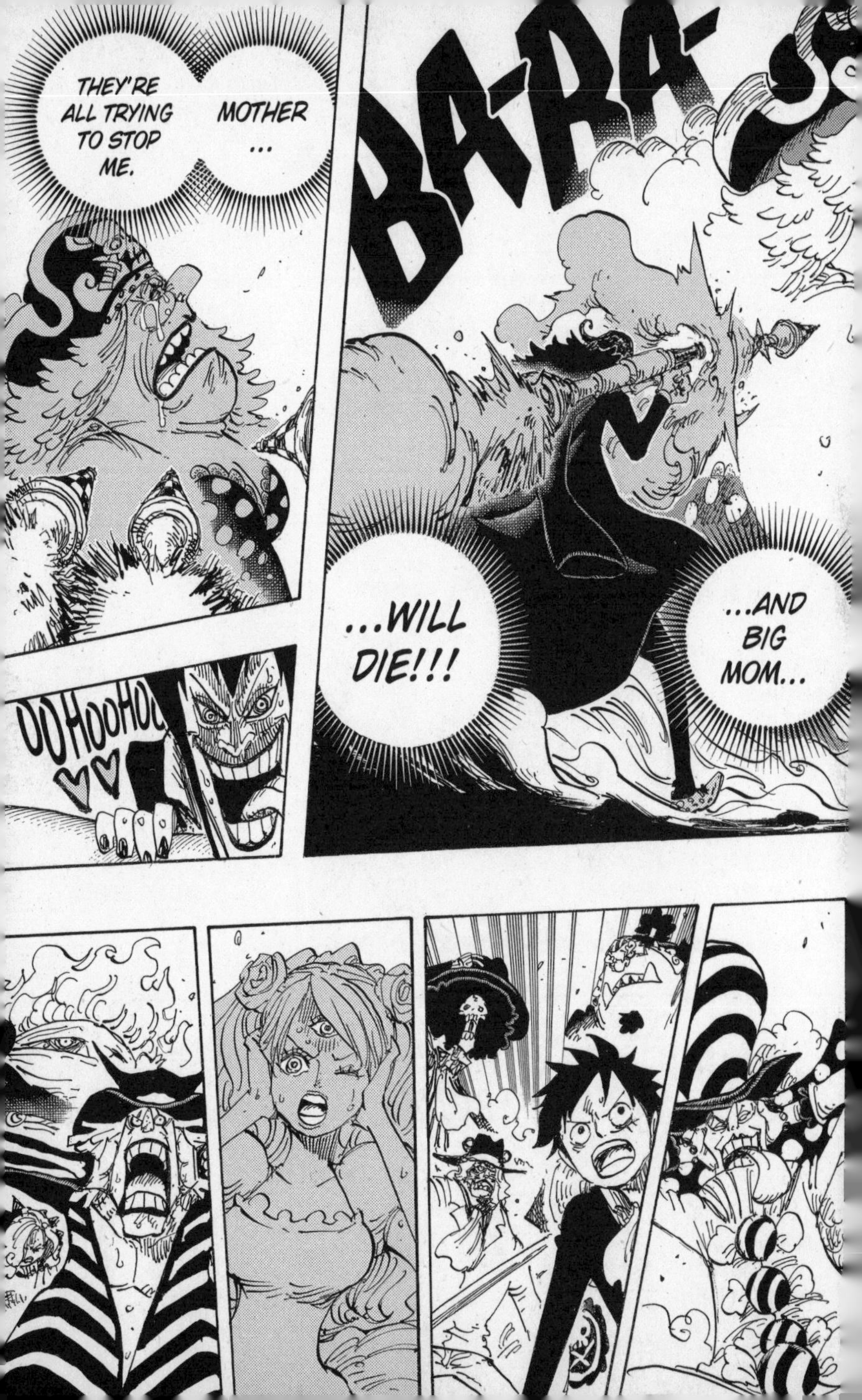
BA-RA-
...AND BIG MOM...
...WILL DIE!!!
MOTHER ...
THEY'RE ALL TRYING TO STOP ME.
OOHOOHO

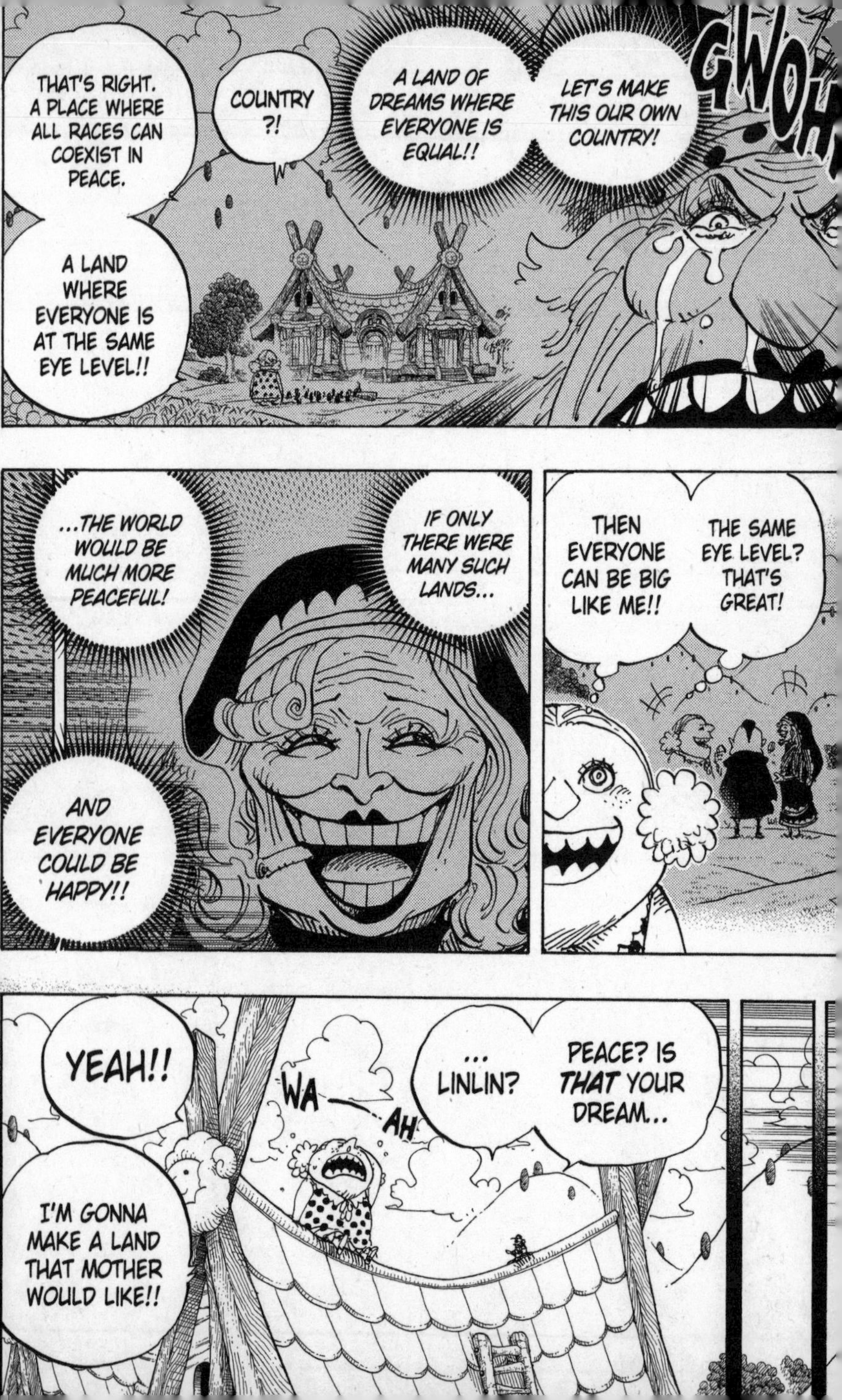
GWOH
LET'S MAKE THIS OUR OWN COUNTRY!
A LAND OF DREAMS WHERE EVERYONE IS EQUAL!!
COUNTRY?!
THAT'S RIGHT. A PLACE WHERE ALL RACES CAN COEXIST IN PEACE.
A LAND WHERE EVERYONE IS AT THE SAME EYE LEVEL!!
THE SAME EYE LEVEL? THAT'S GREAT!
THEN EVERYONE CAN BE BIG LIKE ME!!
IF ONLY THERE WERE MANY SUCH LANDS...
...THE WORLD WOULD BE MUCH MORE PEACEFUL!
AND EVERYONE COULD BE HAPPY!!
PEACE? IS *THAT* YOUR DREAM...
... LINLIN?
WA—AH
YEAH!!
I'M GONNA MAKE A LAND THAT MOTHER WOULD LIKE!!

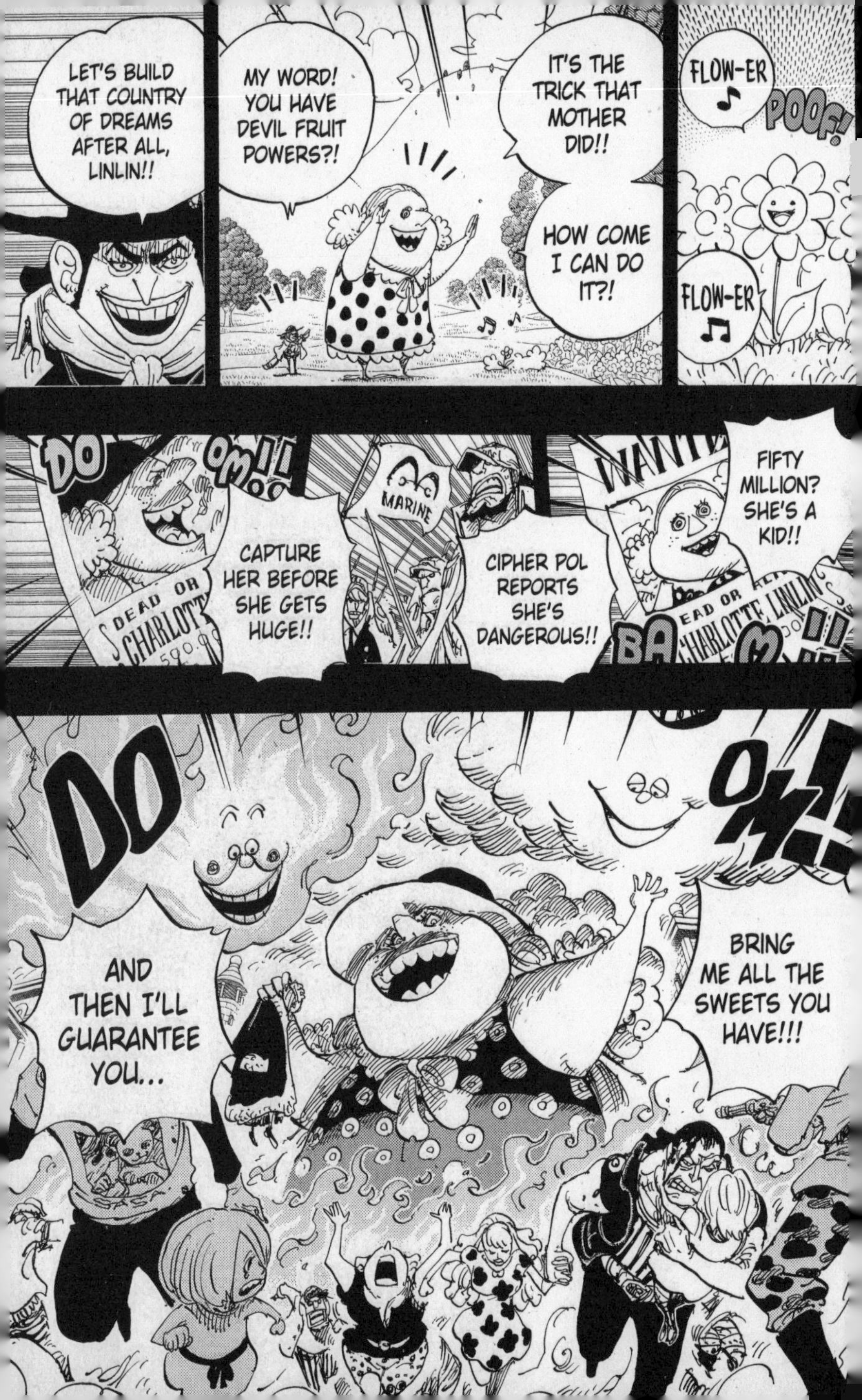
FLOW-ER ♪
POOF!
FLOW-ER ♫
IT'S THE TRICK THAT MOTHER DID!!
HOW COME I CAN DO IT?!
MY WORD! YOU HAVE DEVIL FRUIT POWERS?!
LET'S BUILD THAT COUNTRY OF DREAMS AFTER ALL, LINLIN!!
FIFTY MILLION? SHE'S A KID!!
DEAD OR
CHARLOTTE LINLIN
BA
MARINE
CIPHER POL REPORTS SHE'S DANGEROUS!!
CAPTURE HER BEFORE SHE GETS HUGE!!
DO
DEAD OR
OM!!
BRING ME ALL THE SWEETS YOU HAVE!!!
DO
AND THEN I'LL GUARANTEE YOU...

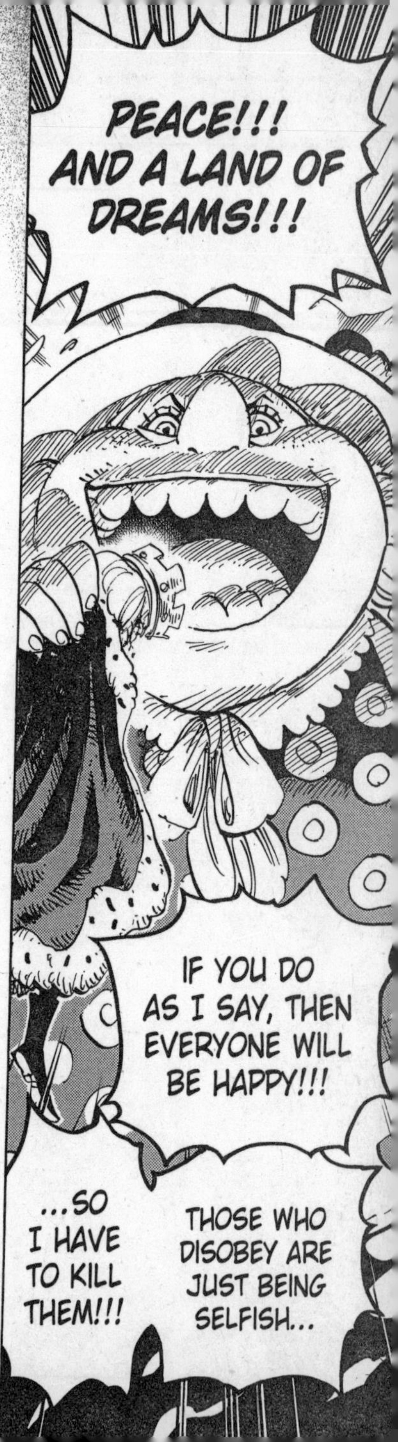
PEACE!!! AND A LAND OF DREAMS!!!
IF YOU DO AS I SAY, THEN EVERYONE WILL BE HAPPY!!!
THOSE WHO DISOBEY ARE JUST BEING SELFISH...
...SO I HAVE TO KILL THEM!!!
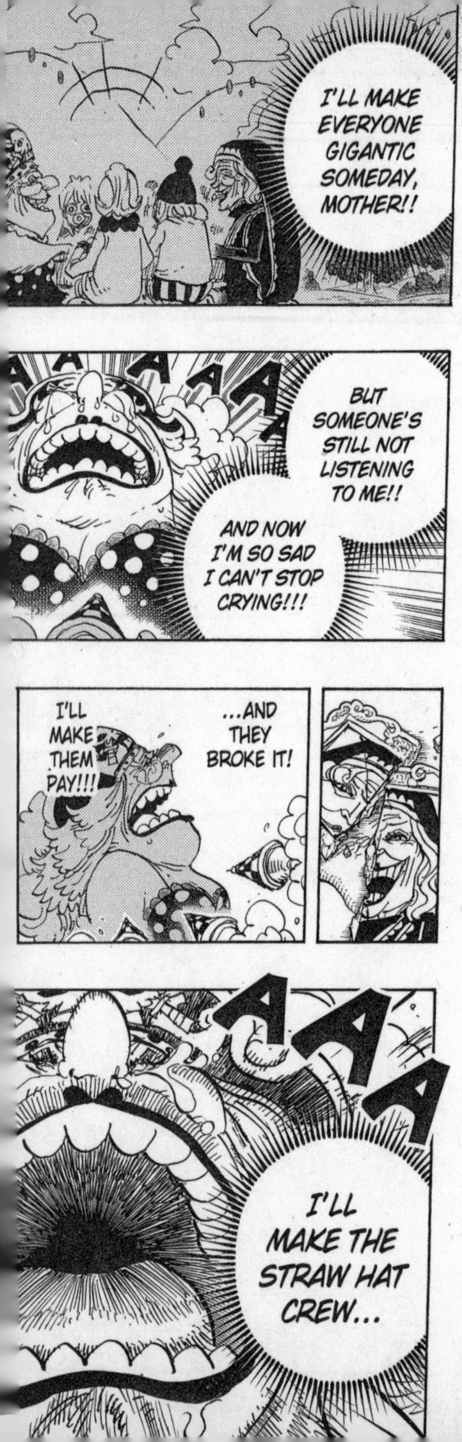
I'LL MAKE EVERYONE GIGANTIC SOMEDAY, MOTHER!!
AAAAA
BUT SOMEONE'S STILL NOT LISTENING TO ME!!
AND NOW I'M SO SAD I CAN'T STOP CRYING!!!
...AND THEY BROKE IT!
I'LL MAKE THEM PAY!!!
AAAA
I'LL MAKE THE STRAW HAT CREW...

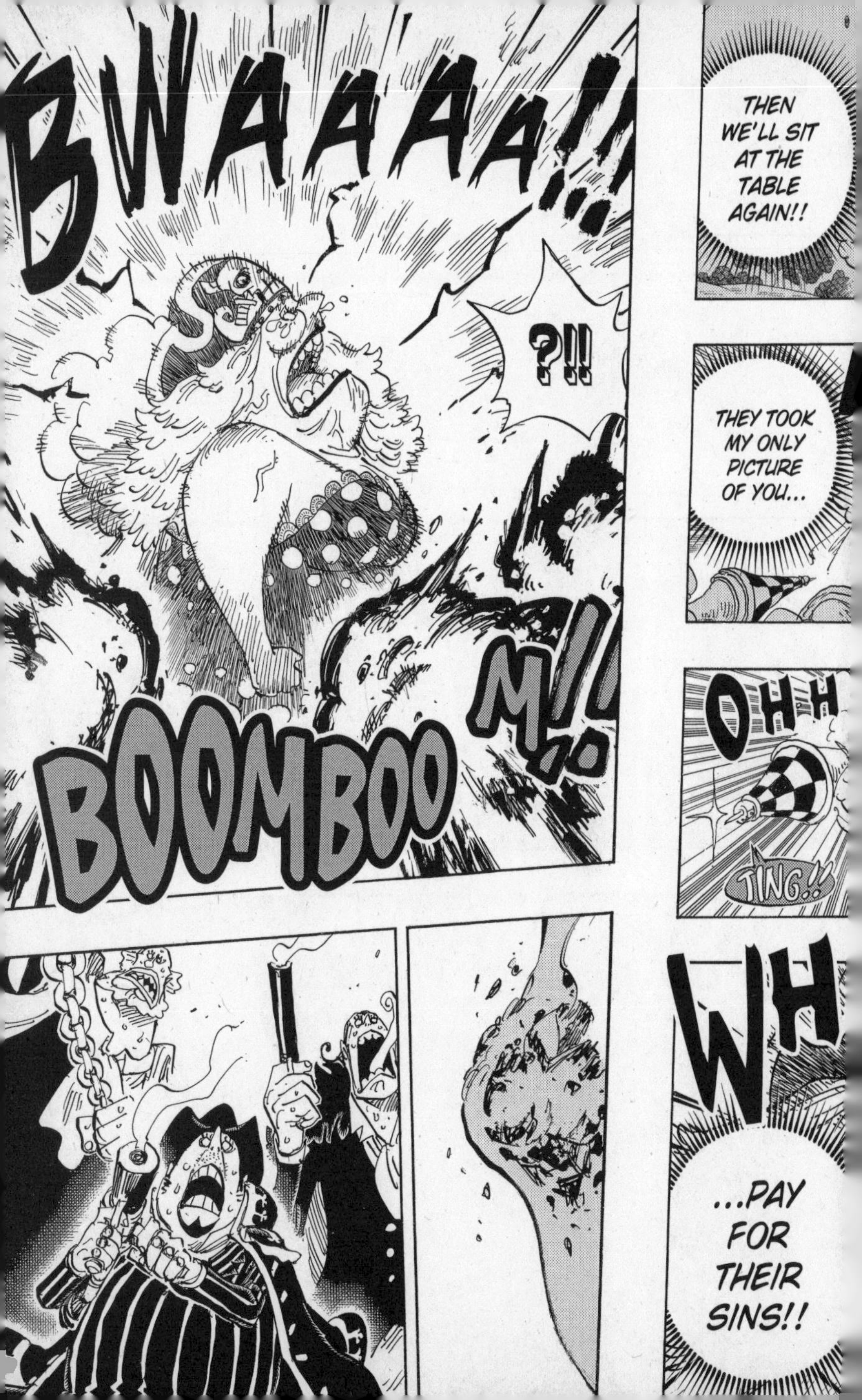
THEN WE'LL SIT AT THE TABLE AGAIN!!
THEY TOOK MY ONLY PICTURE OF YOU...
OHH
TING!!
WH
...PAY FOR THEIR SINS!!
BWAAAA!!
?!!
BOOMBOOM!!

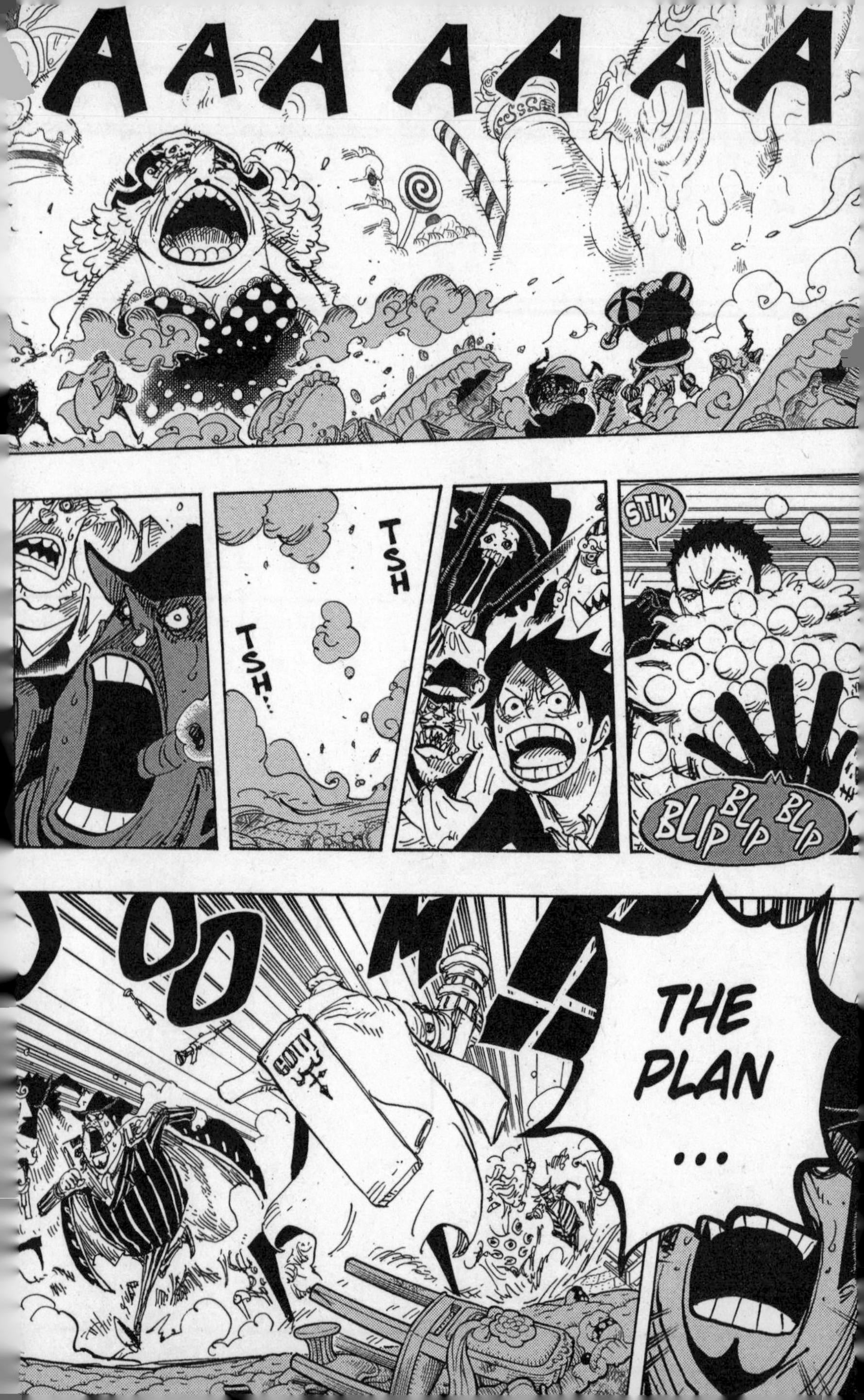
AAAAAAA
STIK
BLIP BLIP BLIP BLIP
TSH
TSH...
THE PLAN ...

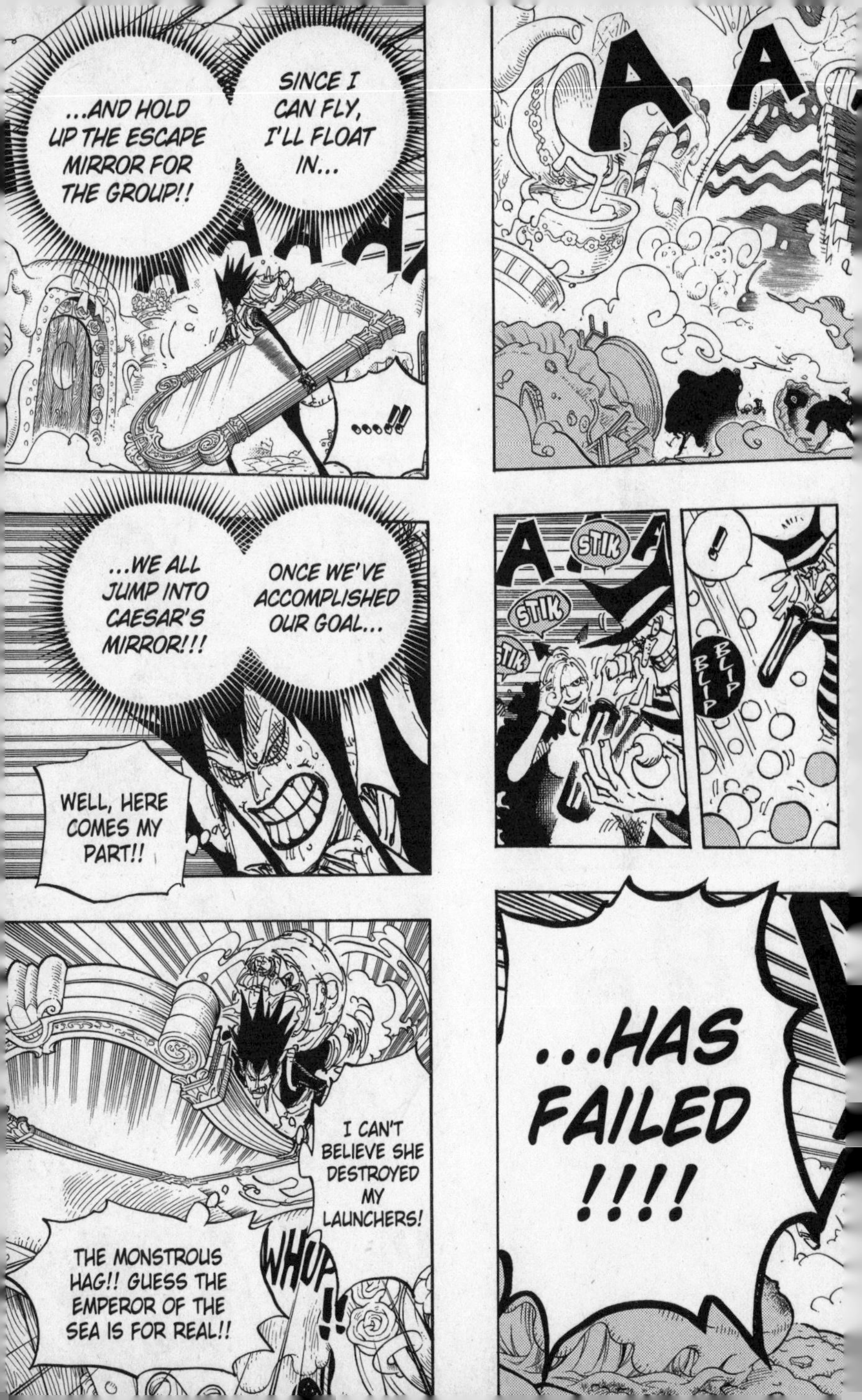
A A
SINCE I CAN FLY, I'LL FLOAT IN...
...AND HOLD UP THE ESCAPE MIRROR FOR THE GROUP!!
AAAA
....!!
A STIK A
STIK
STIK
!
BLIP BLIP
ONCE WE'VE ACCOMPLISHED OUR GOAL...
...WE ALL JUMP INTO CAESAR'S MIRROR!!!
WELL, HERE COMES MY PART!!
...HAS FAILED!!!!
I CAN'T BELIEVE SHE DESTROYED MY LAUNCHERS!
THE MONSTROUS HAG!! GUESS THE EMPEROR OF THE SEA IS FOR REAL!!
WHUP!!

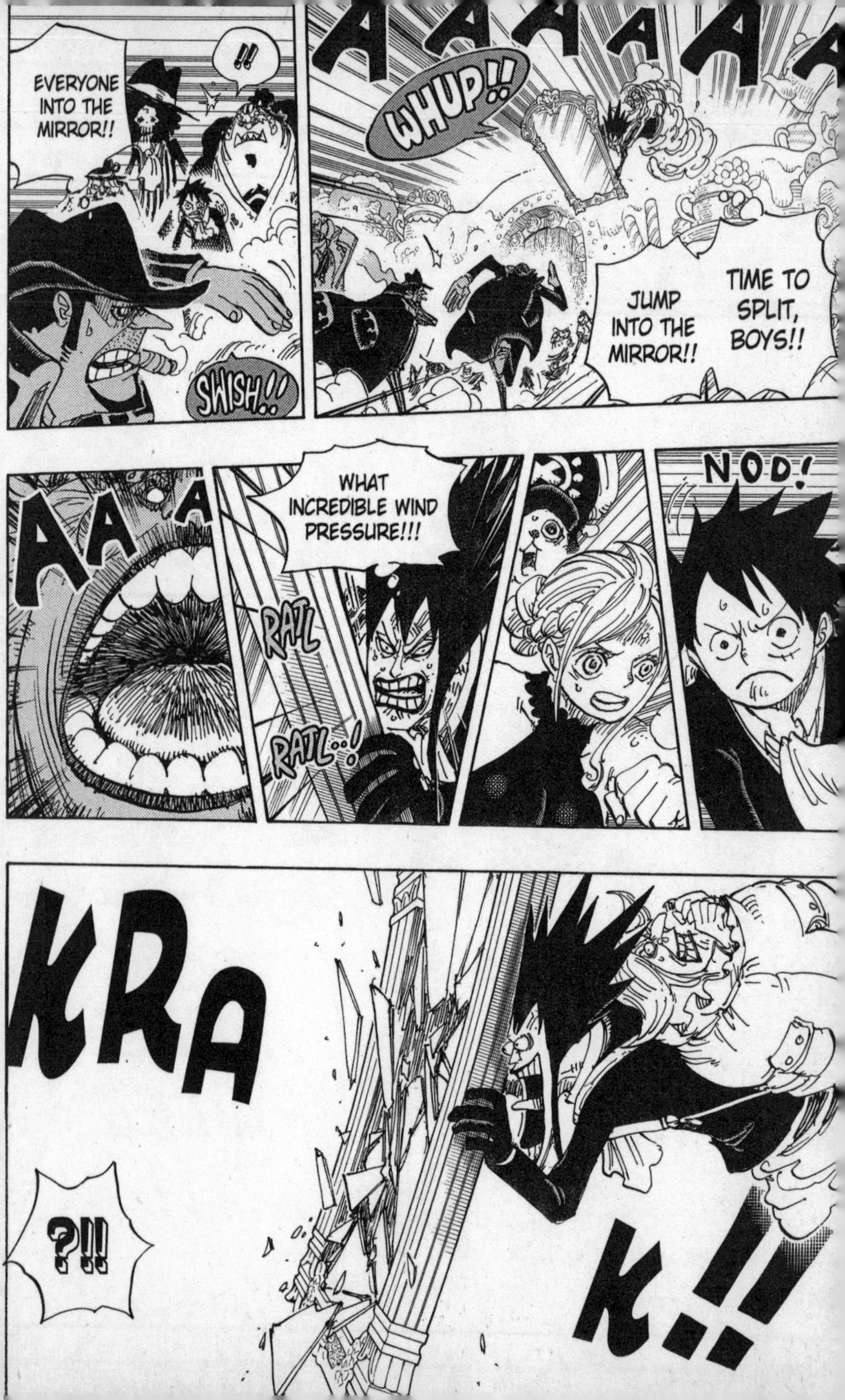
AAAAAAA
WHUP!!
TIME TO SPLIT, BOYS!!
JUMP INTO THE MIRROR!!
!!
EVERYONE INTO THE MIRROR!!
SWISH!!
NOD!
WHAT INCREDIBLE WIND PRESSURE!!!
RATL
RATL..!
AA A
KRA
k..!!
?!!

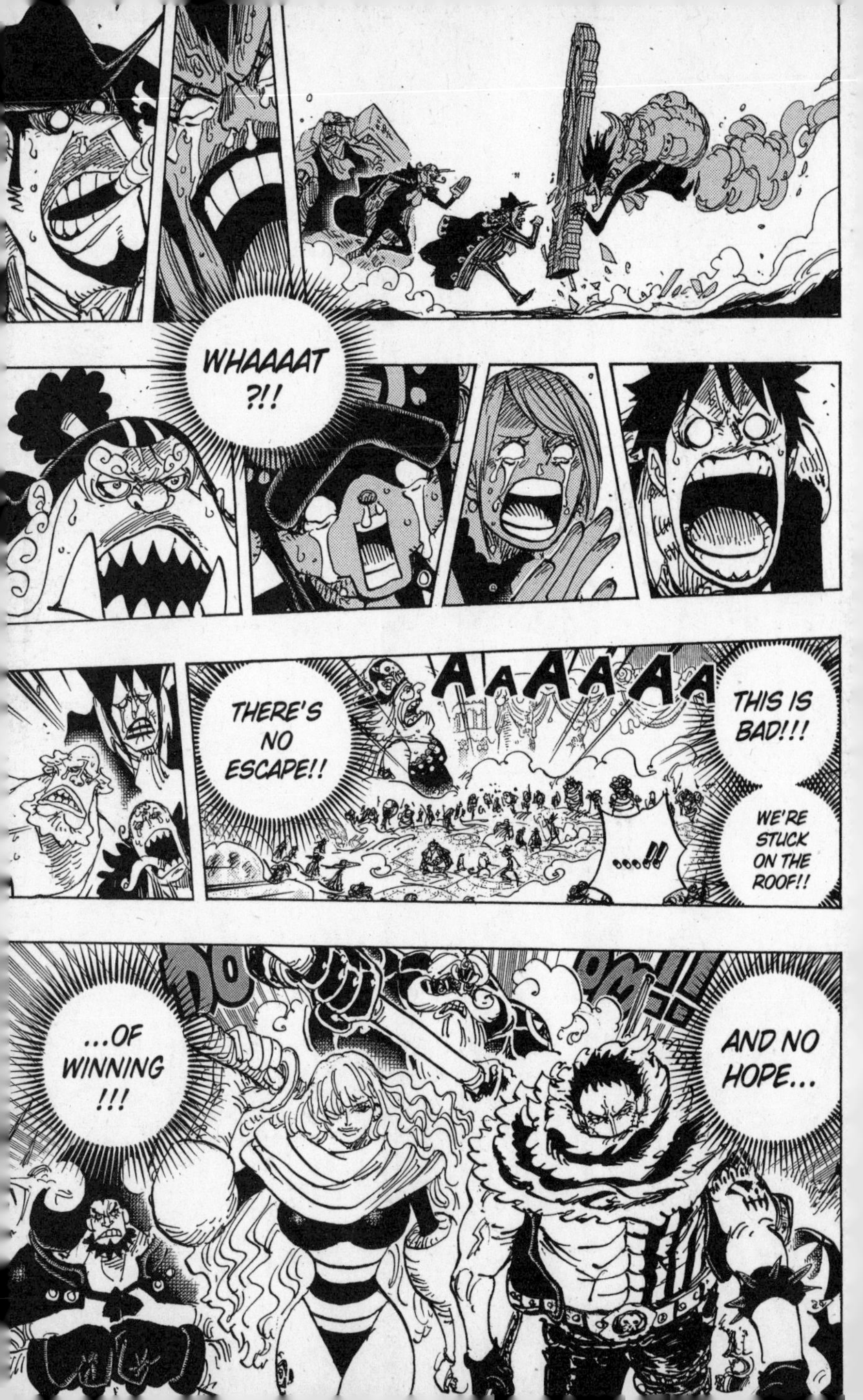
WHAAAAT ?!!
THIS IS BAD!!!
WE'RE STUCK ON THE ROOF!!
...!!
AAAAAA
THERE'S NO ESCAPE!!
AND NO HOPE...
...OF WINNING !!!

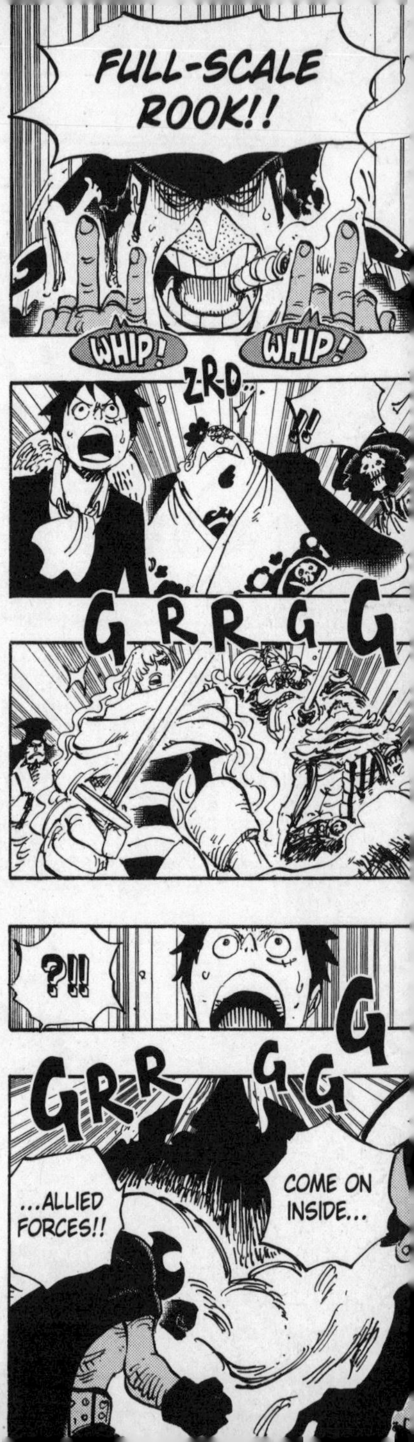
FULL-SCALE ROOK!!
WHIP!
WHIP!
Z-R-D..
!!
G R R G G
?!!
G R R G G G
COME ON INSIDE...
...ALLIED FORCES!!
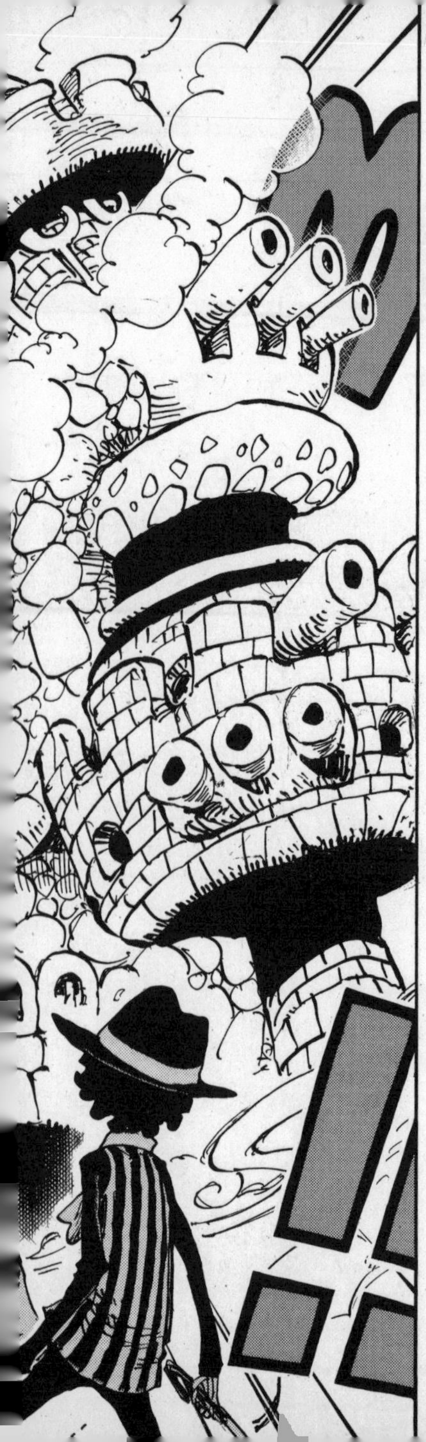
!!

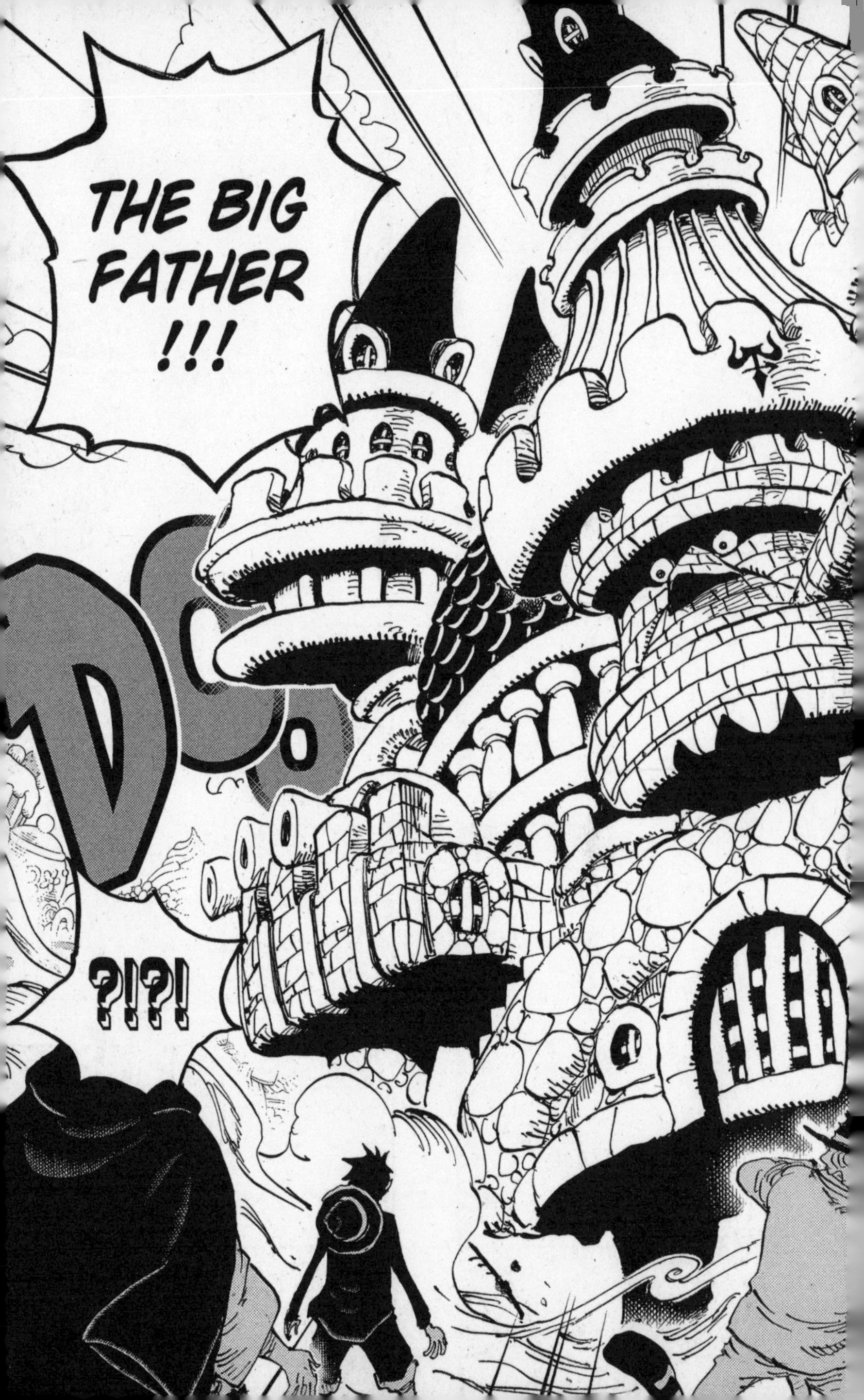
THE BIG FATHER !!!
DO
?!?!

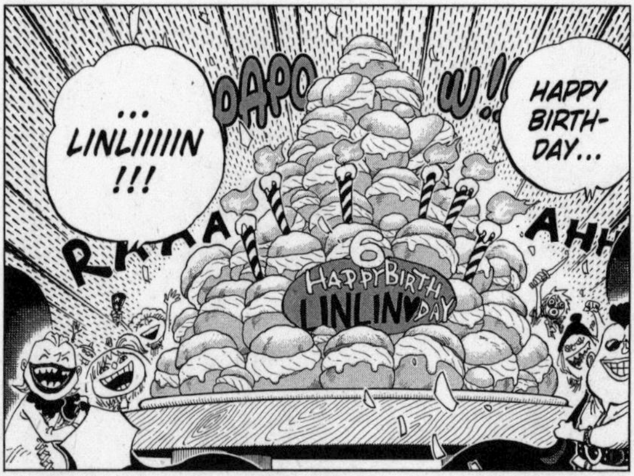
HAPPY BIRTH-DAY...
W!!
DAPO
... LINLIIIIIN !!!
AHH
RAAA
6
HAPPY BIRTHDAY LINLIN

The answers to P134

❶ Buggy's hat ❷ Buggy's hand ❸ Kuzan's shirt ❹ Garp's shirt
❺ Rayleigh's right eye scar ❻ Roger's coat hem ❼ Number of slats on the bench
❽ Chopper hiding behind the bench (freebie answer)

Chapter 869: CASTLING

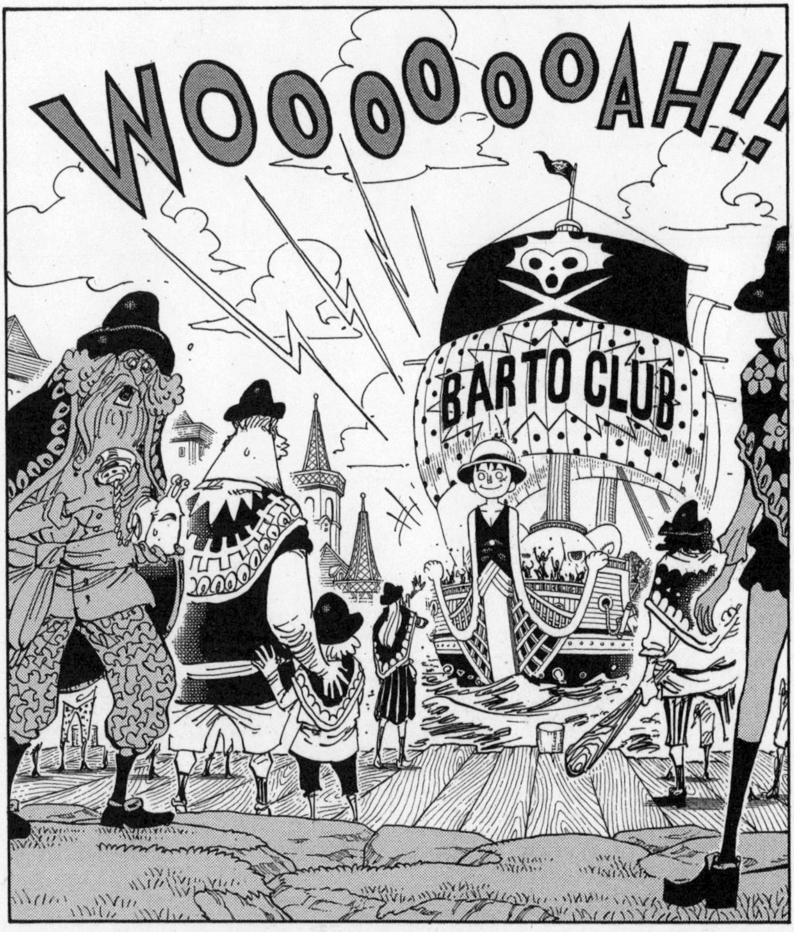
WOOOOOOAH!!!
BARTO CLUB

THE SAGA OF THE SELF-PROCLAIMED STRAW HAT FLEET, VOL. 6, BARTOLOMEO: "IT'S THE USUAL RAUCOUS RUCKUS FROM THE BARTO CLUB"

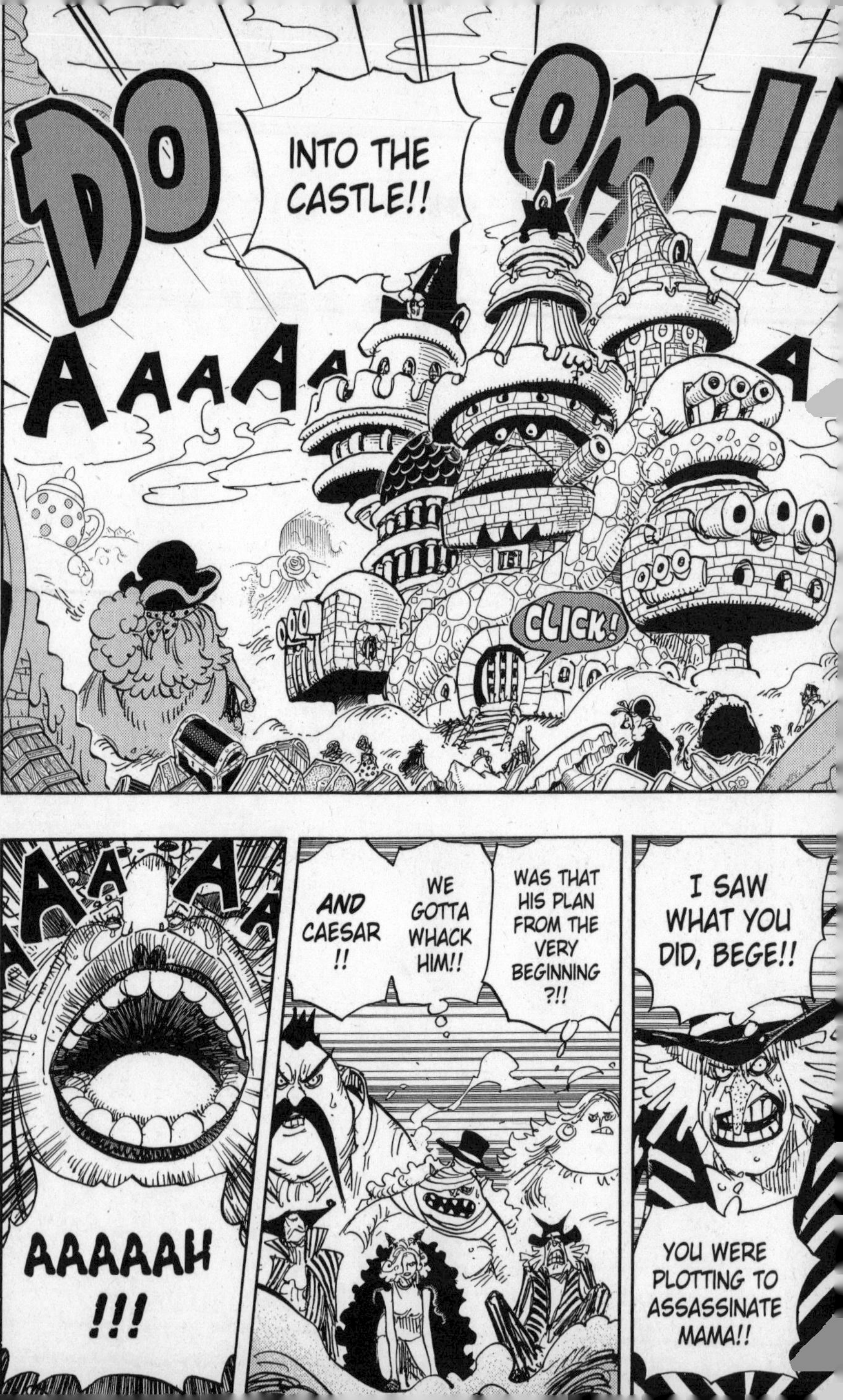
DOOM!!
INTO THE CASTLE!!
AAAAA
CLICK!
I SAW WHAT YOU DID, BEGE!!
YOU WERE PLOTTING TO ASSASSINATE MAMA!!
WAS THAT HIS PLAN FROM THE VERY BEGINNING ?!!
WE GOTTA WHACK HIM!!
AND CAESAR !!
AAAAAH !!!

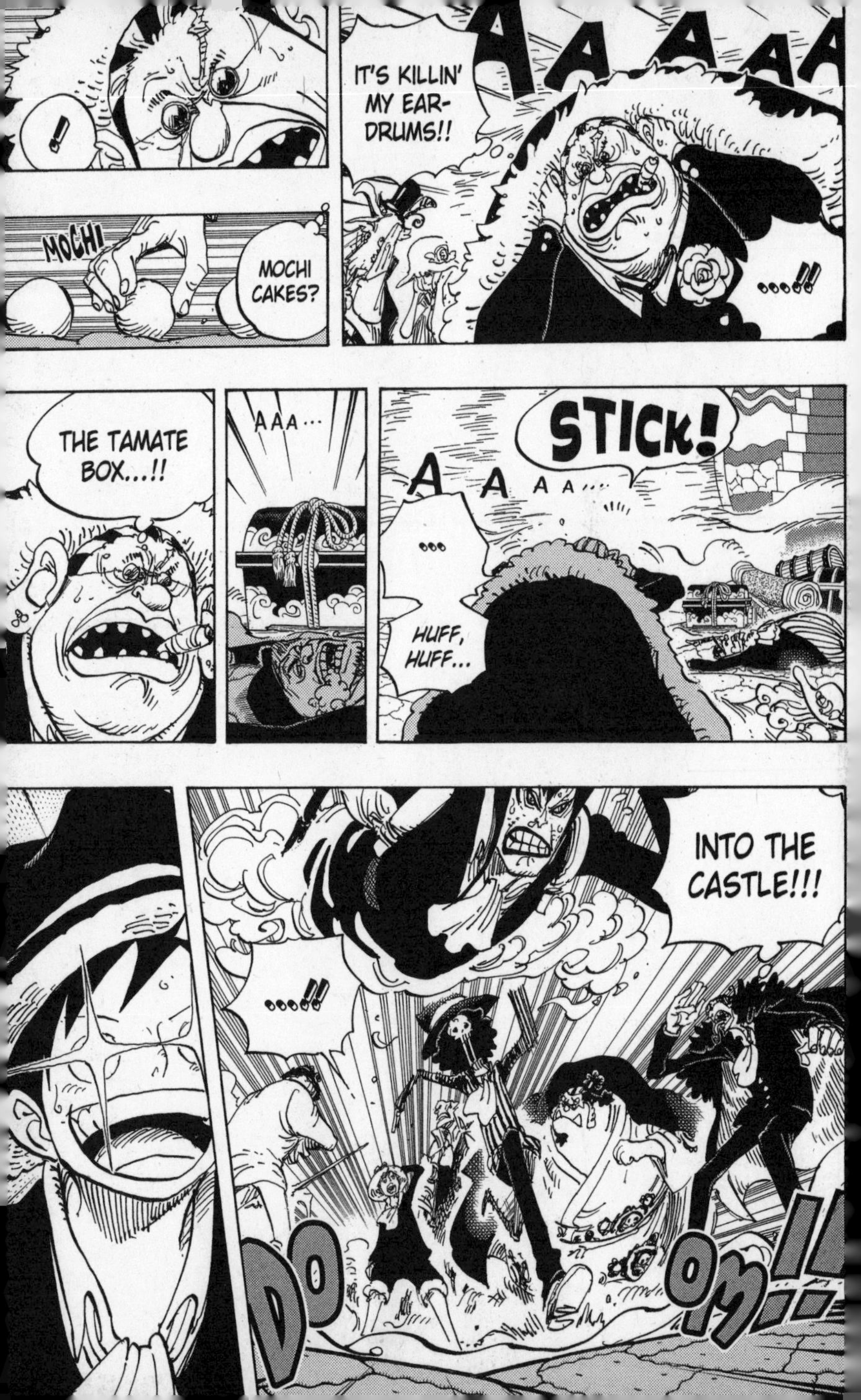
AAAA
IT'S KILLIN' MY EAR-DRUMS!!
...!!
!
MOCHI
MOCHI CAKES?
STICK!
AAAA...
...
HUFF, HUFF...
AAA...
THE TAMATE BOX...!!
INTO THE CASTLE!!!
...!!
DOOM!!

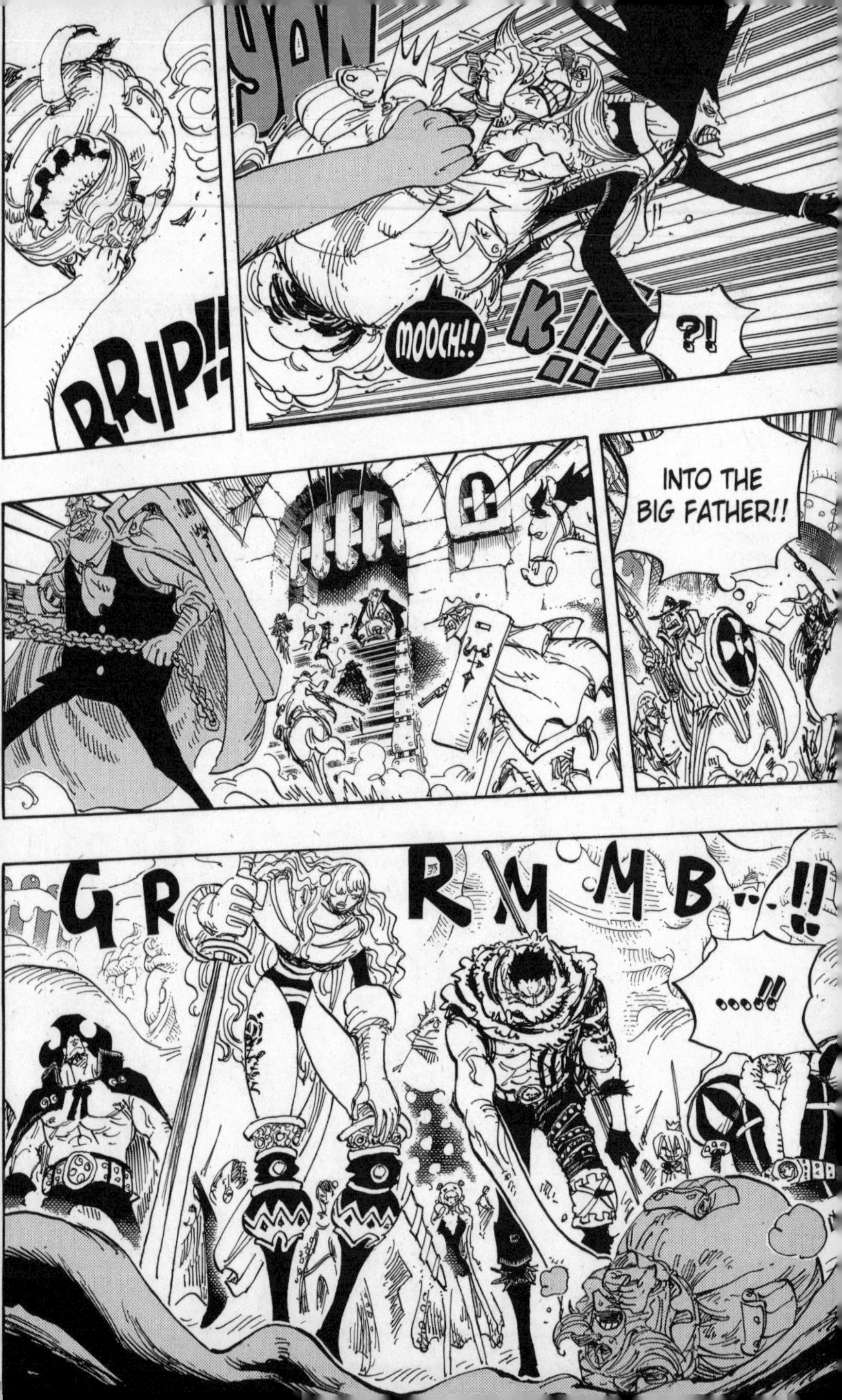
?!
K!!!
MOOCH!!
RRIP!!
INTO THE BIG FATHER!!
GRRUMMB..!!
....!!

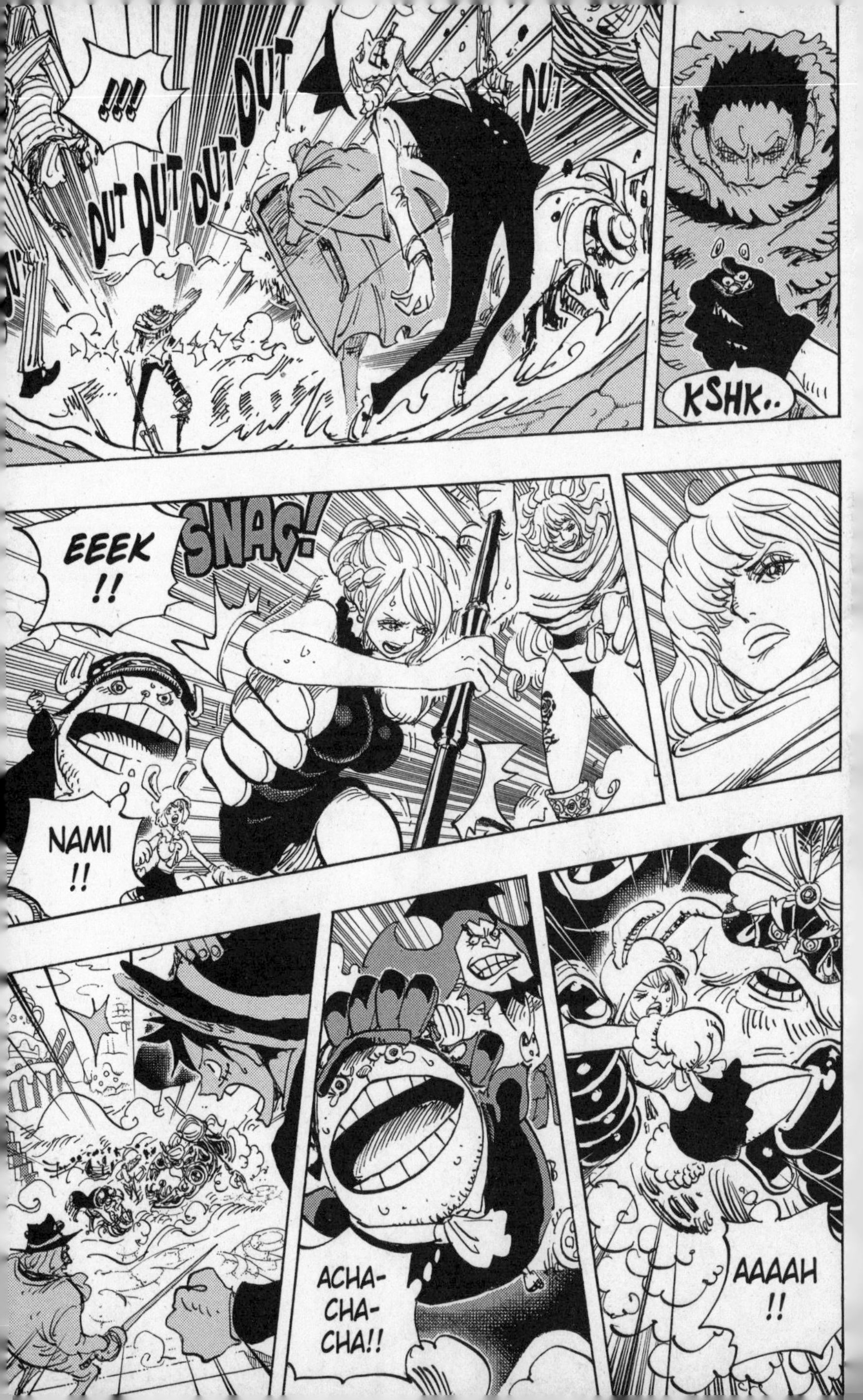

KSHK..
DUT
DUT DUT DUT DUT
!!!
SNAG!
EEEK !!
NAMI !!
AAAAH !!
ACHA-CHA-CHA!!

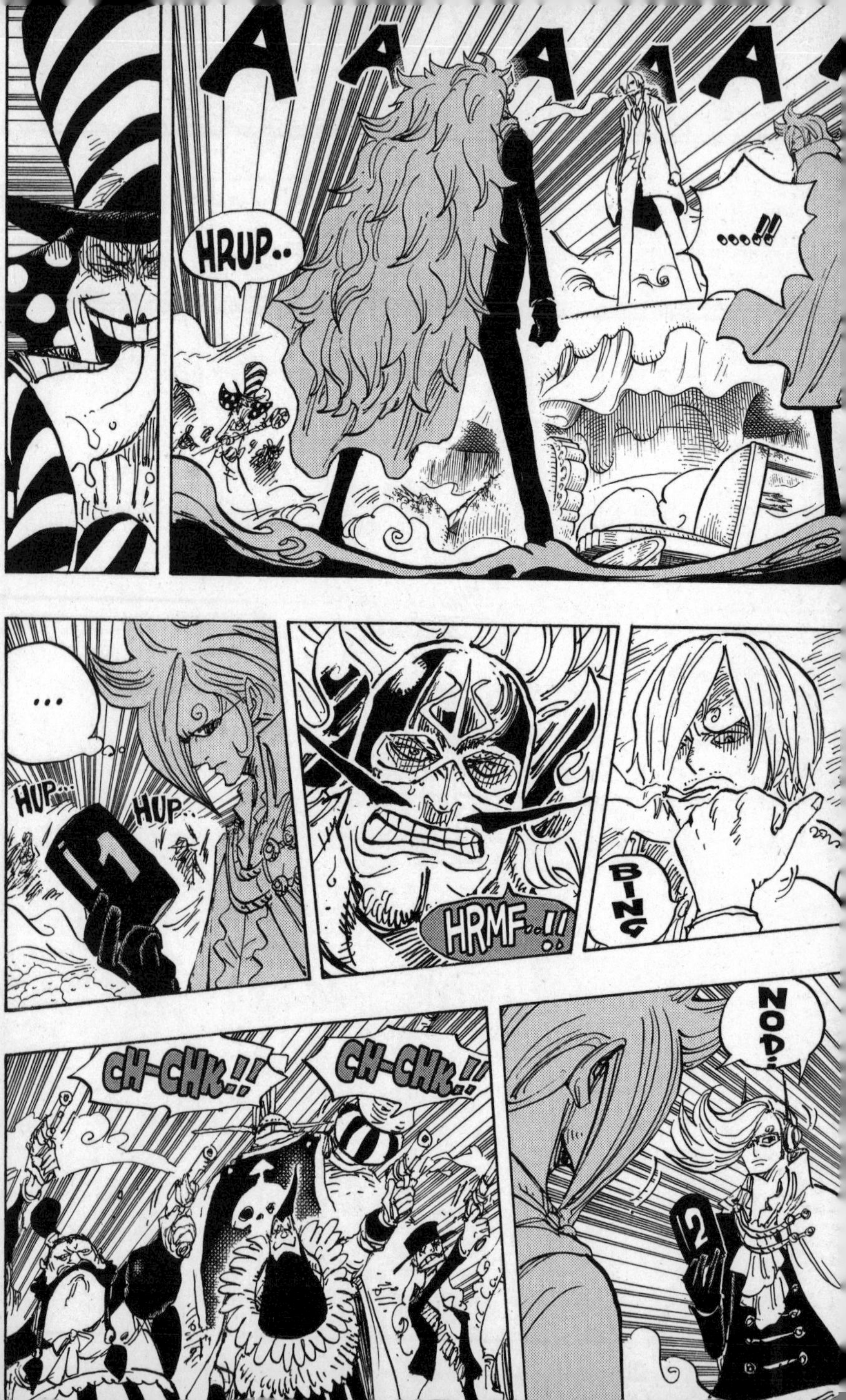
....!!
AAAAA
HRUP..
BING
HRMF..!!
...
HUP...
HUP
NOD..
CH-CHK!!
CH-CHK!!

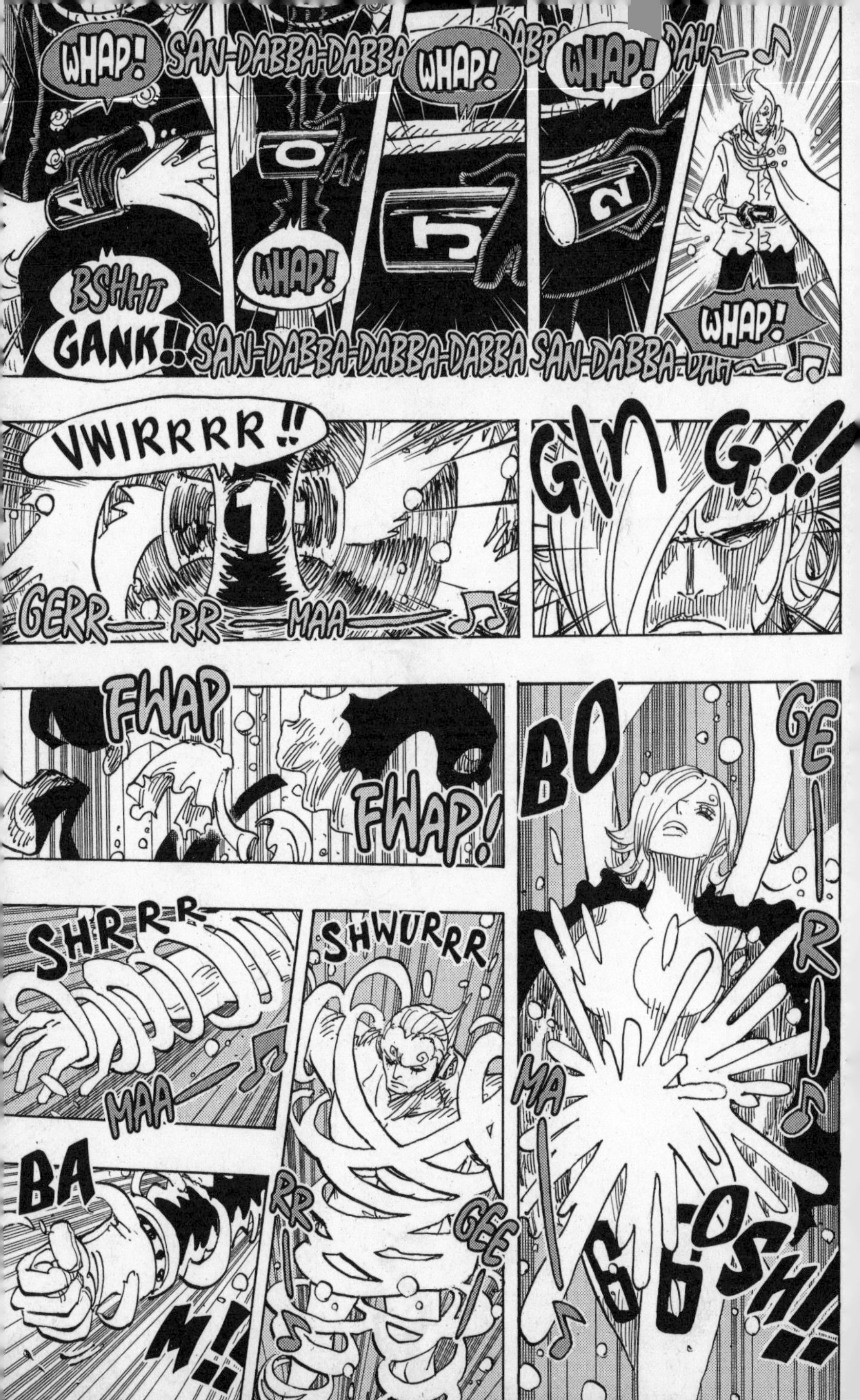
SAN-DABBA-DABBA
DABBA
DAH ♪
WHAP!
WHAP!
SAN-DABBA-DAH ♪
WHAP!
WHAP!
WHAP!
BSHHT
GANK!!
SAN-DABBA-DABBA-DABBA
WHAP!
SAN-DABBA-DABBA-DABBA
GIN G!!
VWIRRRR!!
GERR—RR—MAA ♪
BO
GE—R—♪
MA—♪
GOOSH!!
FWAP!
FWAP
SHWURRR
RR
GEE ♪
SHRRR
MAA ♪
BAM!!

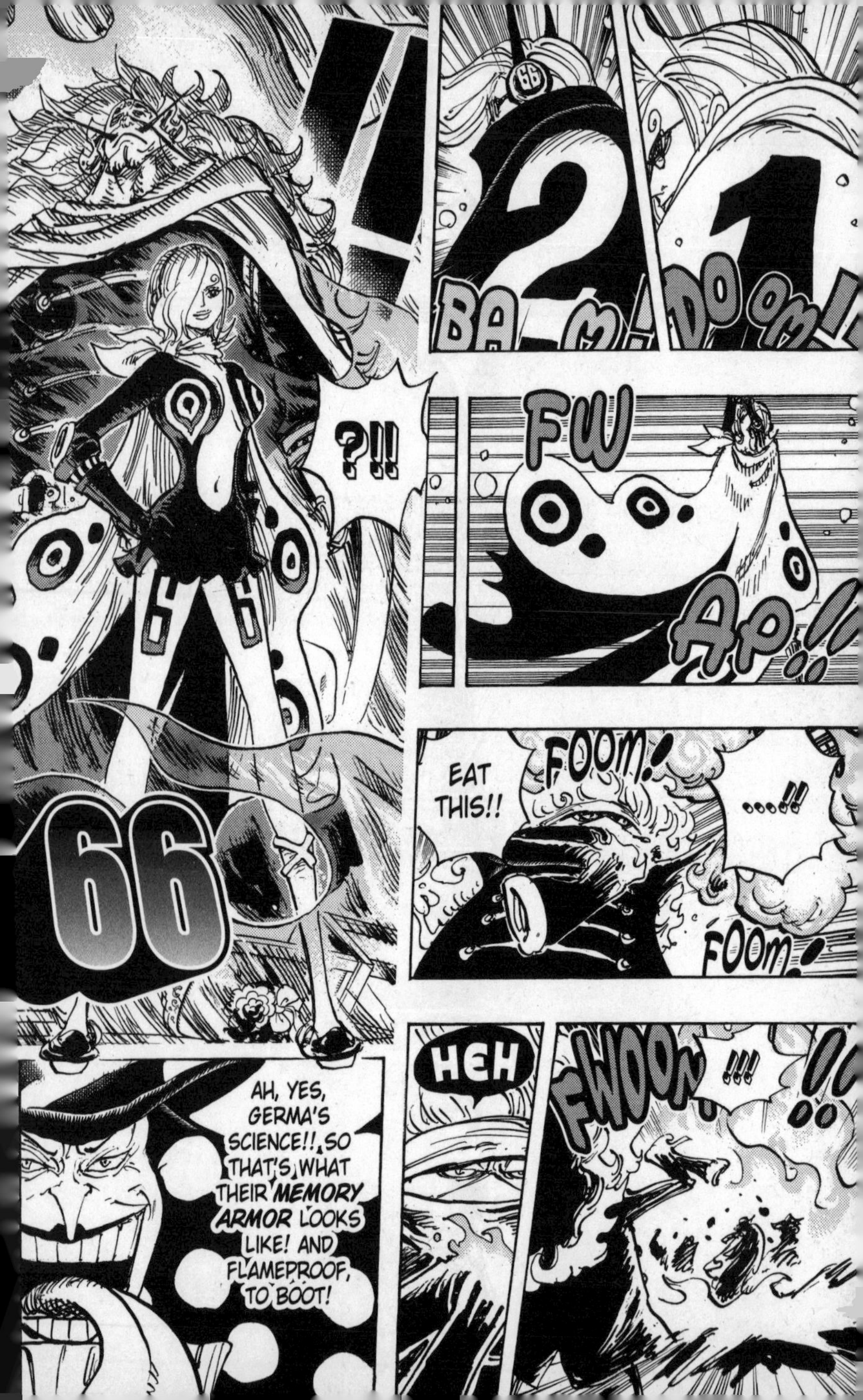
1
DOOM!!
2
BA-M!
FWAP!!
FOOM!
EAT THIS!!
...!!
FOOM!
!!
?!!
66
FWOOM!!!
!!
HEH
AH, YES, GERMA'S SCIENCE!! SO THAT'S WHAT THEIR MEMORY ARMOR LOOKS LIKE! AND FLAMEPROOF, TO BOOT!

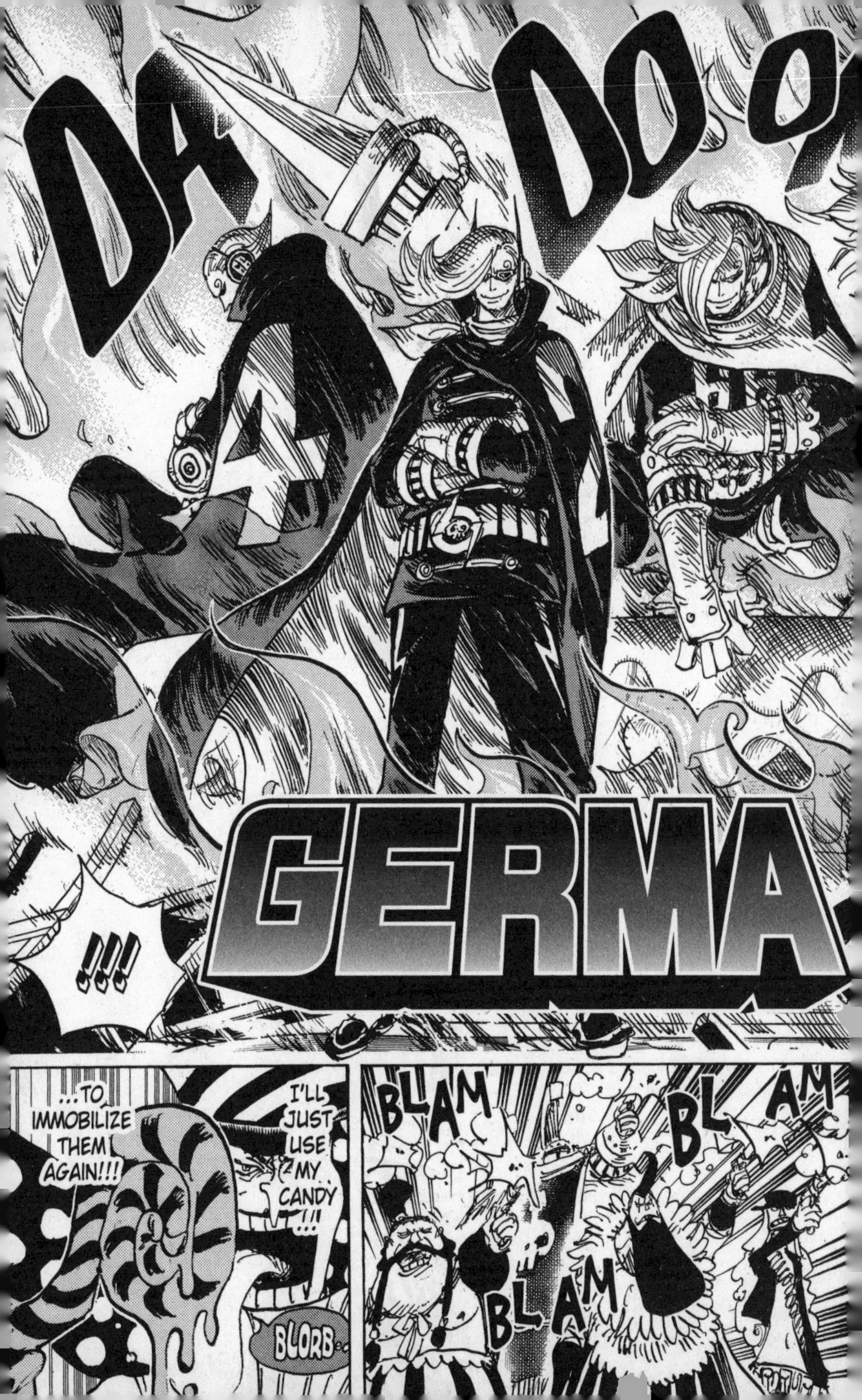
DA
DOO
GERMA
!!!
BLAM
BLAM
BLAM
I'LL JUST USE MY CANDY!!!
...TO IMMOBILIZE THEM AGAIN!!!
BLORB

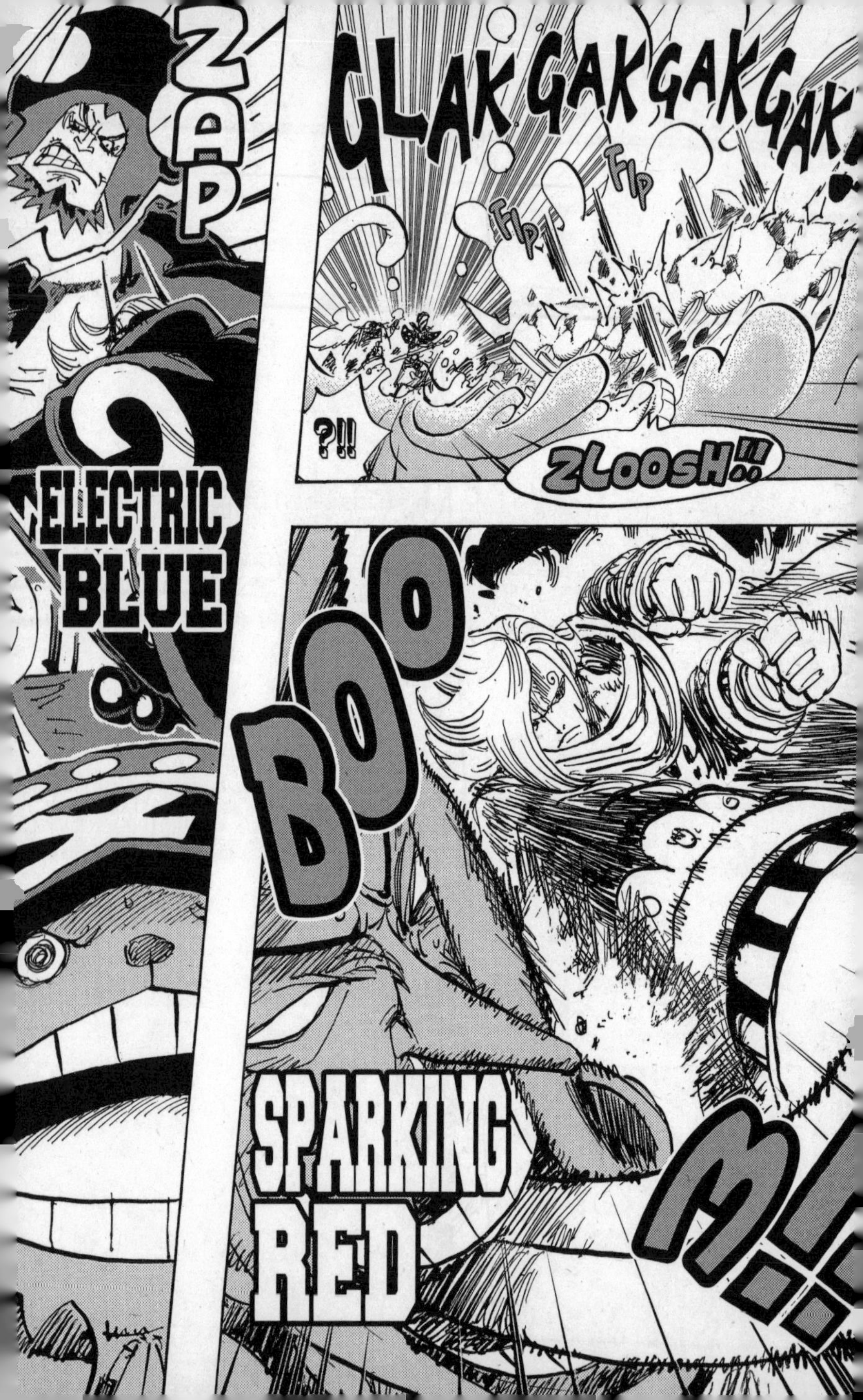
GLAK GAK GAK GAK
Flp
Flp
Flp
?!!
ZLOOSH!!
BOOM!!
SPARKING RED
ZAP
ELECTRIC BLUE

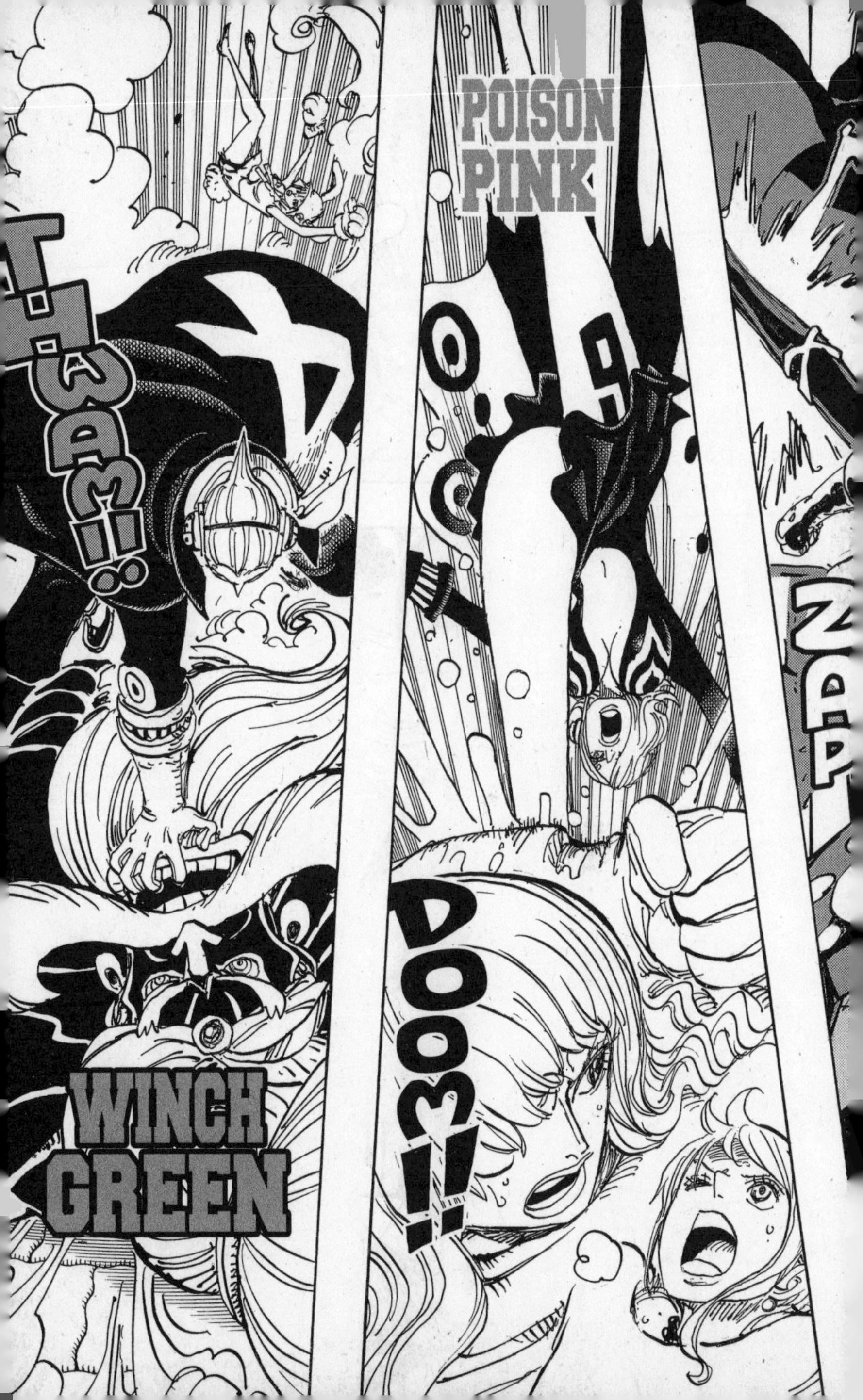
ZAP
POISON PINK
DOOM!!
THWAM!!
WINCH GREEN

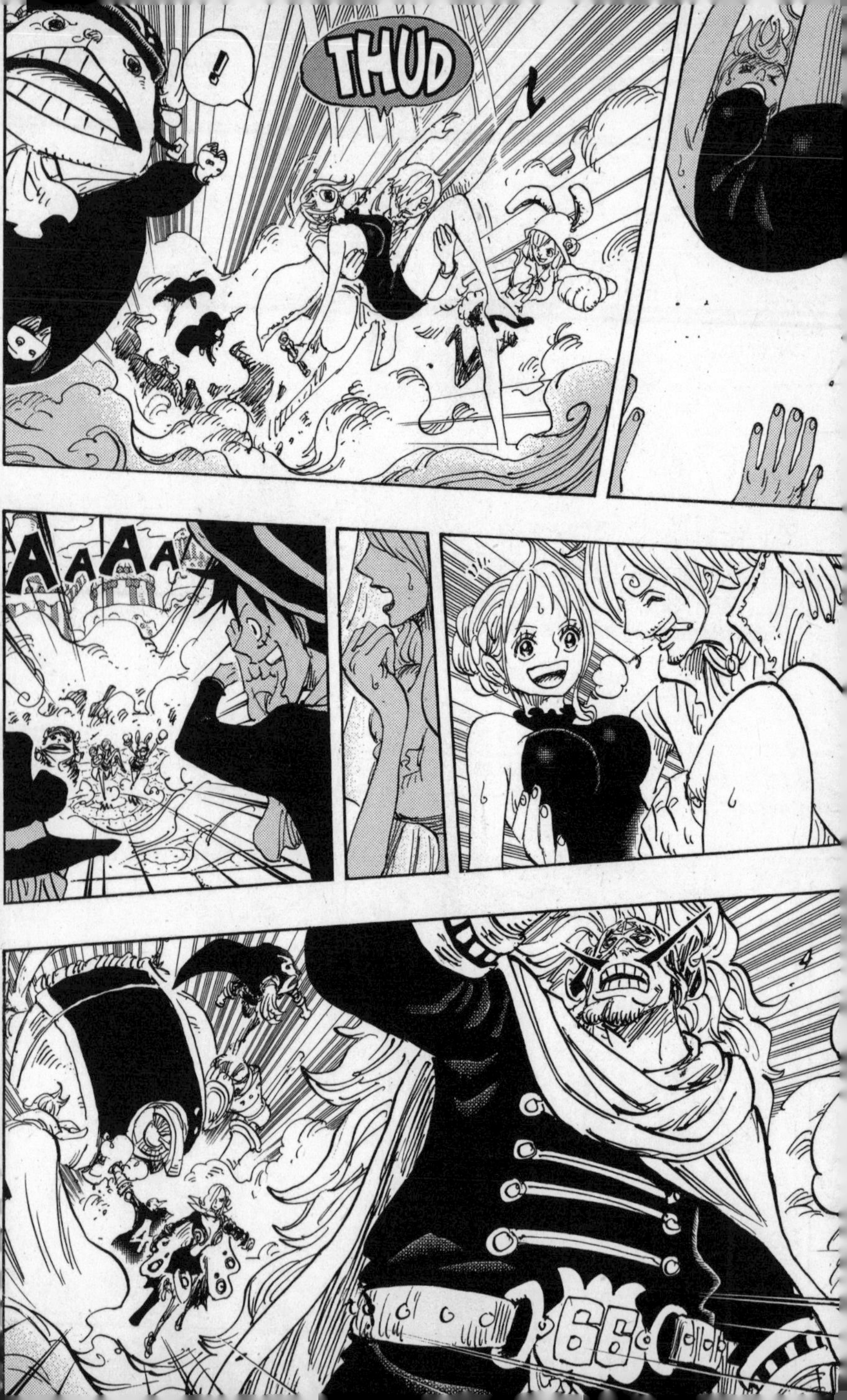
THUD
!
AAAA
66

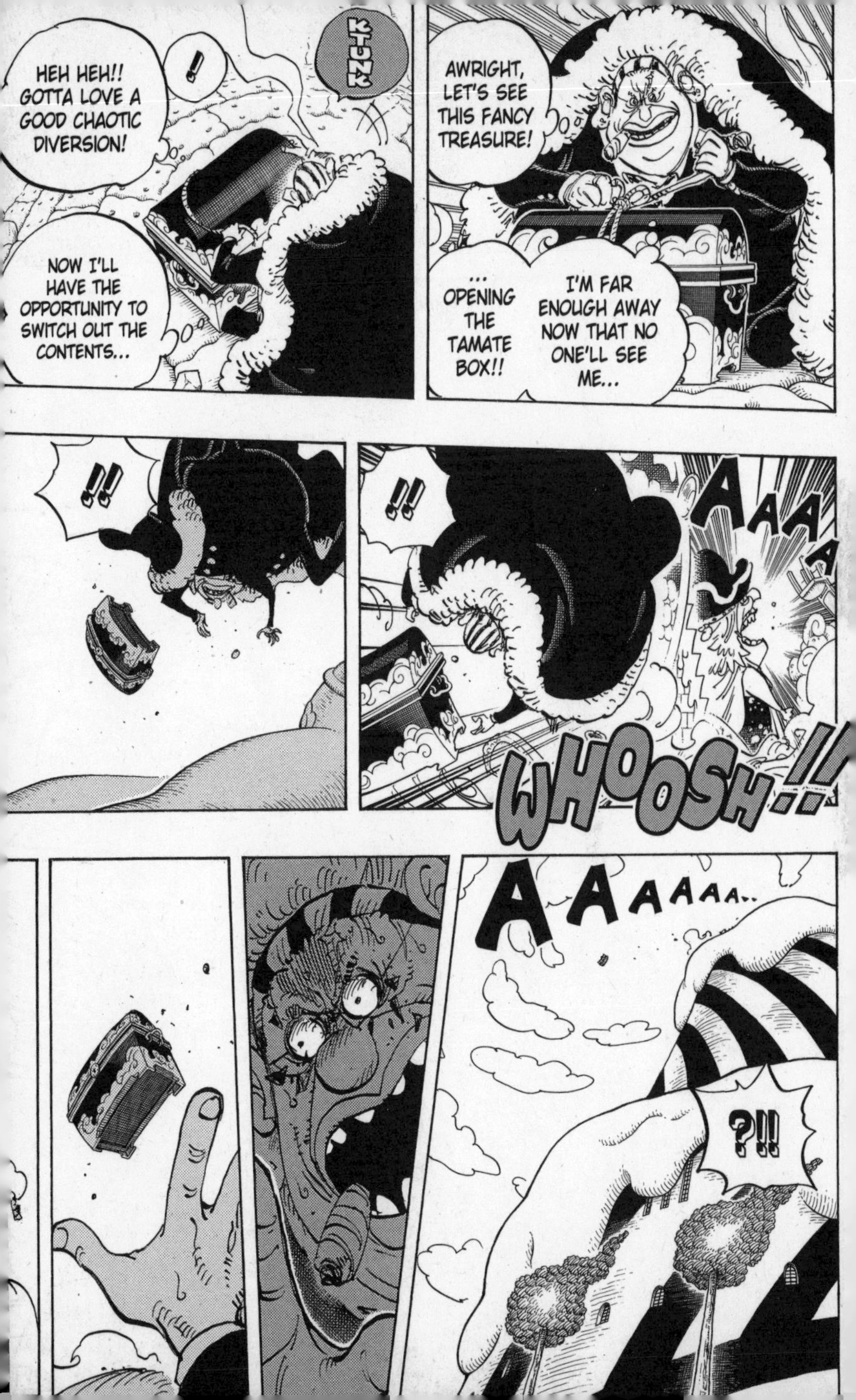
AWRIGHT, LET'S SEE THIS FANCY TREASURE!
I'M FAR ENOUGH AWAY NOW THAT NO ONE'LL SEE ME...
... OPENING THE TAMATE BOX!!
KTUNK
!
HEH HEH!! GOTTA LOVE A GOOD CHAOTIC DIVERSION!
NOW I'LL HAVE THE OPPORTUNITY TO SWITCH OUT THE CONTENTS...
AAAA
!!
WHOOSH!!!
!!
AAAAAA..
?!!

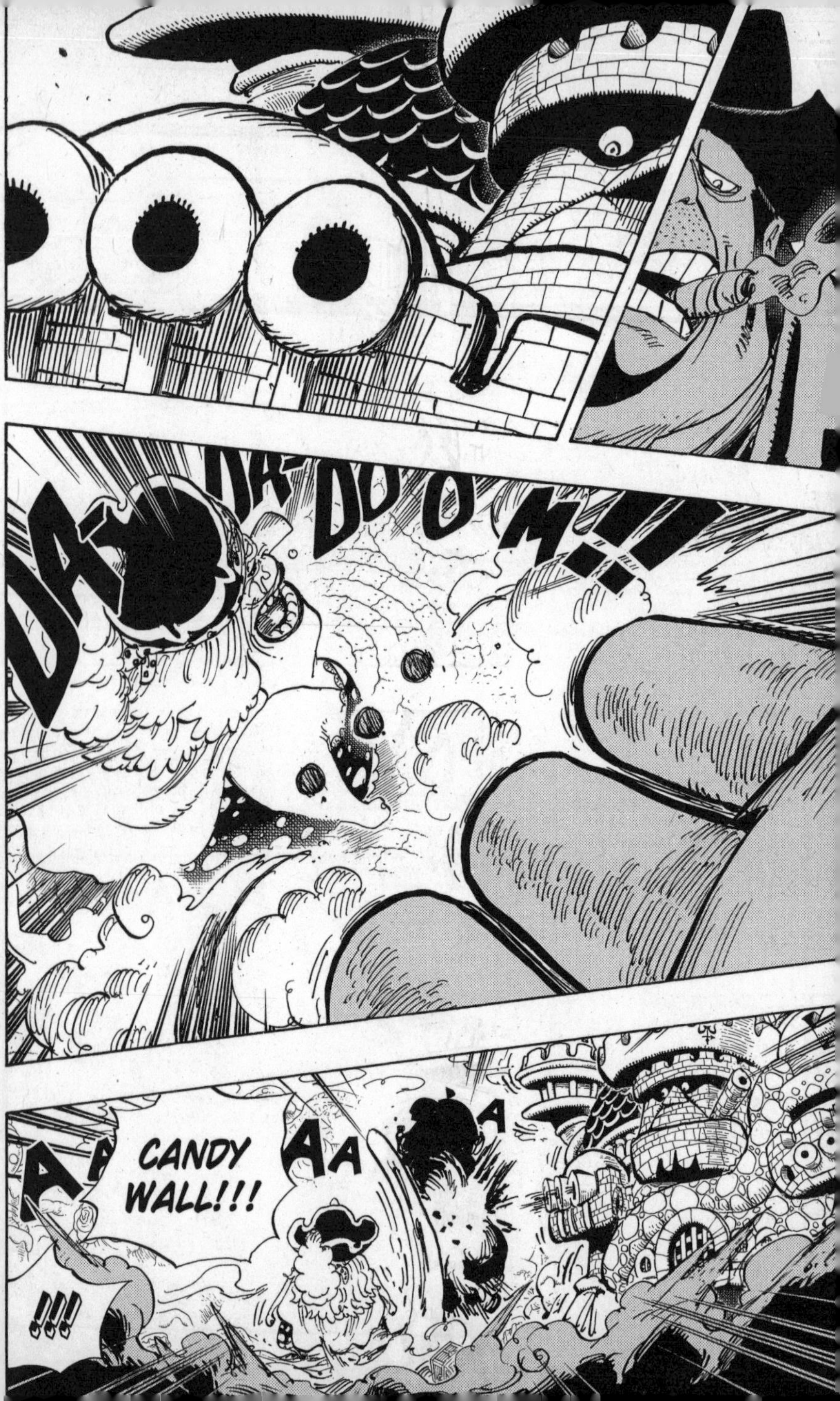
DA-DA-DOOM!!
CANDY WALL!!!
AA
A
!!!

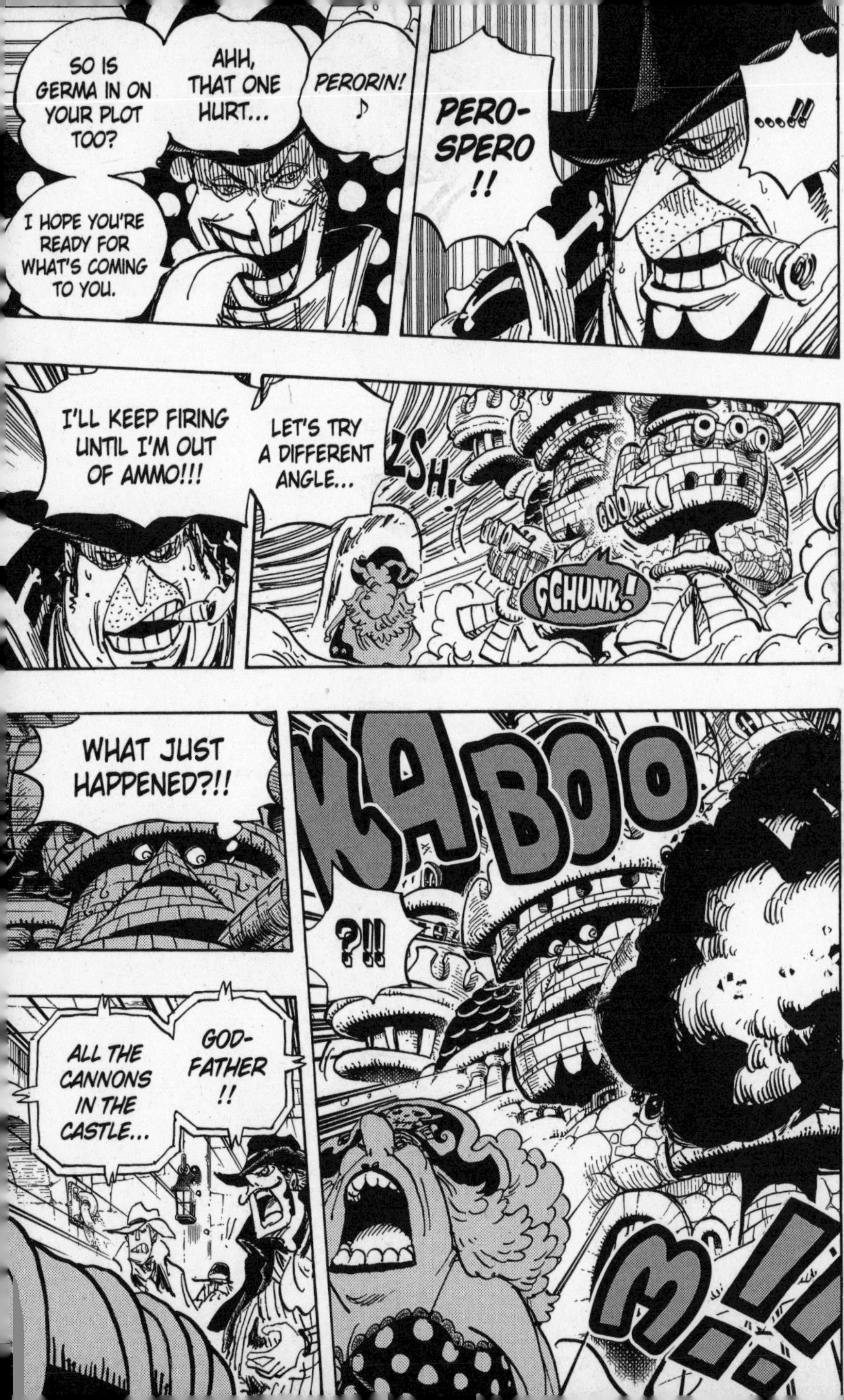
...!!
PERO-SPERO!!
PERORIN! ♪
AHH, THAT ONE HURT...
SO IS GERMA IN ON YOUR PLOT TOO?
I HOPE YOU'RE READY FOR WHAT'S COMING TO YOU.
ZSH
LET'S TRY A DIFFERENT ANGLE...
GCHUNK!
I'LL KEEP FIRING UNTIL I'M OUT OF AMMO!!!
KABOOOM!!
?!!
WHAT JUST HAPPENED?!!
GOD-FATHER!!
ALL THE CANNONS IN THE CASTLE...

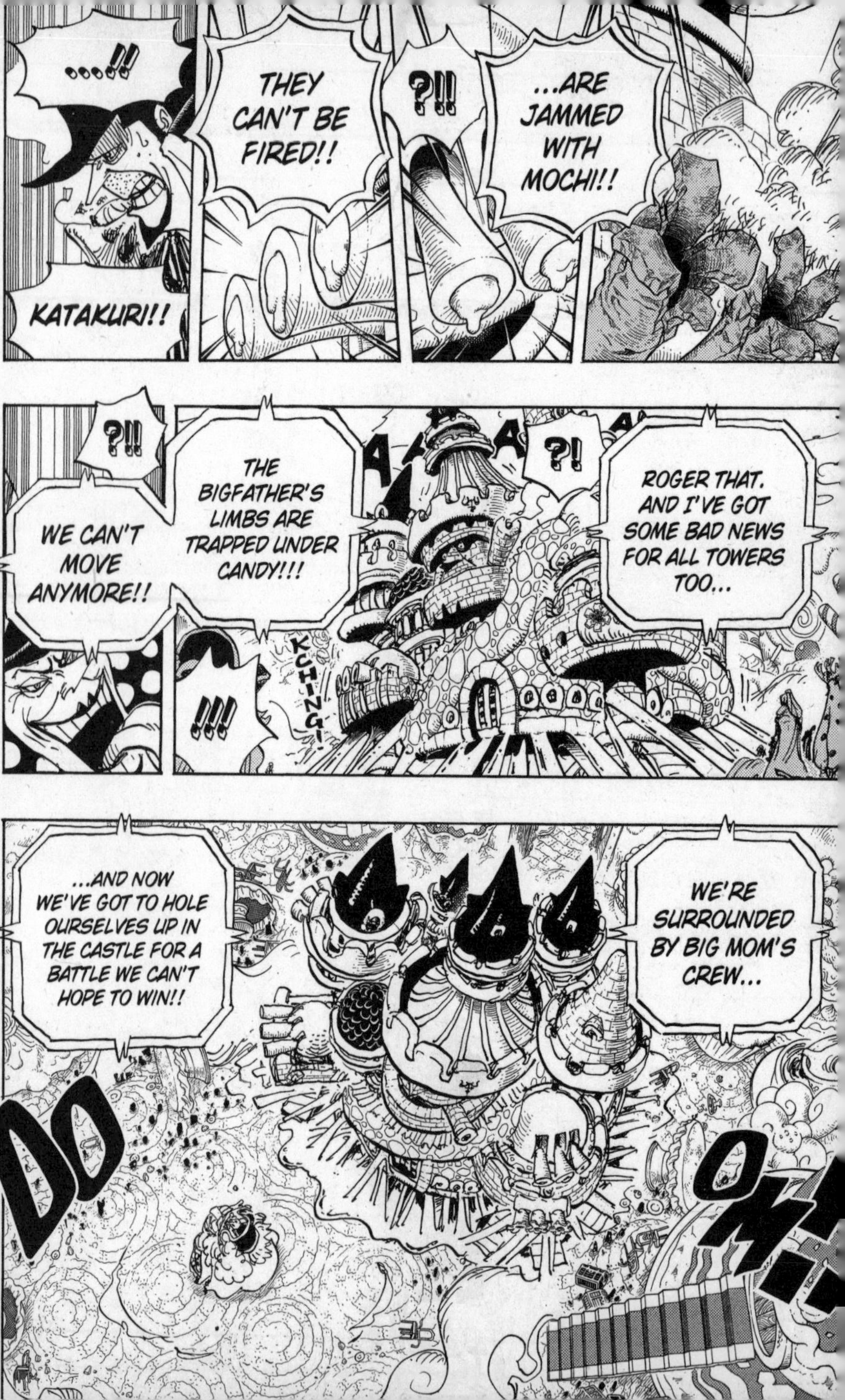
...ARE JAMMED WITH MOCHI!!
?!!
THEY CAN'T BE FIRED!!
...!!
KATAKURI!!
ROGER THAT. AND I'VE GOT SOME BAD NEWS FOR ALL TOWERS TOO...
?!
THE BIGFATHER'S LIMBS ARE TRAPPED UNDER CANDY!!!
KCHING!
!!!
?!!
WE CAN'T MOVE ANYMORE!!
WE'RE SURROUNDED BY BIG MOM'S CREW...
...AND NOW WE'VE GOT TO HOLE OURSELVES UP IN THE CASTLE FOR A BATTLE WE CAN'T HOPE TO WIN!!
DO
OM!!

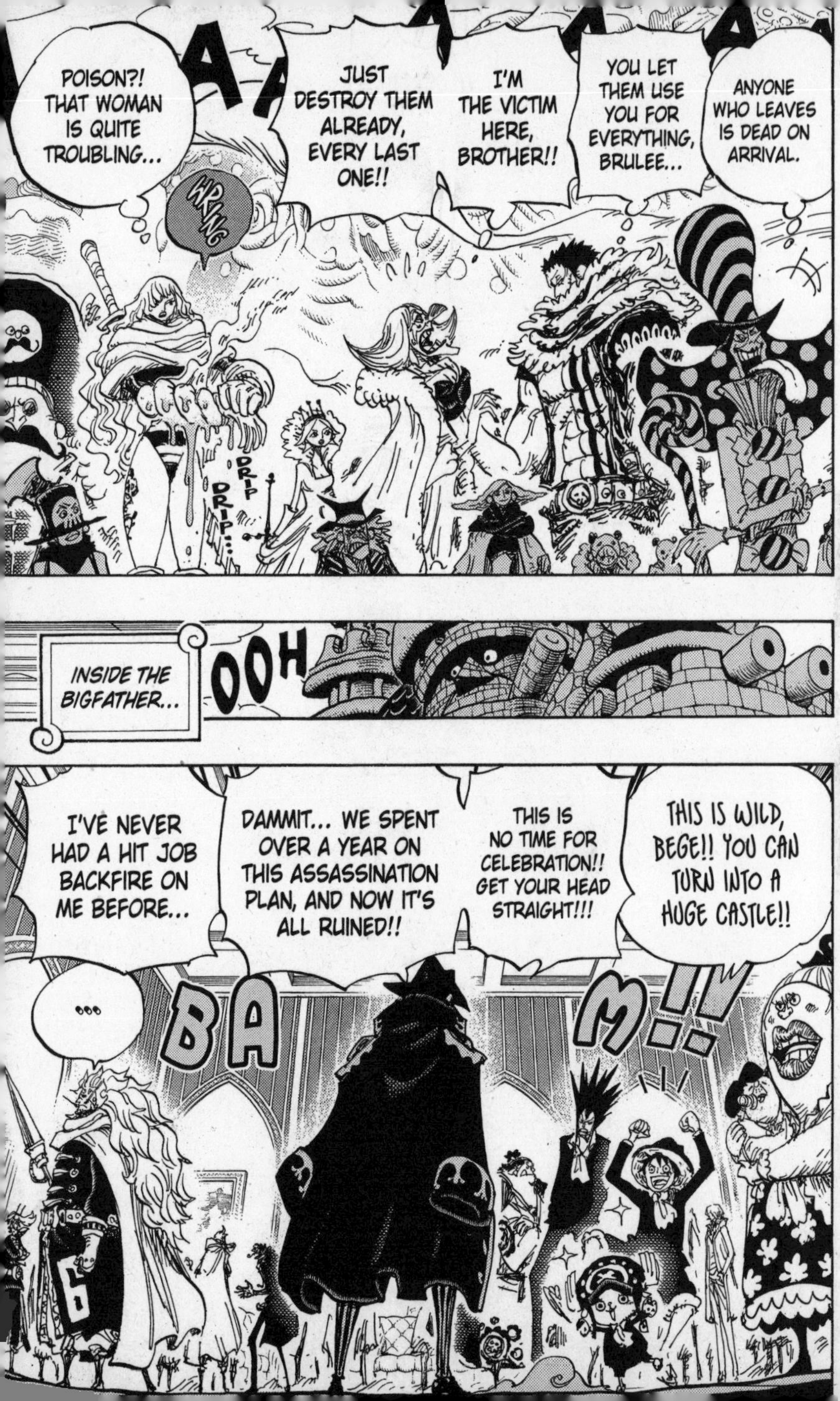
AAAA
ANYONE WHO LEAVES IS DEAD ON ARRIVAL.
YOU LET THEM USE YOU FOR EVERYTHING, BRULEE...
I'M THE VICTIM HERE, BROTHER!!
JUST DESTROY THEM ALREADY, EVERY LAST ONE!!
POISON?! THAT WOMAN IS QUITE TROUBLING...
WRING
DRIP DRIP...
OOH
INSIDE THE BIGFATHER...
THIS IS WILD, BEGE!! YOU CAN TURN INTO A HUGE CASTLE!!
THIS IS NO TIME FOR CELEBRATION!! GET YOUR HEAD STRAIGHT!!!
DAMMIT... WE SPENT OVER A YEAR ON THIS ASSASSINATION PLAN, AND NOW IT'S ALL RUINED!!
I'VE NEVER HAD A HIT JOB BACKFIRE ON ME BEFORE...
BAM!!
...

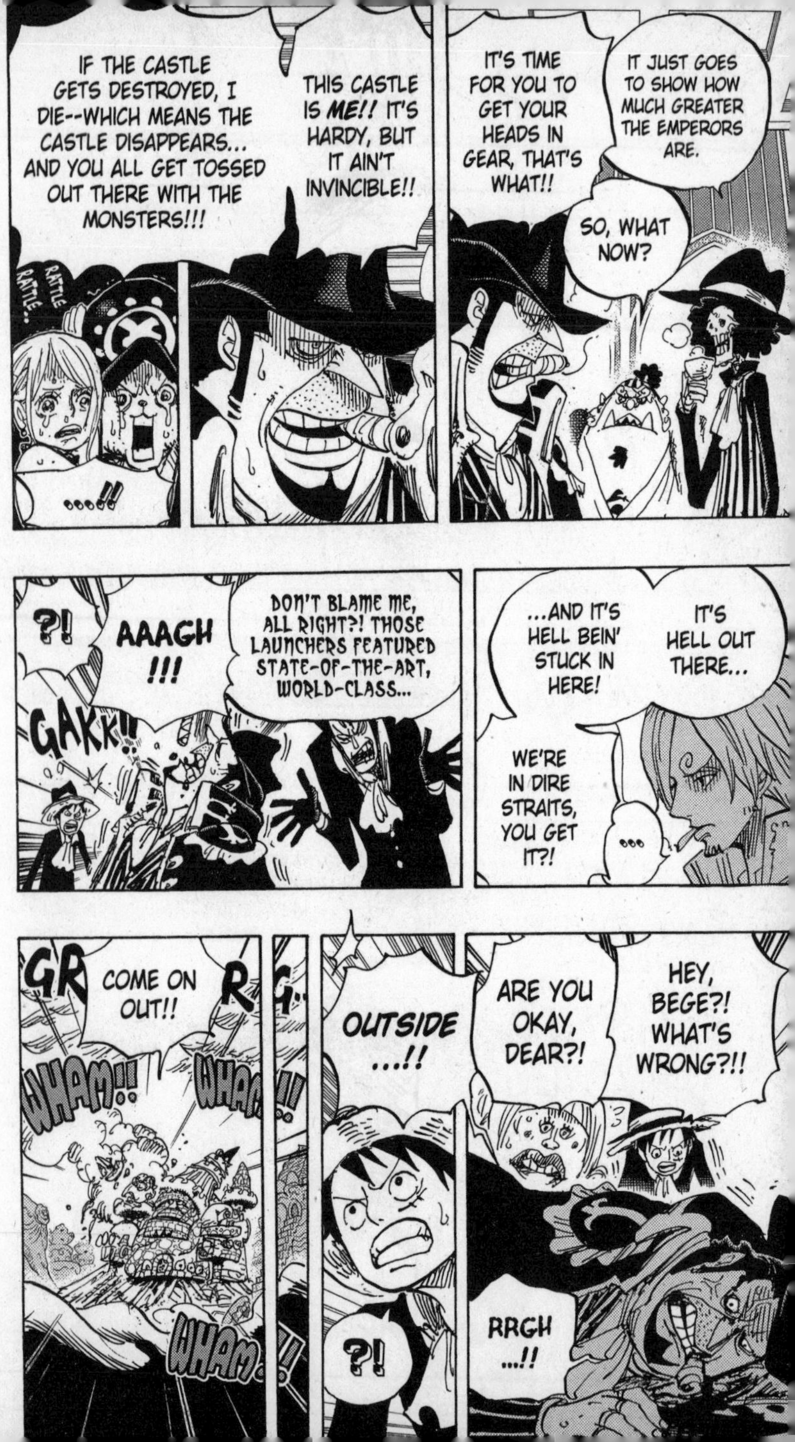

IT JUST GOES TO SHOW HOW MUCH GREATER THE EMPERORS ARE.
SO, WHAT NOW?
IT'S TIME FOR YOU TO GET YOUR HEADS IN GEAR, THAT'S WHAT!!
THIS CASTLE IS ME!! IT'S HARDY, BUT IT AIN'T INVINCIBLE!!
IF THE CASTLE GETS DESTROYED, I DIE--WHICH MEANS THE CASTLE DISAPPEARS... AND YOU ALL GET TOSSED OUT THERE WITH THE MONSTERS!!!
RATTLE RATTLE...
...!!
IT'S HELL OUT THERE...
...AND IT'S HELL BEIN' STUCK IN HERE!
WE'RE IN DIRE STRAITS, YOU GET IT?!
...
DON'T BLAME ME, ALL RIGHT?! THOSE LAUNCHERS FEATURED STATE-OF-THE-ART, WORLD-CLASS...
AAAGH !!!
?!
GAKK!!
HEY, BEGE?! WHAT'S WRONG?!!
ARE YOU OKAY, DEAR?!
RRGH ...!!
OUTSIDE ...!!
?!
COME ON OUT!!
GR
RRG...
WHAM!!
WHAM!!
WHAM...!!

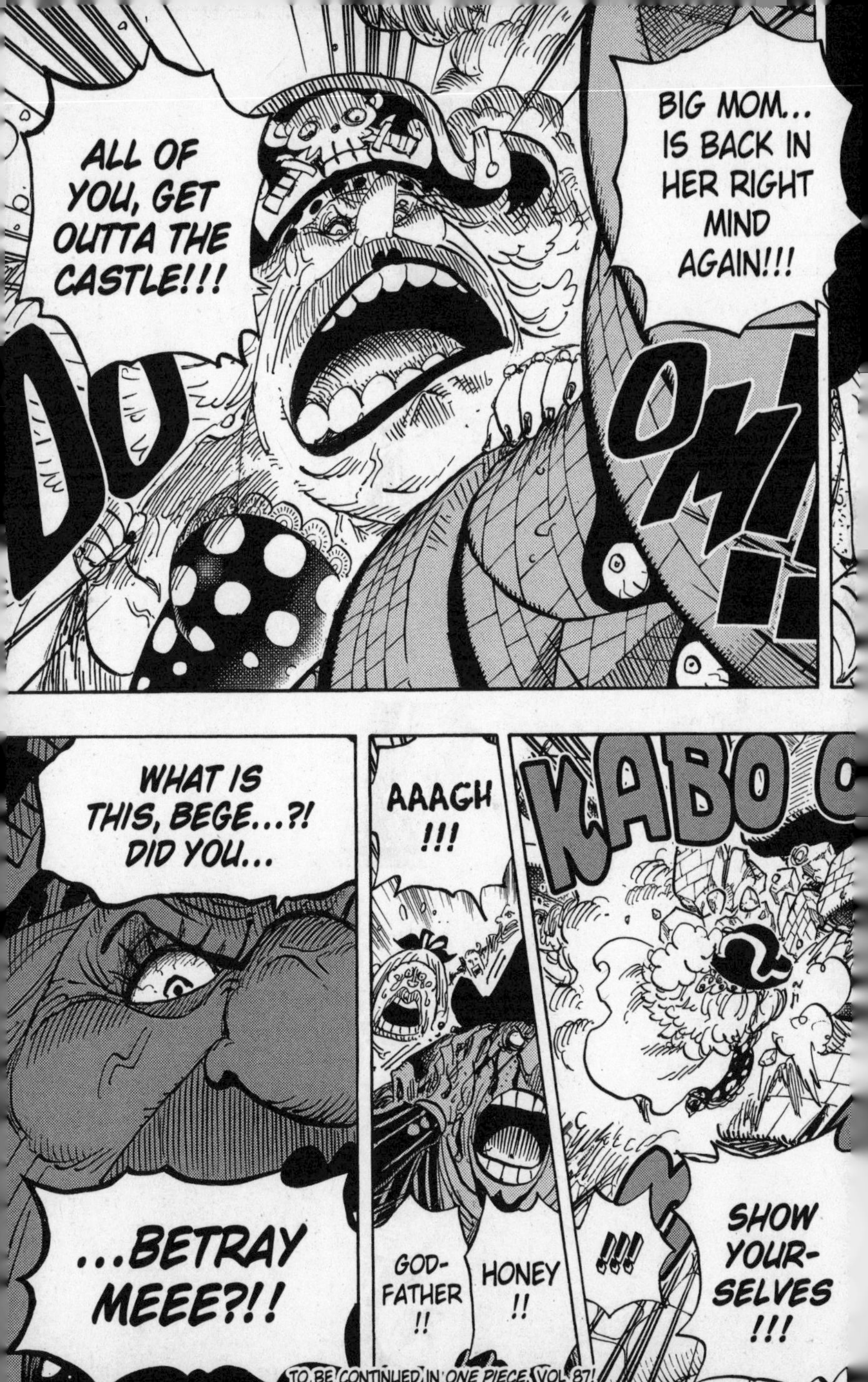
BIG MOM... IS BACK IN HER RIGHT MIND AGAIN!!!
ALL OF YOU, GET OUTTA THE CASTLE!!!
DOOM!!
KABOO
SHOW YOUR-SELVES!!!
!!!
AAAGH!!!
HONEY!!
GOD-FATHER!!
WHAT IS THIS, BEGE...?! DID YOU...
...BETRAY MEEE?!!

TO BE CONTINUED IN ONE PIECE, VOL. 87!

COMING NEXT VOLUME:

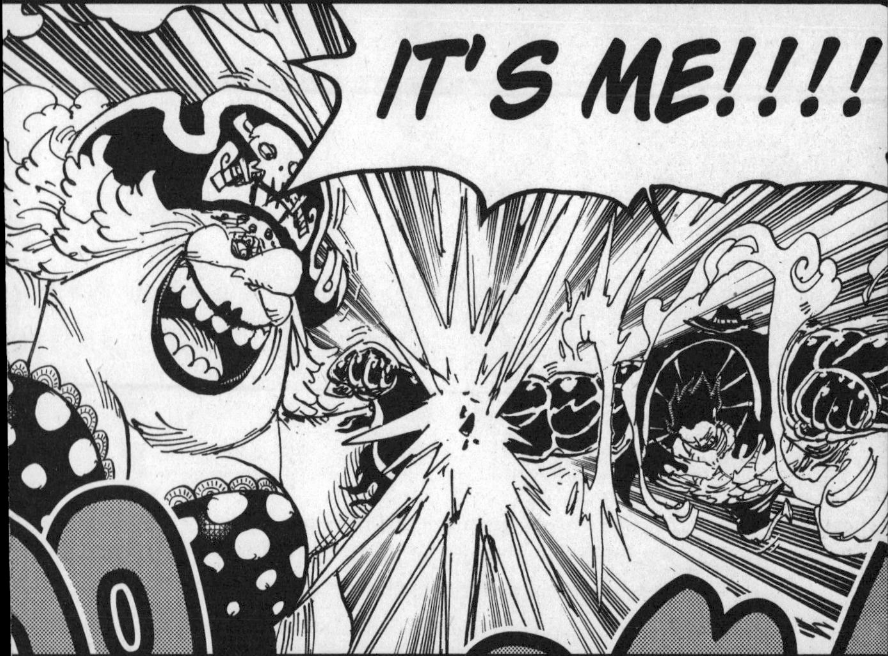
IT'S ME!!!!

The plan to take down Big Mom has failed spectacularly. The Straw Hats and Firetank pirates now find themselves under attack by Big Mom's entire crew. Things look bleak, but Bege has one last plan!

ON SALE AUGUST 2018!

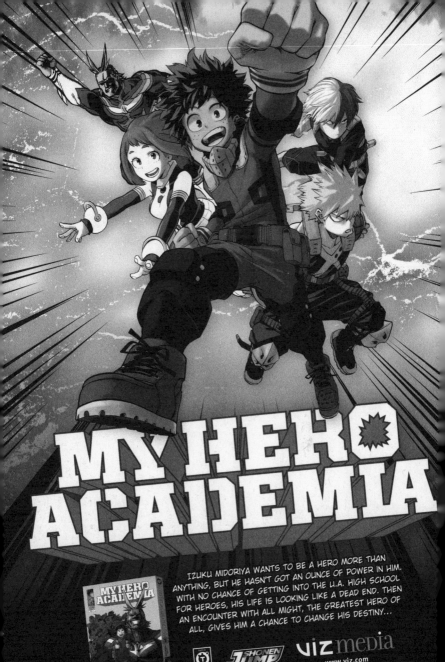

THE ACTION-PACKED SUPERHERO COMEDY ABOUT ONE MAN'S AMBITION TO BE A HERO FOR FUN!
ONE-PUNCH MAN
STORY BY ONE
ART BY YUSUKE MURATA
ONE-PUNCH MAN
01
ONE
YUSUKE MURATA
SHONENJUMP MANGA
Nothing about Saitama passes the eyeball test when it comes to superheroes, from his lifeless expression to his bald head to his unimpressive physique. However, this average-looking guy has a not-so-average problem—he just can't seem to find an opponent strong enough to take on!
Can he finally find an opponent who can go toe-to-toe with him and give his life some meaning? Or is he doomed to a life of superpowered boredom?
SHONEN JUMP
VIZ media
www.viz.com
ONE-PUNCH MAN © 2012 by ONE, Yusuke Murata/SHUEISHA Inc.

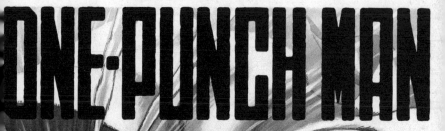

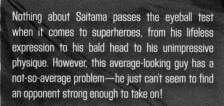

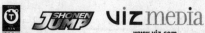

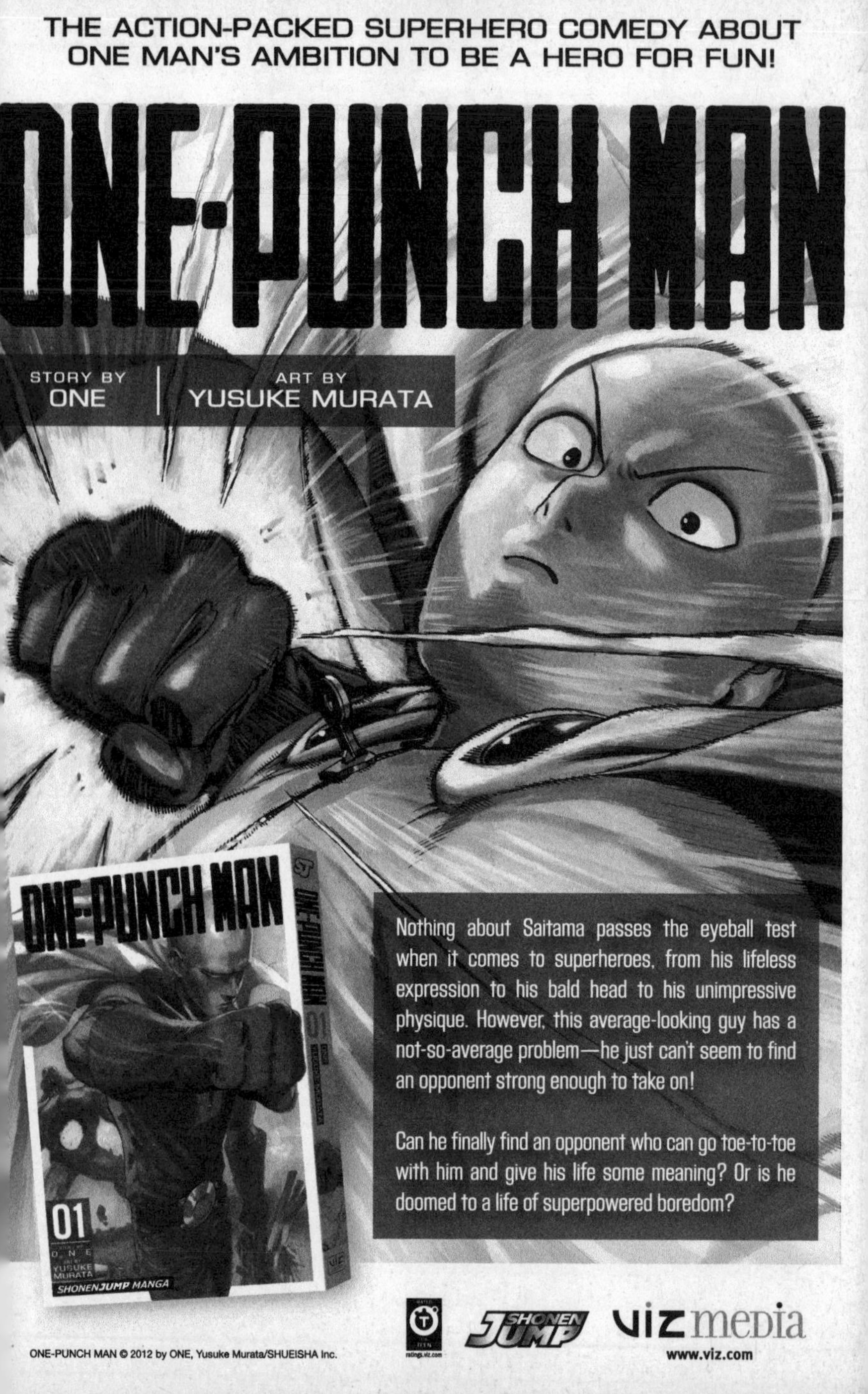

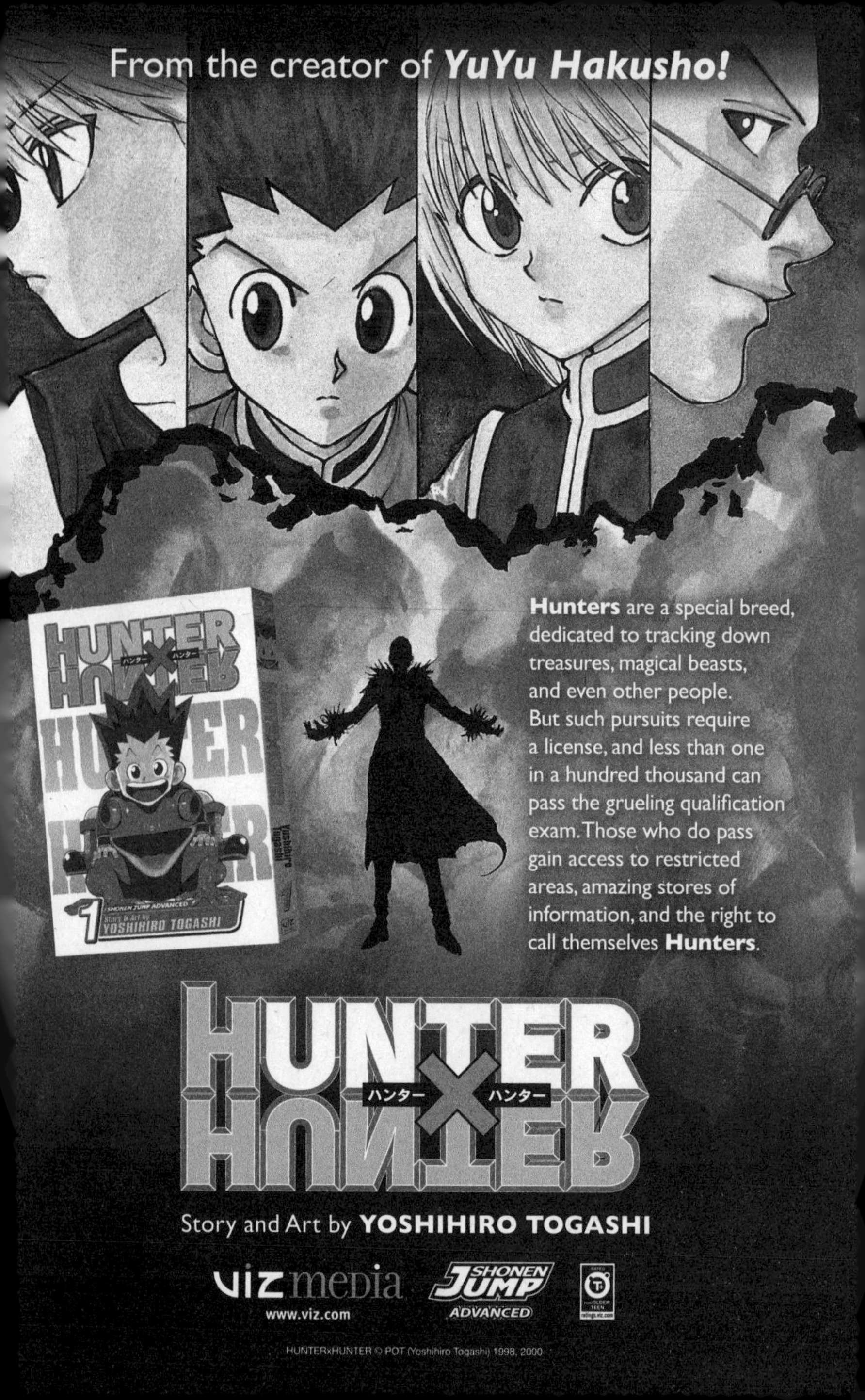
From the creator of YuYu Hakusho!
HUNTER × HUNTER
1
SHONEN JUMP ADVANCED
Story & Art by YOSHIHIRO TOGASHI
Hunters are a special breed, dedicated to tracking down treasures, magical beasts, and even other people. But such pursuits require a license, and less than one in a hundred thousand can pass the grueling qualification exam. Those who do pass gain access to restricted areas, amazing stores of information, and the right to call themselves Hunters.
HUNTER ハンター × ハンター HUNTER
Story and Art by YOSHIHIRO TOGASHI
VIZ media
www.viz.com
SHONEN JUMP ADVANCED
OLDER TEEN
HUNTERxHUNTER © POT (Yoshihiro Togashi) 1998, 2000

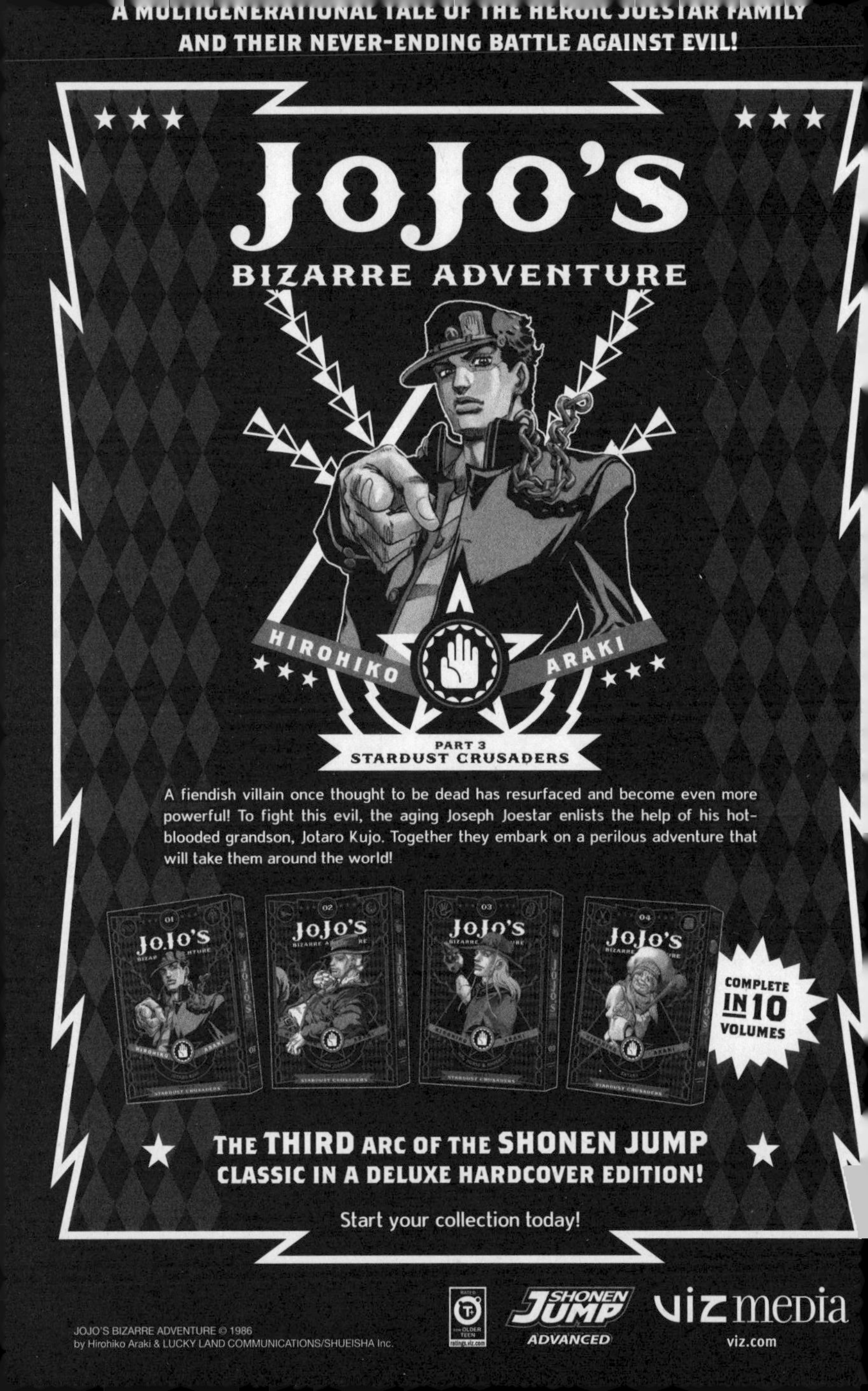

A MULTIGENERATIONAL TALE OF THE HEROIC JOESTAR FAMILY
AND THEIR NEVER-ENDING BATTLE AGAINST EVIL!
JOJO'S
BIZARRE ADVENTURE
HIROHIKO ARAKI
PART 3
STARDUST CRUSADERS
A fiendish villain once thought to be dead has resurfaced and become even more powerful! To fight this evil, the aging Joseph Joestar enlists the help of his hot-blooded grandson, Jotaro Kujo. Together they embark on a perilous adventure that will take them around the world!
COMPLETE IN 10 VOLUMES
THE THIRD ARC OF THE SHONEN JUMP CLASSIC IN A DELUXE HARDCOVER EDITION!
Start your collection today!
SHONEN JUMP ADVANCED
viz media
viz.com
JOJO'S BIZARRE ADVENTURE © 1986
by Hirohiko Araki & LUCKY LAND COMMUNICATIONS/SHUEISHA Inc.

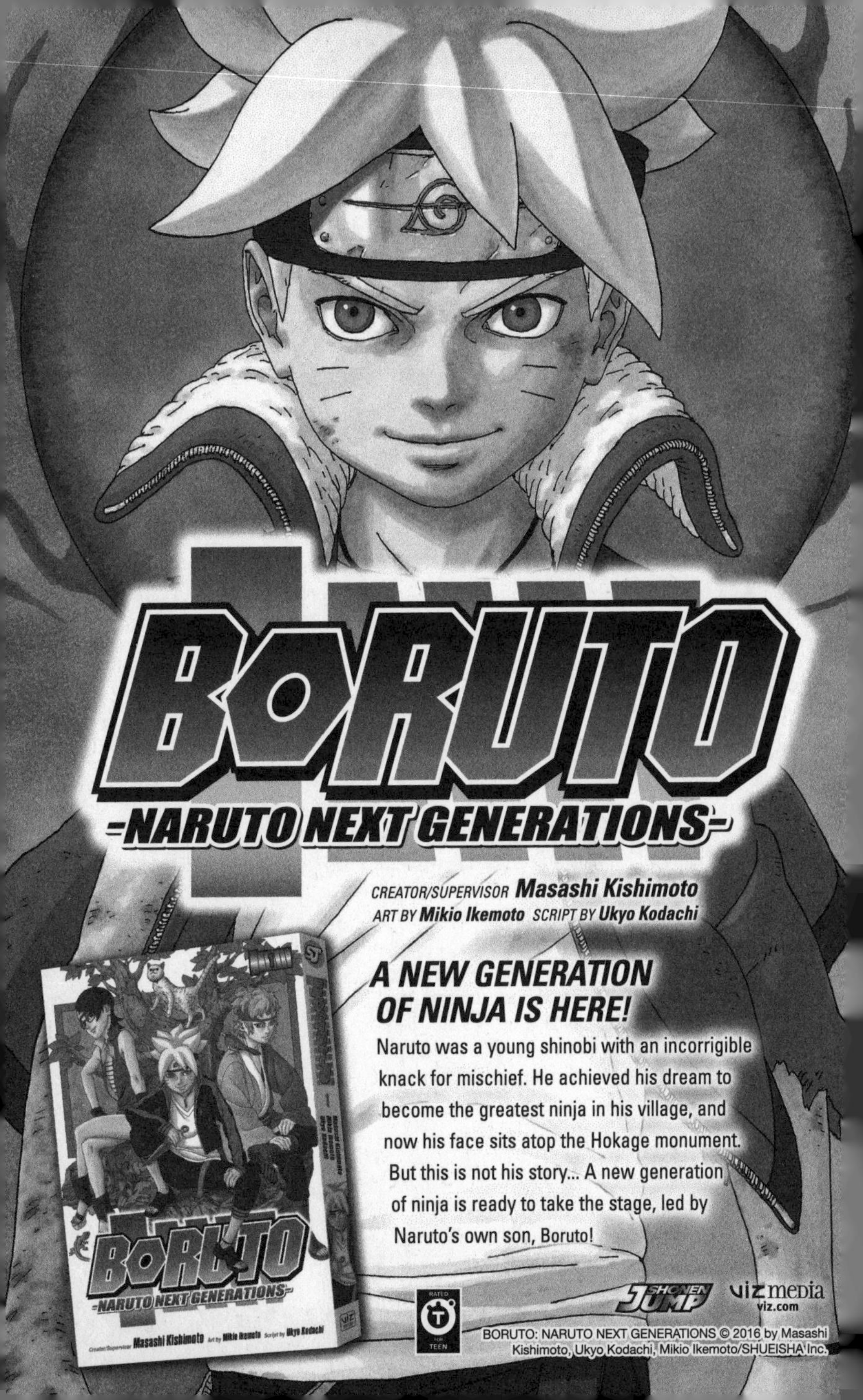

BORUTO
-NARUTO NEXT GENERATIONS-
CREATOR/SUPERVISOR Masashi Kishimoto
ART BY Mikio Ikemoto SCRIPT BY Ukyo Kodachi
A NEW GENERATION OF NINJA IS HERE!
Naruto was a young shinobi with an incorrigible knack for mischief. He achieved his dream to become the greatest ninja in his village, and now his face sits atop the Hokage monument. But this is not his story... A new generation of ninja is ready to take the stage, led by Naruto's own son, Boruto!
BORUTO
-NARUTO NEXT GENERATIONS-
RATED T FOR TEEN
SHONEN JUMP
VIZ media
viz.com
BORUTO: NARUTO NEXT GENERATIONS © 2016 by Masashi Kishimoto, Ukyo Kodachi, Mikio Ikemoto/SHUEISHA Inc.

You're Reading in the Wrong Direction!!

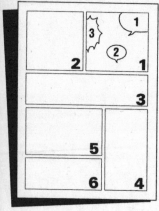

Whoops! Guess what? You're starting at the wrong end of the comic!

...It's true! In keeping with the original Japanese format, **One Piece** is meant to be read from right to left, starting in the upper-right corner.

Unlike English, which is read from left to right, Japanese is read from right to left, meaning that action, sound effects and word-balloon order are completely reversed...something which can make readers unfamiliar with Japanese feel pretty backwards themselves. For this reason, manga or Japanese comics published in the U.S. in English have sometimes been published "flopped"—that is, printed in exact reverse order, as though seen from the other side of a mirror.

By flopping pages, U.S. publishers can avoid confusing readers, but the compromise is not without its downside. For one thing, a character in a flopped manga series who once wore in the original Japanese version a T-shirt emblazoned with "M A Y" (as in "the merry month of") now wears one which reads "Y A M"! Additionally, many manga creators in Japan are themselves unhappy with the process, as some feel the mirror-imaging of their art skews their original intentions.

We are proud to bring you Eiichiro Oda's **One Piece** in the original unflopped format. For now, though, turn to the other side of the book and let the journey begin...!

—Editor